Devils and Realist vol. 3

story by Madoka Takadono
art by Utako Yukihiro

Cast of Characters

William

A brilliant realist from a famous noble family. As the descendant of King Solomon, he is an Elector with the authority to choose the representative king of Hell.

Kevin

William's capable butler. He has served the Twining family for generations, and manages all of William's affairs. He has recently been appointed head pastor at Stradford School.

Dantalion

Seventy-first Pillar of Hell, who commands its leading 36 armies. He is Grand Duke of the Underworld and a candidate to represent the king. At school, students rely on him during sporting events.

Sytry

Twelfth Pillar of Hell, who leads 60 armies. Sytry is Prince of Hell and a candidate to represent the king. He is treated like a princess at school because of his beautiful appearance.

Isaac

William's classmate who is obsessed with supernatural phenomena.

The Story So Far

The demons Dantalion and Sytry appear before William, claiming that William is an Elector with the power to select the representative king of Hell. Both insist they will not leave William's side until he chooses one of them, and the demons decide to enjoy their time masquerading as students. William isn't interested in having anything to do with either of them, but he gets dragged into incident after incident. To further complicate things, William's butler suddenly takes over as the academy's pastor...

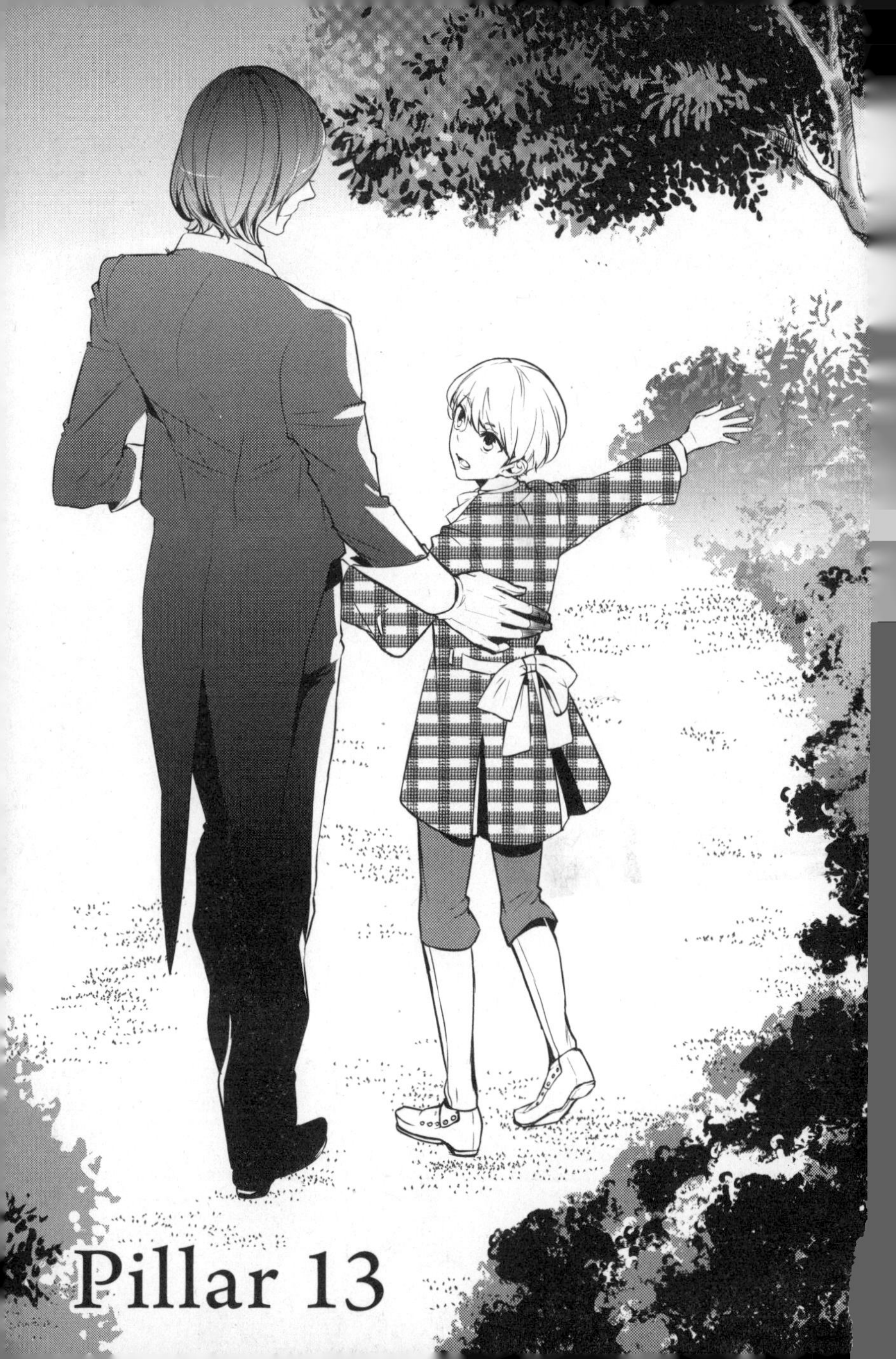
Pillar 13

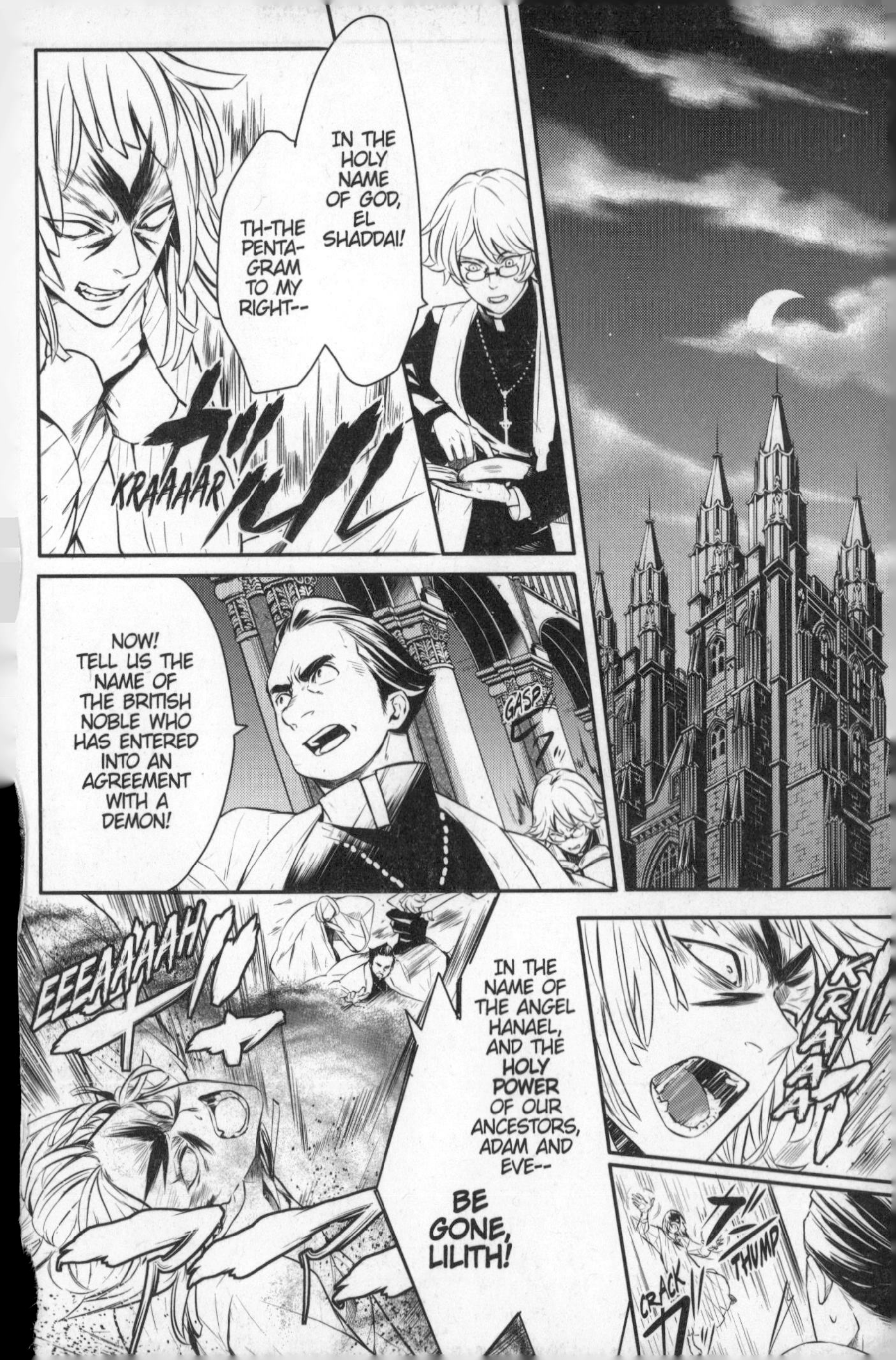
IN THE HOLY NAME OF GOD, EL SHADDAI!
TH-THE PENTAGRAM TO MY RIGHT--
KRAAAAR
GASP
NOW! TELL US THE NAME OF THE BRITISH NOBLE WHO HAS ENTERED INTO AN AGREEMENT WITH A DEMON!
KRAAAA
THUMP
CRACK
IN THE NAME OF THE ANGEL HANAEL, AND THE HOLY POWER OF OUR ANCESTORS, ADAM AND EVE--
BE GONE, LILITH!
EEEAAAAAH

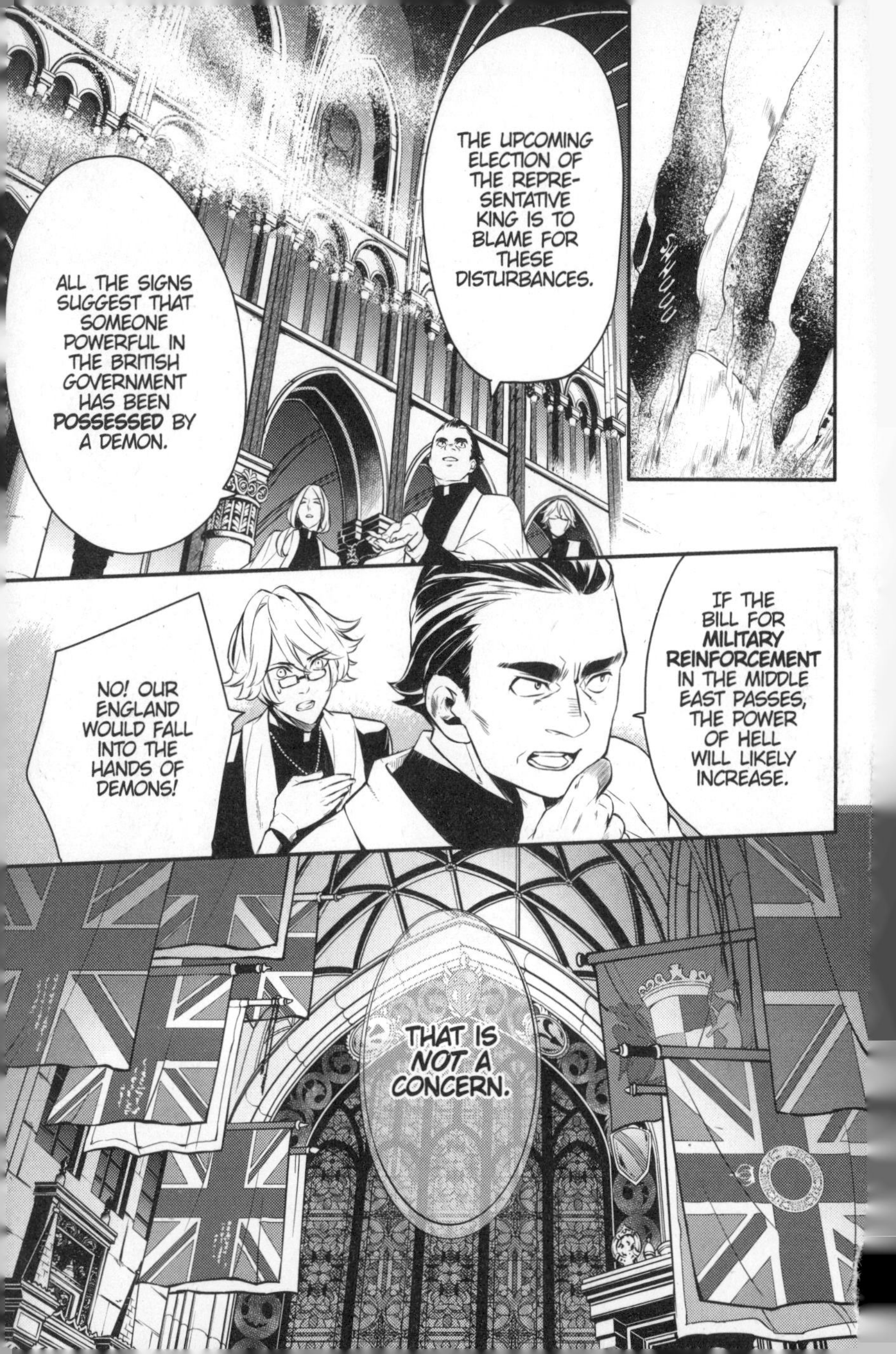
SHHUUU
THE UPCOMING ELECTION OF THE REPRESENTATIVE KING IS TO BLAME FOR THESE DISTURBANCES.
ALL THE SIGNS SUGGEST THAT SOMEONE POWERFUL IN THE BRITISH GOVERNMENT HAS BEEN **POSSESSED** BY A DEMON.
IF THE BILL FOR **MILITARY REINFORCEMENT** IN THE MIDDLE EAST PASSES, THE POWER OF HELL WILL LIKELY INCREASE.
NO! OUR ENGLAND WOULD FALL INTO THE HANDS OF DEMONS!
THAT IS *NOT* A CONCERN.

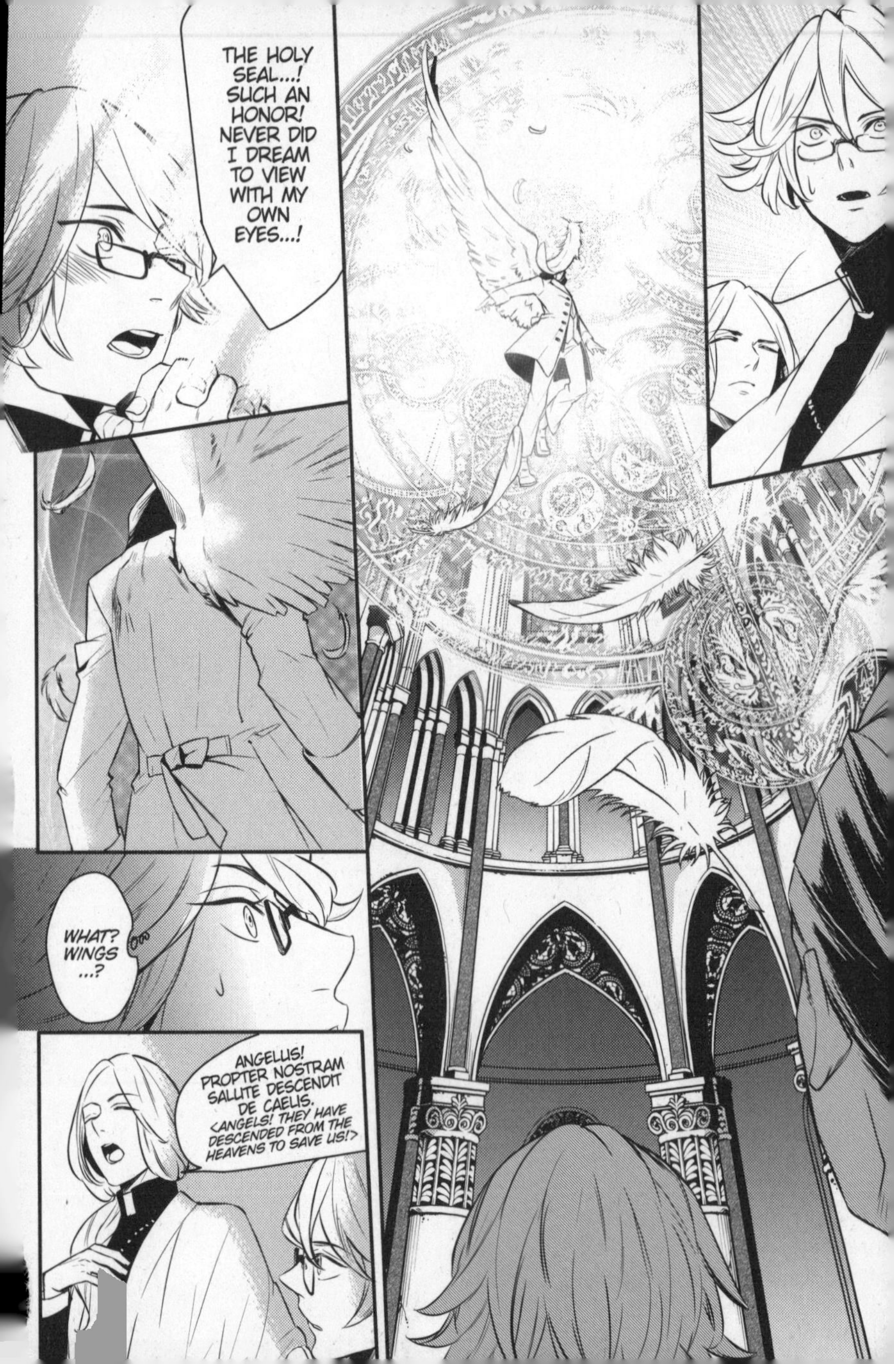
THE HOLY SEAL...! SUCH AN HONOR! NEVER DID I DREAM TO VIEW WITH MY OWN EYES...!
WHAT? WINGS ...?
ANGELUS! PROPTER NOSTRAM SALUTE DESCENDIT DE CAELIS.
<ANGELS! THEY HAVE DESCENDED FROM THE HEAVENS TO SAVE US!>

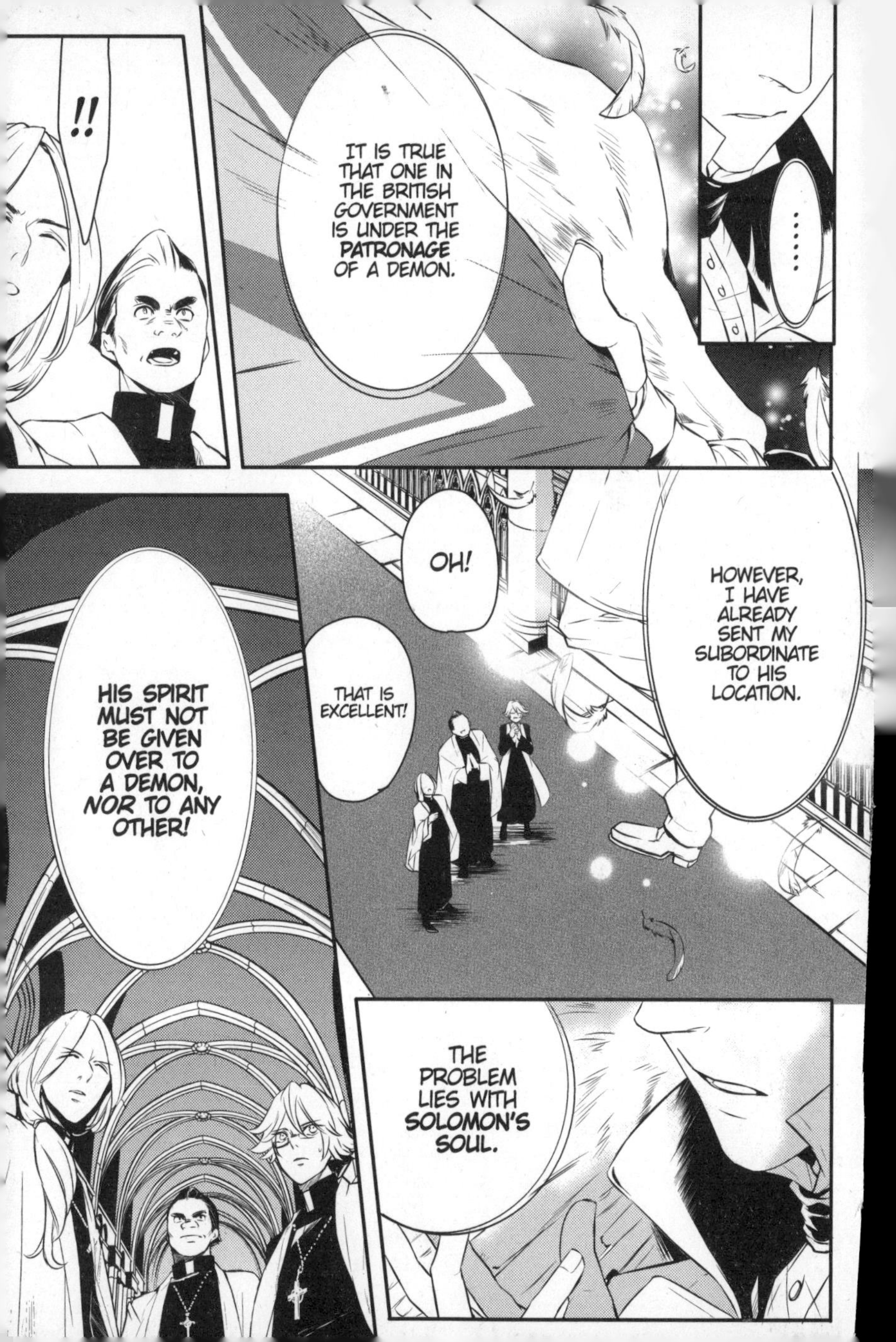
......
IT IS TRUE THAT ONE IN THE BRITISH GOVERNMENT IS UNDER THE PATRONAGE OF A DEMON.
!!
HOWEVER, I HAVE ALREADY SENT MY SUBORDINATE TO HIS LOCATION.
OH!
THAT IS EXCELLENT!
THE PROBLEM LIES WITH SOLOMON'S SOUL.
HIS SPIRIT MUST NOT BE GIVEN OVER TO A DEMON, NOR TO ANY OTHER!

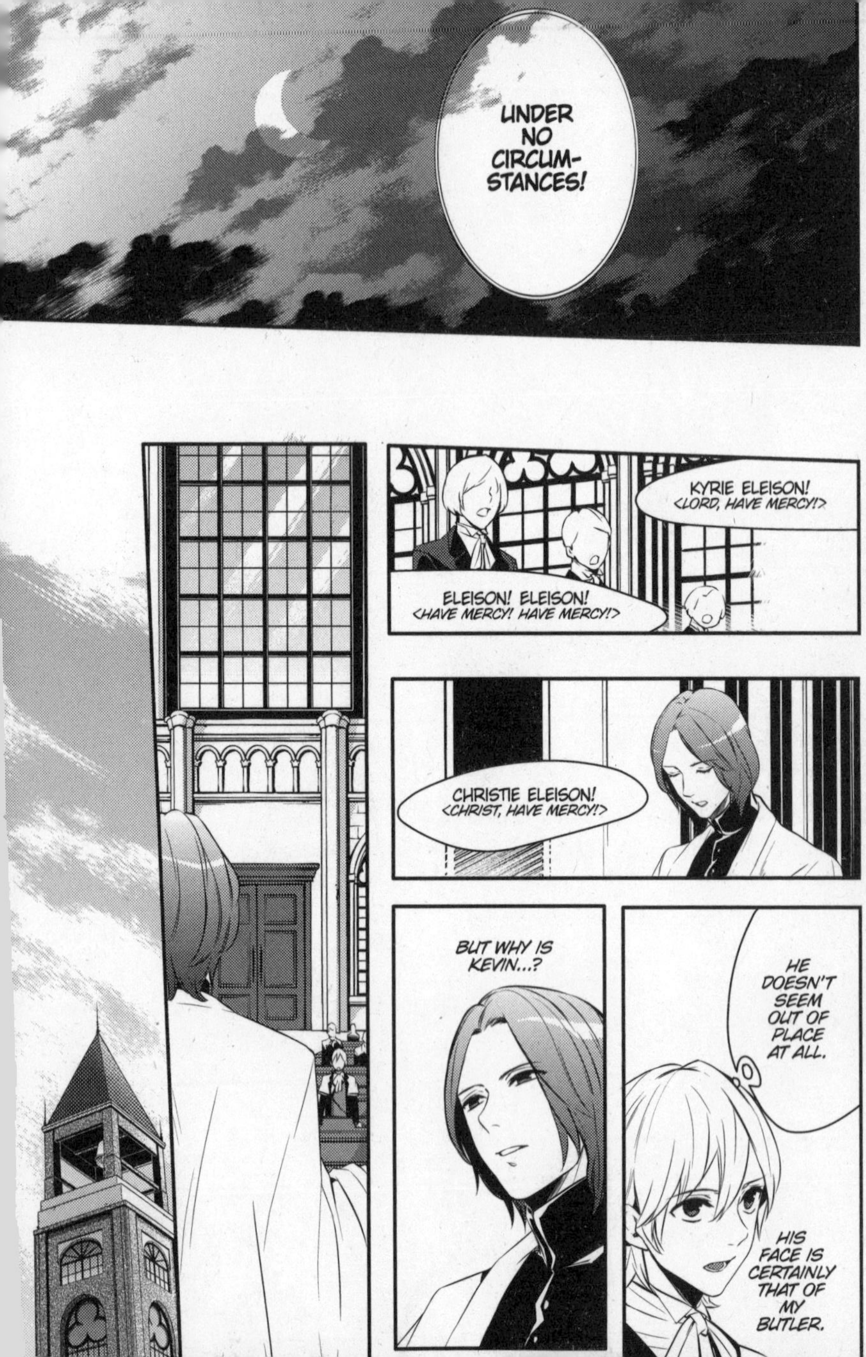
UNDER NO CIRCUMSTANCES!
KYRIE ELEISON! <LORD, HAVE MERCY!>
ELEISON! ELEISON! <HAVE MERCY! HAVE MERCY!>
CHRISTIE ELEISON! <CHRIST, HAVE MERCY!>
HE DOESN'T SEEM OUT OF PLACE AT ALL.
HIS FACE IS CERTAINLY THAT OF MY BUTLER.
BUT WHY IS KEVIN...?

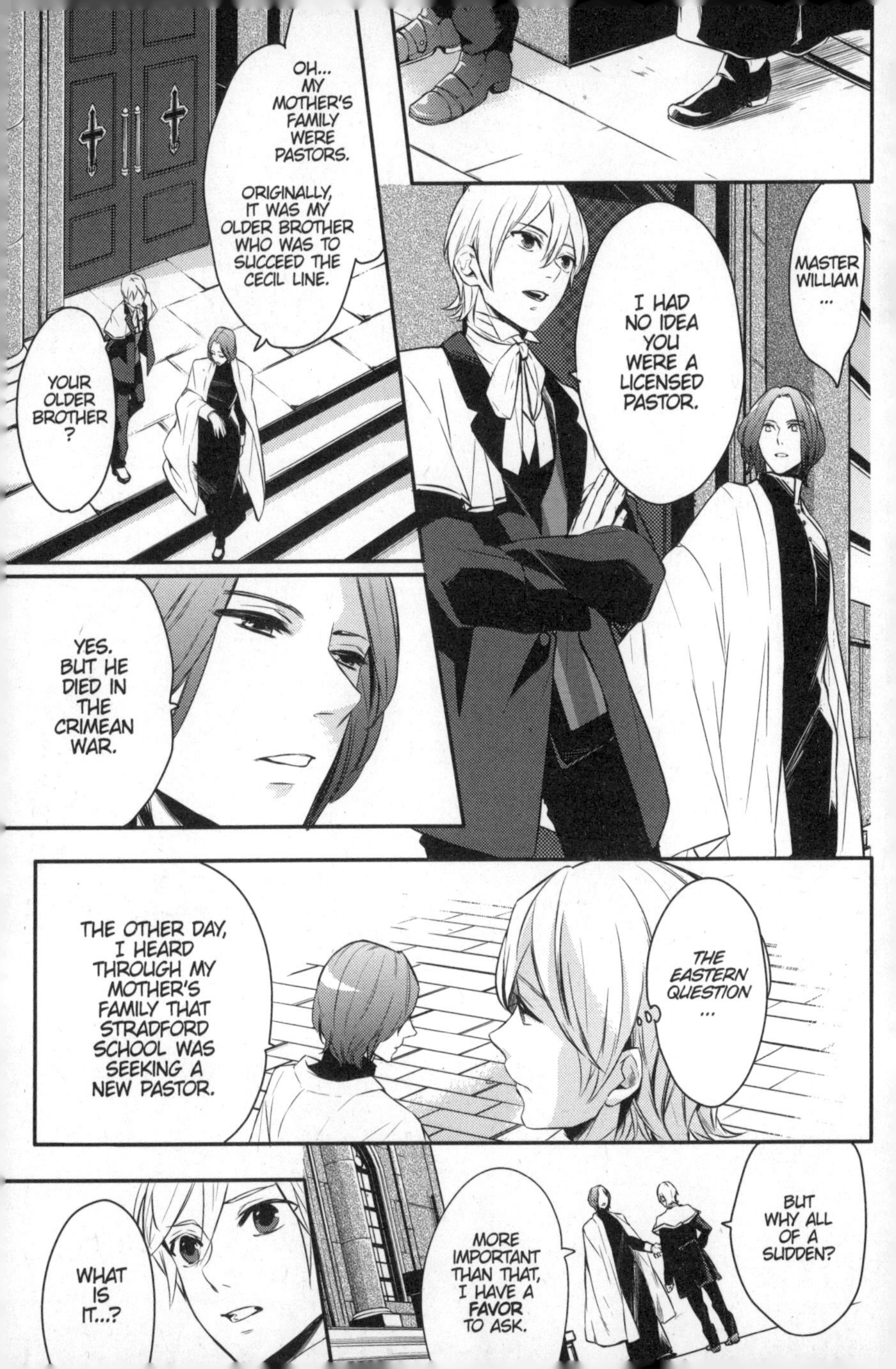
MASTER WILLIAM ...
I HAD NO IDEA YOU WERE A LICENSED PASTOR.
OH... MY MOTHER'S FAMILY WERE PASTORS.
ORIGINALLY, IT WAS MY OLDER BROTHER WHO WAS TO SUCCEED THE CECIL LINE.
YOUR OLDER BROTHER ?
YES. BUT HE DIED IN THE CRIMEAN WAR.
THE EASTERN QUESTION ...
THE OTHER DAY, I HEARD THROUGH MY MOTHER'S FAMILY THAT STRADFORD SCHOOL WAS SEEKING A NEW PASTOR.
BUT WHY ALL OF A SUDDEN?
MORE IMPORTANT THAN THAT, I HAVE A FAVOR TO ASK.
WHAT IS IT...?

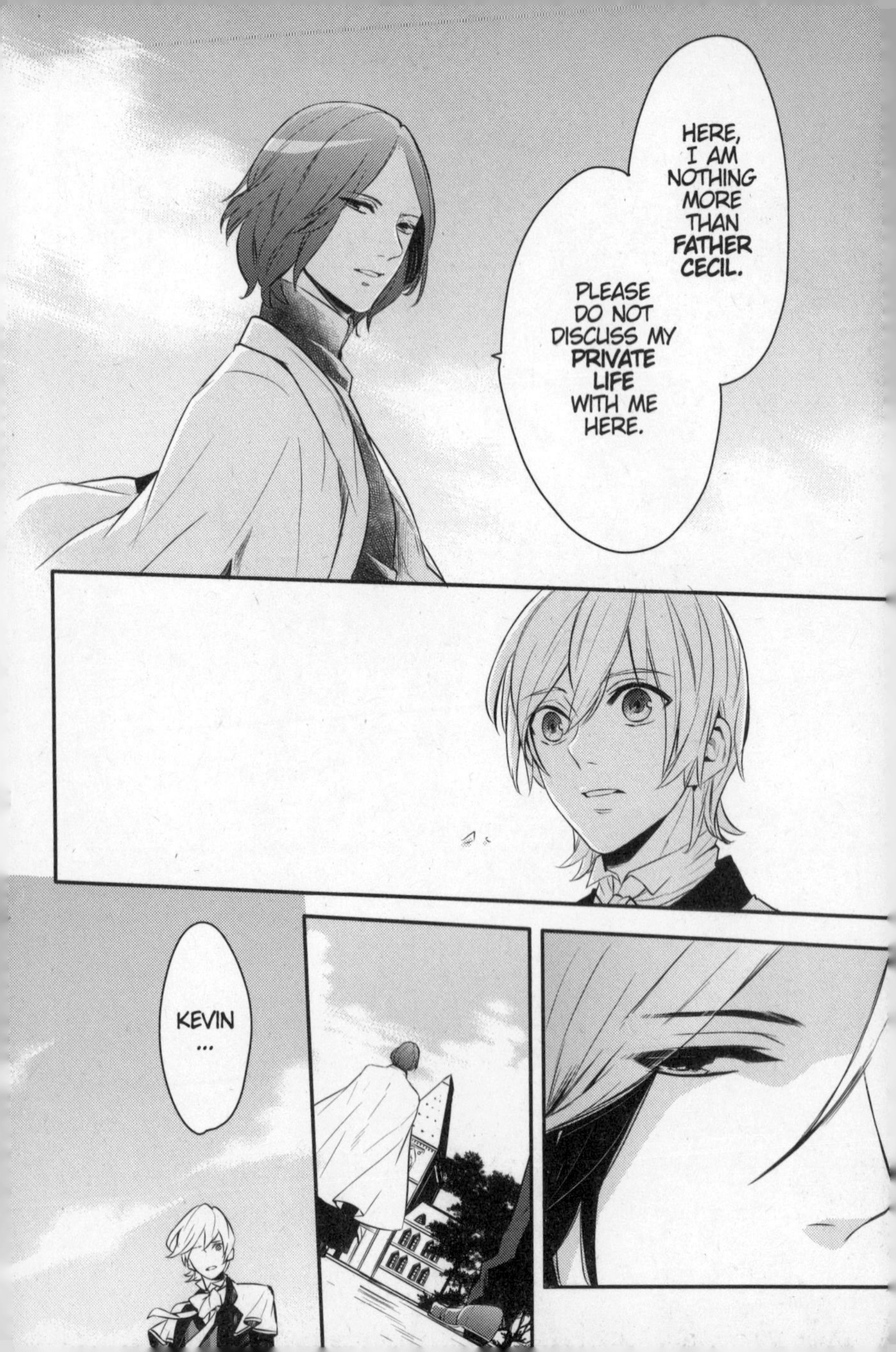
HERE, I AM NOTHING MORE THAN FATHER CECIL.
PLEASE DO NOT DISCUSS MY PRIVATE LIFE WITH ME HERE.
KEVIN ...

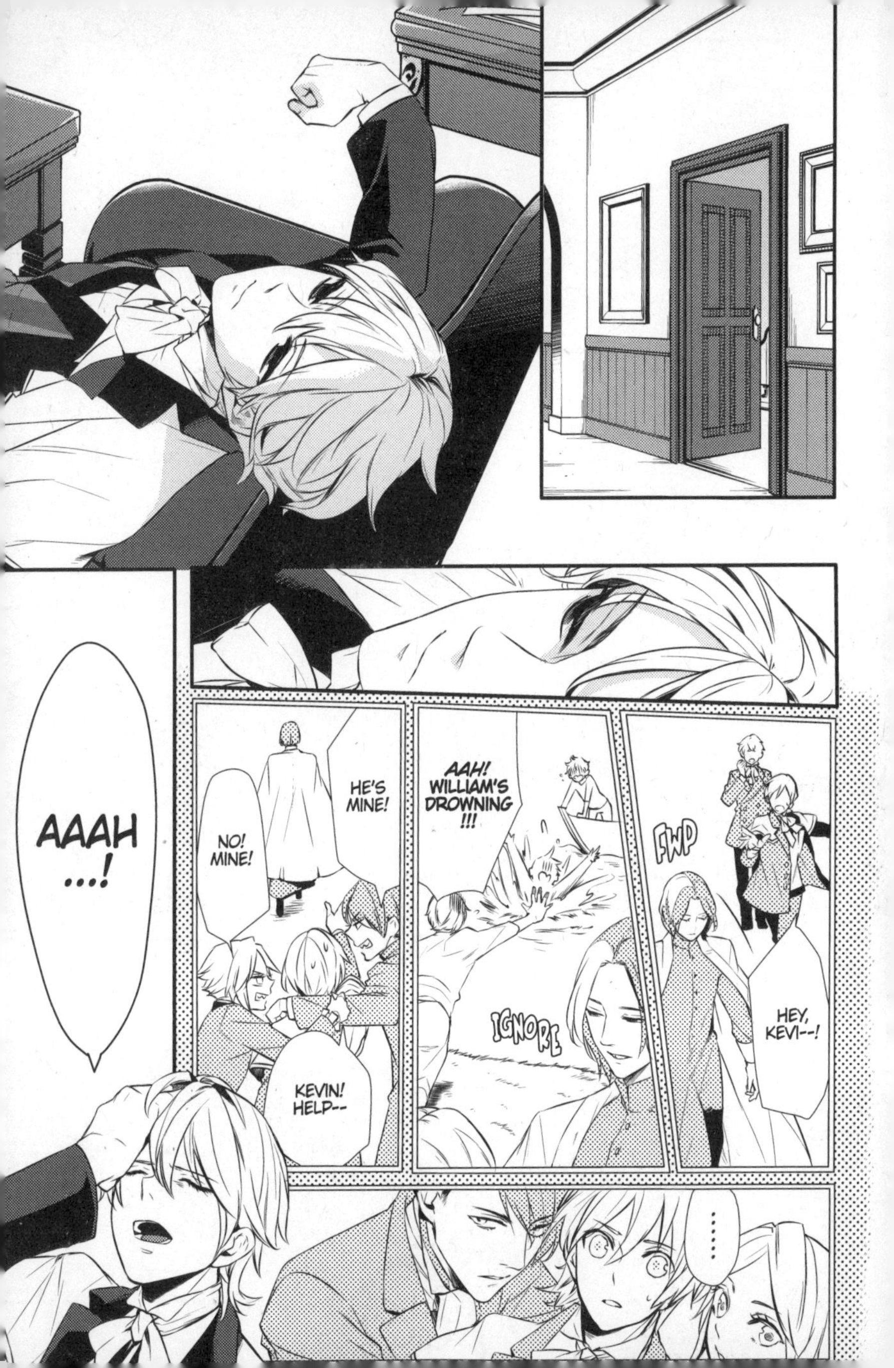
FWP
HEY, KEVI--!
AAH! WILLIAM'S DROWNING !!!
IGNORE
HE'S MINE!
NO! MINE!
KEVIN! HELP--
......
AAAH ...!

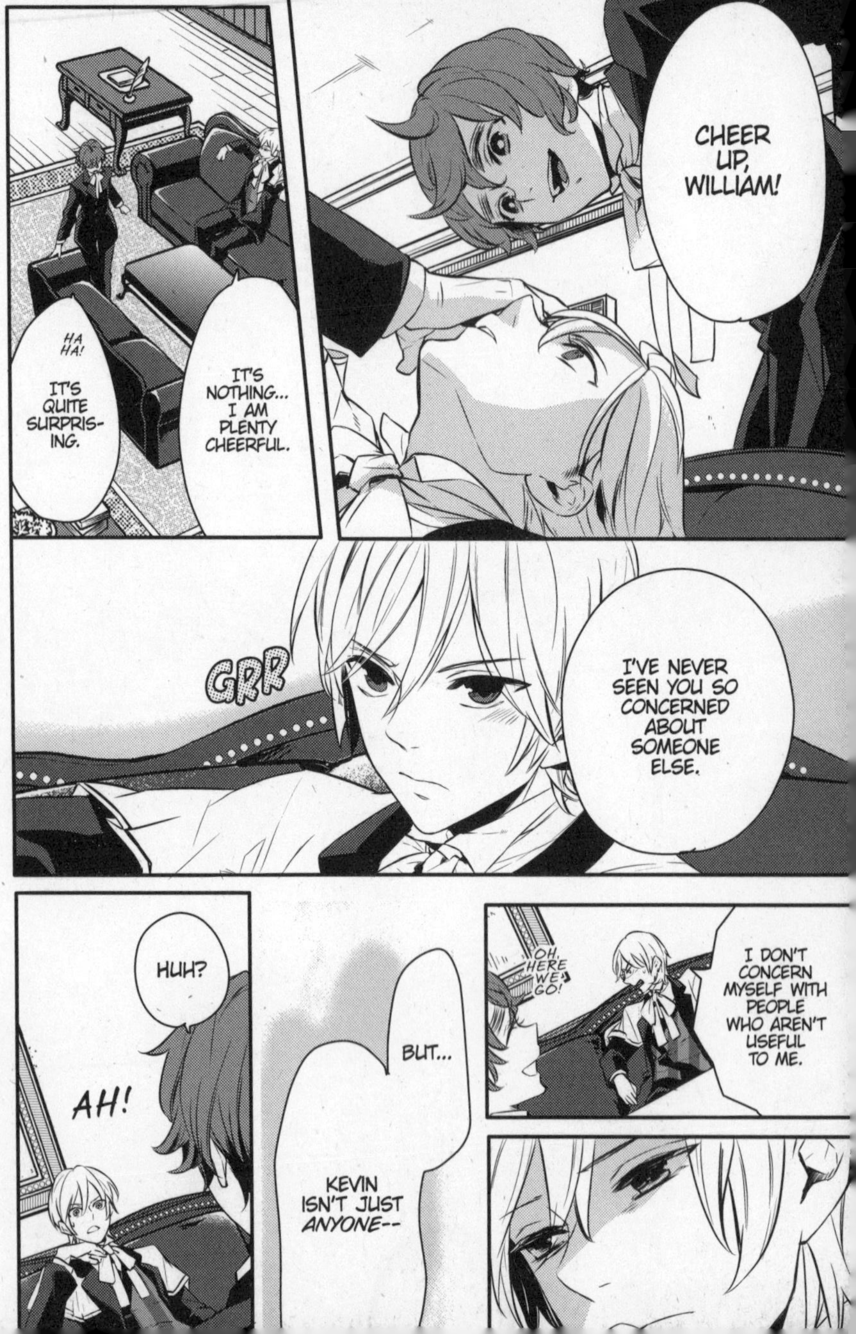
CHEER UP, WILLIAM!
IT'S NOTHING... I AM PLENTY CHEERFUL.
HA HA!
IT'S QUITE SURPRIS-ING.
I'VE NEVER SEEN YOU SO CONCERNED ABOUT SOMEONE ELSE.
GRR
I DON'T CONCERN MYSELF WITH PEOPLE WHO AREN'T USEFUL TO ME.
OH, HERE WE GO!
BUT...
KEVIN ISN'T JUST *ANYONE*--
HUH?
AH!

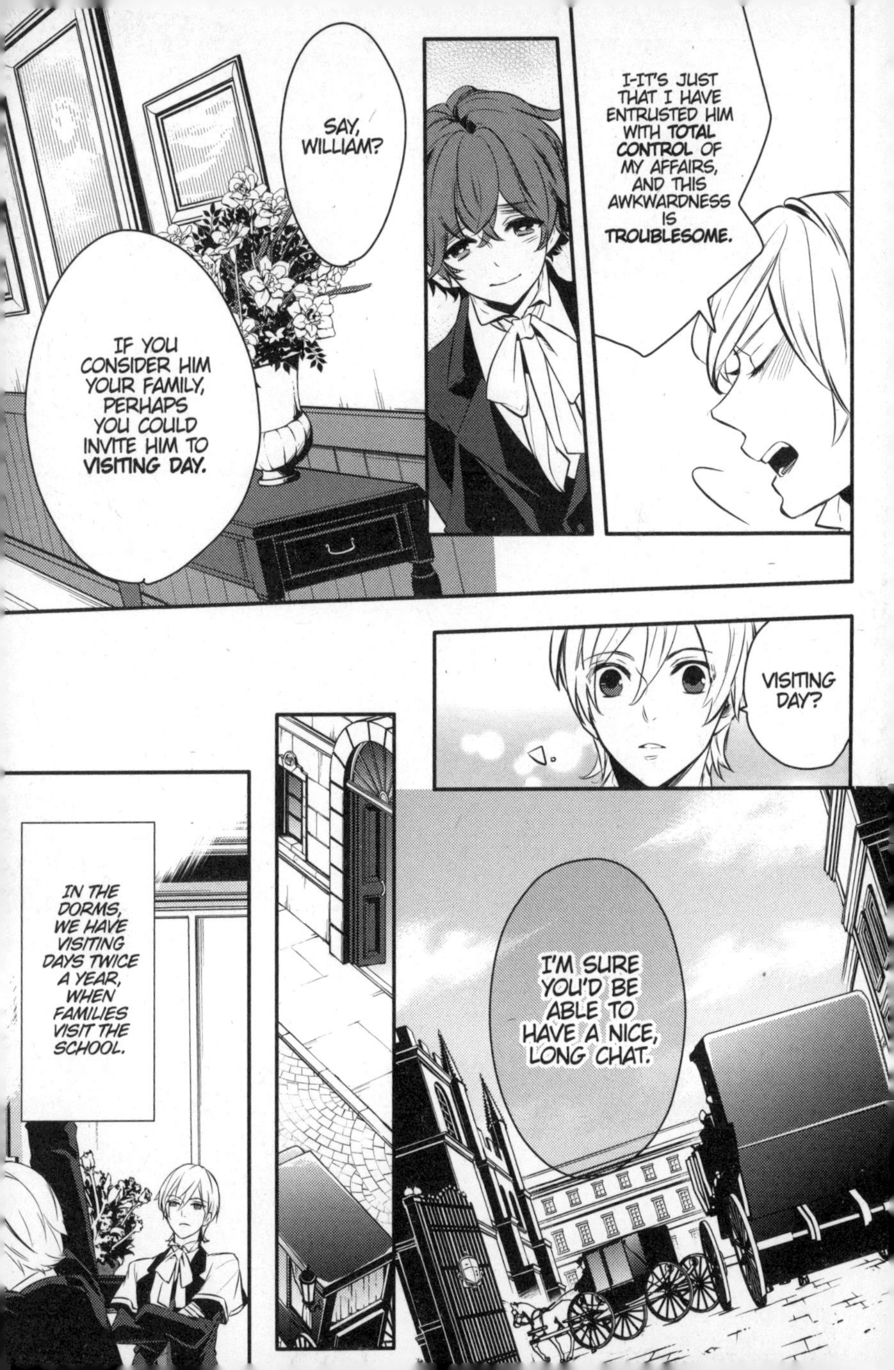
I-IT'S JUST THAT I HAVE ENTRUSTED HIM WITH TOTAL CONTROL OF MY AFFAIRS, AND THIS AWKWARDNESS IS TROUBLESOME.
SAY, WILLIAM?
IF YOU CONSIDER HIM YOUR FAMILY, PERHAPS YOU COULD INVITE HIM TO VISITING DAY.
VISITING DAY?
I'M SURE YOU'D BE ABLE TO HAVE A NICE, LONG CHAT.
IN THE DORMS, WE HAVE VISITING DAYS TWICE A YEAR, WHEN FAMILIES VISIT THE SCHOOL.

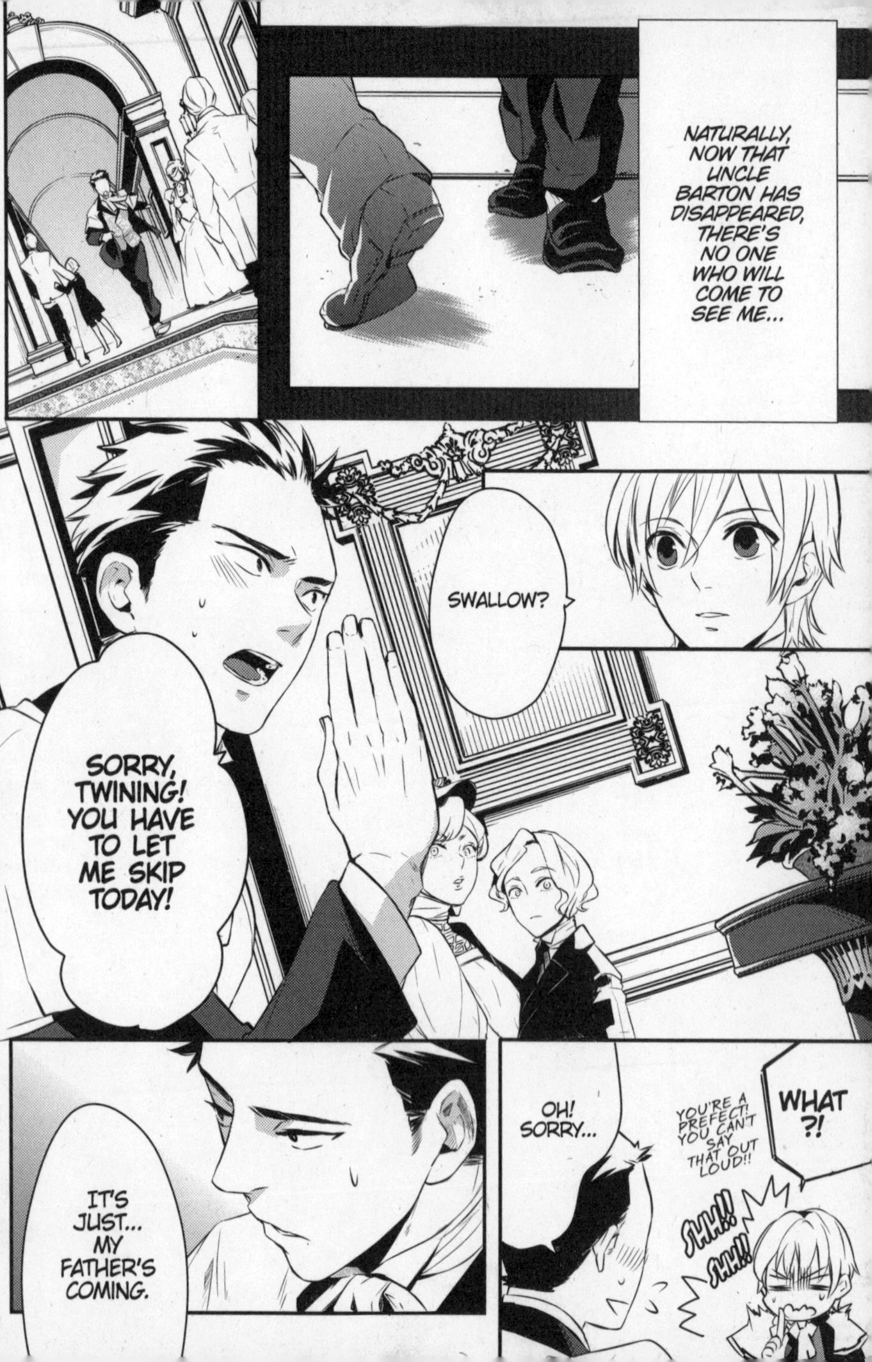
NATURALLY, NOW THAT UNCLE BARTON HAS DISAPPEARED, THERE'S NO ONE WHO WILL COME TO SEE ME...
SWALLOW?
SORRY, TWINING! YOU HAVE TO LET ME SKIP TODAY!
WHAT ?!
YOU'RE A PREFECT! YOU CAN'T SAY THAT OUT LOUD!!
SHH!!
SHH!!
OH! SORRY...
IT'S JUST... MY FATHER'S COMING.

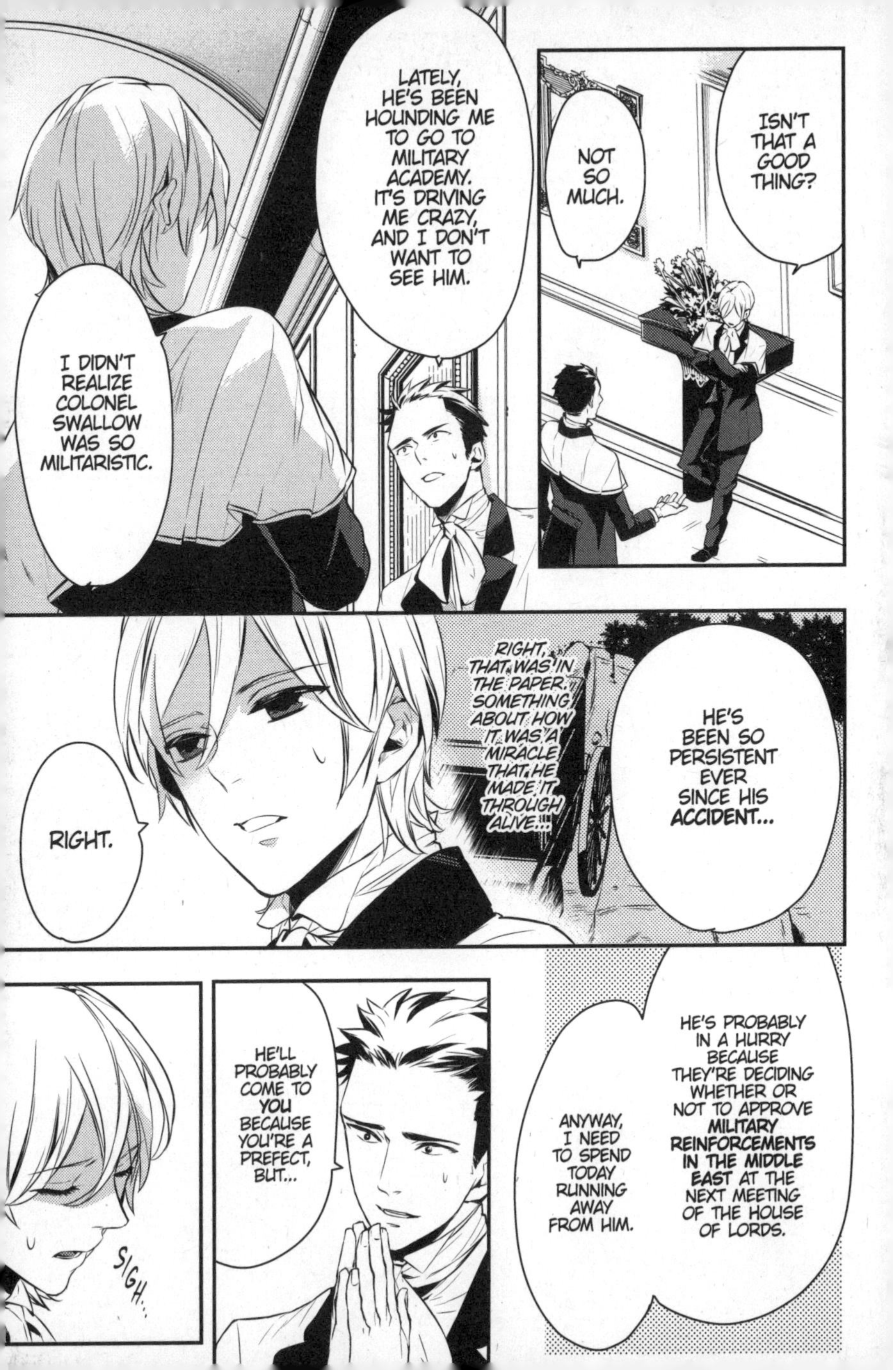
ISN'T THAT A GOOD THING?
NOT SO MUCH.
LATELY, HE'S BEEN HOUNDING ME TO GO TO MILITARY ACADEMY. IT'S DRIVING ME CRAZY, AND I DON'T WANT TO SEE HIM.
I DIDN'T REALIZE COLONEL SWALLOW WAS SO MILITARISTIC.
HE'S BEEN SO PERSISTENT EVER SINCE HIS **ACCIDENT...**
RIGHT, THAT WAS IN THE PAPER. SOMETHING ABOUT HOW IT WAS A MIRACLE THAT HE MADE IT THROUGH ALIVE...
RIGHT.
HE'S PROBABLY IN A HURRY BECAUSE THEY'RE DECIDING WHETHER OR NOT TO APPROVE **MILITARY REINFORCEMENTS IN THE MIDDLE EAST** AT THE NEXT MEETING OF THE HOUSE OF LORDS.
ANYWAY, I NEED TO SPEND TODAY RUNNING AWAY FROM HIM.
HE'LL PROBABLY COME TO **YOU** BECAUSE YOU'RE A PREFECT, BUT...
SIGH...

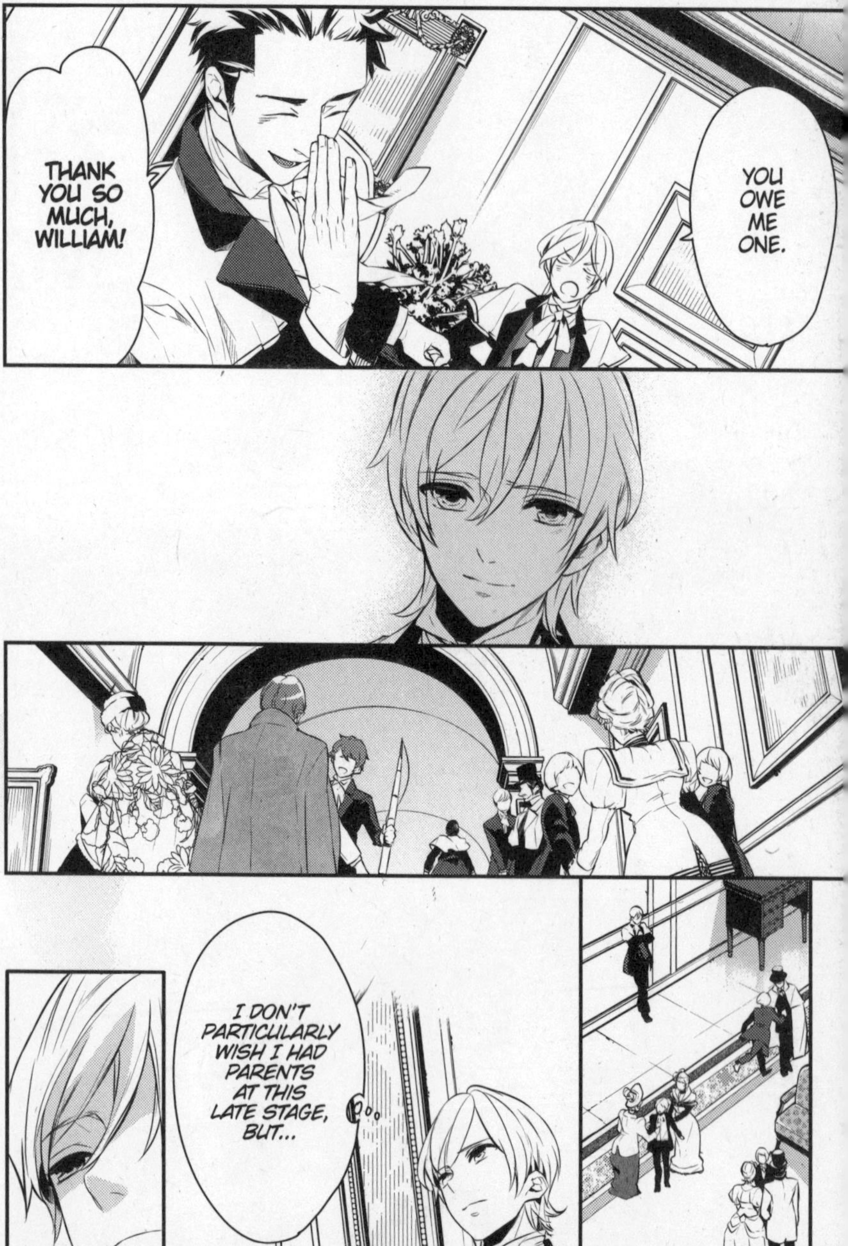
YOU OWE ME ONE.
THANK YOU SO MUCH, WILLIAM!
I DON'T PARTICULARLY WISH I HAD PARENTS AT THIS LATE STAGE, BUT...

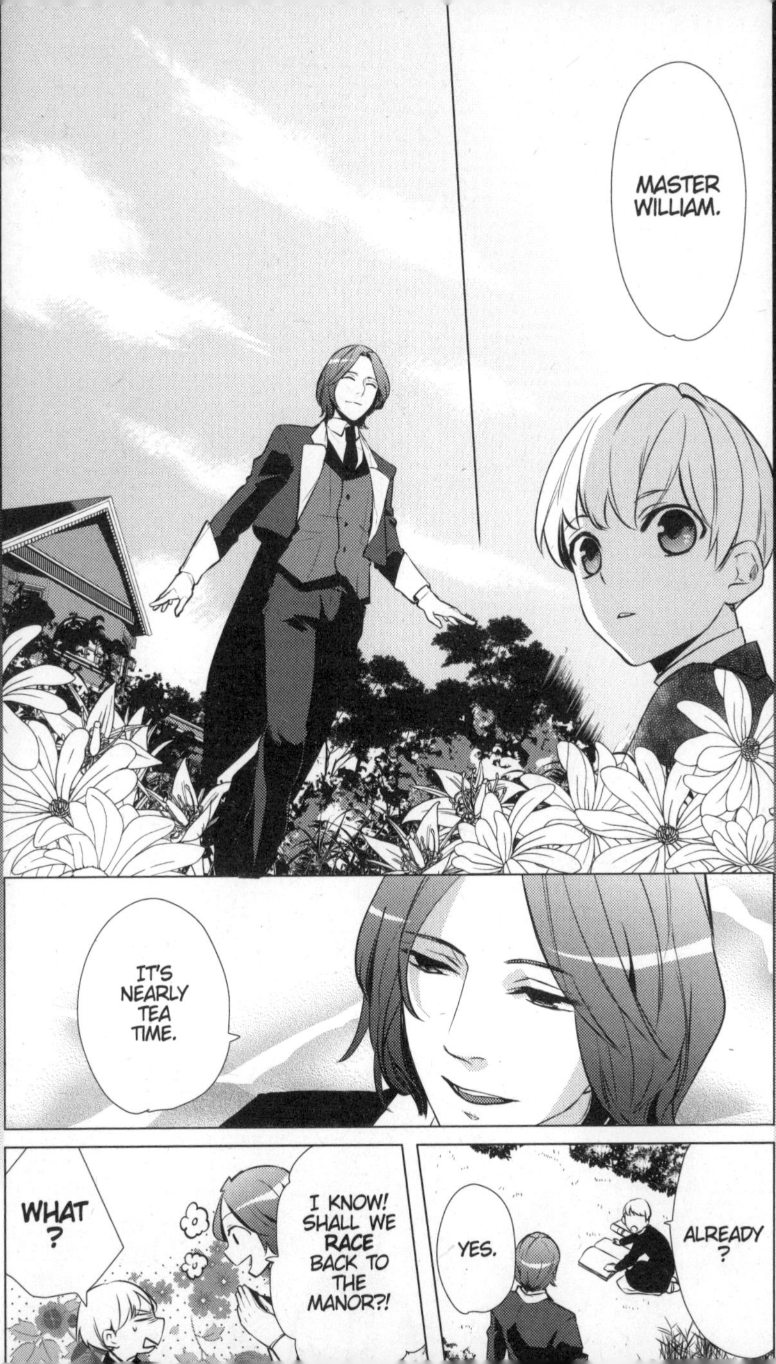
MASTER WILLIAM.
IT'S NEARLY TEA TIME.
ALREADY ?
YES.
I KNOW! SHALL WE RACE BACK TO THE MANOR?!
WHAT ?

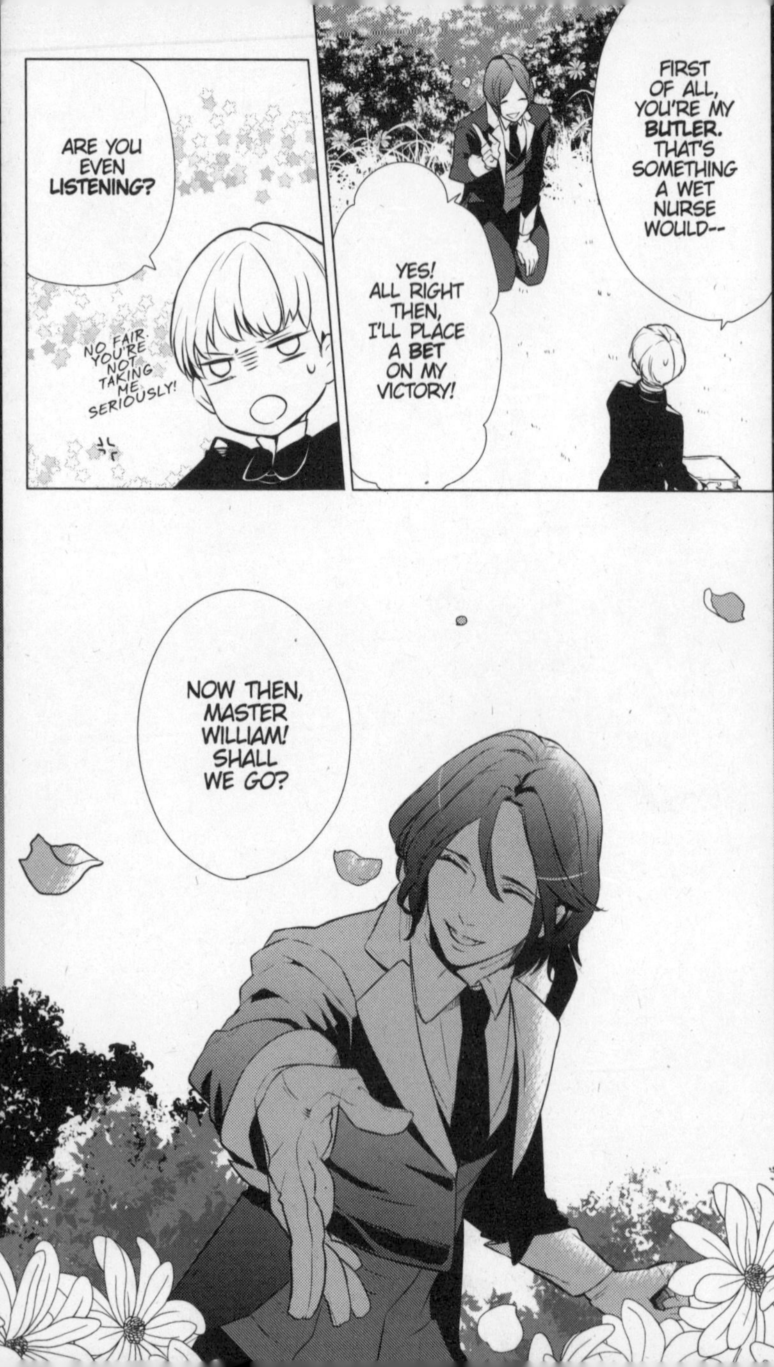
FIRST OF ALL, YOU'RE MY BUTLER. THAT'S SOMETHING A WET NURSE WOULD--
YES! ALL RIGHT THEN, I'LL PLACE A BET ON MY VICTORY!
ARE YOU EVEN LISTENING?
NO FAIR. YOU'RE NOT TAKING ME SERIOUSLY!
NOW THEN, MASTER WILLIAM! SHALL WE GO?

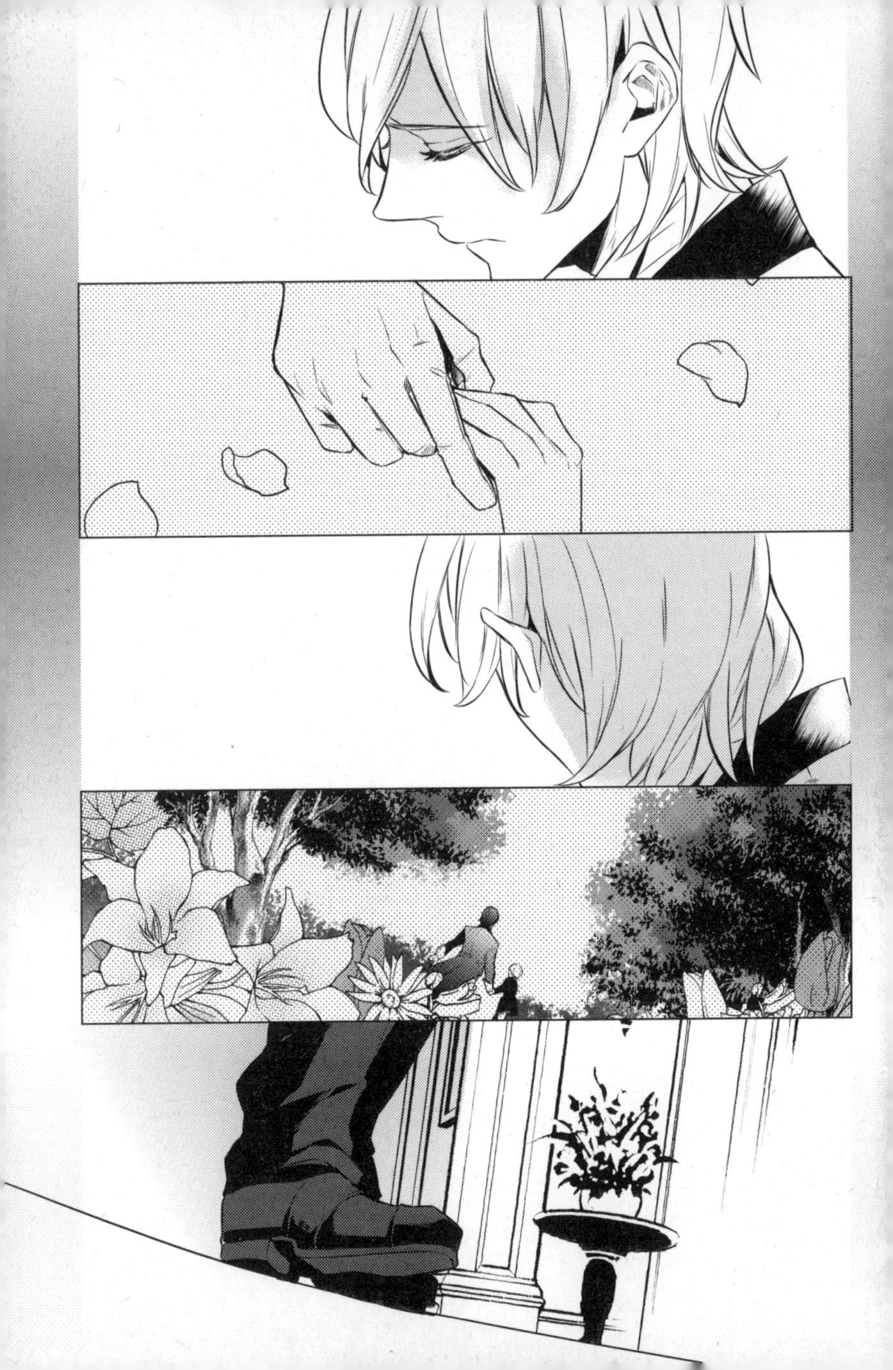

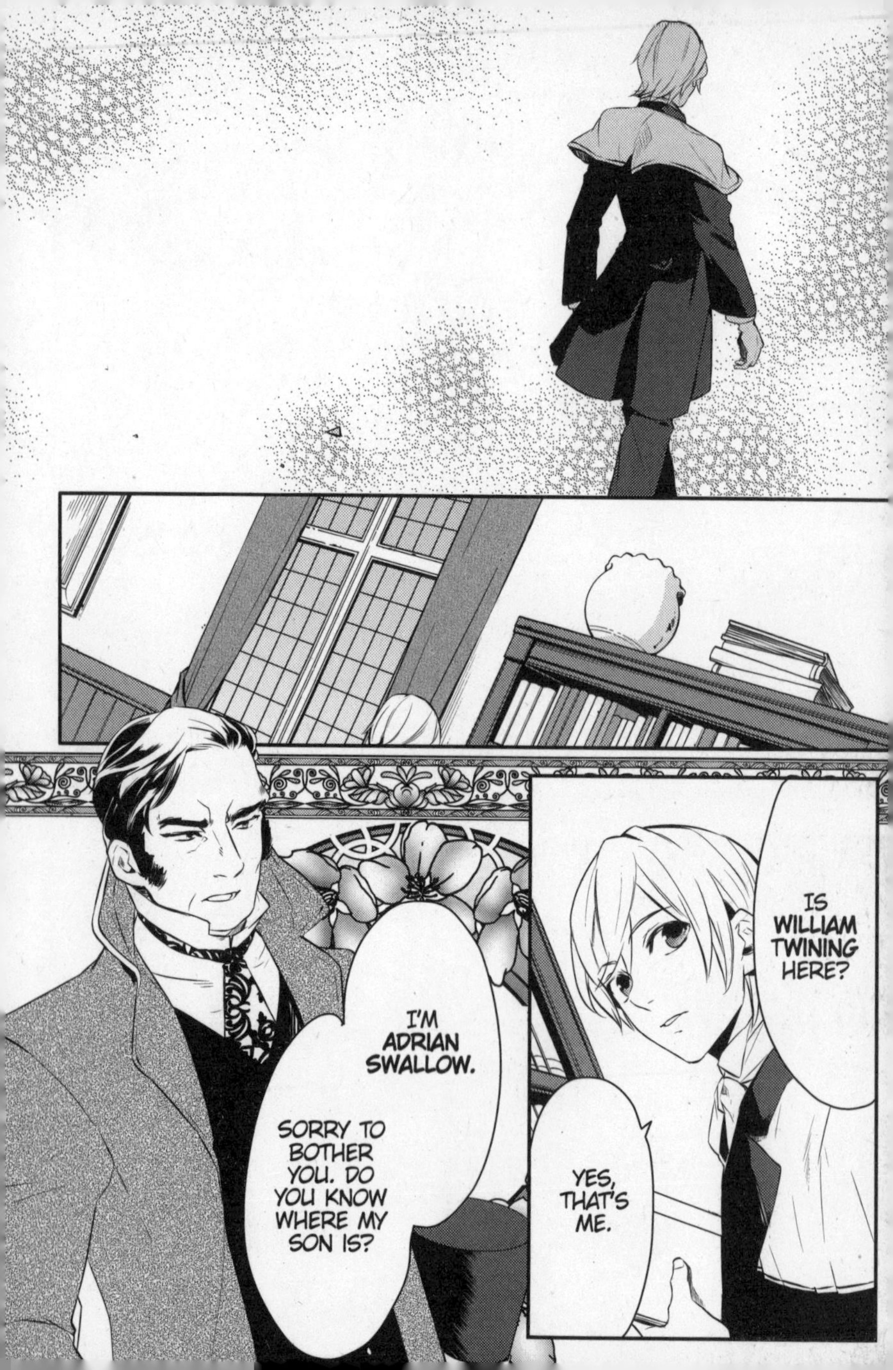
IS WILLIAM TWINING HERE?
YES, THAT'S ME.
I'M ADRIAN SWALLOW.
SORRY TO BOTHER YOU. DO YOU KNOW WHERE MY SON IS?

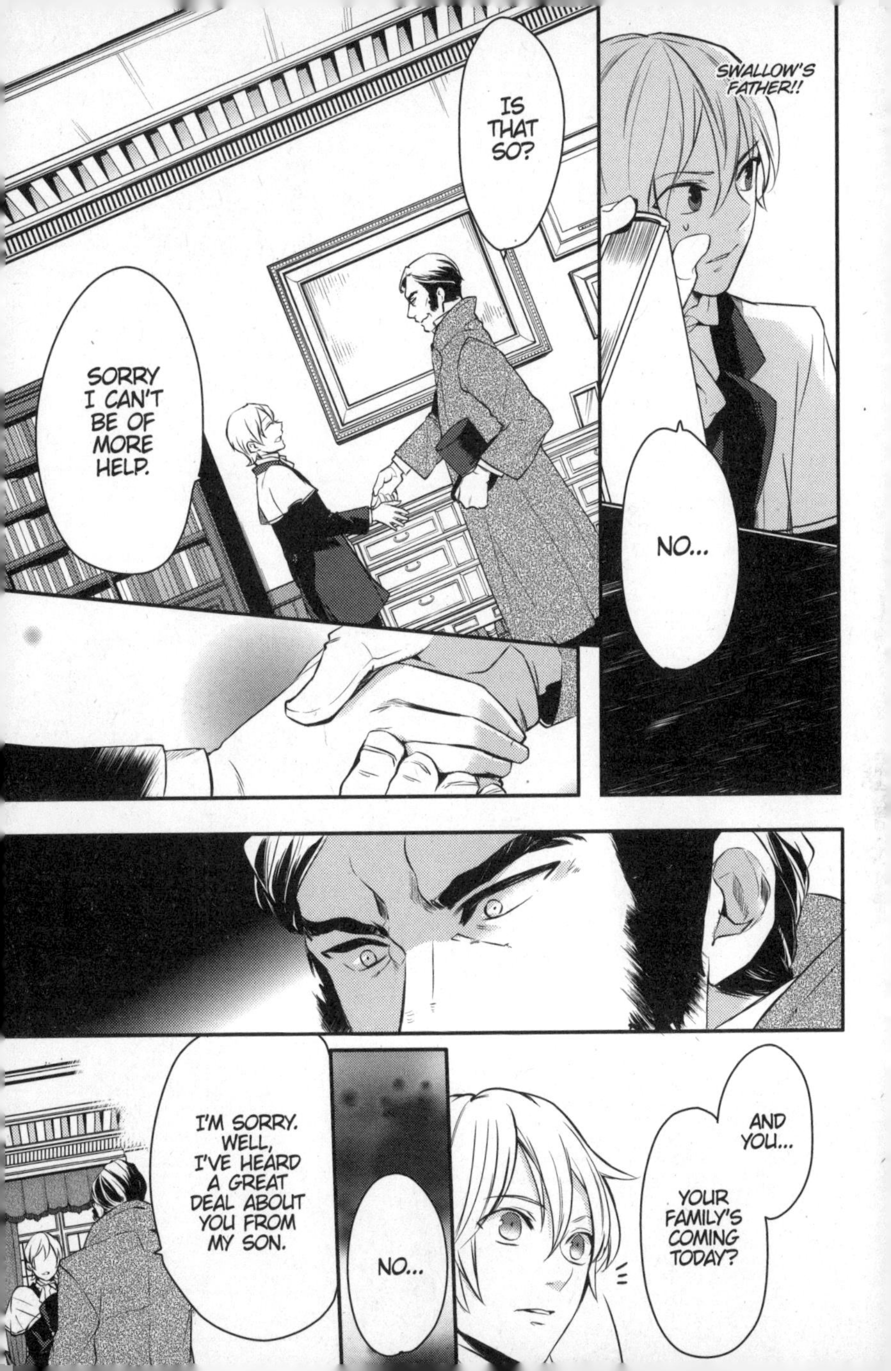
SWALLOW'S FATHER!!
NO...
IS THAT SO?
SORRY I CAN'T BE OF MORE HELP.
AND YOU...
YOUR FAMILY'S COMING TODAY?
NO...
I'M SORRY. WELL, I'VE HEARD A GREAT DEAL ABOUT YOU FROM MY SON.

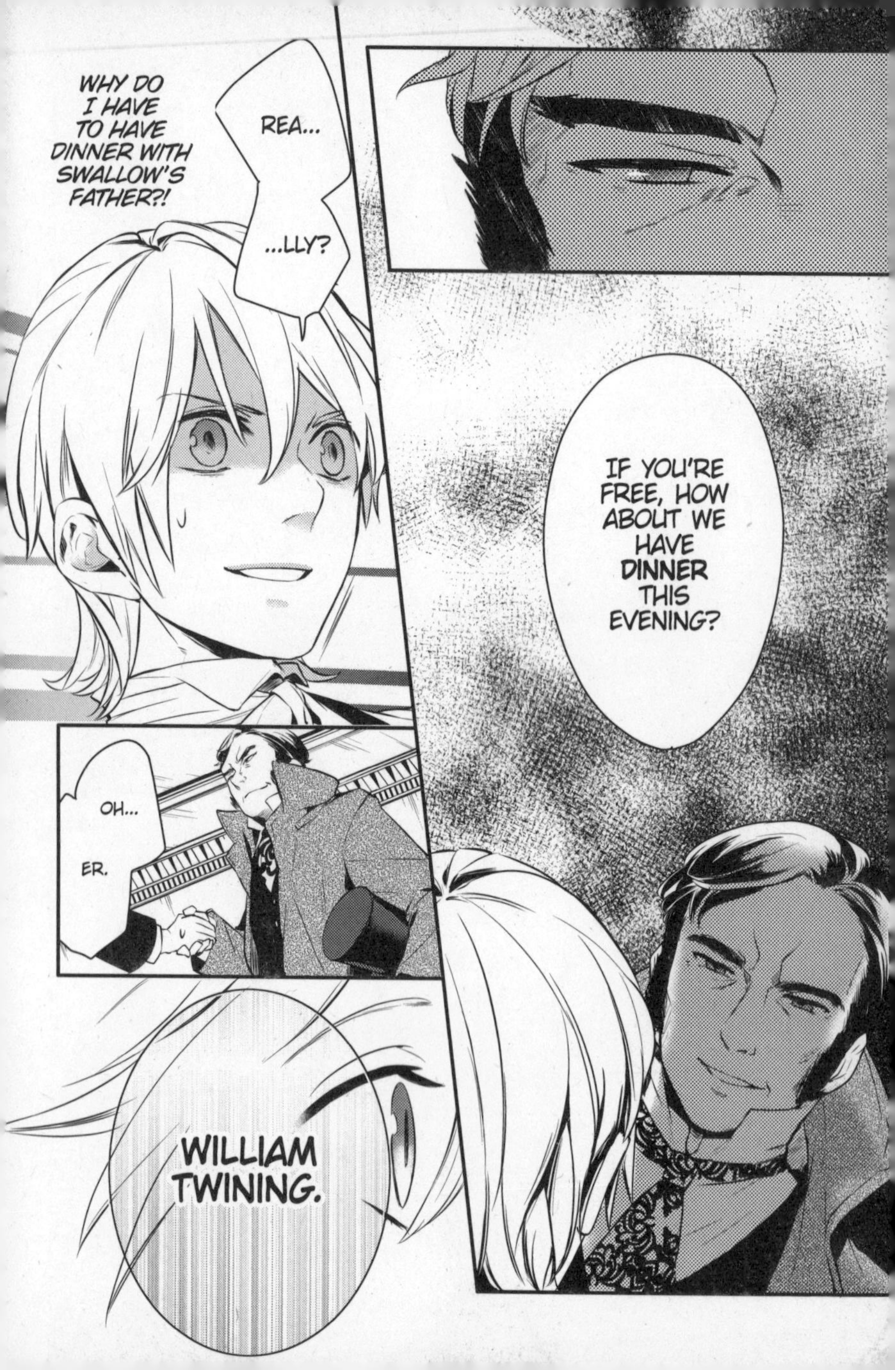
IF YOU'RE FREE, HOW ABOUT WE HAVE DINNER THIS EVENING?
REA...
...LLY?
WHY DO I HAVE TO HAVE DINNER WITH SWALLOW'S FATHER?!
OH...
ER.
WILLIAM TWINING.

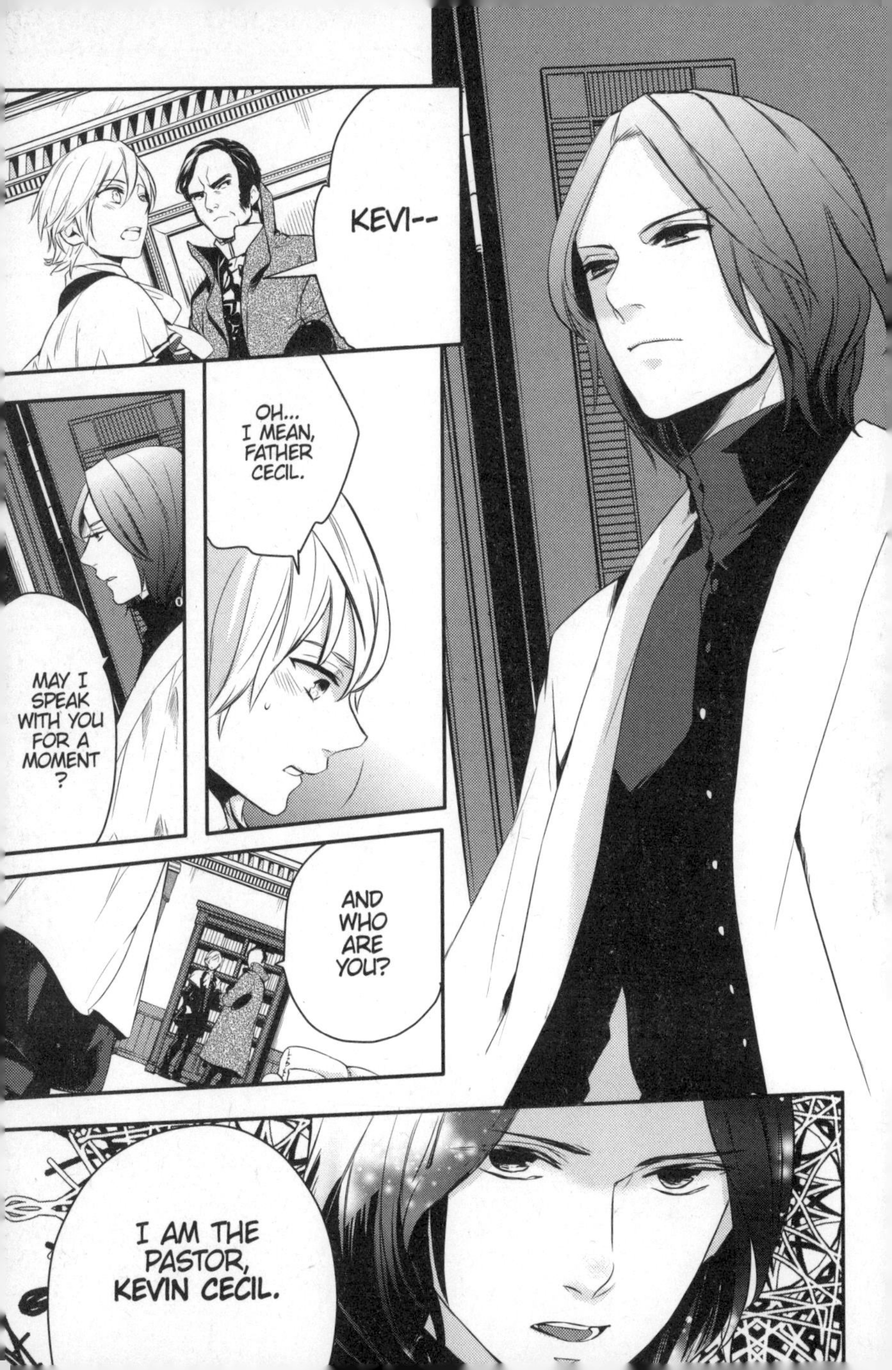
KEVI--
OH... I MEAN, FATHER CECIL.
MAY I SPEAK WITH YOU FOR A MOMENT?
AND WHO ARE YOU?
I AM THE PASTOR, KEVIN CECIL.

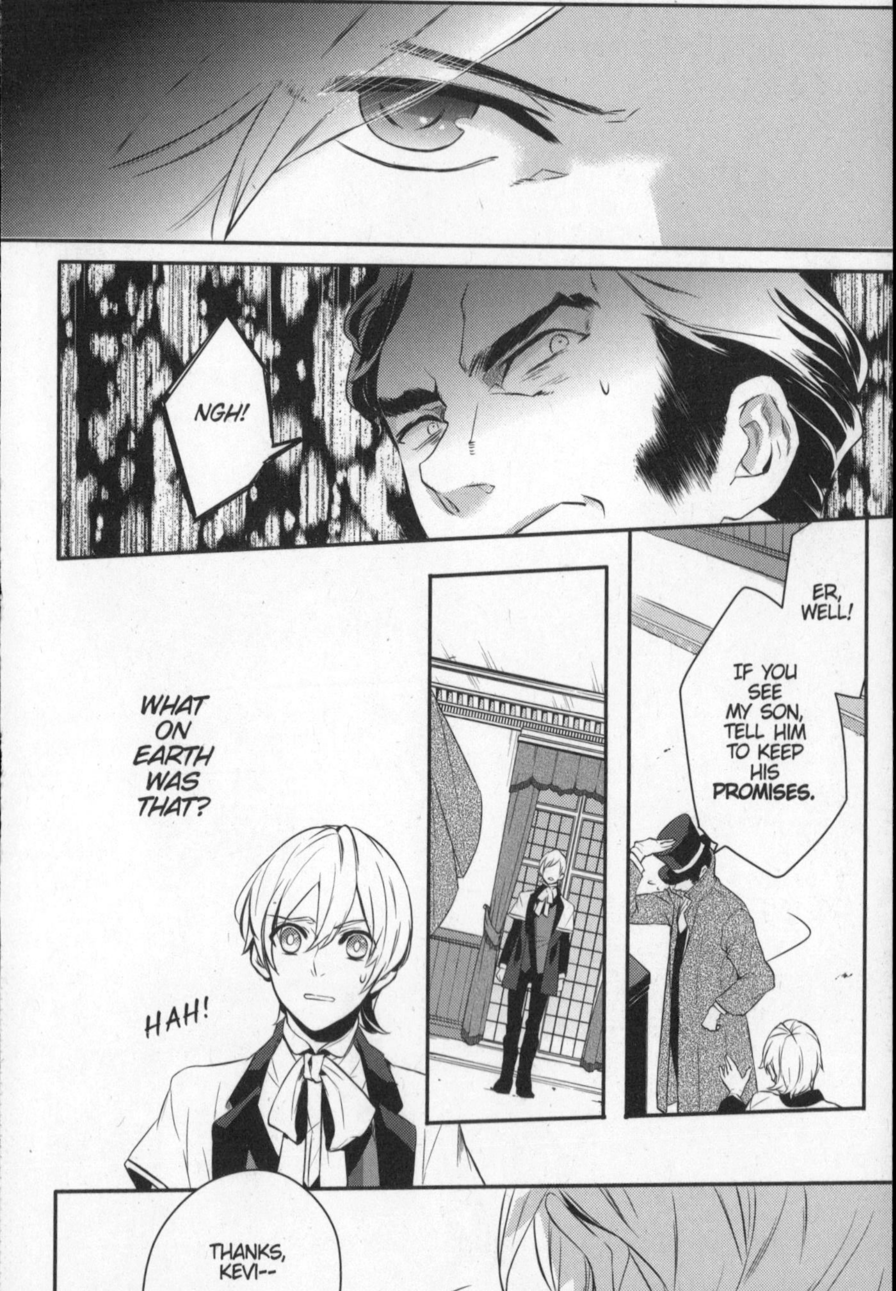
NGH!
ER, WELL!
IF YOU SEE MY SON, TELL HIM TO KEEP HIS PROMISES.
WHAT ON EARTH WAS THAT?
HAH!
THANKS, KEVI--

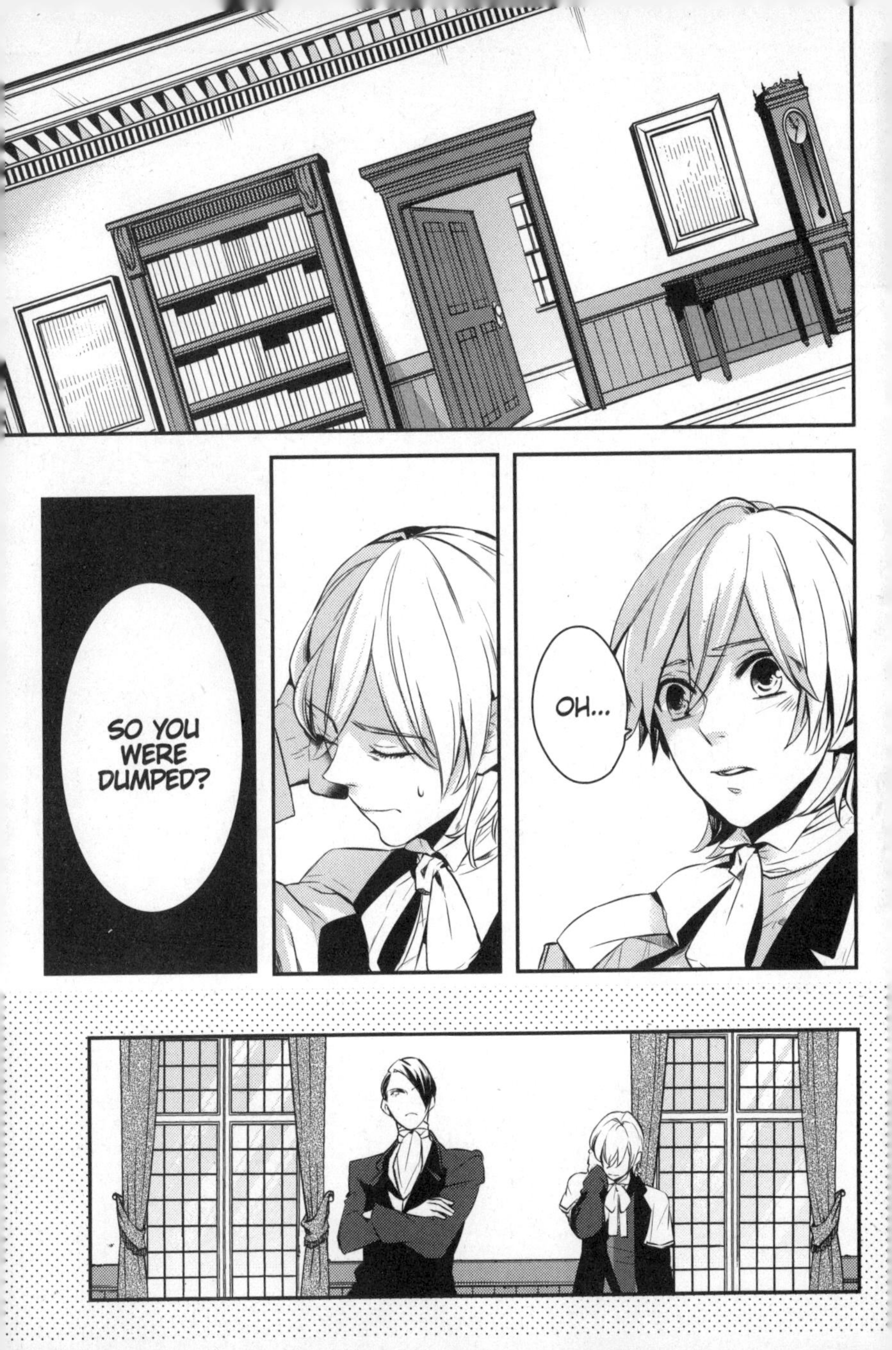
OH...
SO YOU WERE DUMPED?

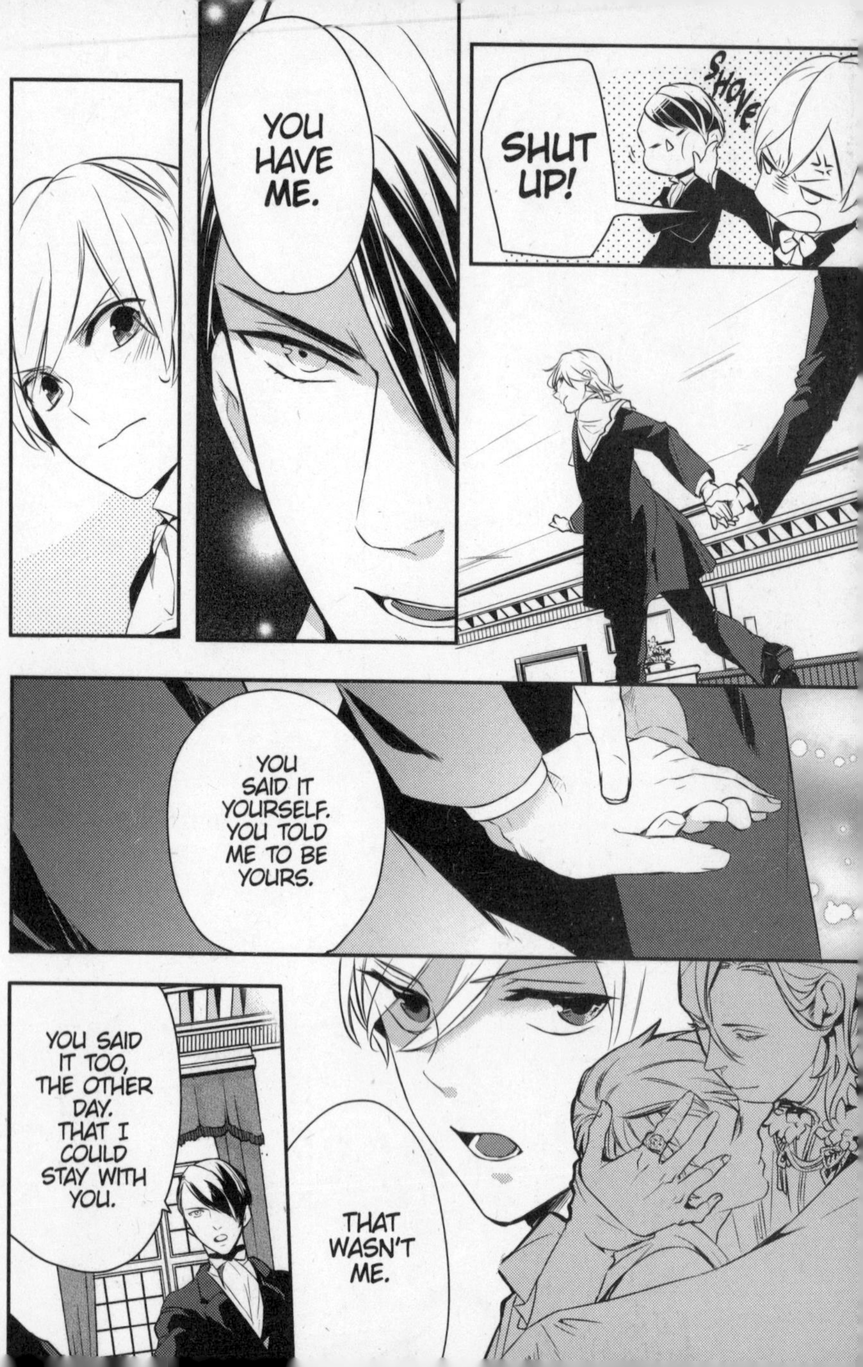

SHOVE
SHUT UP!
YOU HAVE ME.
YOU SAID IT YOURSELF. YOU TOLD ME TO BE YOURS.
THAT WASN'T ME.
YOU SAID IT TOO, THE OTHER DAY. THAT I COULD STAY WITH YOU.

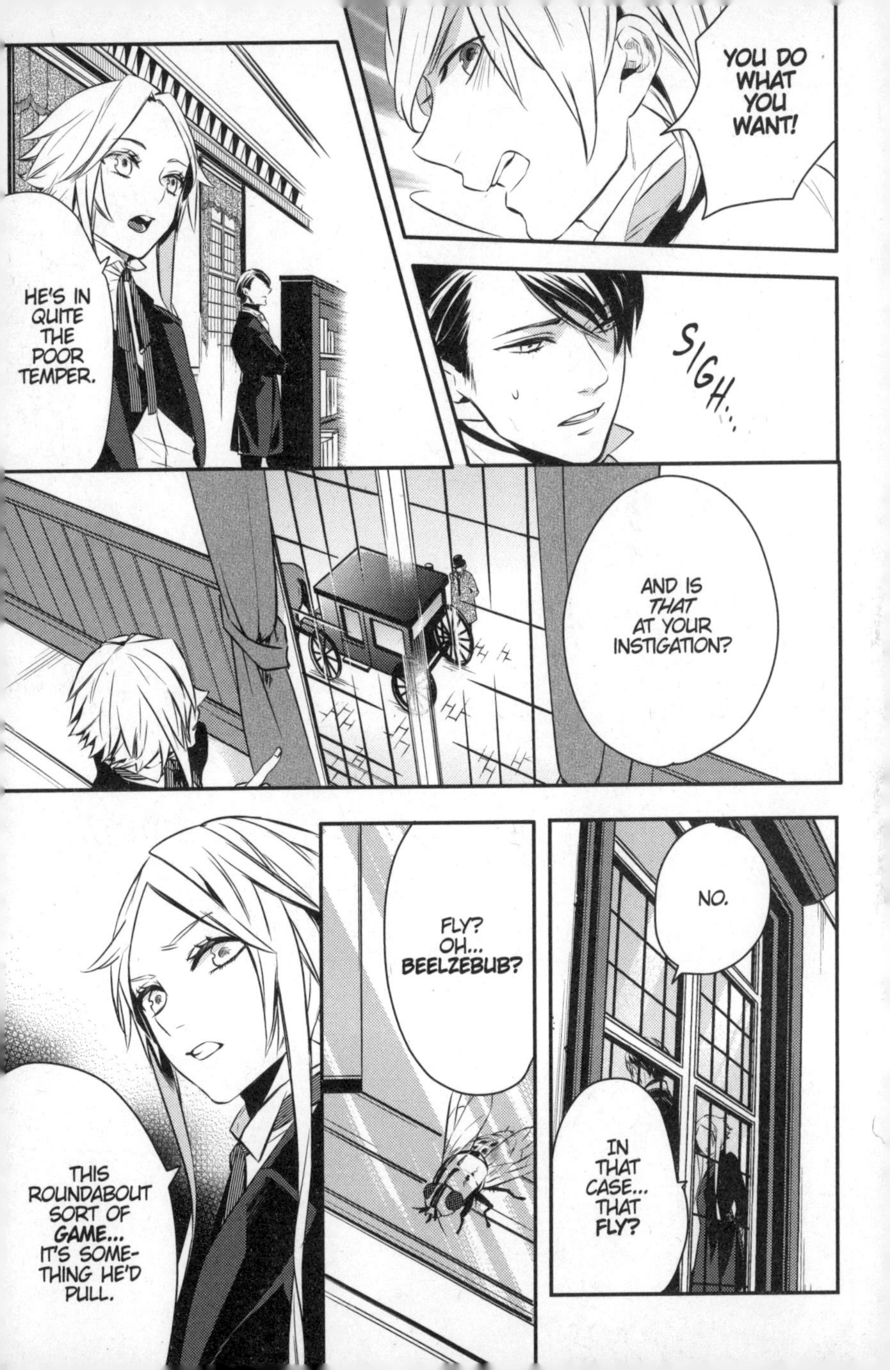
YOU DO WHAT YOU WANT!
SIGH...
HE'S IN QUITE THE POOR TEMPER.
AND IS THAT AT YOUR INSTIGATION?
NO.
IN THAT CASE... THAT FLY?
FLY? OH... BEELZEBUB?
THIS ROUNDABOUT SORT OF GAME... IT'S SOMETHING HE'D PULL.

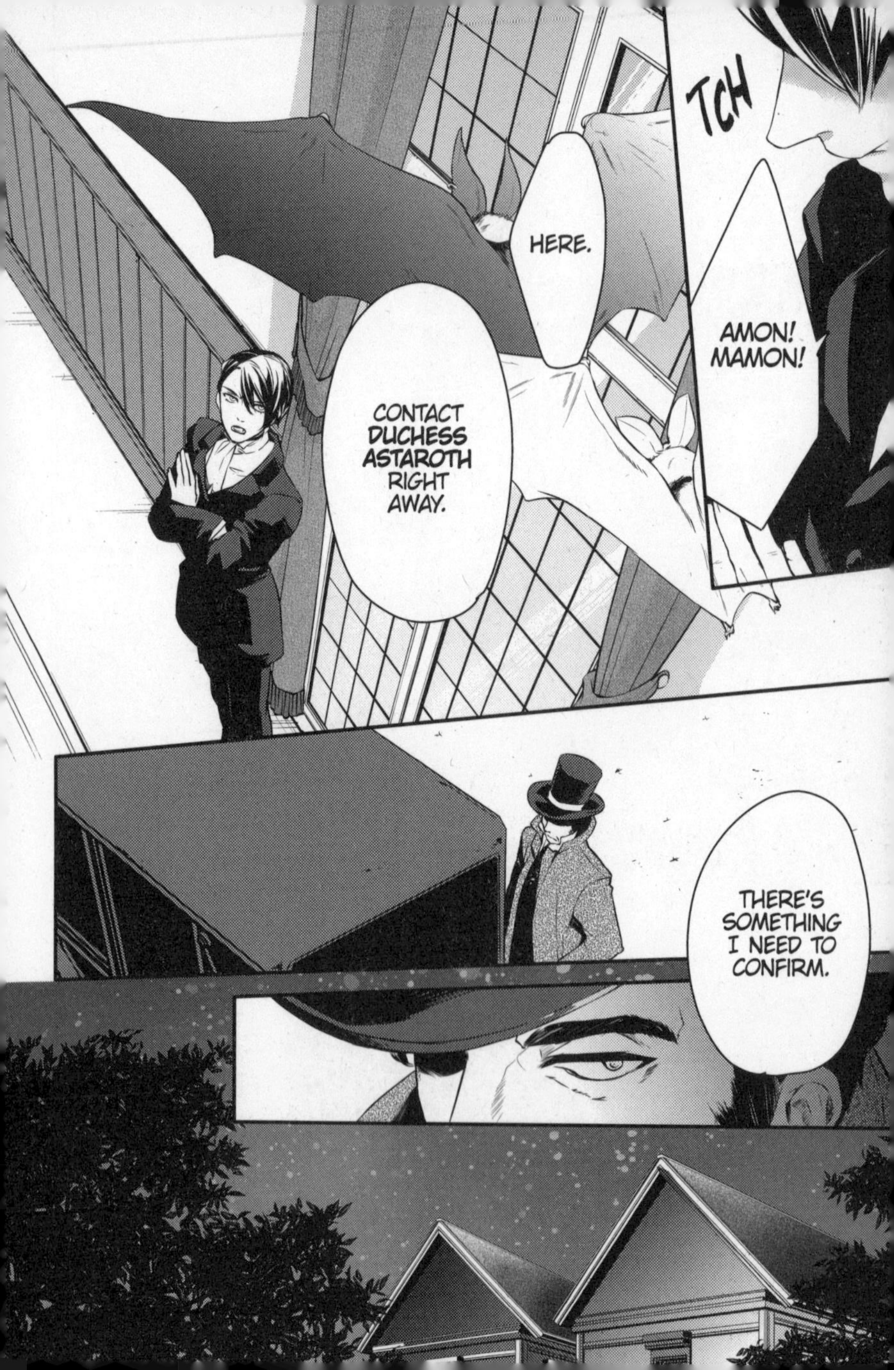
TCH
AMON! MAMON!
HERE.
CONTACT DUCHESS ASTAROTH RIGHT AWAY.
THERE'S SOMETHING I NEED TO CONFIRM.

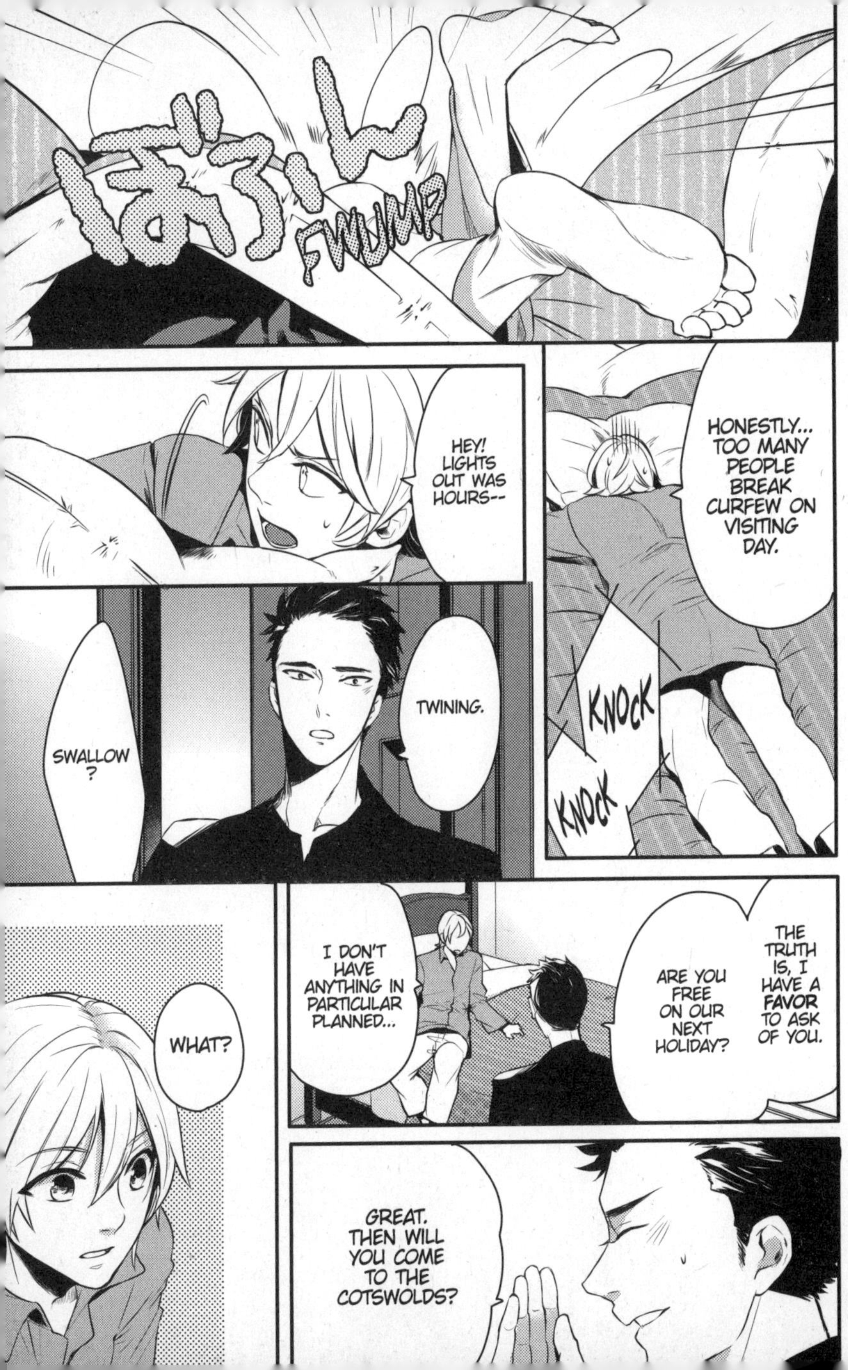
ぼふん
FWUMP
HONESTLY... TOO MANY PEOPLE BREAK CURFEW ON VISITING DAY.
KNOCK
KNOCK
HEY! LIGHTS OUT WAS HOURS--
TWINING.
SWALLOW?
THE TRUTH IS, I HAVE A FAVOR TO ASK OF YOU.
ARE YOU FREE ON OUR NEXT HOLIDAY?
I DON'T HAVE ANYTHING IN PARTICULAR PLANNED...
GREAT. THEN WILL YOU COME TO THE COTSWOLDS?
WHAT?

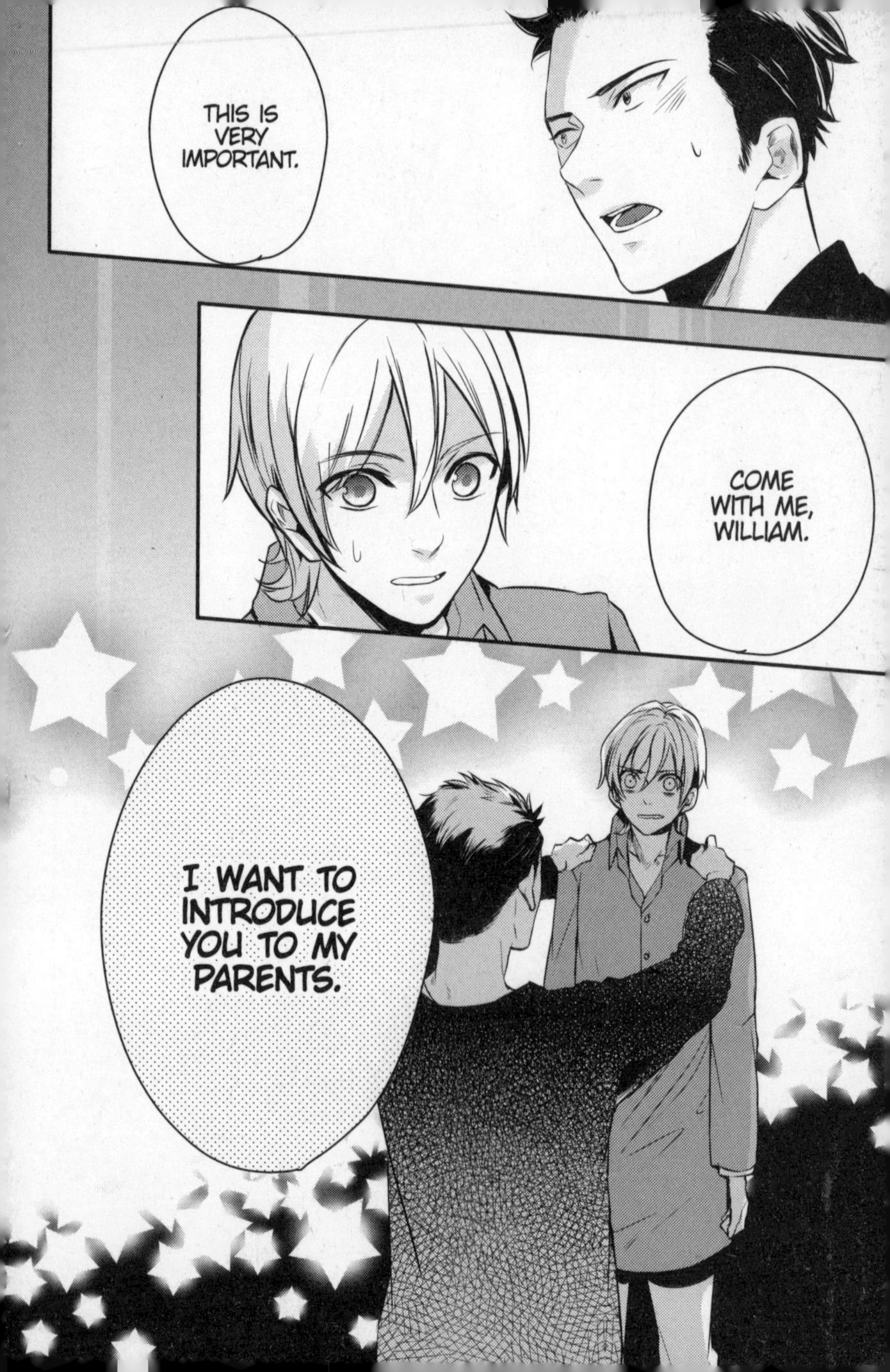
THIS IS VERY IMPORTANT.
COME WITH ME, WILLIAM.
I WANT TO INTRODUCE YOU TO MY PARENTS.

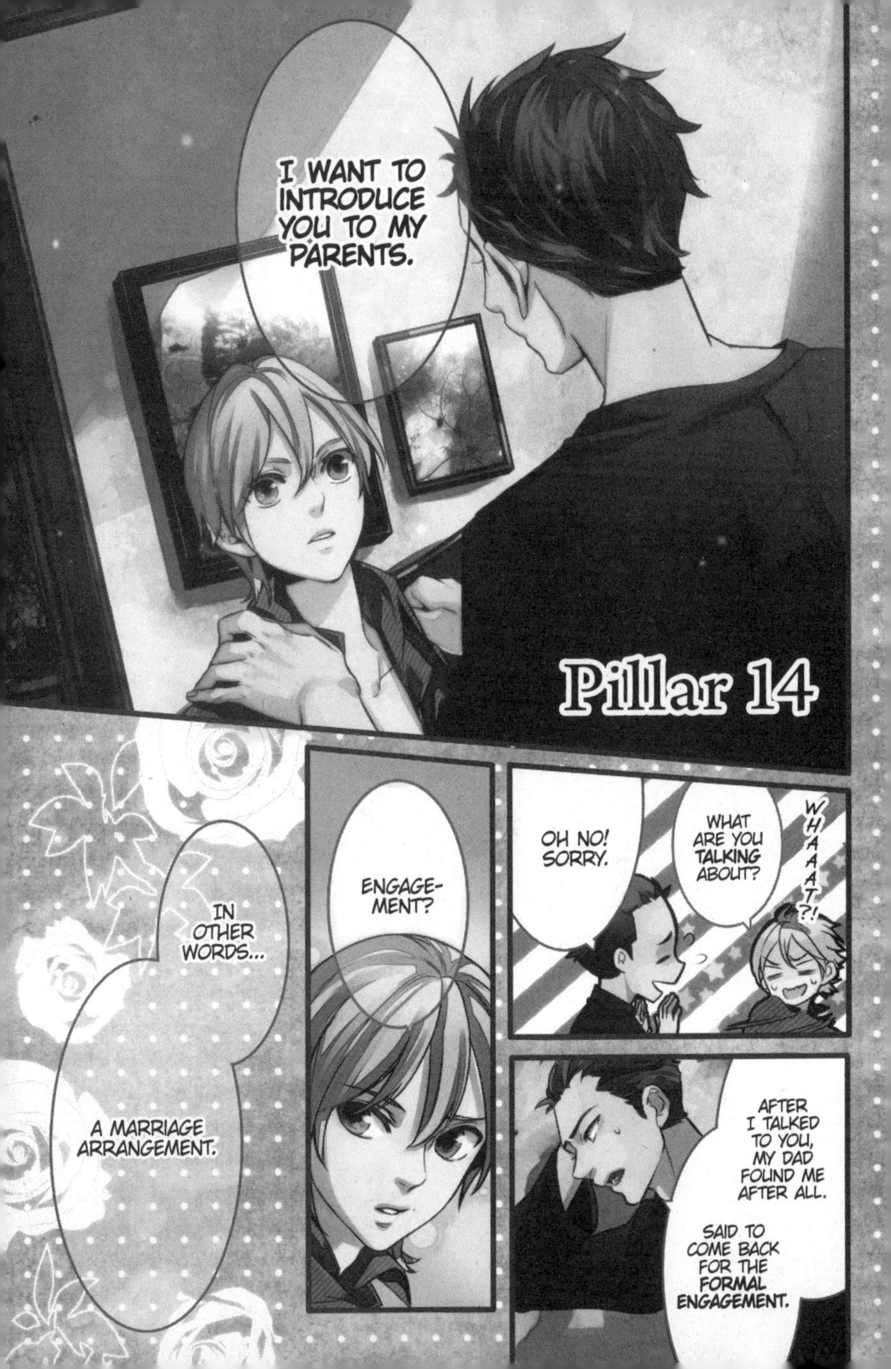
I WANT TO INTRODUCE YOU TO MY PARENTS.
Pillar 14
WHAAAAT?!
WHAT ARE YOU TALKING ABOUT?
OH NO! SORRY.
AFTER I TALKED TO YOU, MY DAD FOUND ME AFTER ALL.
SAID TO COME BACK FOR THE FORMAL ENGAGEMENT.
ENGAGE-MENT?
IN OTHER WORDS...
A MARRIAGE ARRANGEMENT.

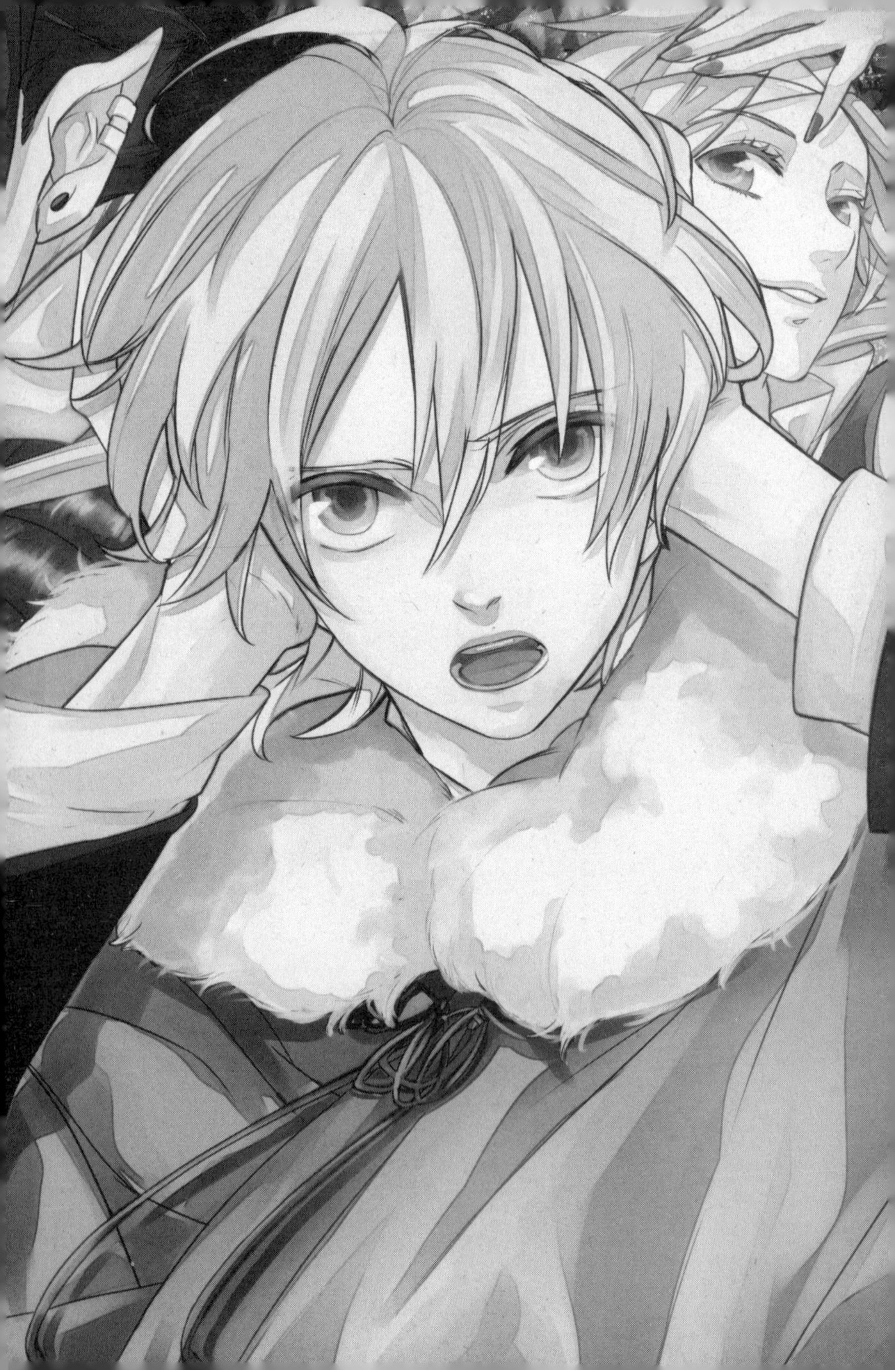

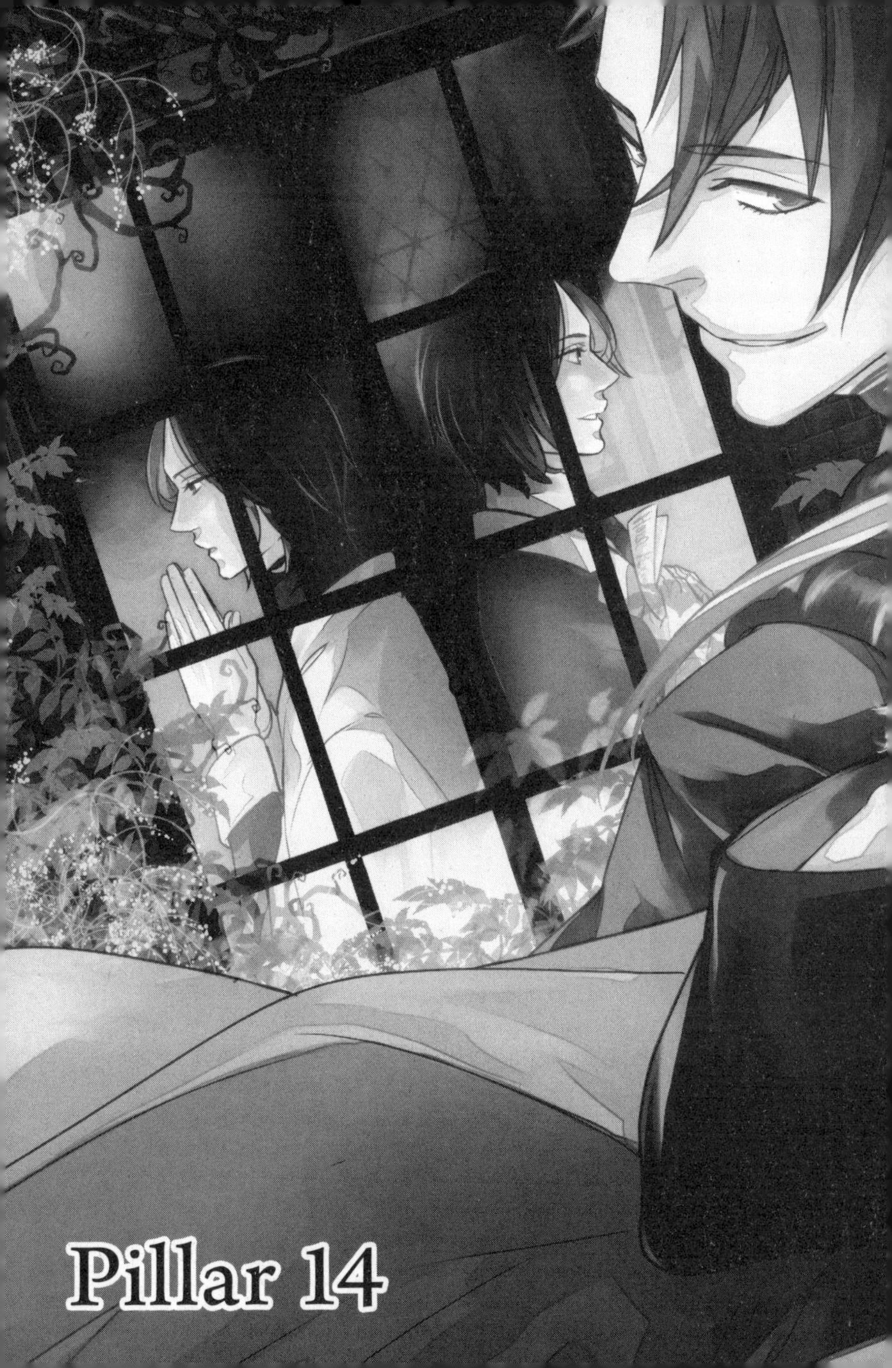

Pillar 14

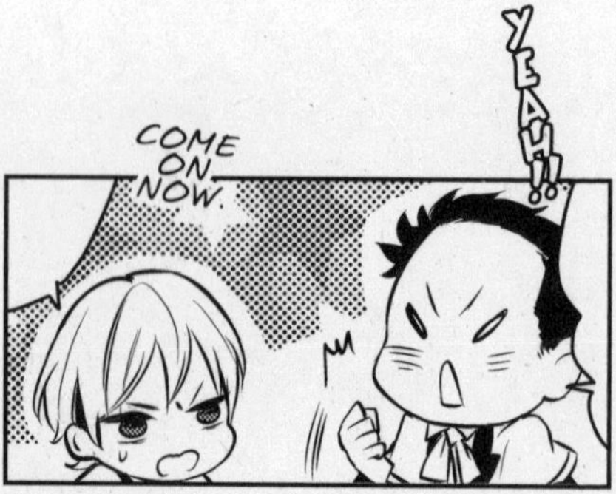
YEAH!!
COME ON NOW.

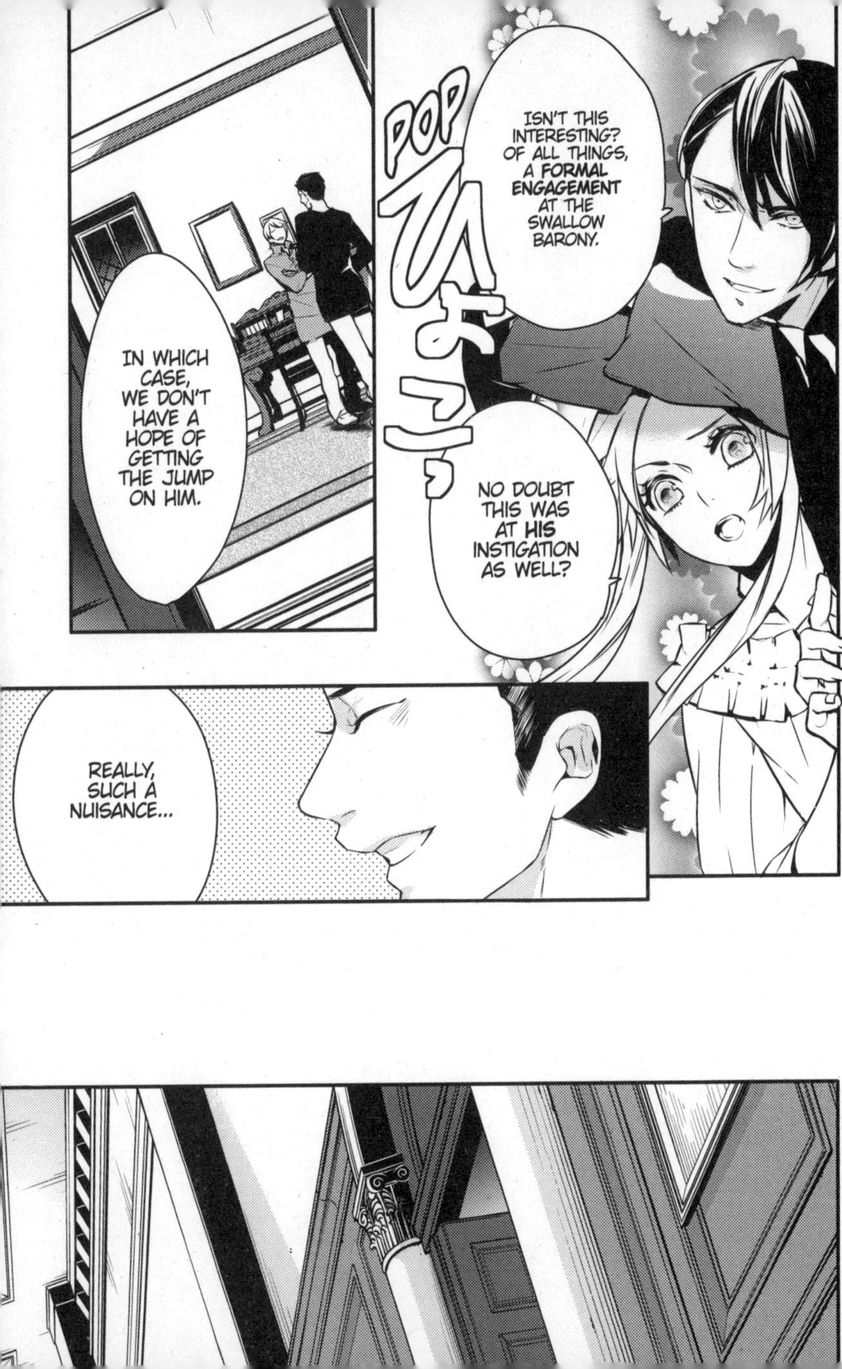
ISN'T THIS INTERESTING? OF ALL THINGS, A **FORMAL ENGAGEMENT** AT THE SWALLOW BARONY.
POP
ひょこっ
NO DOUBT THIS WAS AT **HIS** INSTIGATION AS WELL?
IN WHICH CASE, WE DON'T HAVE A HOPE OF GETTING THE JUMP ON HIM.
REALLY, SUCH A NUISANCE...

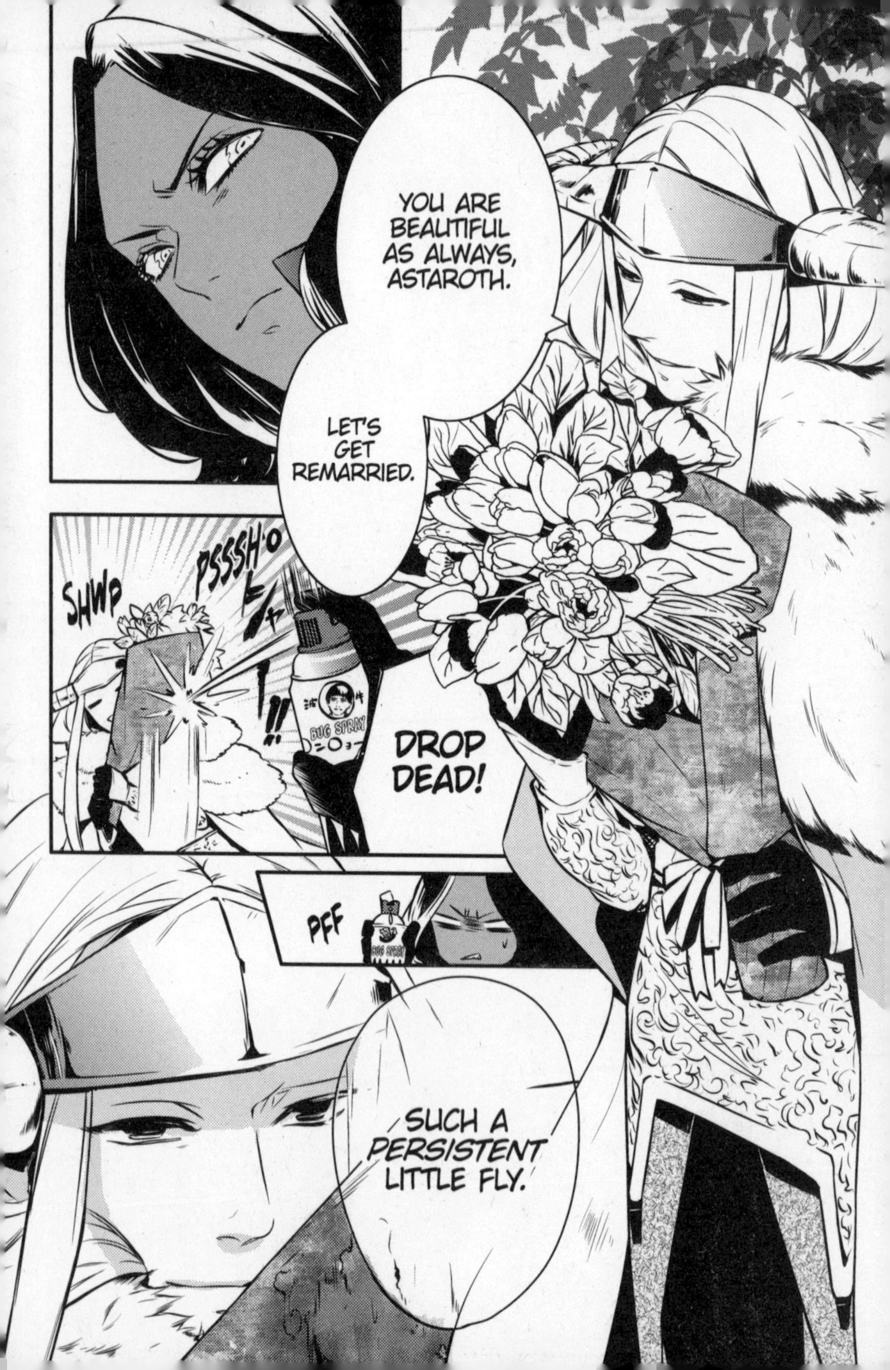
YOU ARE BEAUTIFUL AS ALWAYS, ASTAROTH.
LET'S GET REMARRIED.
PSSSSH
SHWP
DROP DEAD!
BUG SPRAY
PFF
BUG SPRAY
SUCH A PERSISTENT LITTLE FLY.

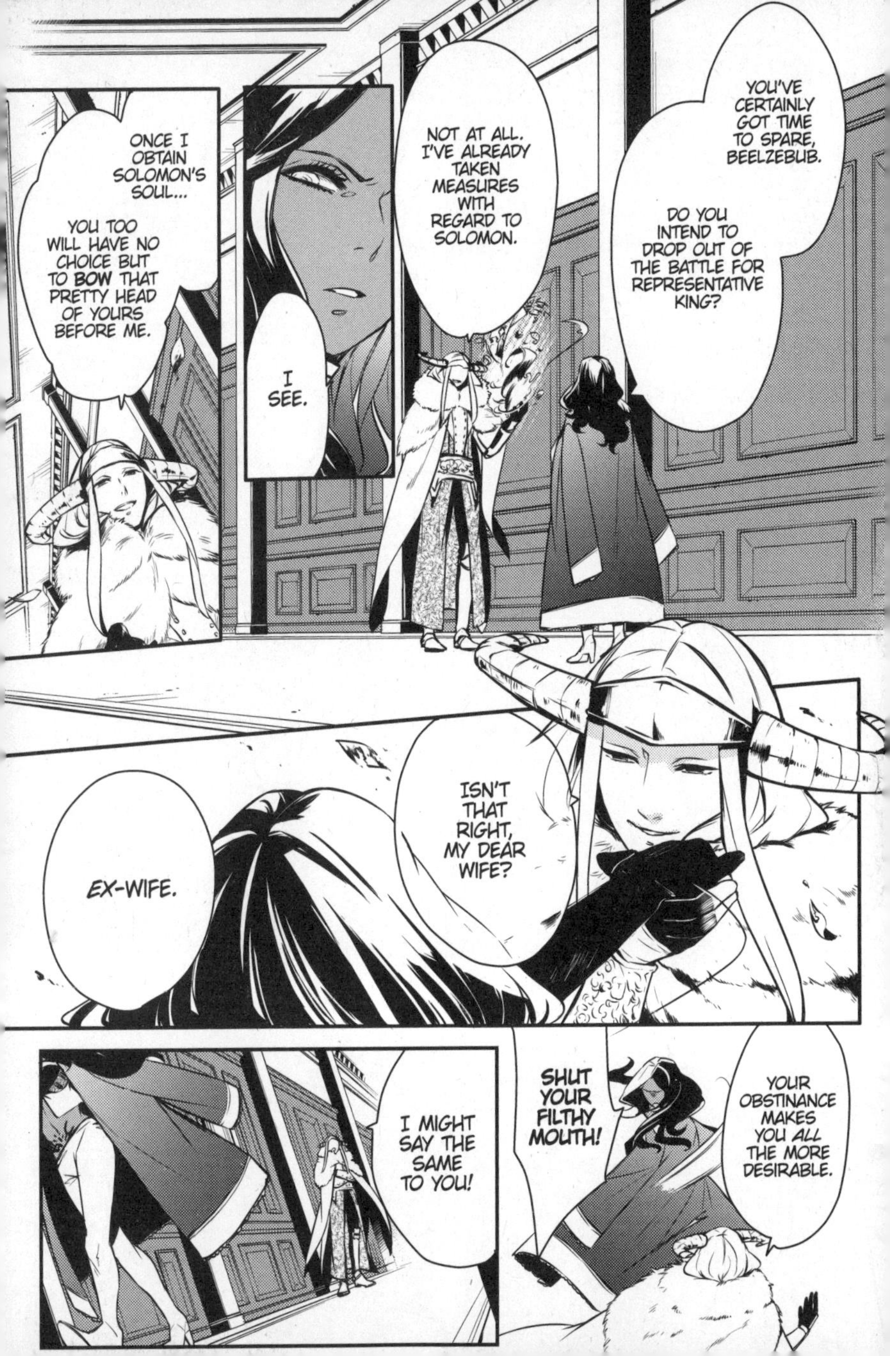
YOU'VE CERTAINLY GOT TIME TO SPARE, BEELZEBUB.
DO YOU INTEND TO DROP OUT OF THE BATTLE FOR REPRESENTATIVE KING?
NOT AT ALL. I'VE ALREADY TAKEN MEASURES WITH REGARD TO SOLOMON.
I SEE.
ONCE I OBTAIN SOLOMON'S SOUL...
YOU TOO WILL HAVE NO CHOICE BUT TO **BOW** THAT PRETTY HEAD OF YOURS BEFORE ME.
ISN'T THAT RIGHT, MY DEAR WIFE?
EX-WIFE.
YOUR OBSTINANCE MAKES YOU *ALL* THE MORE DESIRABLE.
SHUT YOUR FILTHY MOUTH!
I MIGHT SAY THE SAME TO YOU!

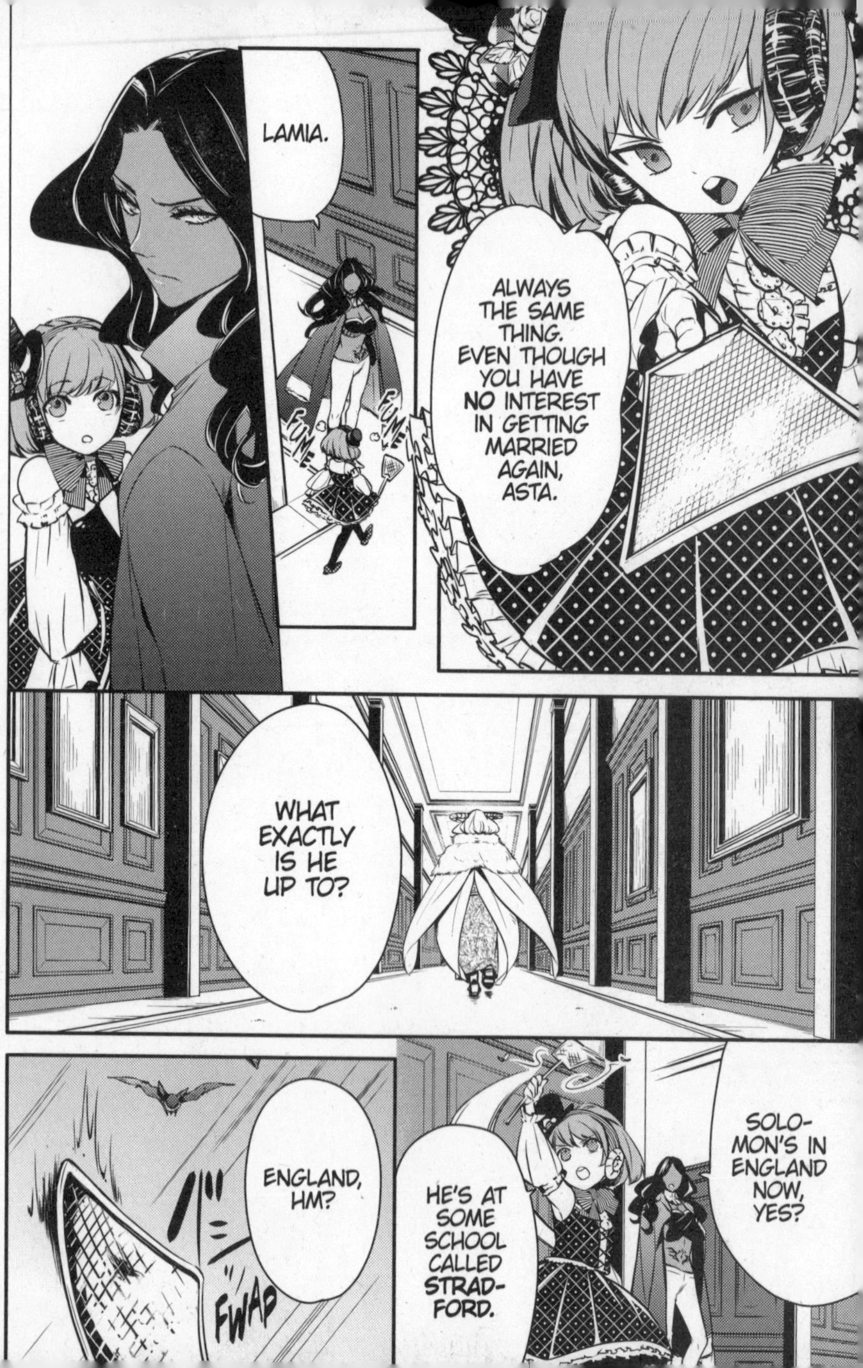
ALWAYS THE SAME THING. EVEN THOUGH YOU HAVE NO INTEREST IN GETTING MARRIED AGAIN, ASTA.
LAMIA.
FUME
FUME
WHAT EXACTLY IS HE UP TO?
SOLO-MON'S IN ENGLAND NOW, YES?
HE'S AT SOME SCHOOL CALLED STRAD-FORD.
ENGLAND, HM?
FWAP

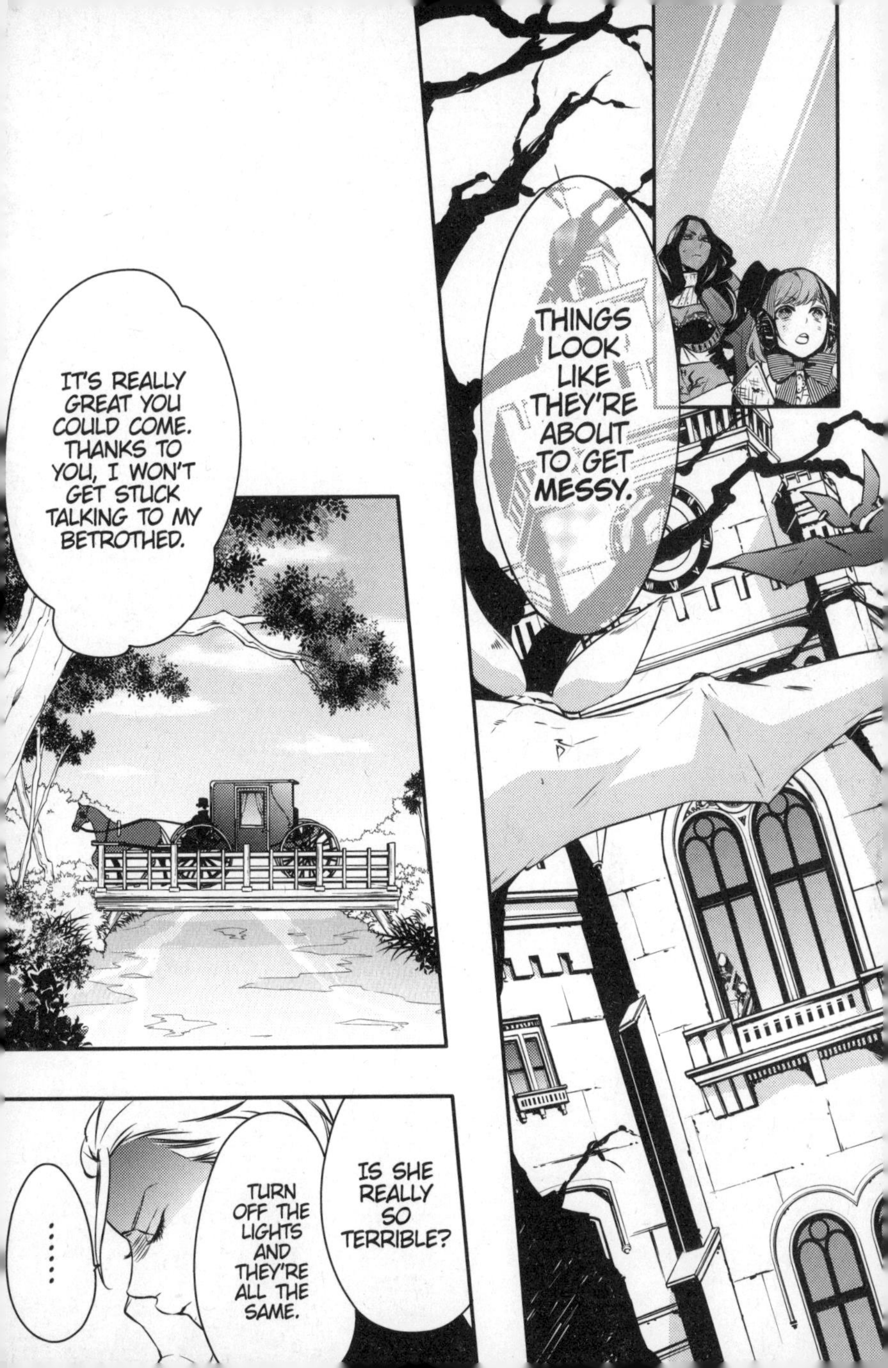
THINGS LOOK LIKE THEY'RE ABOUT TO GET MESSY.
IT'S REALLY GREAT YOU COULD COME. THANKS TO YOU, I WON'T GET STUCK TALKING TO MY BETROTHED.
IS SHE REALLY SO TERRIBLE?
TURN OFF THE LIGHTS AND THEY'RE ALL THE SAME.
......

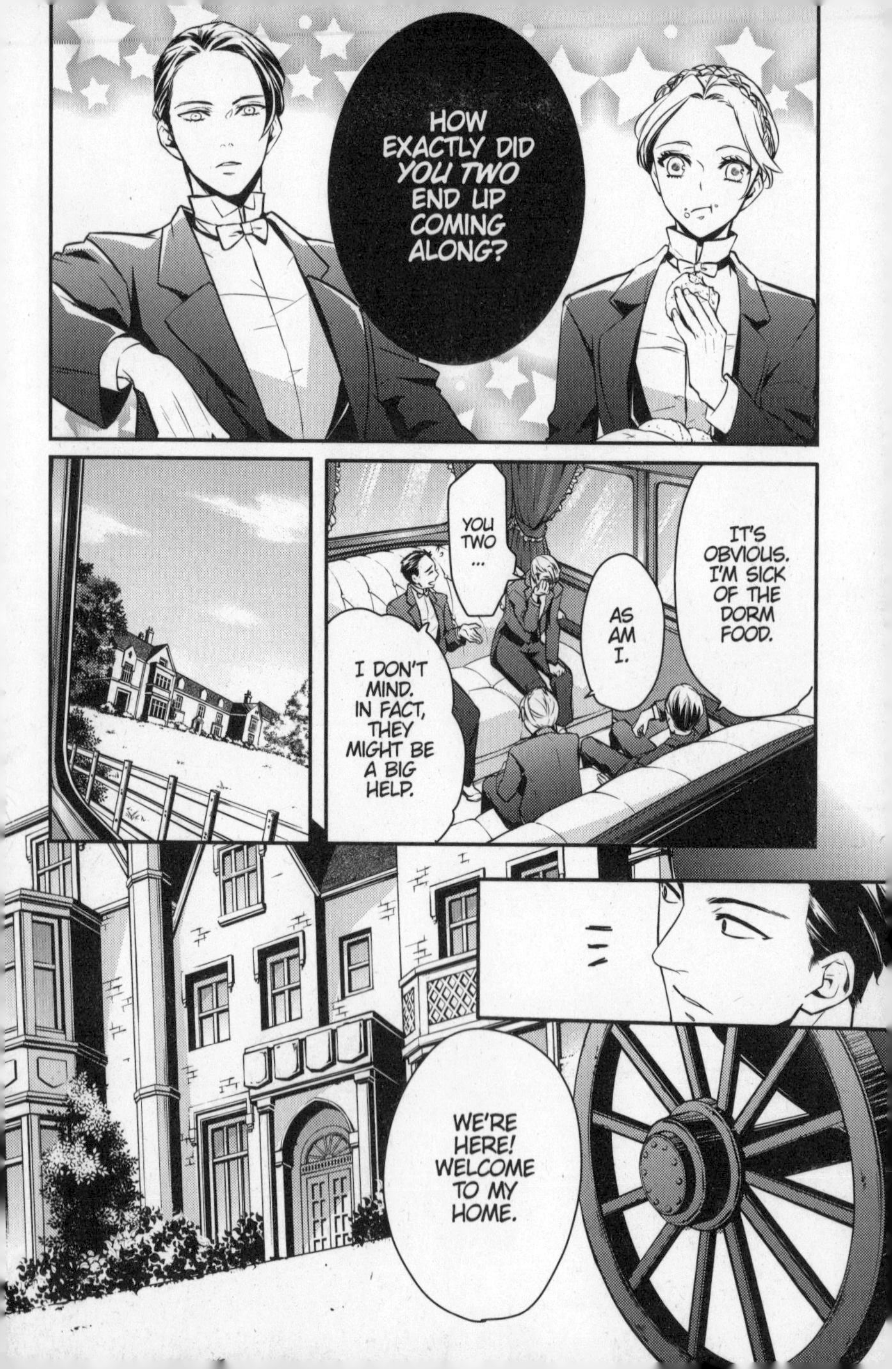
HOW EXACTLY DID *YOU TWO* END UP COMING ALONG?
IT'S OBVIOUS. I'M SICK OF THE DORM FOOD.
AS AM I.
YOU TWO ...
I DON'T MIND. IN FACT, THEY MIGHT BE A BIG HELP.
WE'RE HERE! WELCOME TO MY HOME.

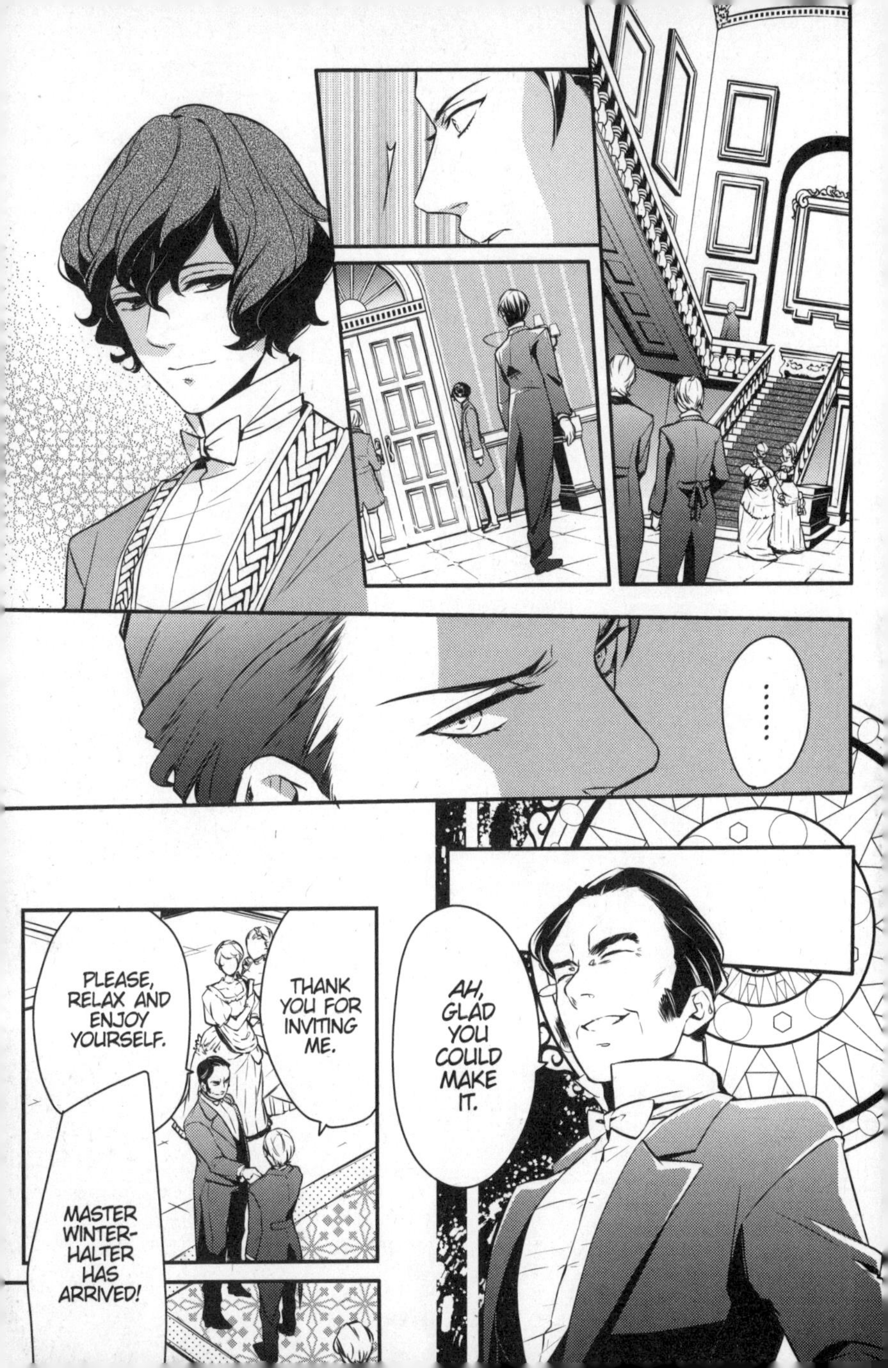
......
AH, GLAD YOU COULD MAKE IT.
THANK YOU FOR INVITING ME.
PLEASE, RELAX AND ENJOY YOURSELF.
MASTER WINTER-HALTER HAS ARRIVED!

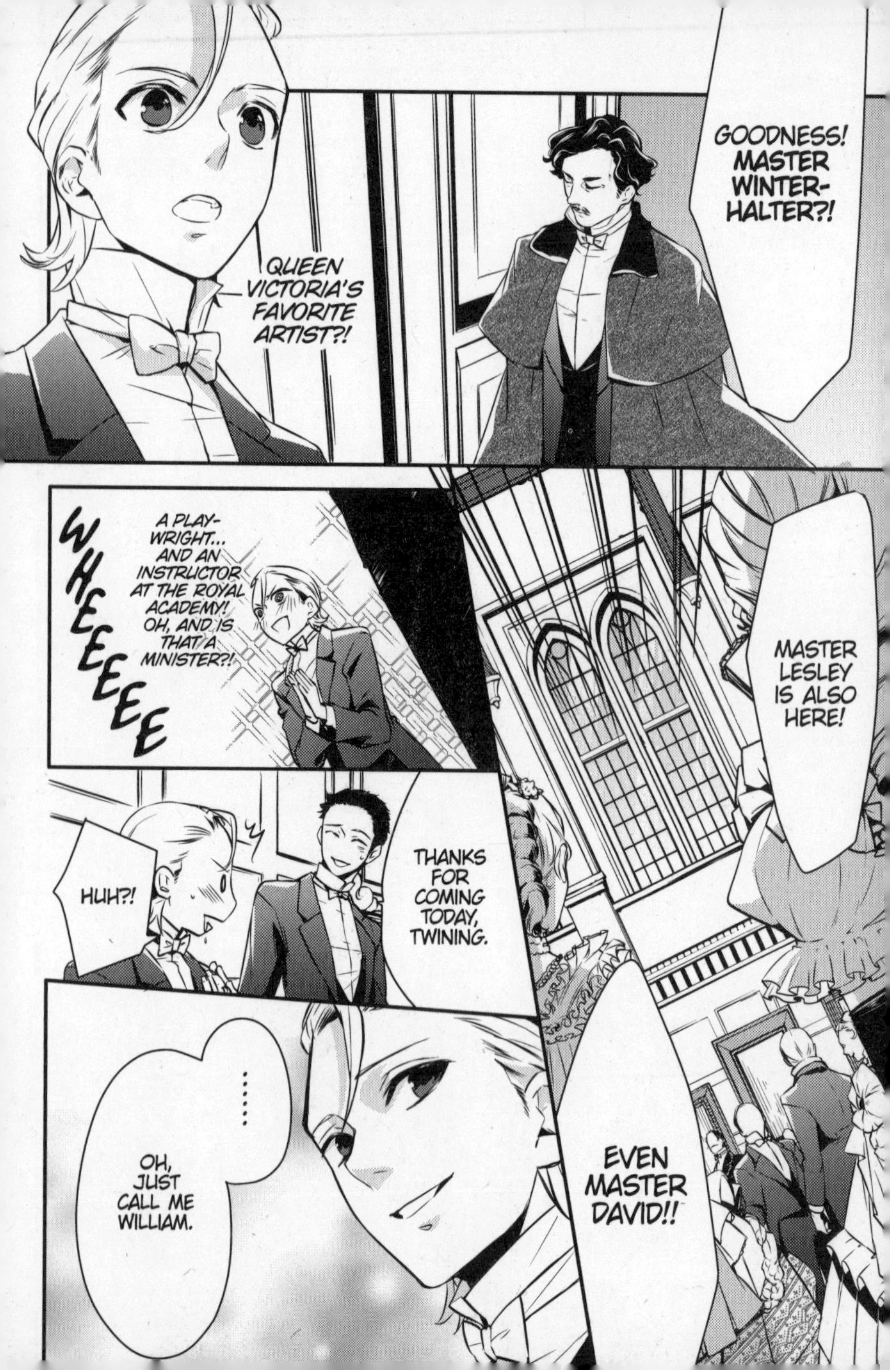
GOODNESS! MASTER WINTER-HALTER?!
QUEEN VICTORIA'S FAVORITE ARTIST?!
MASTER LESLEY IS ALSO HERE!
EVEN MASTER DAVID!!
A PLAY-WRIGHT... AND AN INSTRUCTOR AT THE ROYAL ACADEMY! OH, AND IS THAT A MINISTER?!
WHEEEEEE
THANKS FOR COMING TODAY, TWINING.
HUH?!
......
OH, JUST CALL ME WILLIAM.

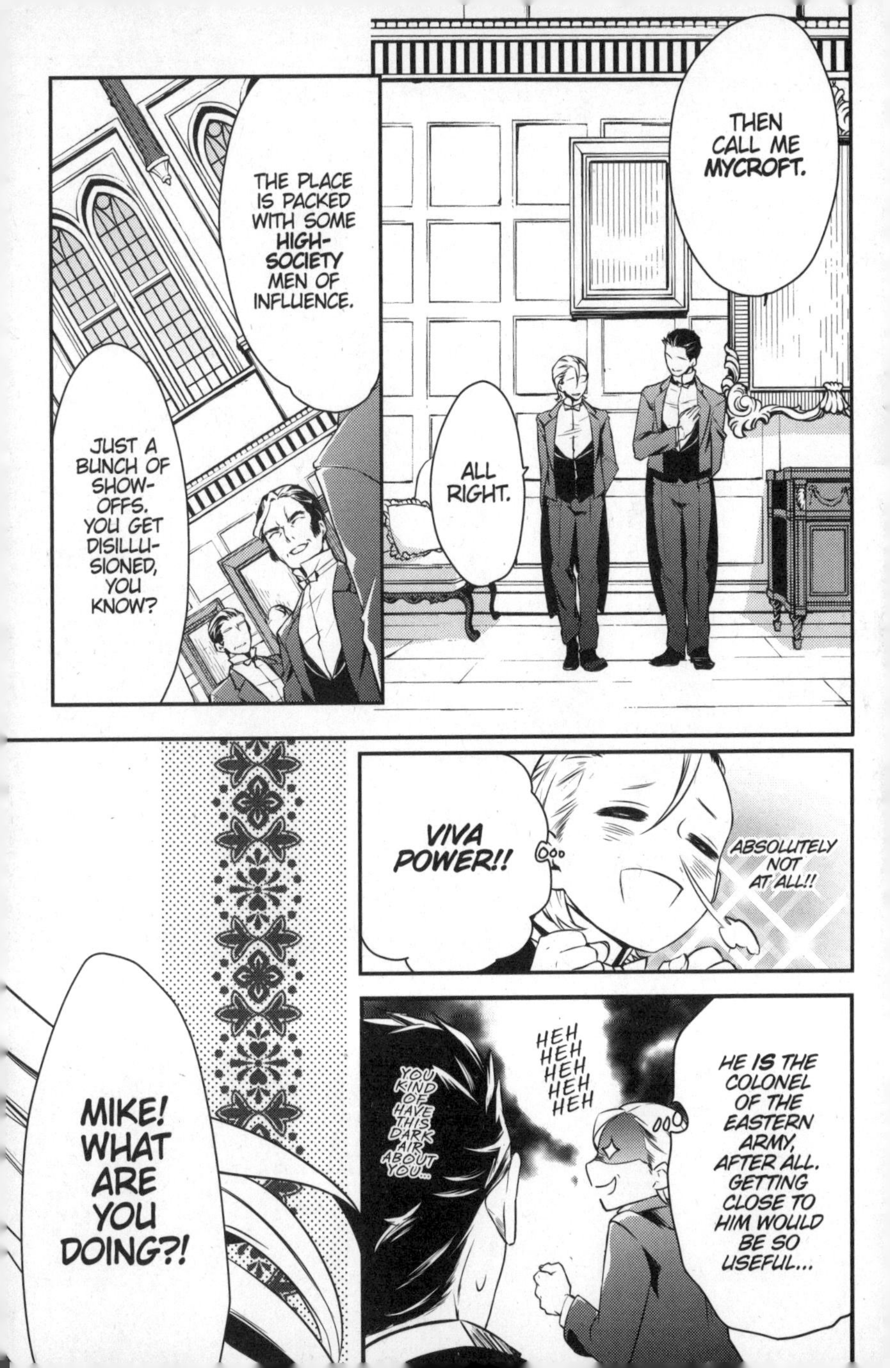
THEN CALL ME MYCROFT.
ALL RIGHT.
THE PLACE IS PACKED WITH SOME HIGH-SOCIETY MEN OF INFLUENCE.
JUST A BUNCH OF SHOW-OFFS. YOU GET DISILLUSIONED, YOU KNOW?
ABSOLUTELY NOT AT ALL!!
VIVA POWER!!
HE IS THE COLONEL OF THE EASTERN ARMY, AFTER ALL. GETTING CLOSE TO HIM WOULD BE SO USEFUL...
HEH HEH HEH HEH HEH
YOU KIND OF HAVE THIS DARK AIR ABOUT YOU...
MIKE! WHAT ARE YOU DOING?!

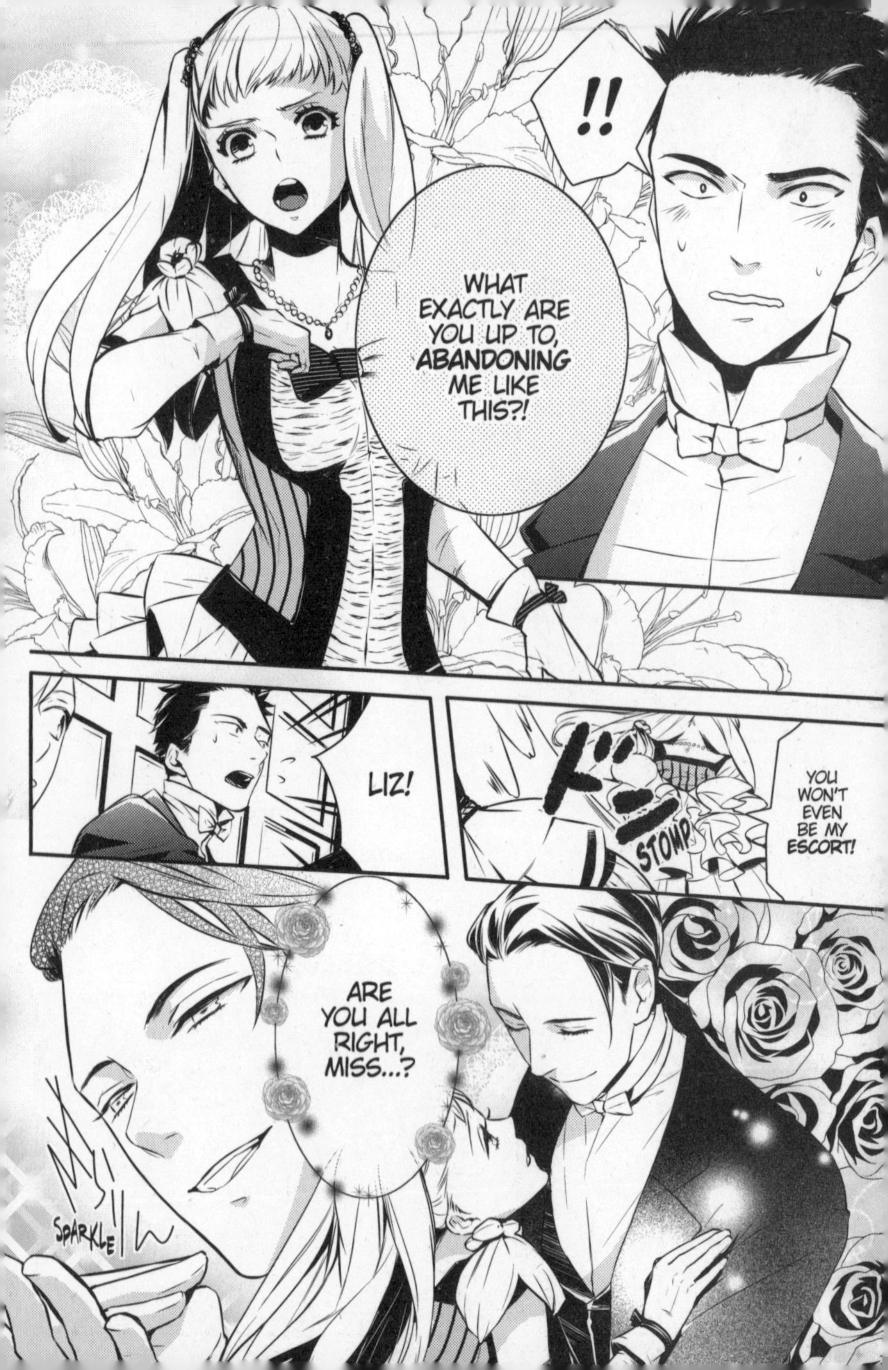
!!
WHAT EXACTLY ARE YOU UP TO, ABANDONING ME LIKE THIS?!
STOMP
YOU WON'T EVEN BE MY ESCORT!
LIZ!
ARE YOU ALL RIGHT, MISS...?
SPARKLE

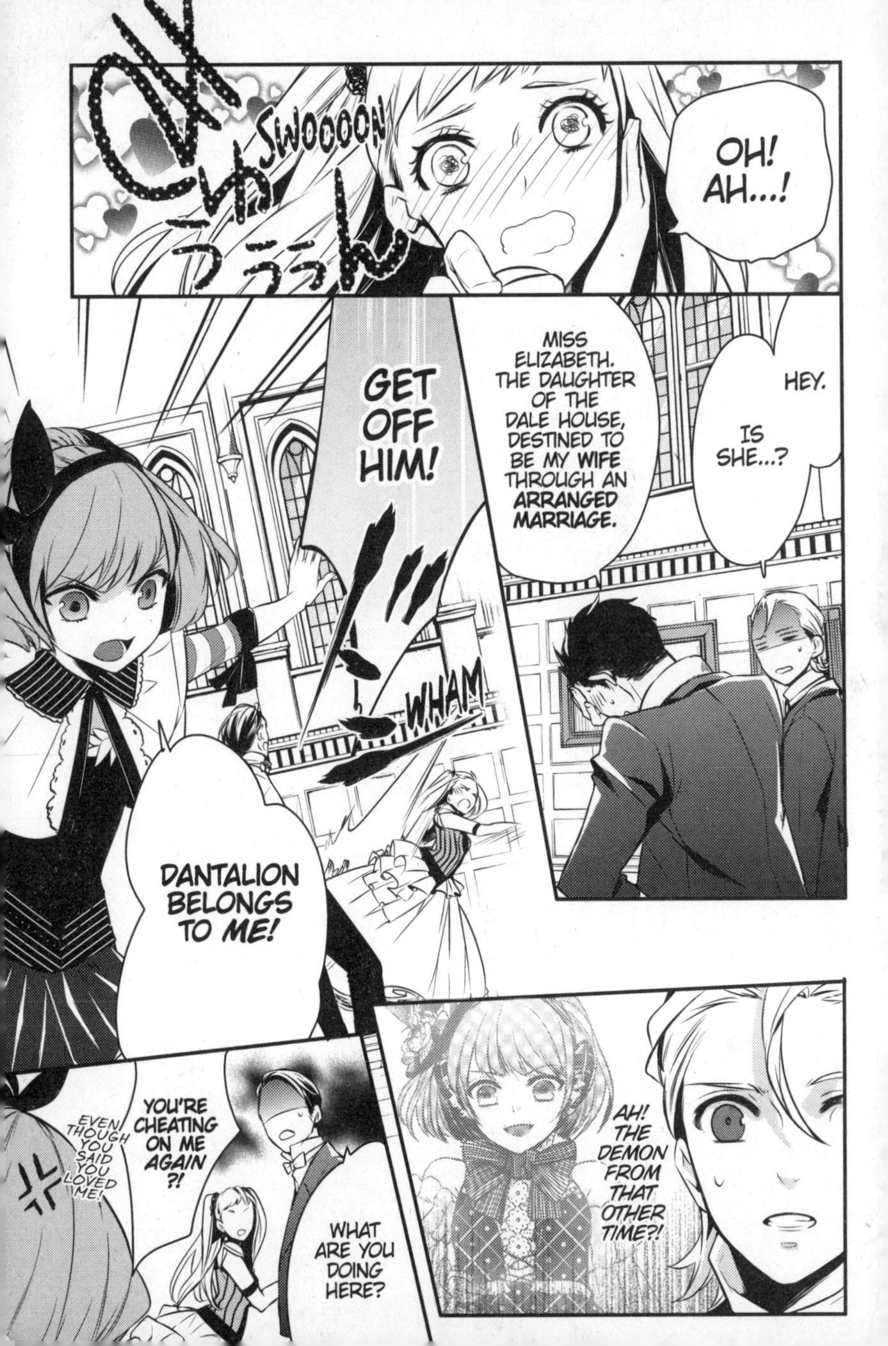

OH! AH...!
SWOOOON
HEY.
IS SHE...?
MISS ELIZABETH. THE DAUGHTER OF THE DALE HOUSE, DESTINED TO BE MY WIFE THROUGH AN ARRANGED MARRIAGE.
GET OFF HIM!
WHAM
DANTALION BELONGS TO ME!
AH! THE DEMON FROM THAT OTHER TIME?!
YOU'RE CHEATING ON ME AGAIN?!
EVEN THOUGH YOU SAID YOU LOVED ME!
WHAT ARE YOU DOING HERE?

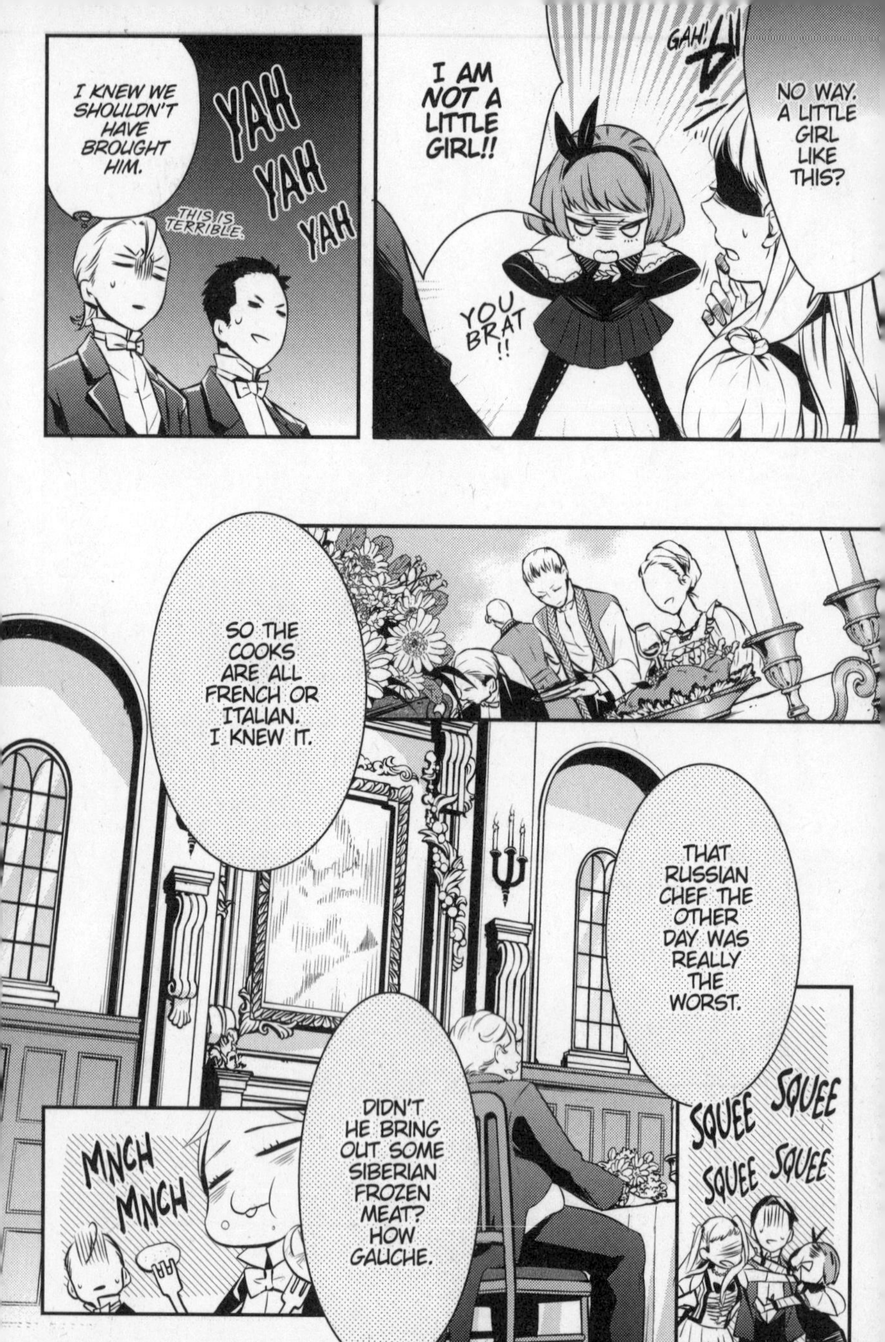
GAH!
NO WAY. A LITTLE GIRL LIKE THIS?
I AM NOT A LITTLE GIRL!!
YOU BRAT!!
I KNEW WE SHOULDN'T HAVE BROUGHT HIM.
YAH YAH YAH
THIS IS TERRIBLE.
SO THE COOKS ARE ALL FRENCH OR ITALIAN. I KNEW IT.
THAT RUSSIAN CHEF THE OTHER DAY WAS REALLY THE WORST.
DIDN'T HE BRING OUT SOME SIBERIAN FROZEN MEAT? HOW GAUCHE.
SQUEE SQUEE
SQUEE SQUEE
MNCH MNCH

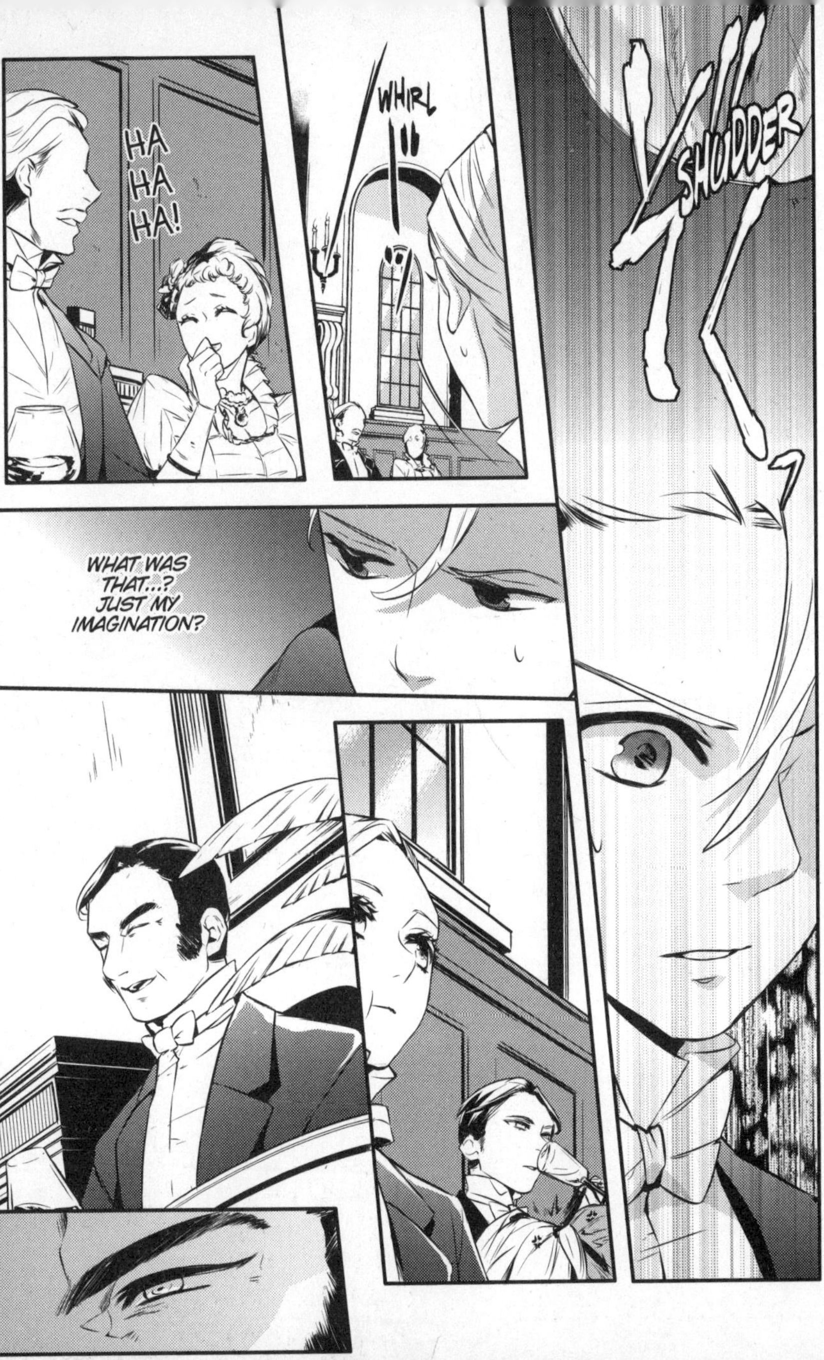
SHUDDER
WHIRL
HA HA HA!
WHAT WAS THAT...? JUST MY IMAGINATION?

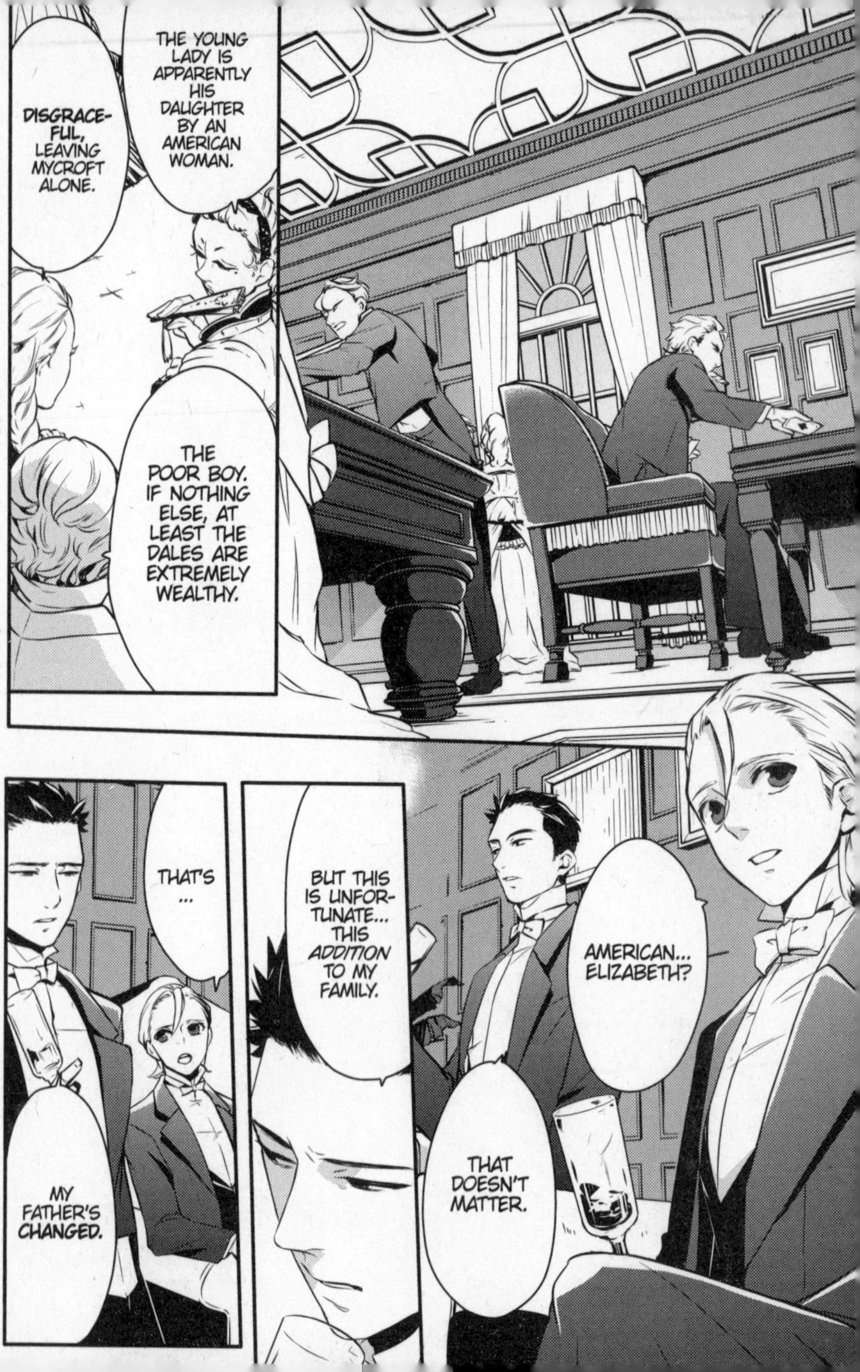
THE YOUNG LADY IS APPARENTLY HIS DAUGHTER BY AN AMERICAN WOMAN.
DISGRACE-FUL, LEAVING MYCROFT ALONE.
THE POOR BOY. IF NOTHING ELSE, AT LEAST THE DALES ARE EXTREMELY WEALTHY.
AMERICAN... ELIZABETH?
BUT THIS IS UNFORTU-NATE... THIS *ADDITION* TO MY FAMILY.
THAT DOESN'T MATTER.
THAT'S ...
MY FATHER'S CHANGED.

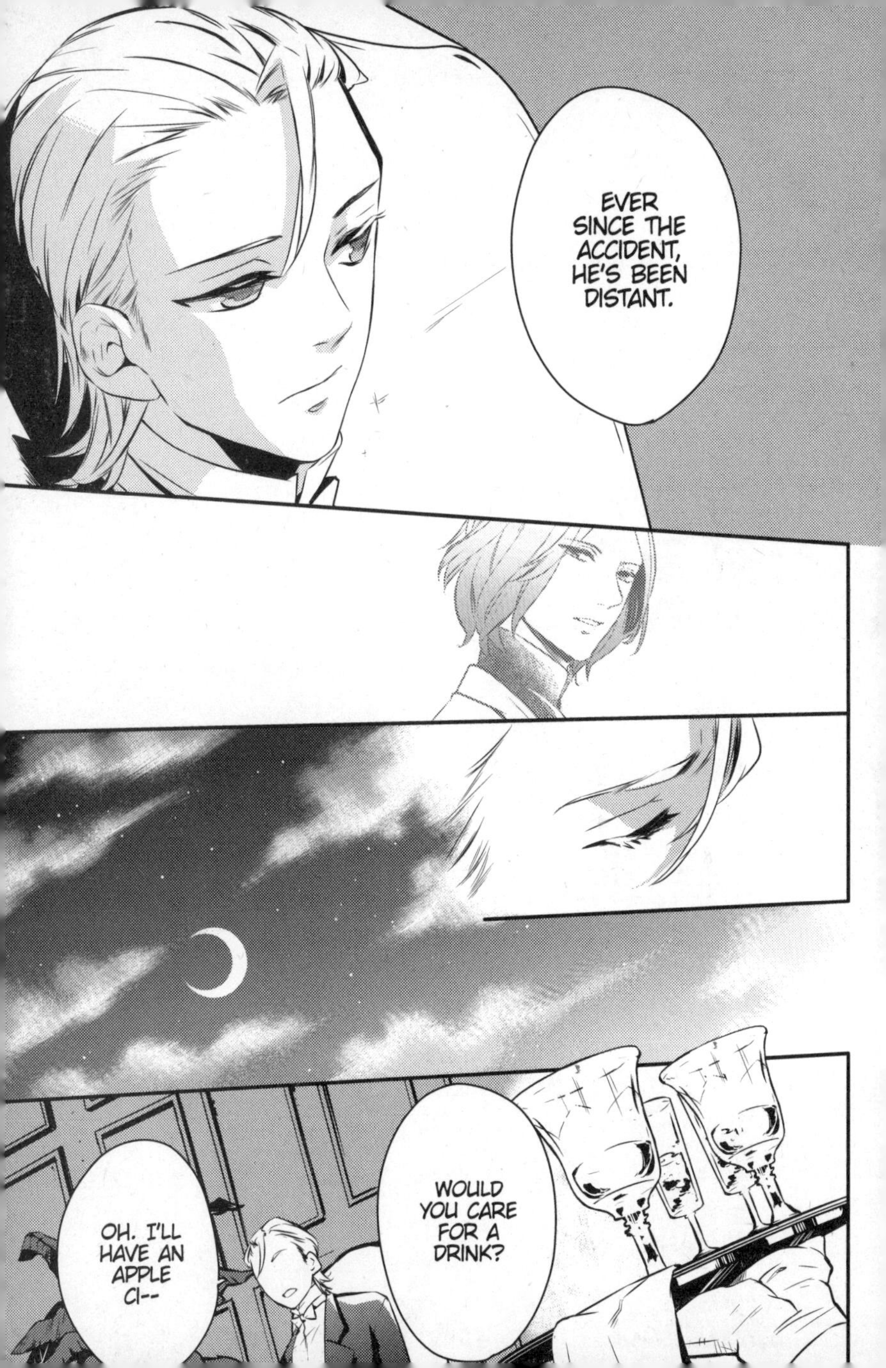
EVER SINCE THE ACCIDENT, HE'S BEEN DISTANT.
WOULD YOU CARE FOR A DRINK?
OH. I'LL HAVE AN APPLE CI--

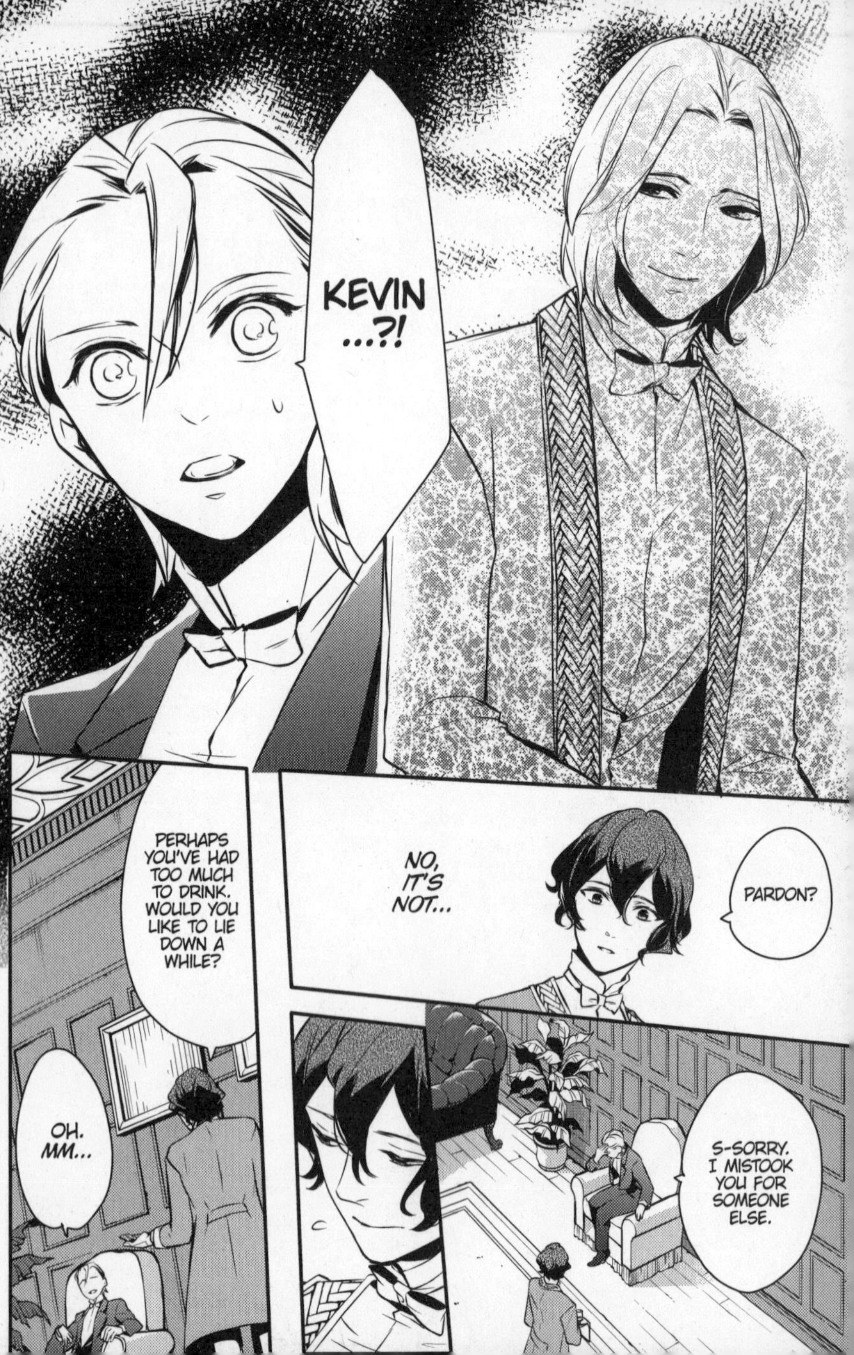
KEVIN ...?!
PARDON?
NO, IT'S NOT...
S-SORRY. I MISTOOK YOU FOR SOMEONE ELSE.
PERHAPS YOU'VE HAD TOO MUCH TO DRINK. WOULD YOU LIKE TO LIE DOWN A WHILE?
OH. MM...

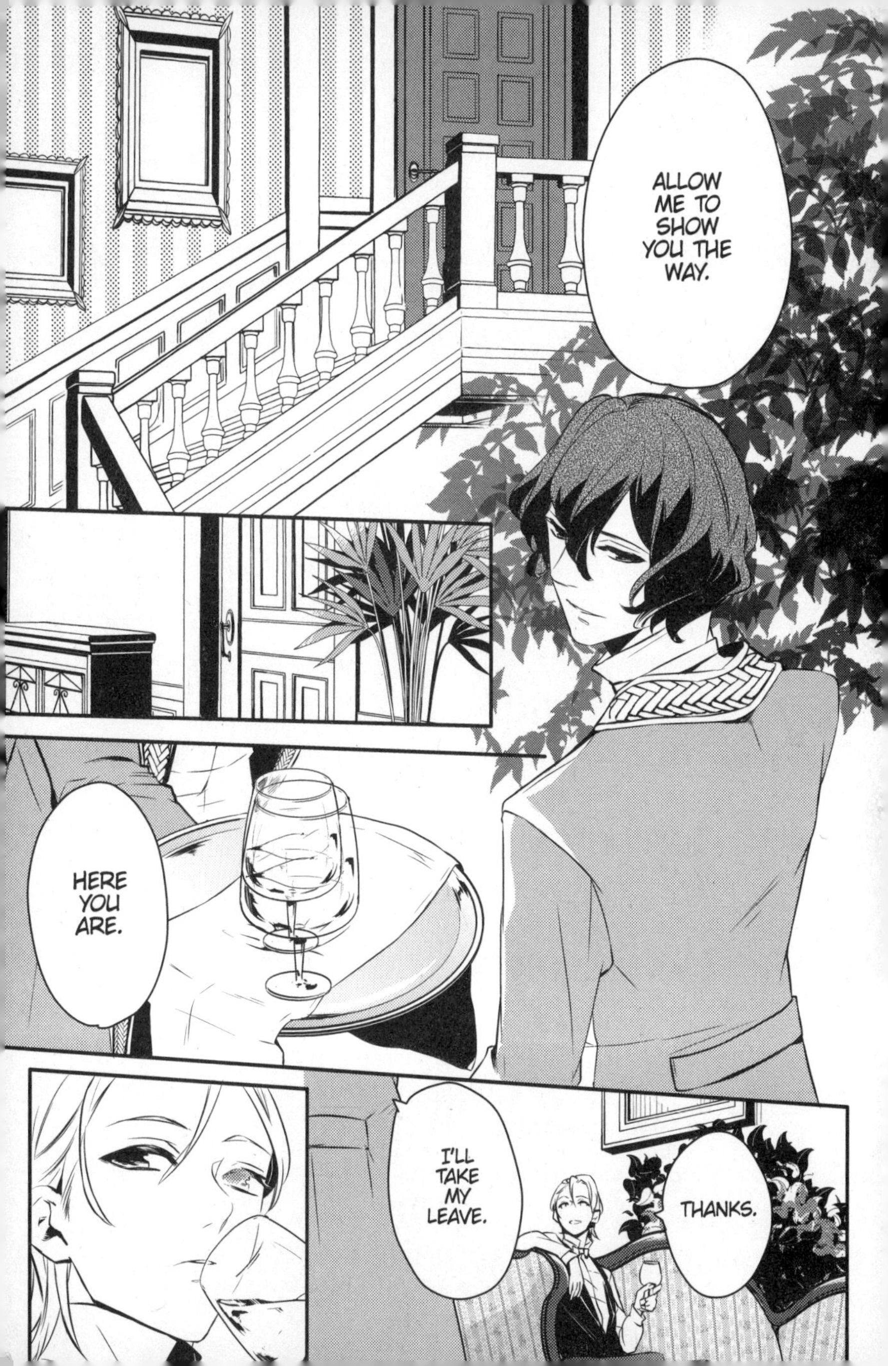
ALLOW ME TO SHOW YOU THE WAY.
HERE YOU ARE.
THANKS.
I'LL TAKE MY LEAVE.

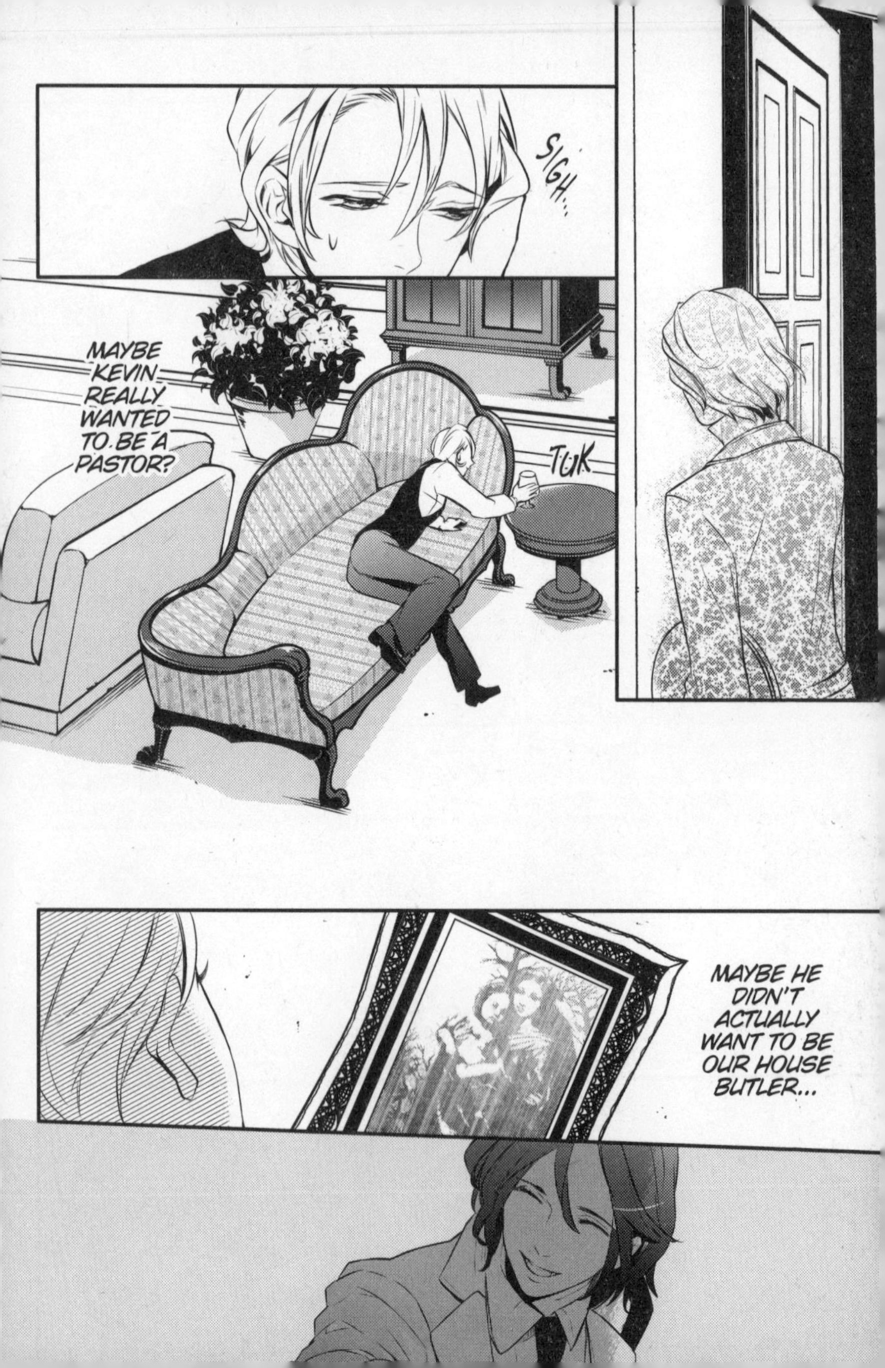
SIGH...
MAYBE KEVIN REALLY WANTED TO BE A PASTOR?
TUK
MAYBE HE DIDN'T ACTUALLY WANT TO BE OUR HOUSE BUTLER...

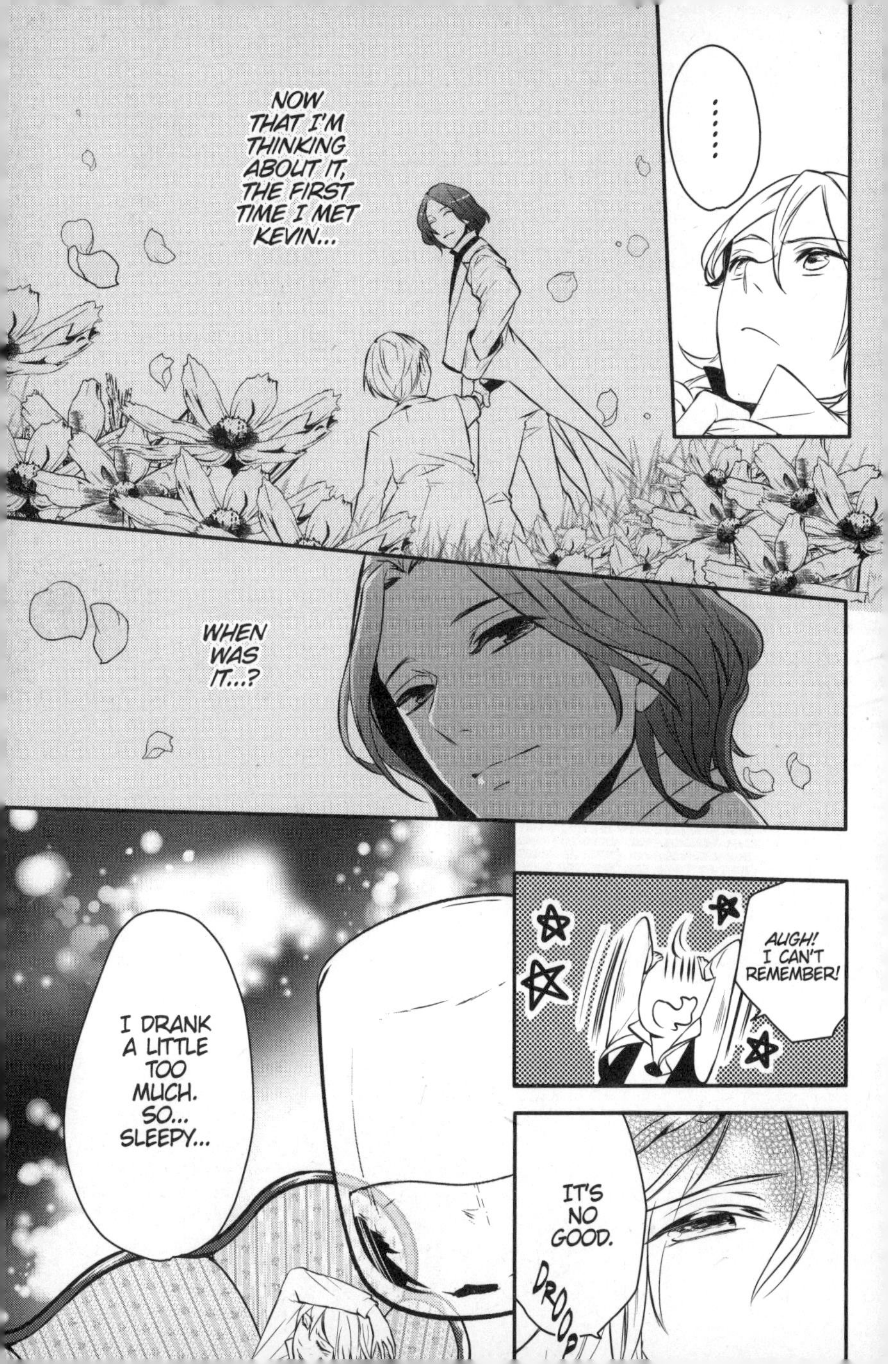
......
NOW THAT I'M THINKING ABOUT IT, THE FIRST TIME I MET KEVIN...
WHEN WAS IT...?
AUGH! I CAN'T REMEMBER!
IT'S NO GOOD.
DROOP
I DRANK A LITTLE TOO MUCH. SO... SLEEPY...

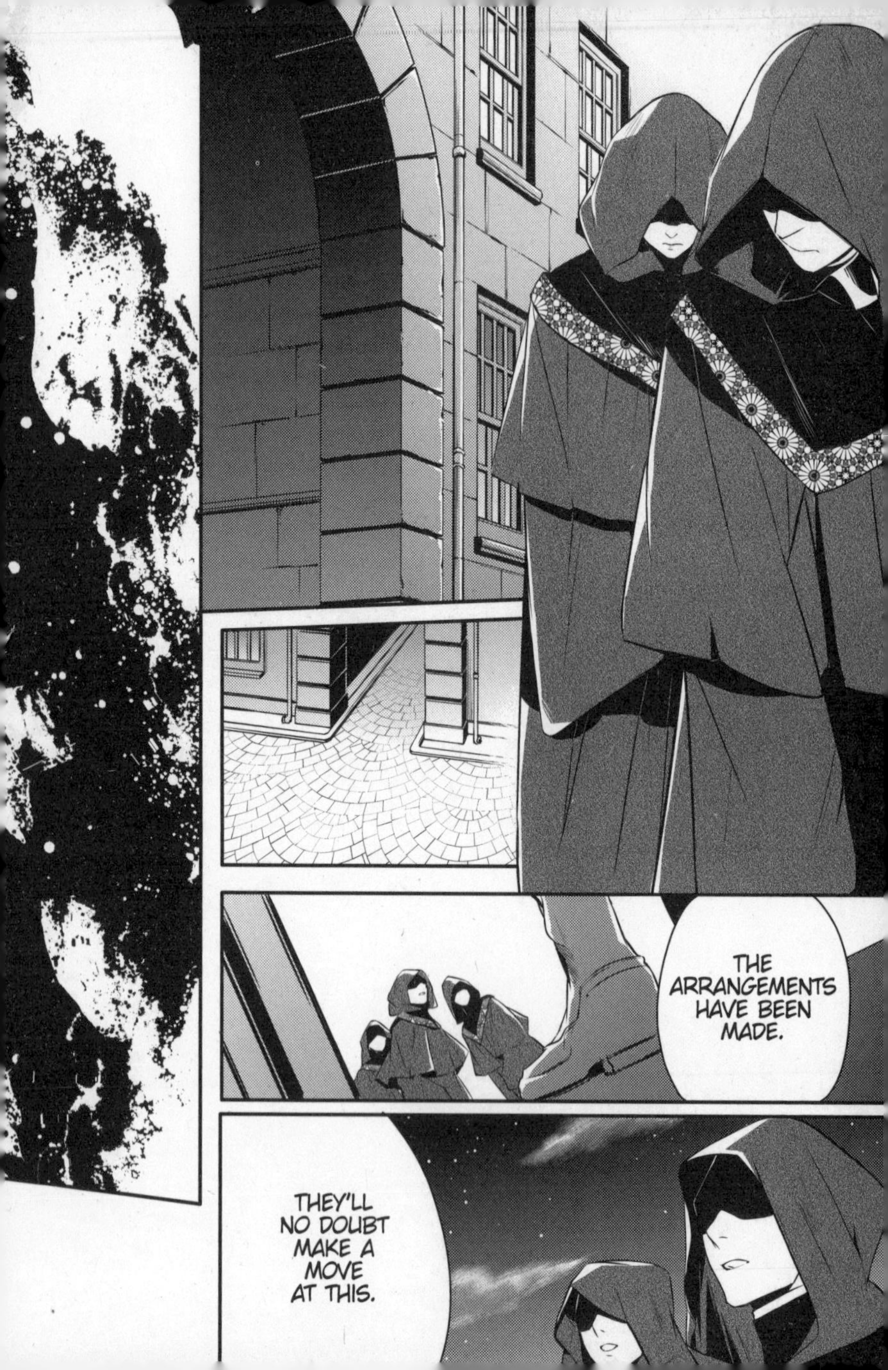
THE ARRANGEMENTS HAVE BEEN MADE.
THEY'LL NO DOUBT MAKE A MOVE AT THIS.

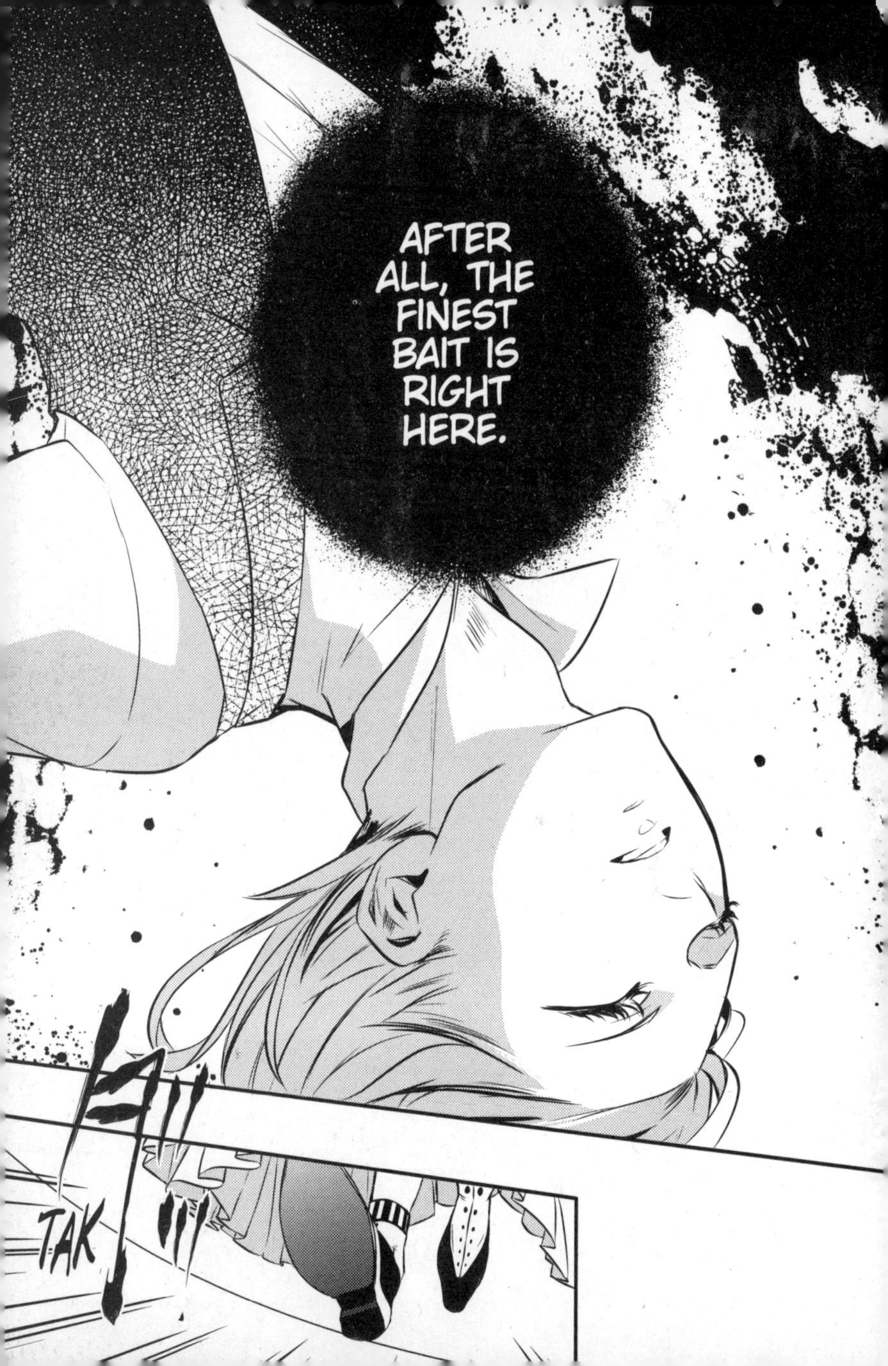
AFTER ALL, THE FINEST BAIT IS RIGHT HERE.
TAK

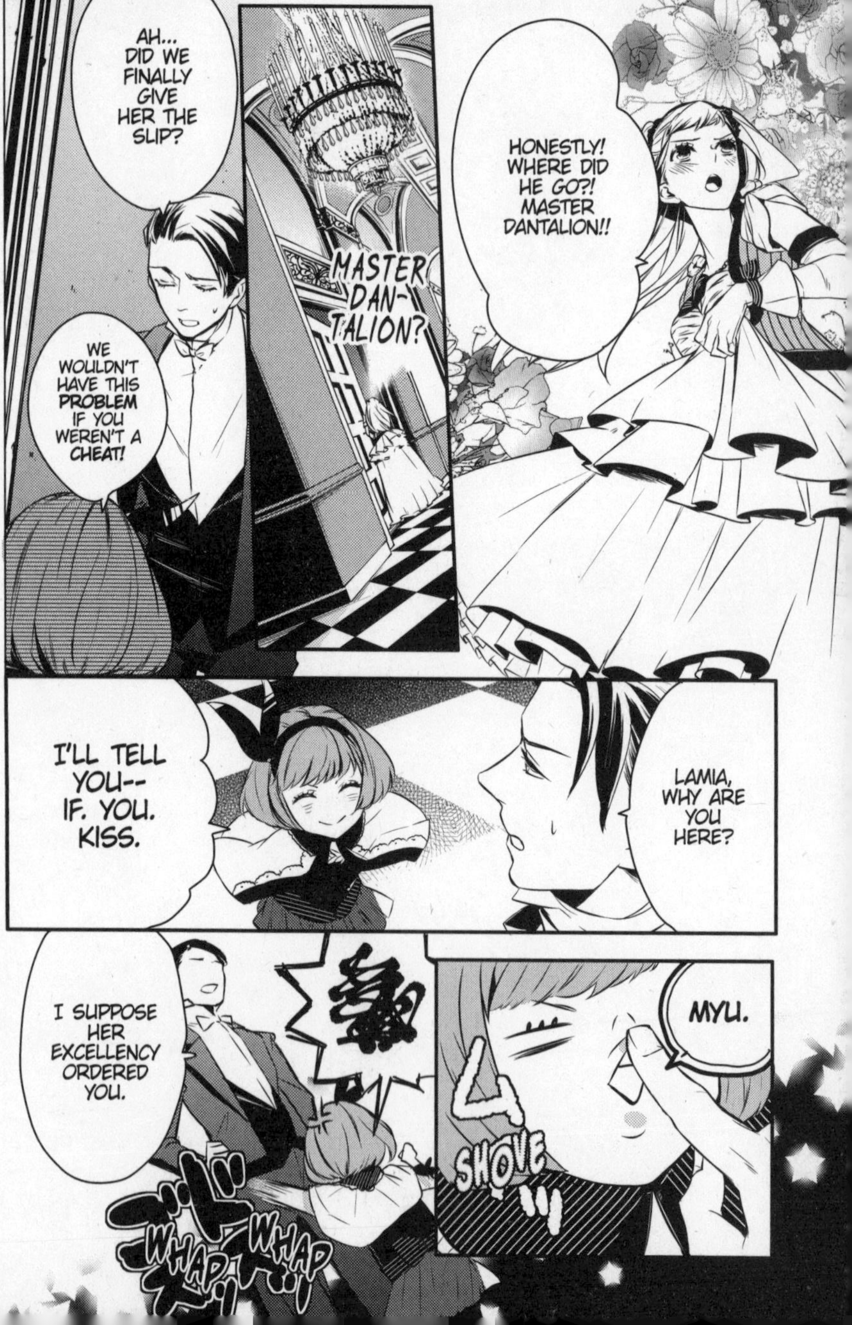
HONESTLY! WHERE DID HE GO?! MASTER DANTALION!!
MASTER DAN-TALION?
AH... DID WE FINALLY GIVE HER THE SLIP?
WE WOULDN'T HAVE THIS PROBLEM IF YOU WEREN'T A CHEAT!
LAMIA, WHY ARE YOU HERE?
I'LL TELL YOU-- IF. YOU. KISS.
MYU.
SHOVE
I SUPPOSE HER EXCELLENCY ORDERED YOU.
WHAP
WHAP

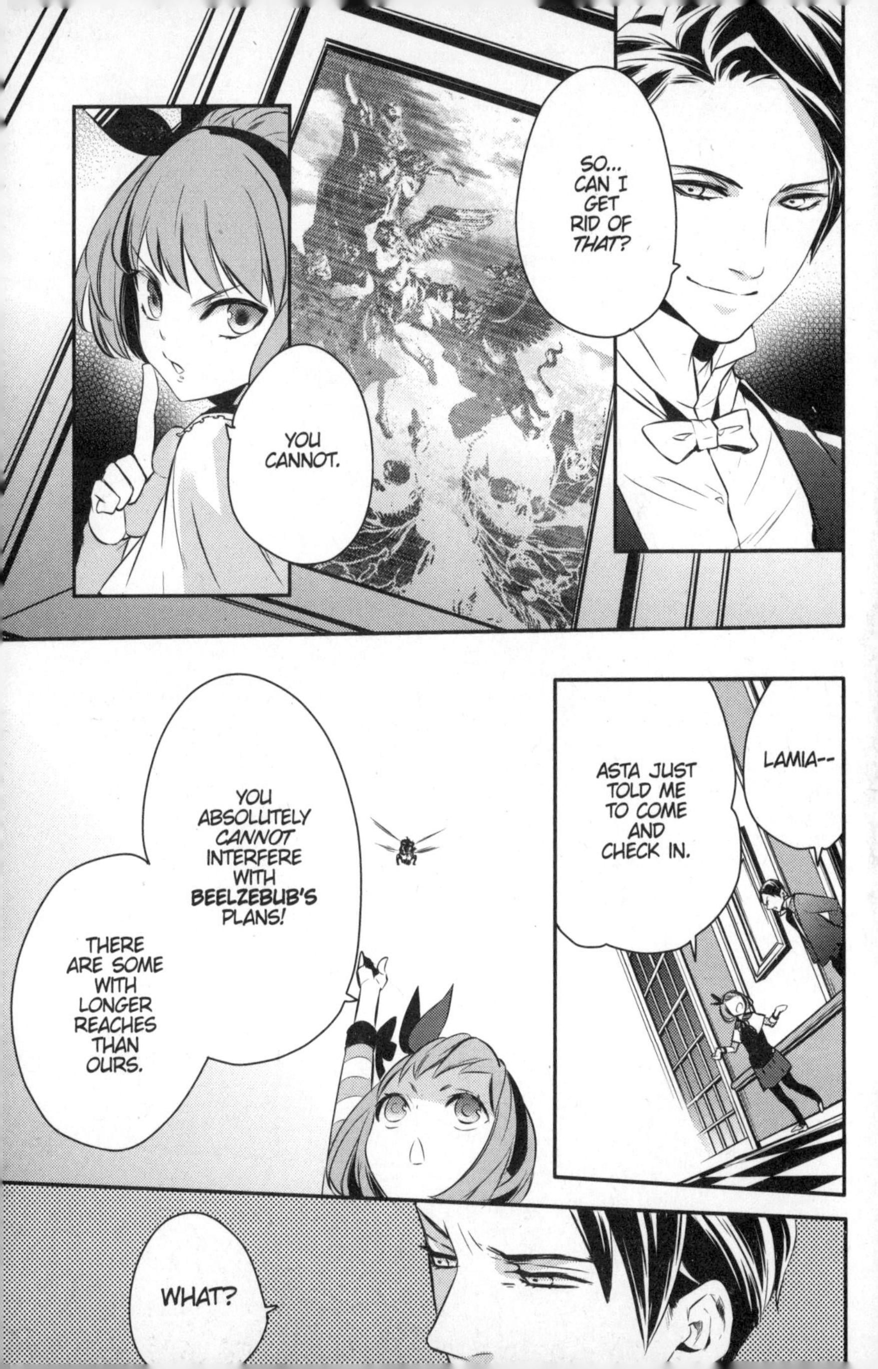
SO... CAN I GET RID OF *THAT*?
YOU CANNOT.
LAMIA--
ASTA JUST TOLD ME TO COME AND CHECK IN.
YOU ABSOLUTELY *CANNOT* INTERFERE WITH BEELZEBUB'S PLANS!
THERE ARE SOME WITH LONGER REACHES THAN OURS.
WHAT?

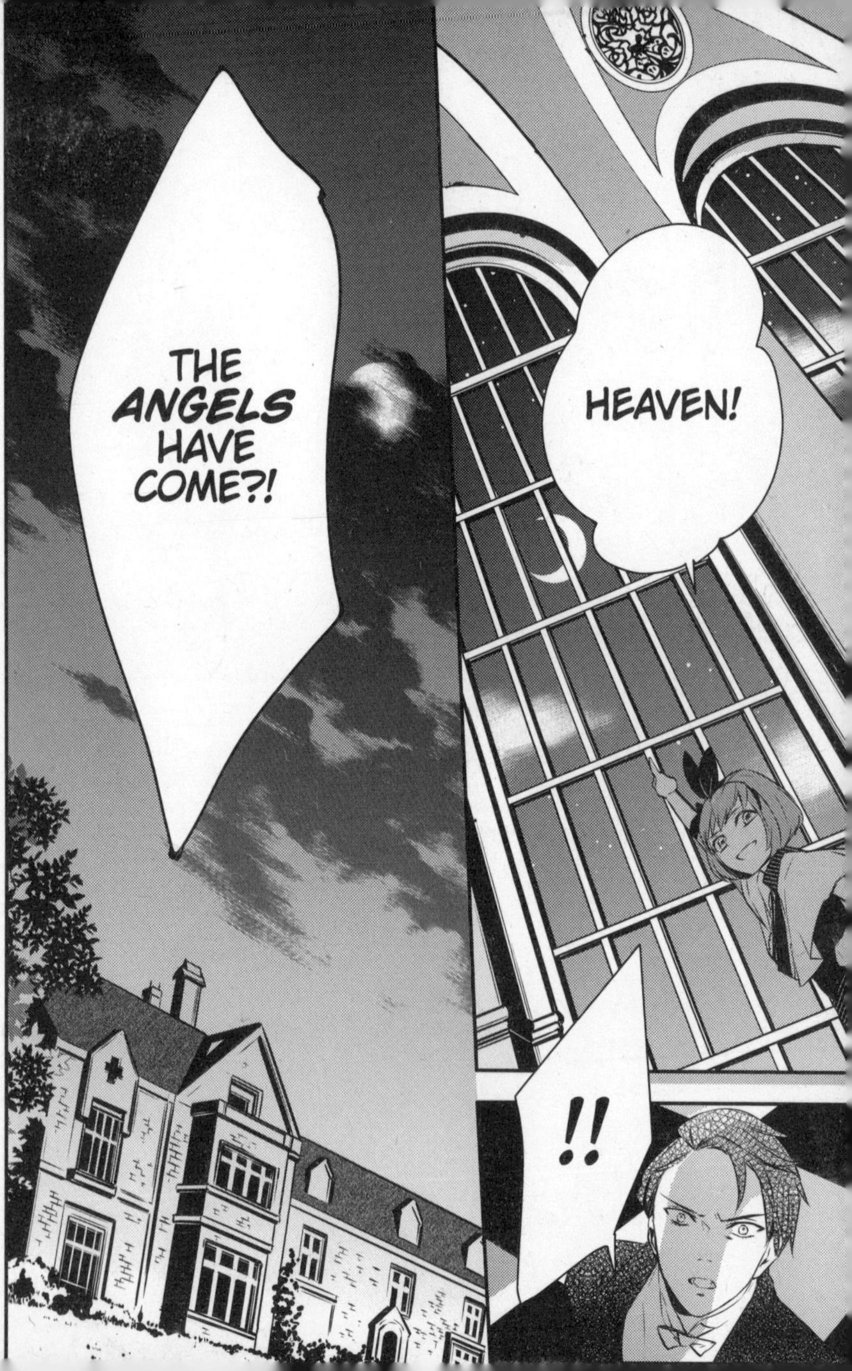
HEAVEN!
!!
THE ANGELS HAVE COME?!

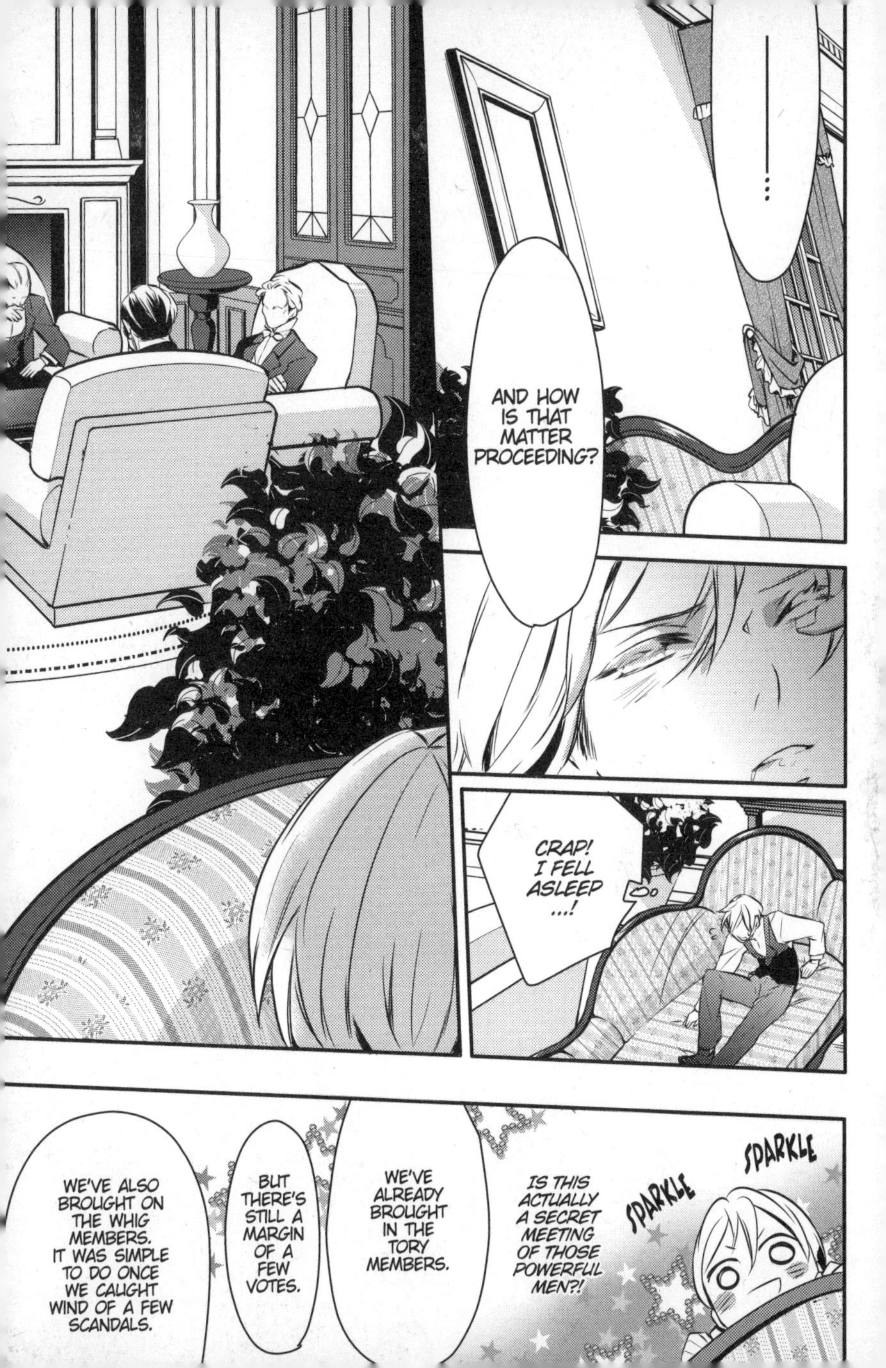
......
AND HOW IS THAT MATTER PROCEEDING?
CRAP! I FELL ASLEEP ...!
SPARKLE
SPARKLE
IS THIS ACTUALLY A SECRET MEETING OF THOSE POWERFUL MEN?!
WE'VE ALREADY BROUGHT IN THE TORY MEMBERS.
BUT THERE'S STILL A MARGIN OF A FEW VOTES.
WE'VE ALSO BROUGHT ON THE WHIG MEMBERS. IT WAS SIMPLE TO DO ONCE WE CAUGHT WIND OF A FEW SCANDALS.

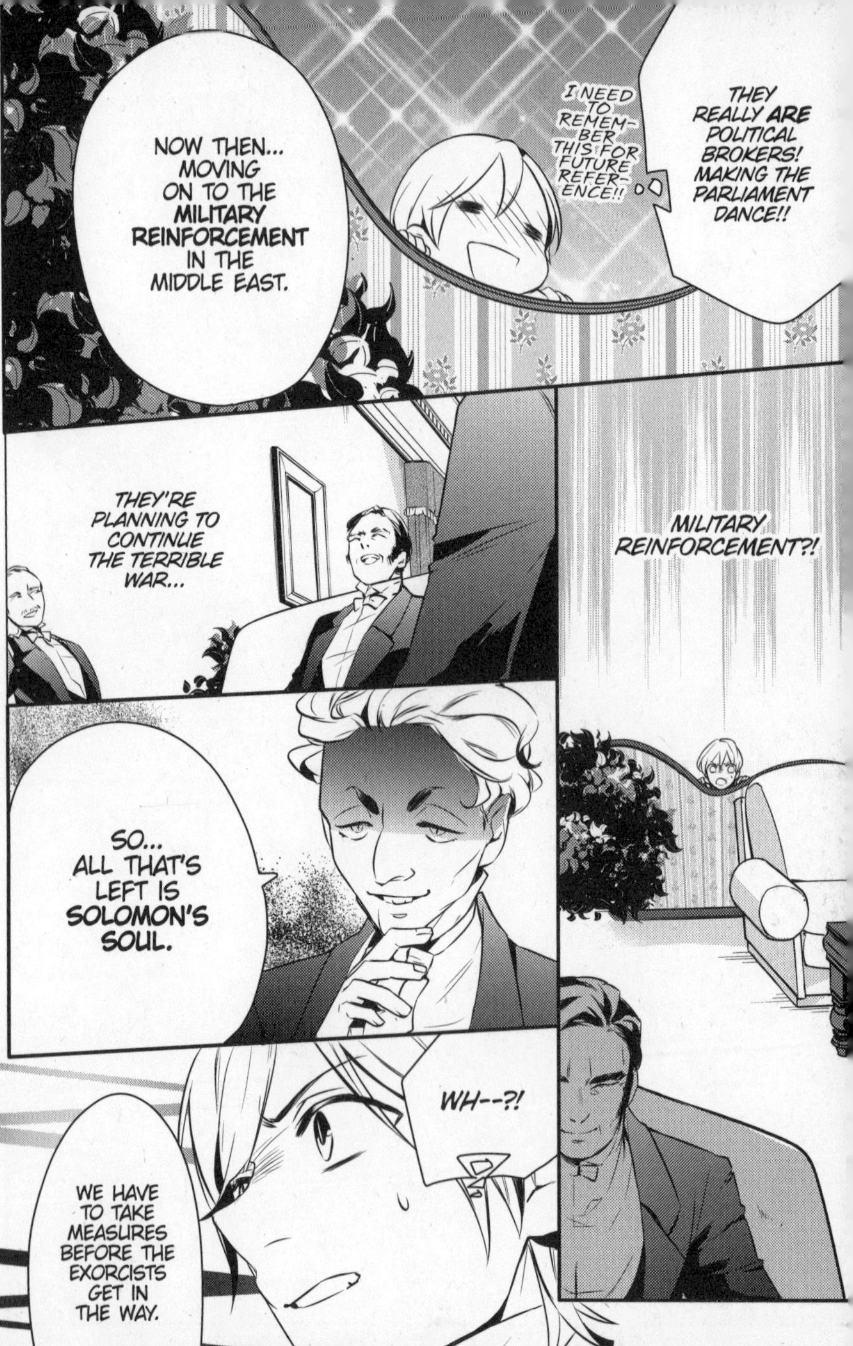
THEY REALLY ARE POLITICAL BROKERS! MAKING THE PARLIAMENT DANCE!!
I NEED TO REMEMBER THIS FOR FUTURE REFERENCE!!
NOW THEN... MOVING ON TO THE MILITARY REINFORCEMENT IN THE MIDDLE EAST.
MILITARY REINFORCEMENT?!
THEY'RE PLANNING TO CONTINUE THE TERRIBLE WAR...
SO... ALL THAT'S LEFT IS SOLOMON'S SOUL.
WH--?!
WE HAVE TO TAKE MEASURES BEFORE THE EXORCISTS GET IN THE WAY.

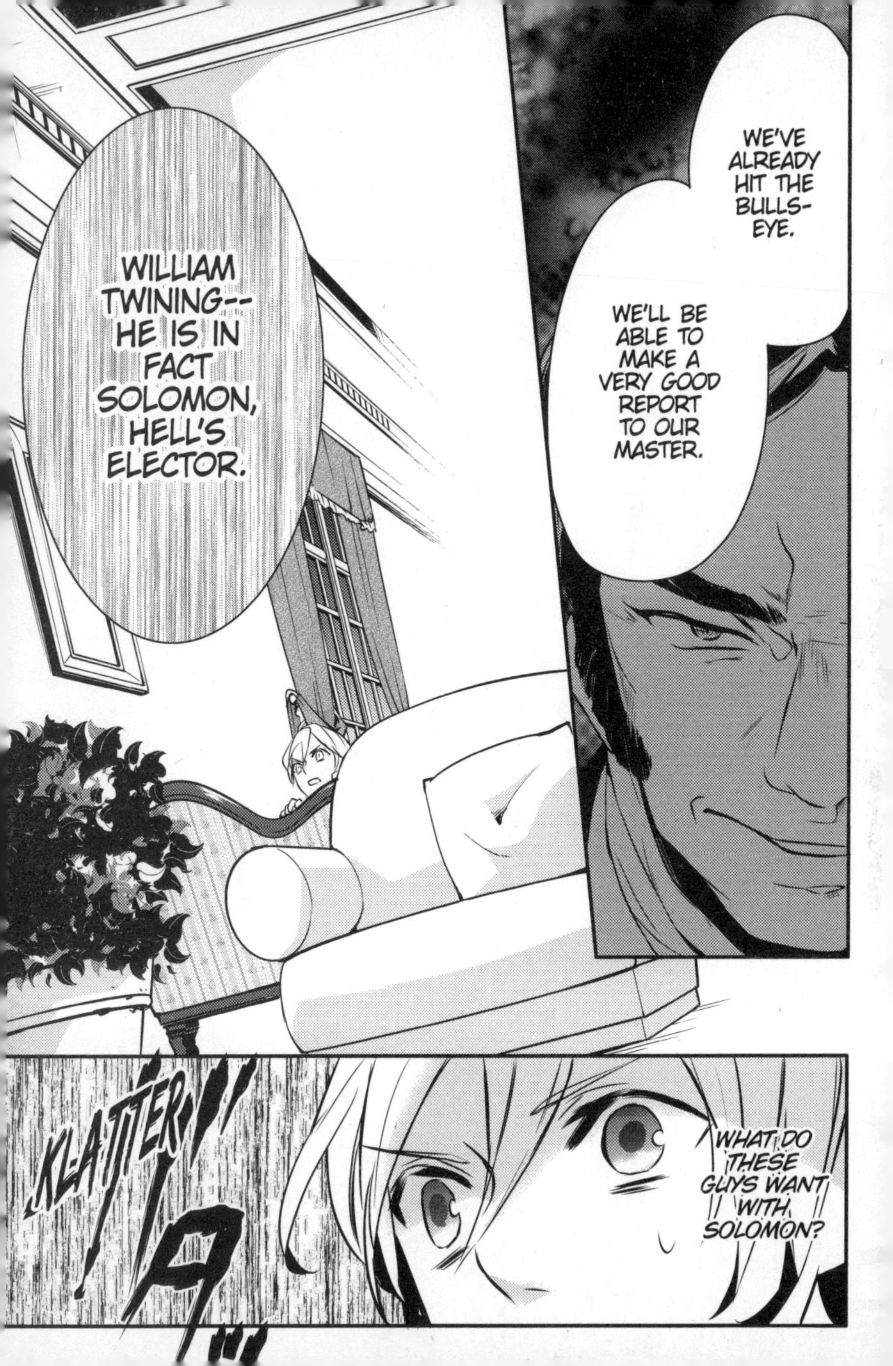
WE'VE ALREADY HIT THE BULLS-EYE.
WE'LL BE ABLE TO MAKE A VERY GOOD REPORT TO OUR MASTER.
WILLIAM TWINING-- HE IS IN FACT SOLOMON, HELL'S ELECTOR.
WHAT DO THESE GUYS WANT WITH SOLOMON?
KL-ATTER!!

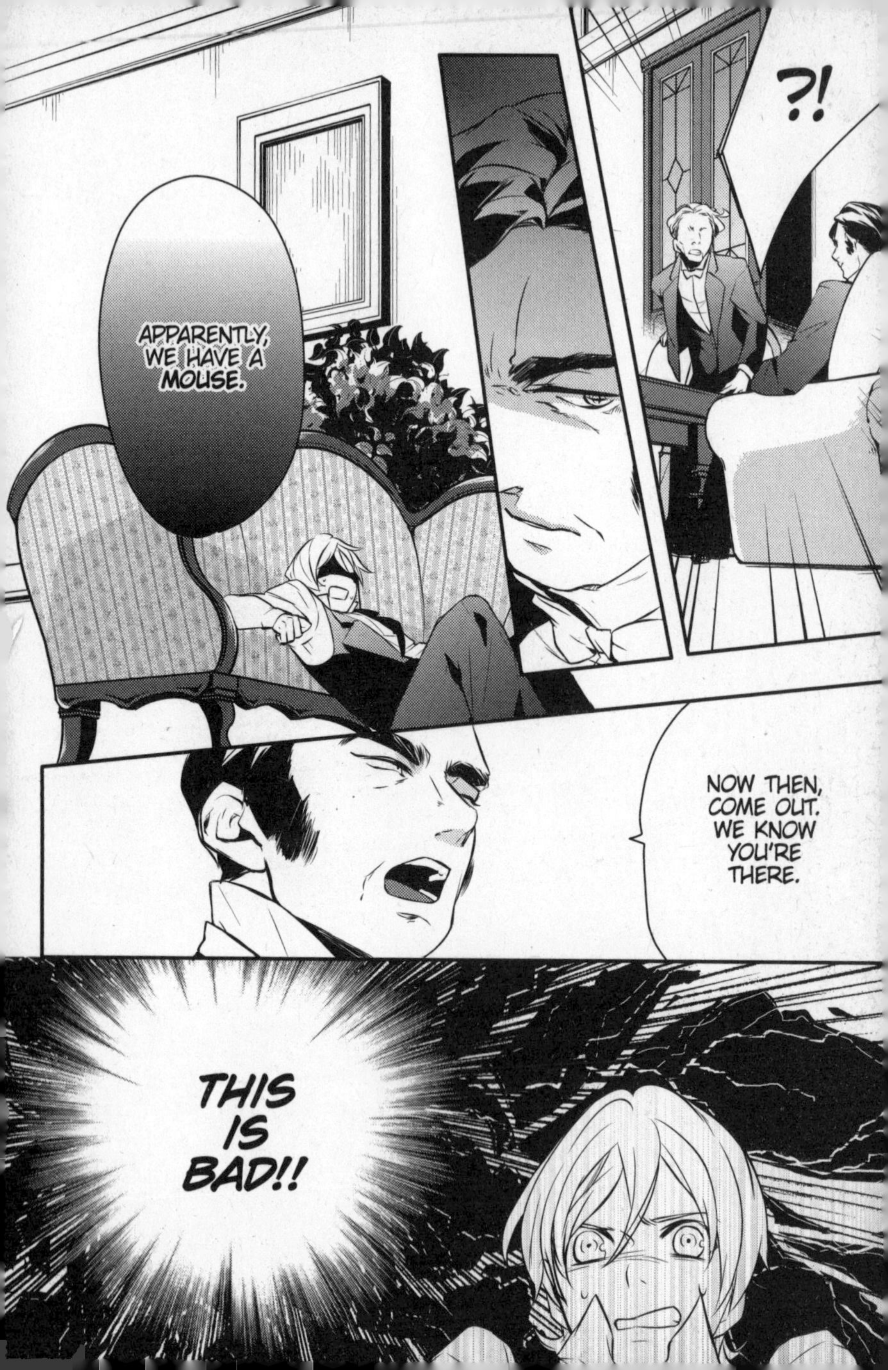
?!
APPARENTLY, WE HAVE A MOUSE.
NOW THEN, COME OUT. WE KNOW YOU'RE THERE.
THIS IS BAD!!

魔界王子
devils and realist

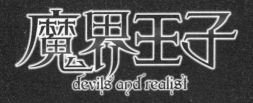

--SIR.

FATHER...

Miracle ... from falling accident

FA... THER...?

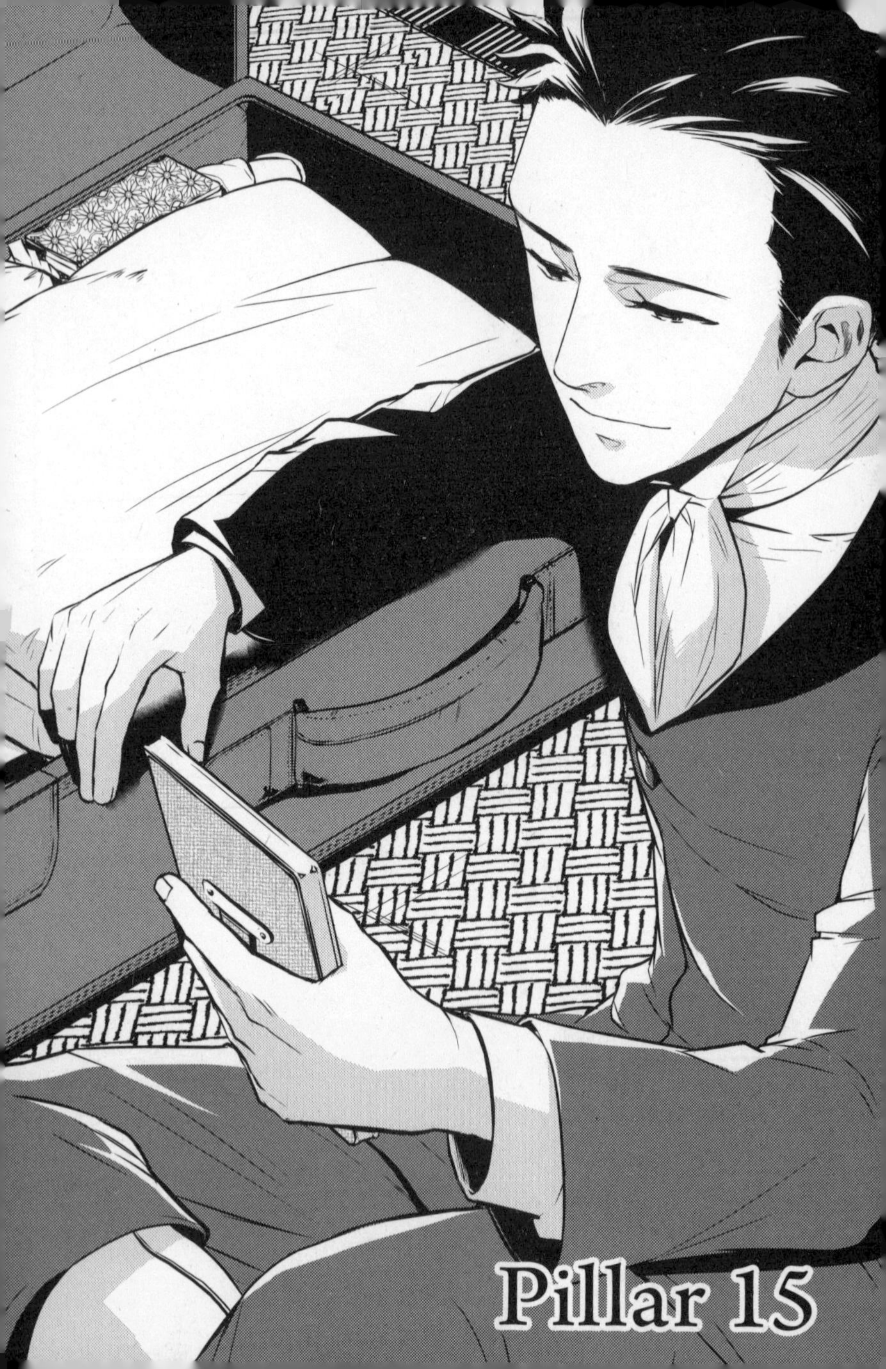

Pillar 15

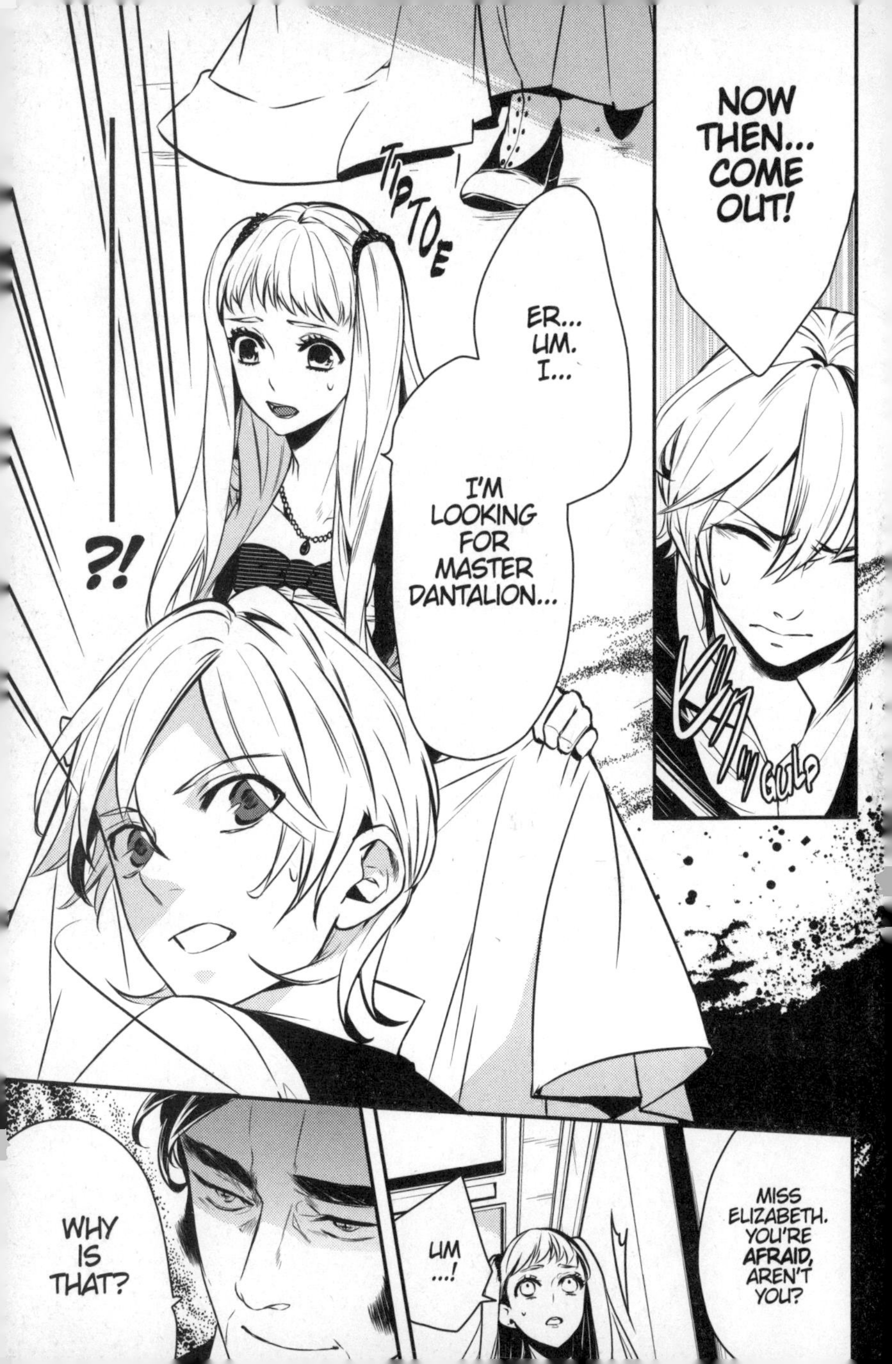
NOW THEN... COME OUT!
GULP
TIPTOE
ER... UM. I...
I'M LOOKING FOR MASTER DANTALION...
?!
MISS ELIZABETH. YOU'RE AFRAID, AREN'T YOU?
UM ...!
WHY IS THAT?

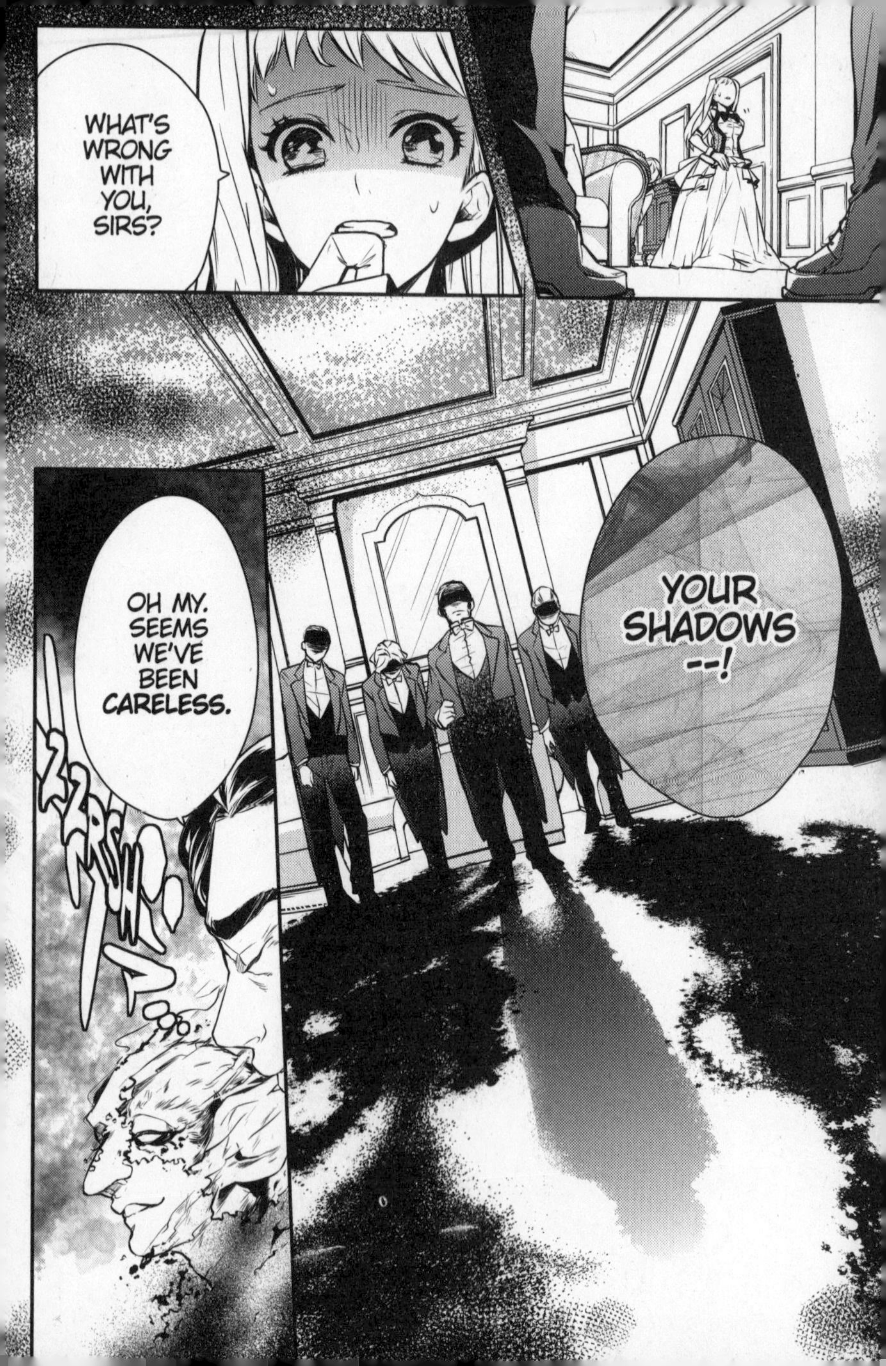
WHAT'S WRONG WITH YOU, SIRS?
YOUR SHADOWS --!
OH MY. SEEMS WE'VE BEEN CARELESS.

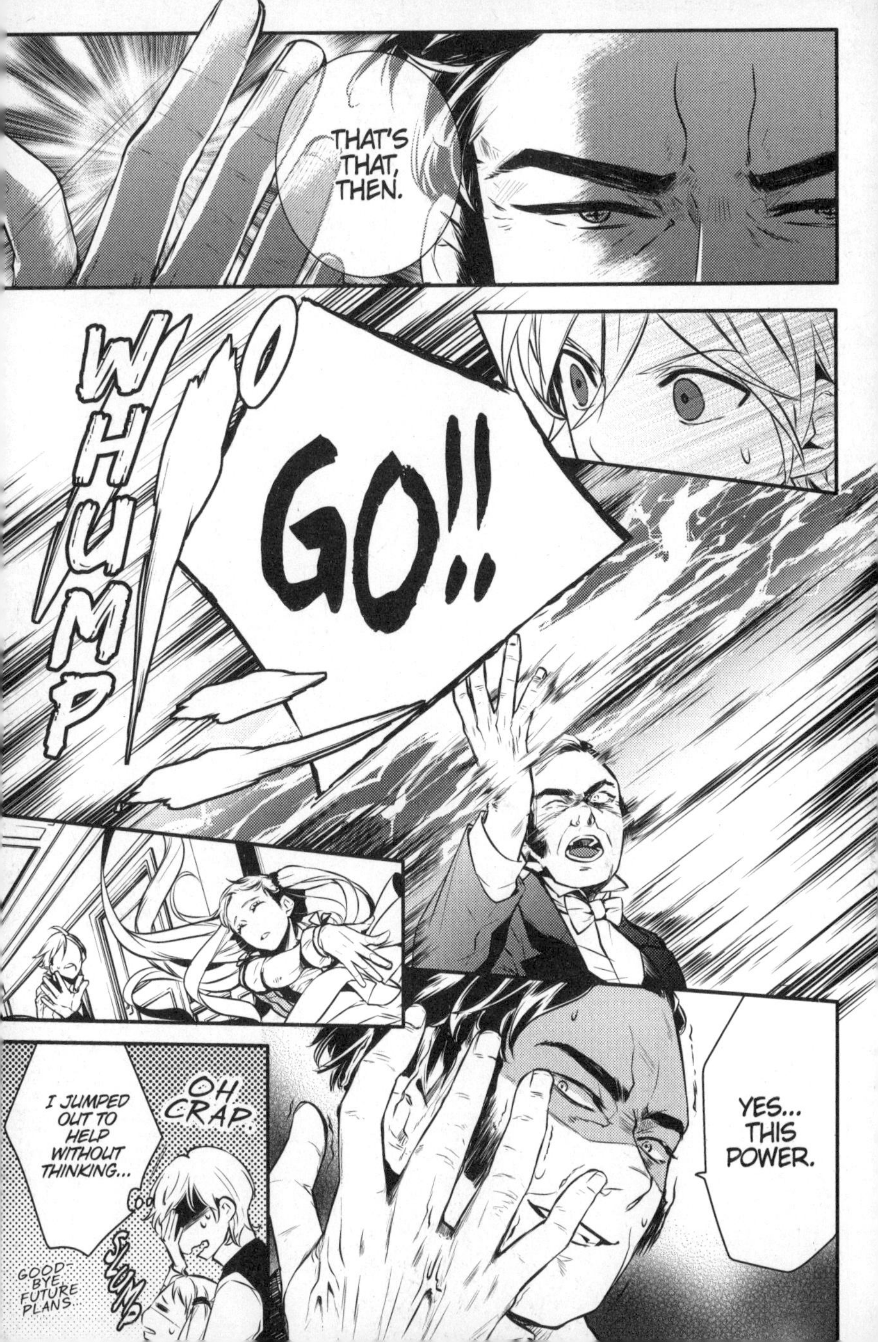
THAT'S THAT, THEN.
GO!!
WHUMP
YES... THIS POWER.
OH CRAP.
I JUMPED OUT TO HELP WITHOUT THINKING...
SLUMP
GOOD-BYE FUTURE PLANS.

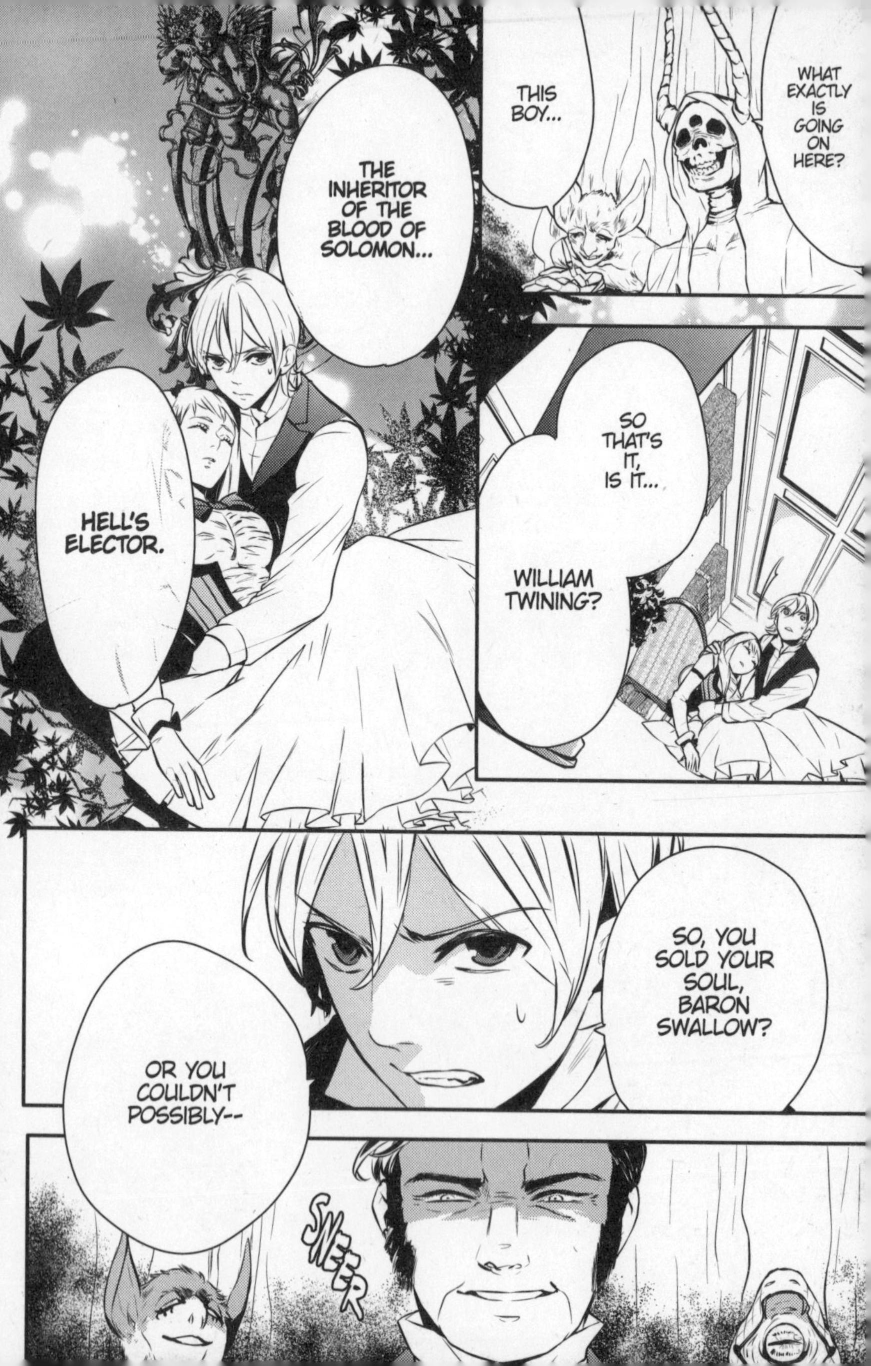
WHAT EXACTLY IS GOING ON HERE?
THIS BOY...
SO THAT'S IT, IS IT...
WILLIAM TWINING?
THE INHERITOR OF THE BLOOD OF SOLOMON...
HELL'S ELECTOR.
SO, YOU SOLD YOUR SOUL, BARON SWALLOW?
OR YOU COULDN'T POSSIBLY--
SNEER

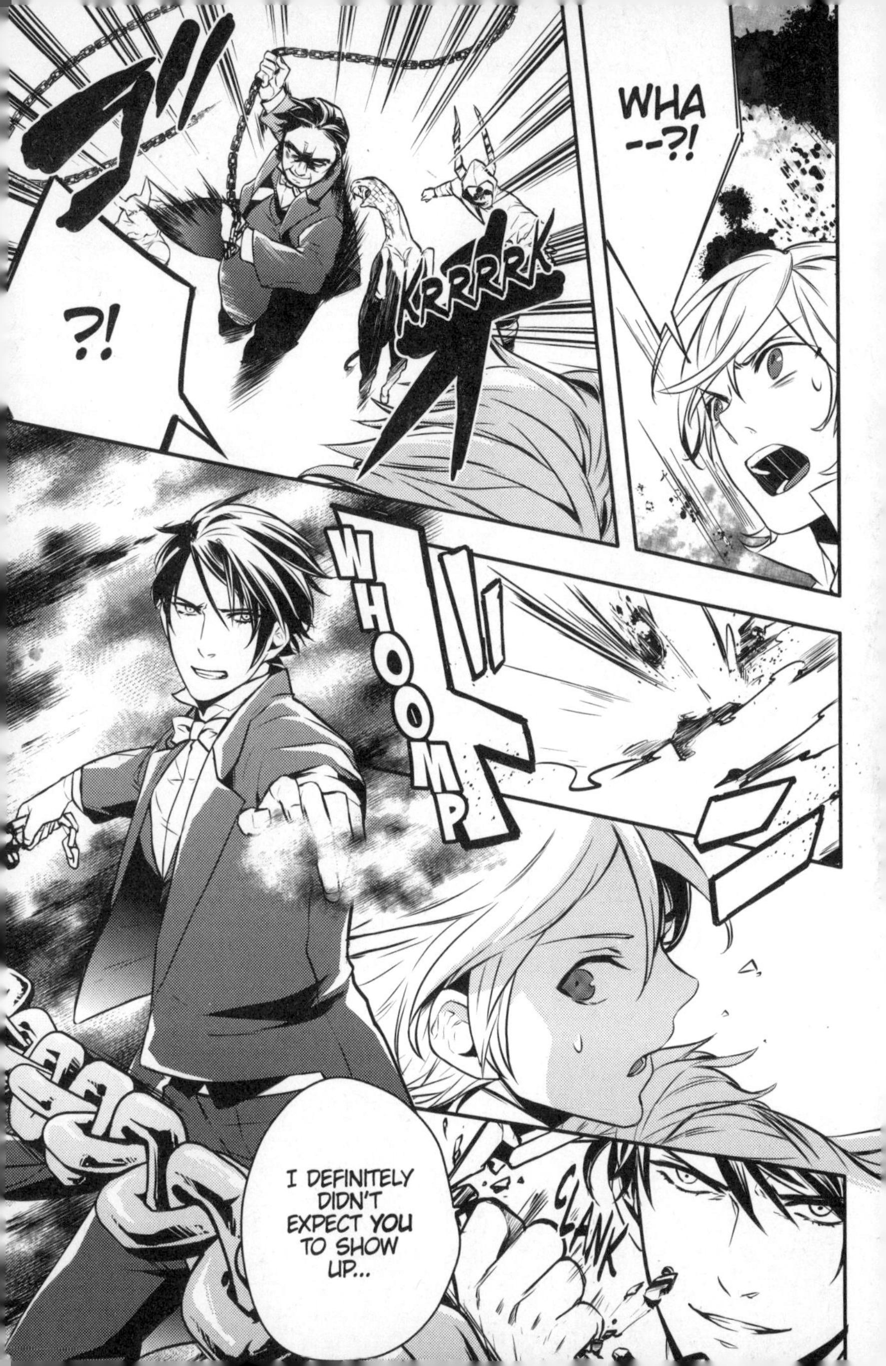
WHA --?!
?!
KRRRRK
WHOOMP
CLANK
I DEFINITELY DIDN'T EXPECT YOU TO SHOW UP...

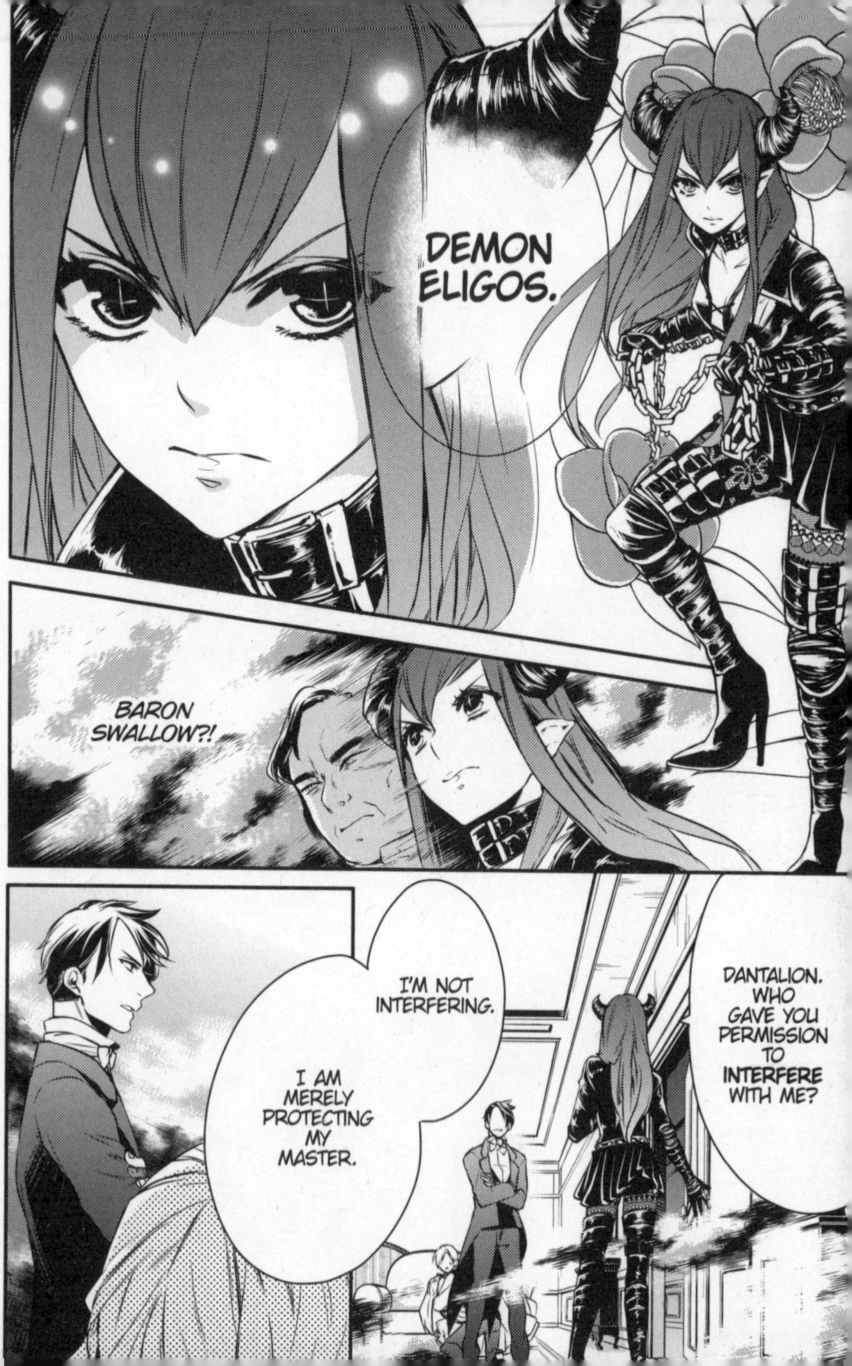
DEMON ELIGOS.
BARON SWALLOW?!
DANTALION. WHO GAVE YOU PERMISSION TO INTERFERE WITH ME?
I'M NOT INTERFERING.
I AM MERELY PROTECTING MY MASTER.

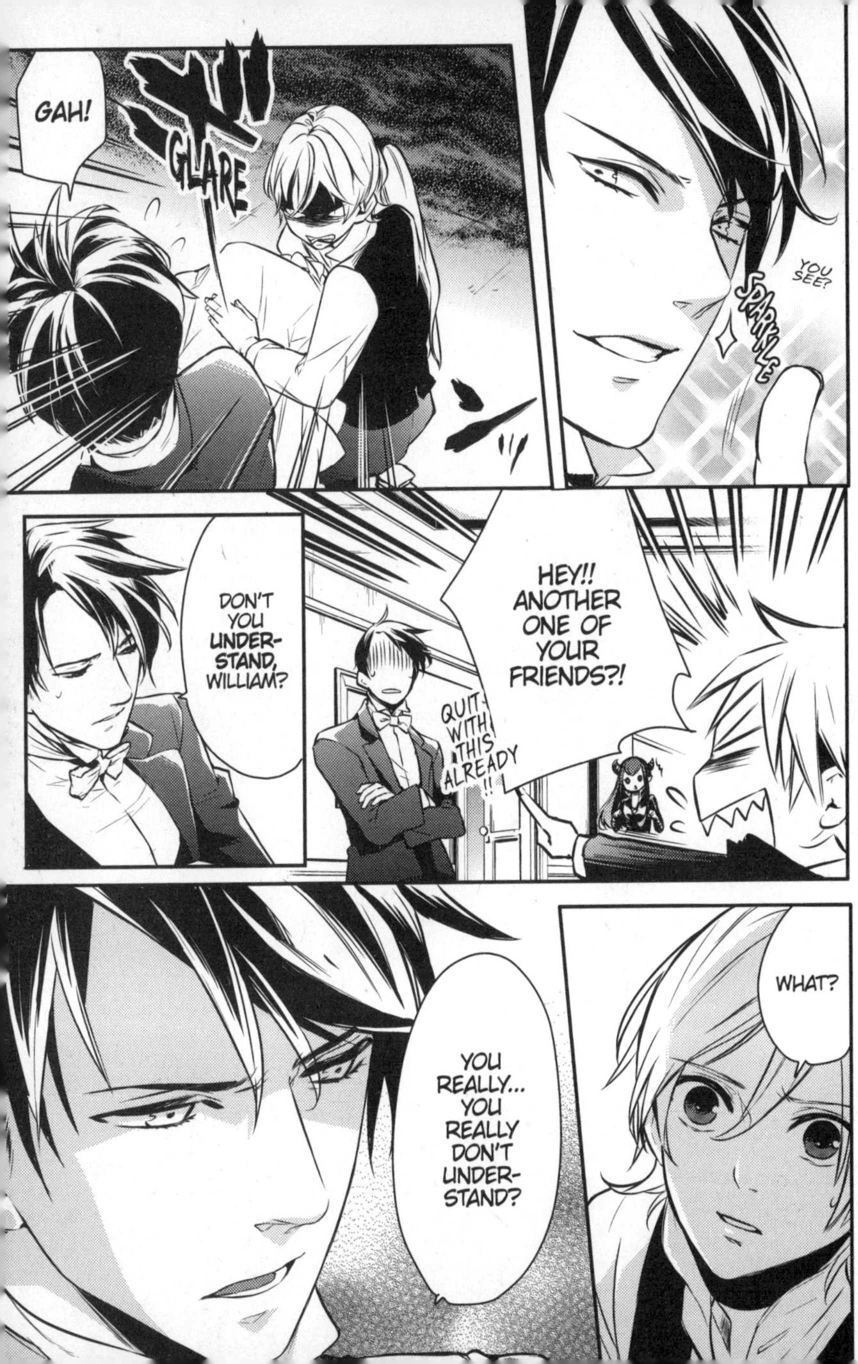
YOU SEE?
SPARKLE
GAH!
GLARE
HEY!! ANOTHER ONE OF YOUR FRIENDS?!
QUIT WITH THIS ALREADY!!
DON'T YOU UNDER-STAND, WILLIAM?
WHAT?
YOU REALLY... YOU REALLY DON'T UNDER-STAND?

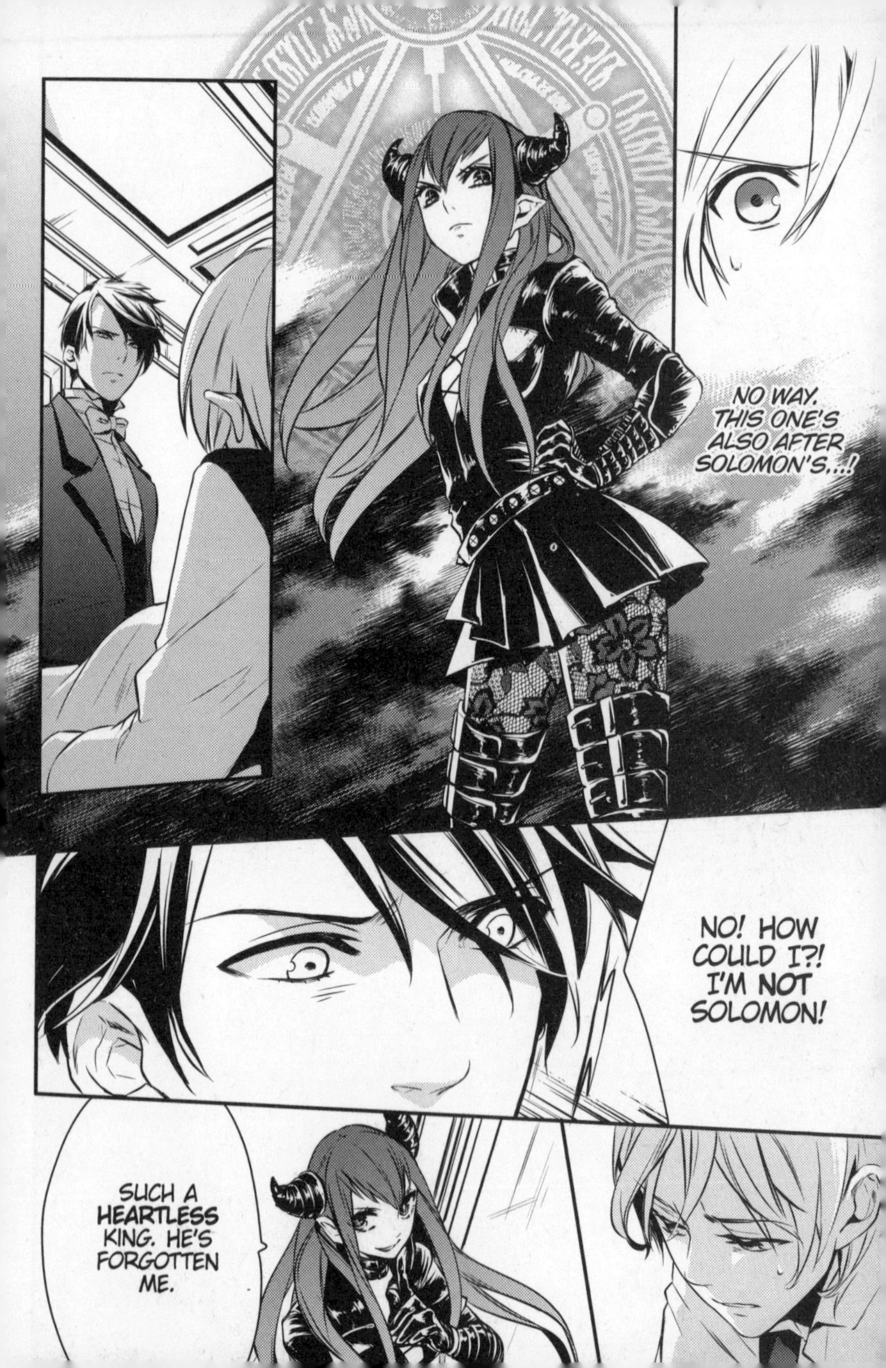
NO WAY. THIS ONE'S ALSO AFTER SOLOMON'S...!
NO! HOW COULD I?! I'M NOT SOLOMON!
SUCH A HEARTLESS KING. HE'S FORGOTTEN ME.

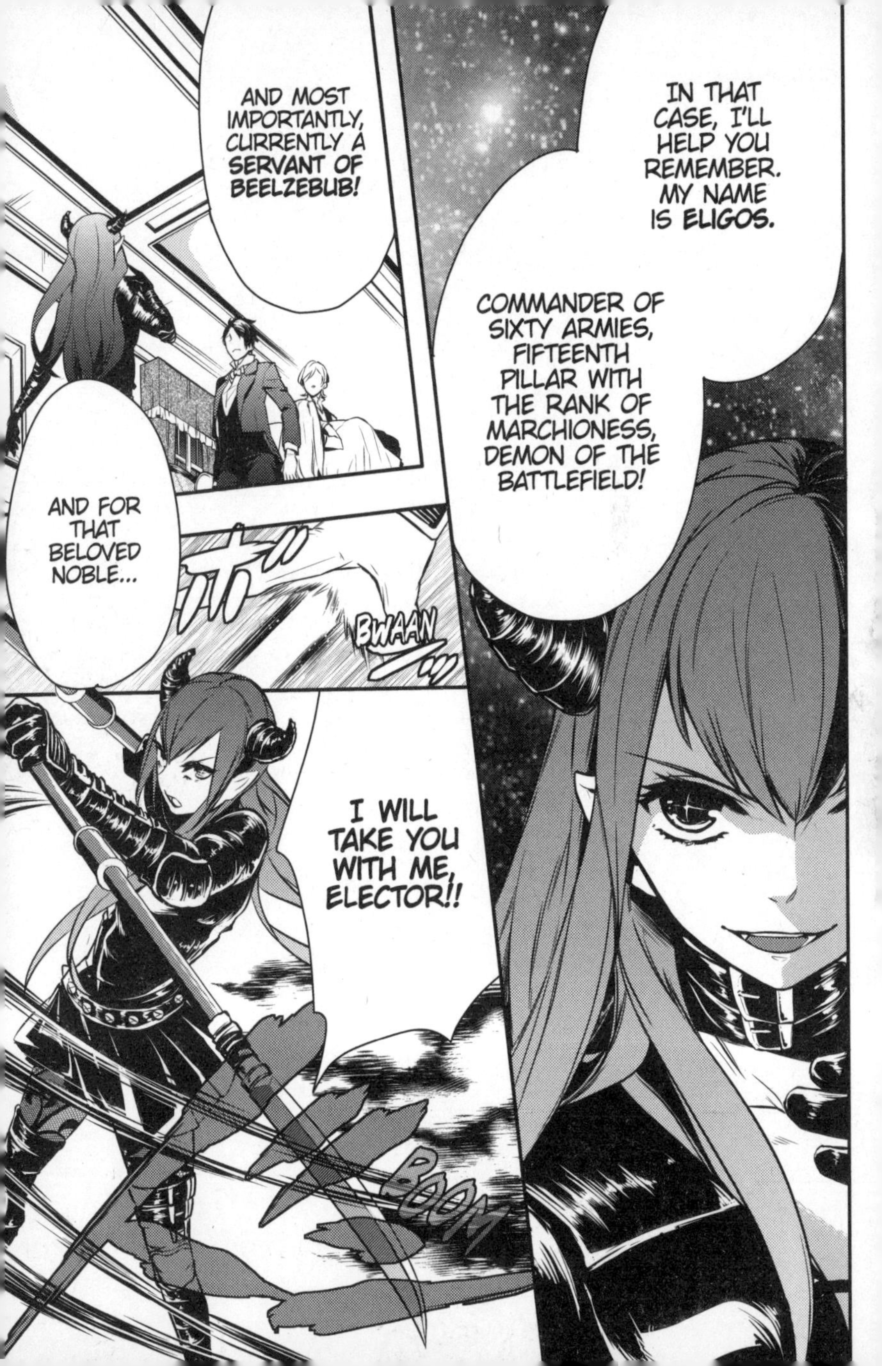
IN THAT CASE, I'LL HELP YOU REMEMBER. MY NAME IS ELIGOS.
COMMANDER OF SIXTY ARMIES, FIFTEENTH PILLAR WITH THE RANK OF MARCHIONESS, DEMON OF THE BATTLEFIELD!
AND MOST IMPORTANTLY, CURRENTLY A SERVANT OF BEELZEBUB!
AND FOR THAT BELOVED NOBLE...
BWAAN
I WILL TAKE YOU WITH ME, ELECTOR!!
BOOM

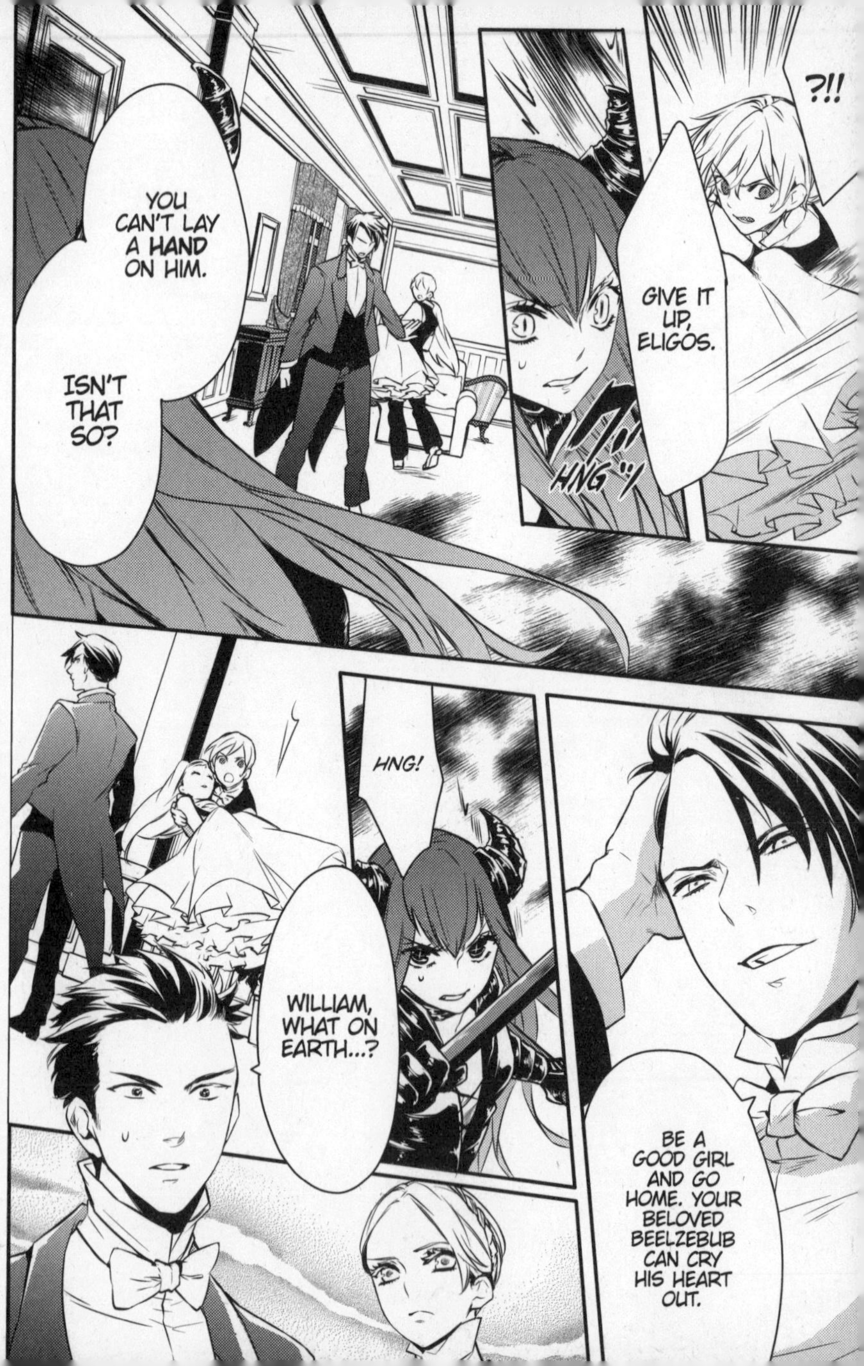
?!!
GIVE IT UP, ELIGOS.
HNG
YOU CAN'T LAY A HAND ON HIM.
ISN'T THAT SO?
BE A GOOD GIRL AND GO HOME. YOUR BELOVED BEELZEBUB CAN CRY HIS HEART OUT.
HNG!
WILLIAM, WHAT ON EARTH...?

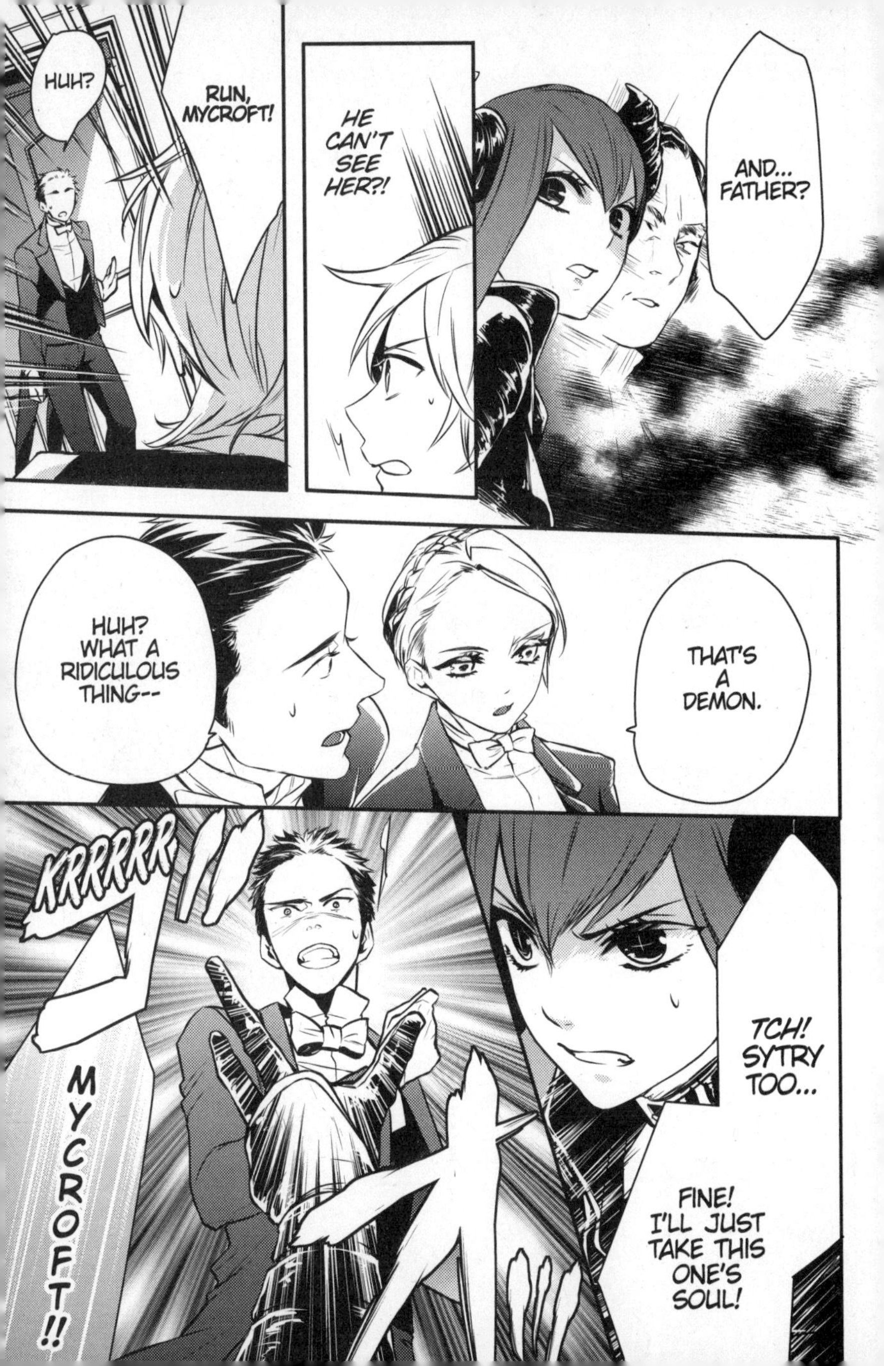
AND... FATHER?
HE CAN'T SEE HER?!
RUN, MYCROFT!
HUH?
THAT'S A DEMON.
HUH? WHAT A RIDICULOUS THING--
TCH! SYTRY TOO...
FINE! I'LL JUST TAKE THIS ONE'S SOUL!
KRRRRR
MYCROFT!!

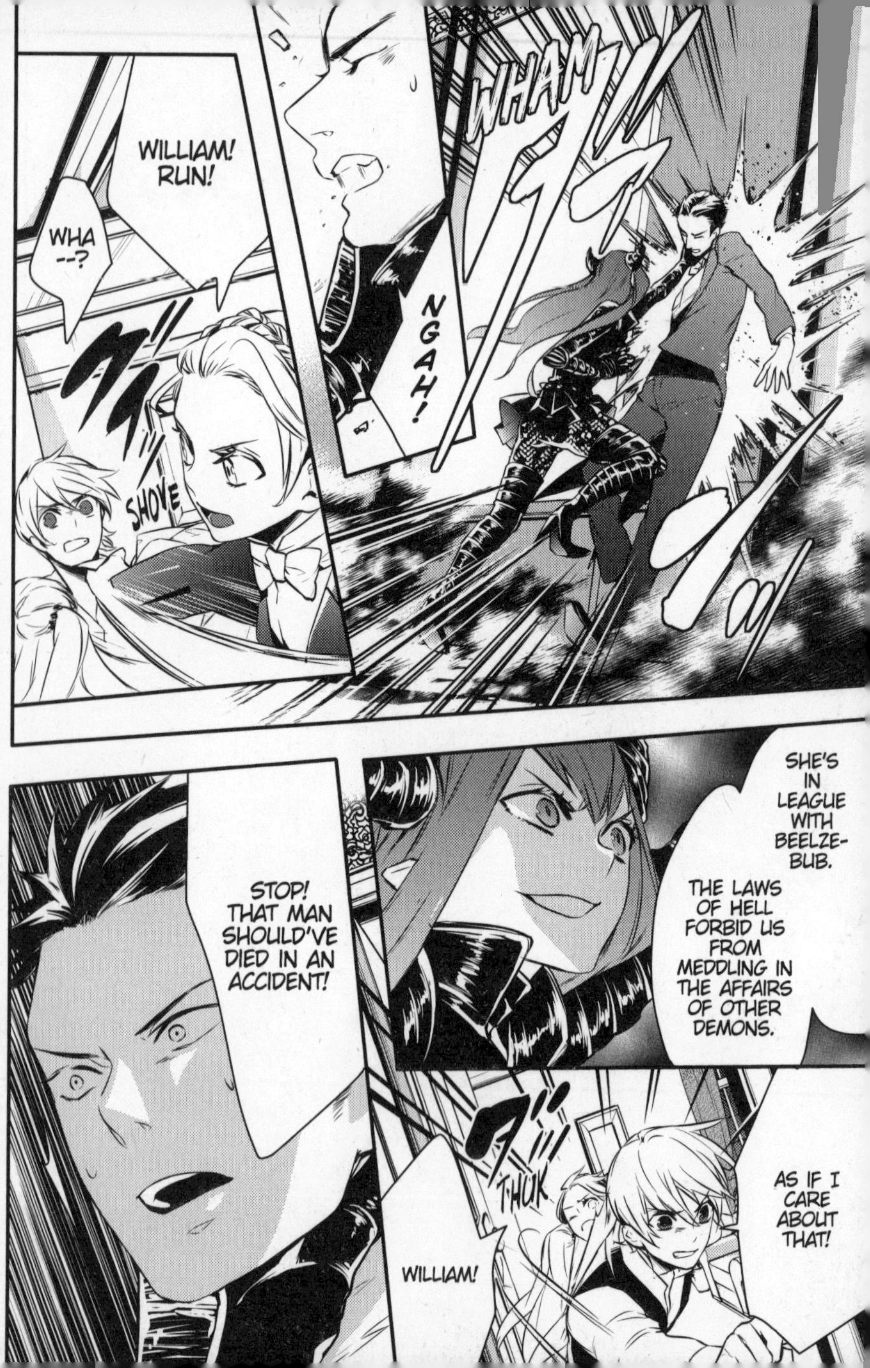
WHAM
NGAH!
WILLIAM! RUN!
WHA--?
SHOVE
SHE'S IN LEAGUE WITH BEELZE-BUB.
THE LAWS OF HELL FORBID US FROM MEDDLING IN THE AFFAIRS OF OTHER DEMONS.
AS IF I CARE ABOUT THAT!
THUK
WILLIAM!
STOP! THAT MAN SHOULD'VE DIED IN AN ACCIDENT!

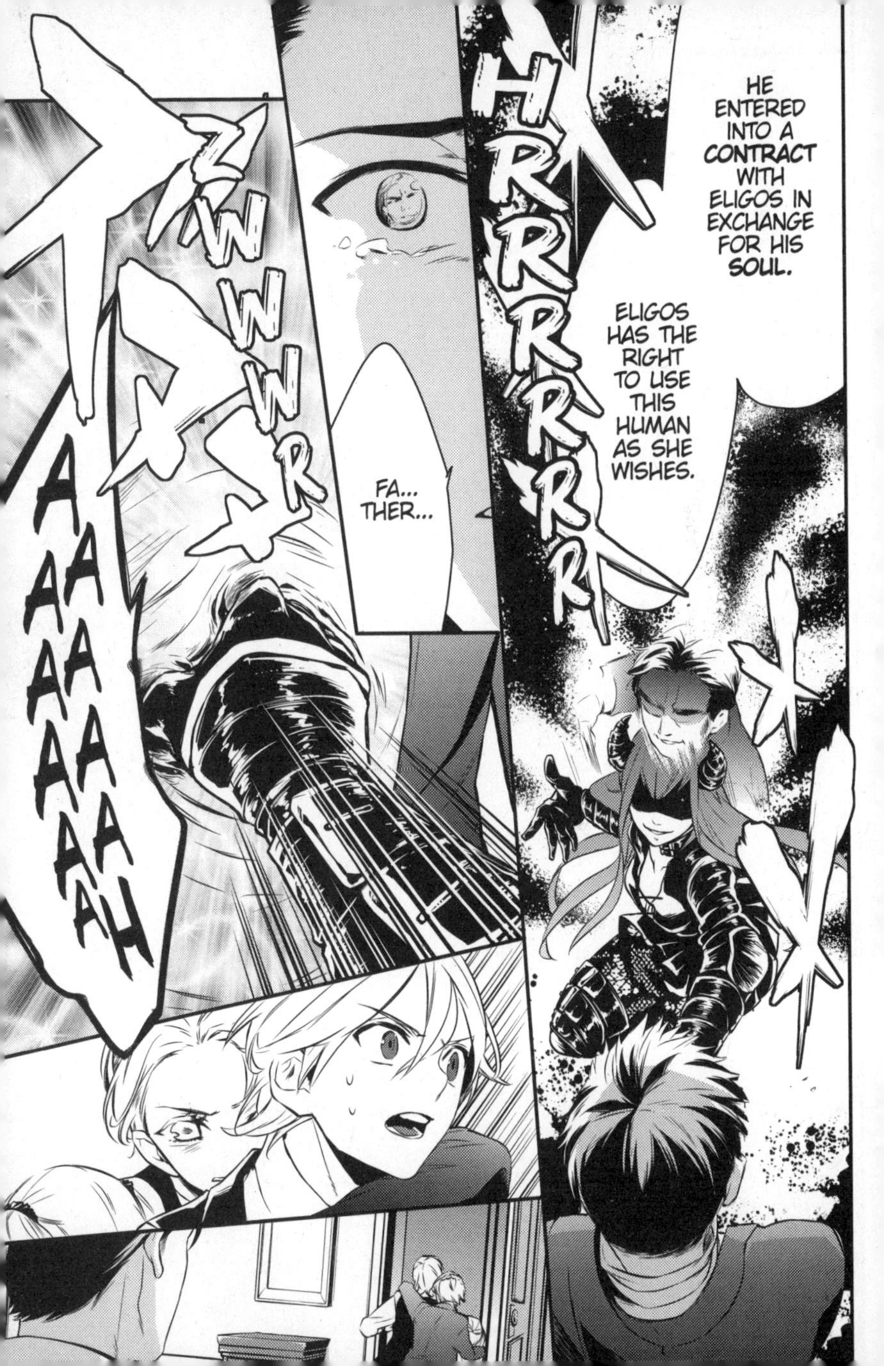
HRRRRRRR
HE ENTERED INTO A CONTRACT WITH ELIGOS IN EXCHANGE FOR HIS SOUL.
ELIGOS HAS THE RIGHT TO USE THIS HUMAN AS SHE WISHES.
FA... THER...
ZWWWWR
AAAAAAAAAAH

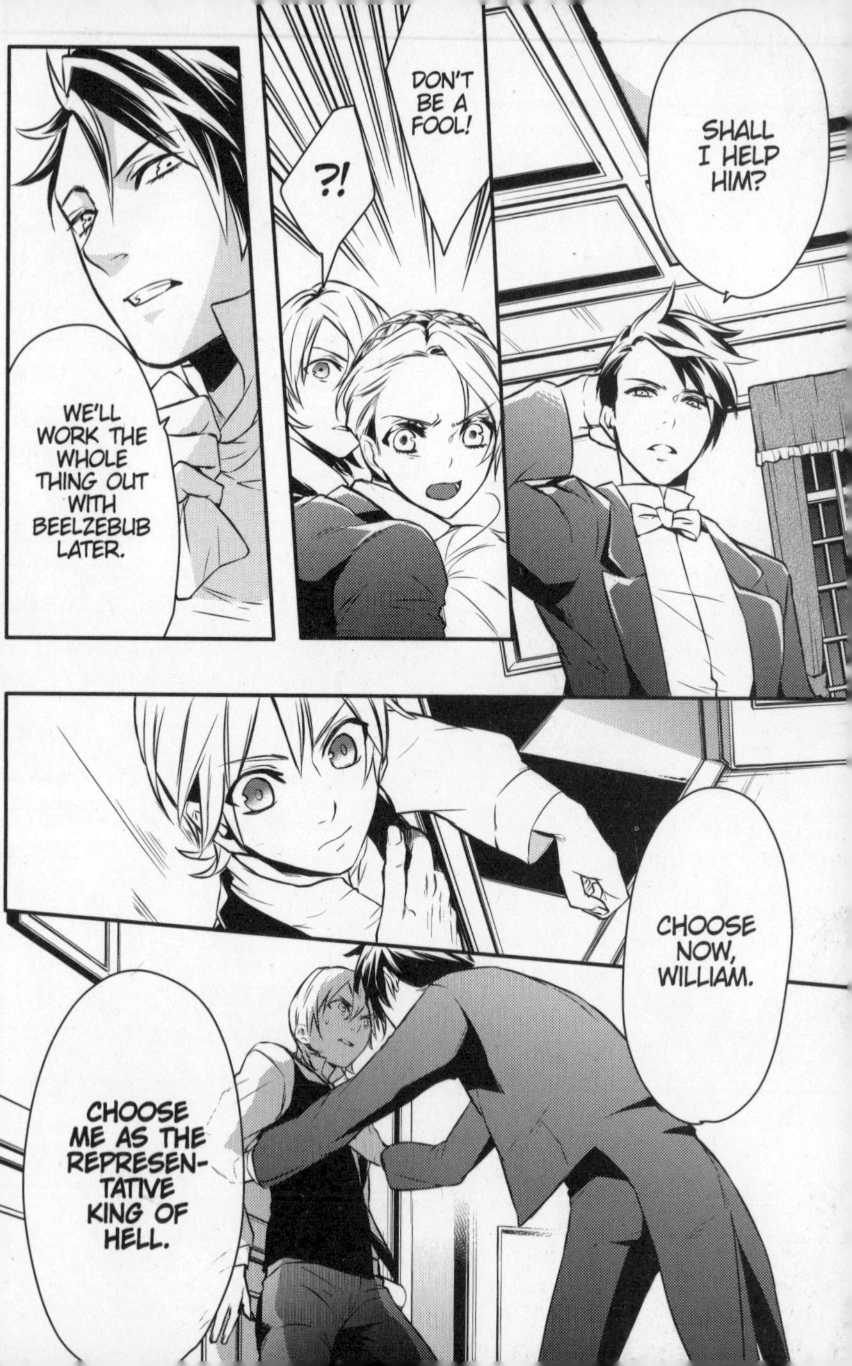
SHALL I HELP HIM?
DON'T BE A FOOL!
?!
WE'LL WORK THE WHOLE THING OUT WITH BEELZEBUB LATER.
CHOOSE NOW, WILLIAM.
CHOOSE ME AS THE REPRESEN-TATIVE KING OF HELL.

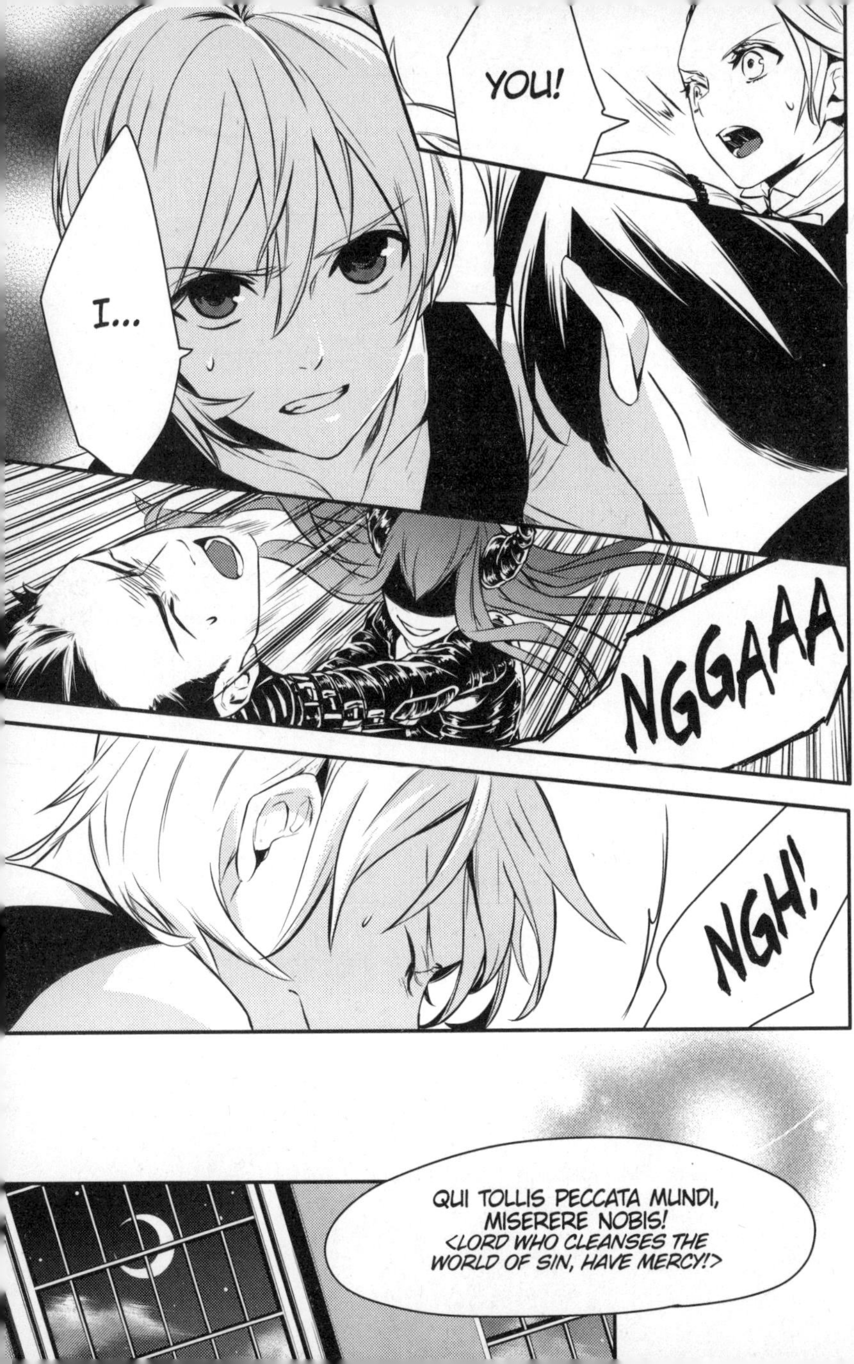
YOU!
I...
NGGAAA
NGH!
QUI TOLLIS PECCATA MUNDI, MISERERE NOBIS!
<LORD WHO CLEANSES THE WORLD OF SIN, HAVE MERCY!>

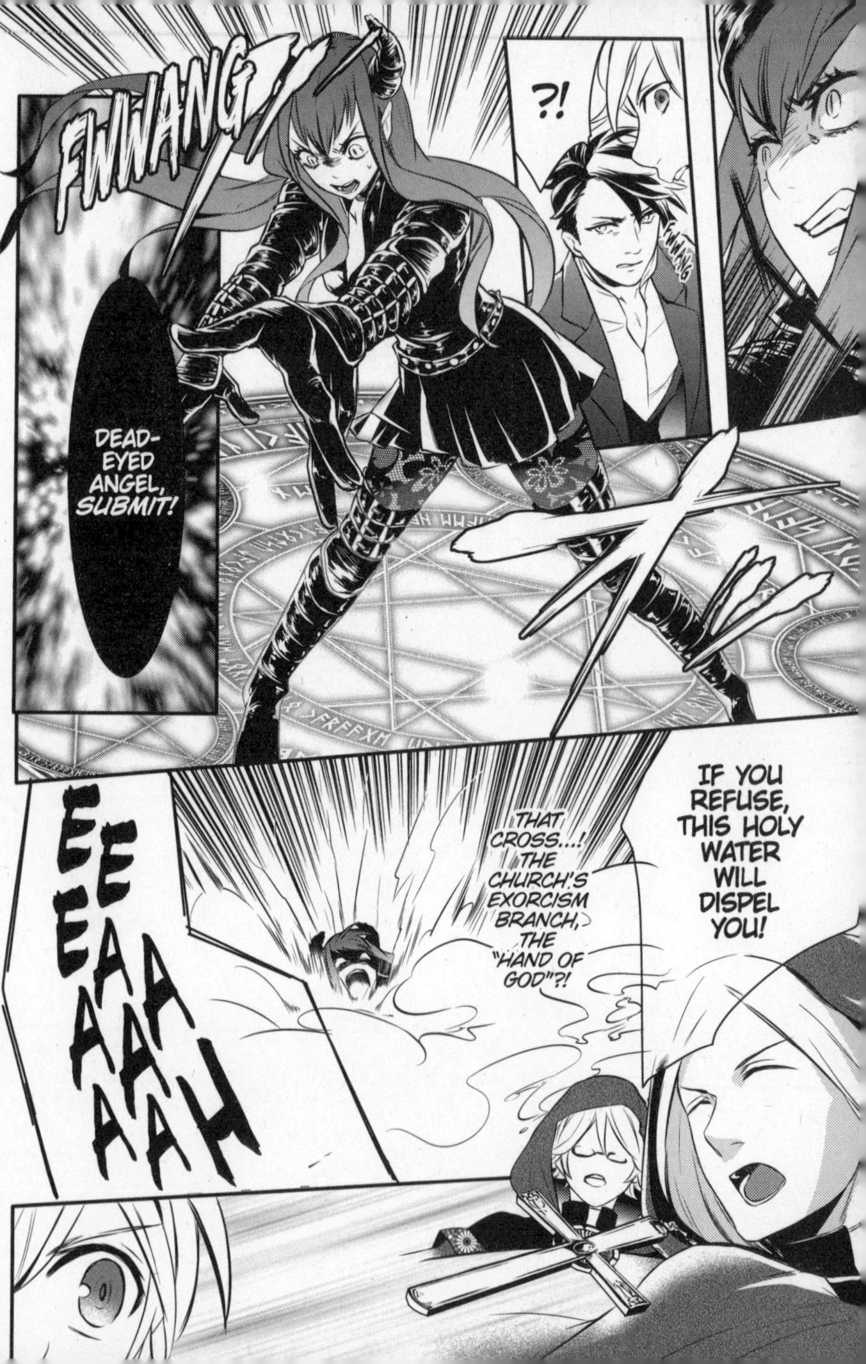
?!
FWWANG
FWWANG
DEAD-EYED ANGEL, SUBMIT!
IF YOU REFUSE, THIS HOLY WATER WILL DISPEL YOU!
THAT CROSS...! THE CHURCH'S EXORCISM BRANCH, THE "HAND OF GOD"?!
EEEAAAAAAH

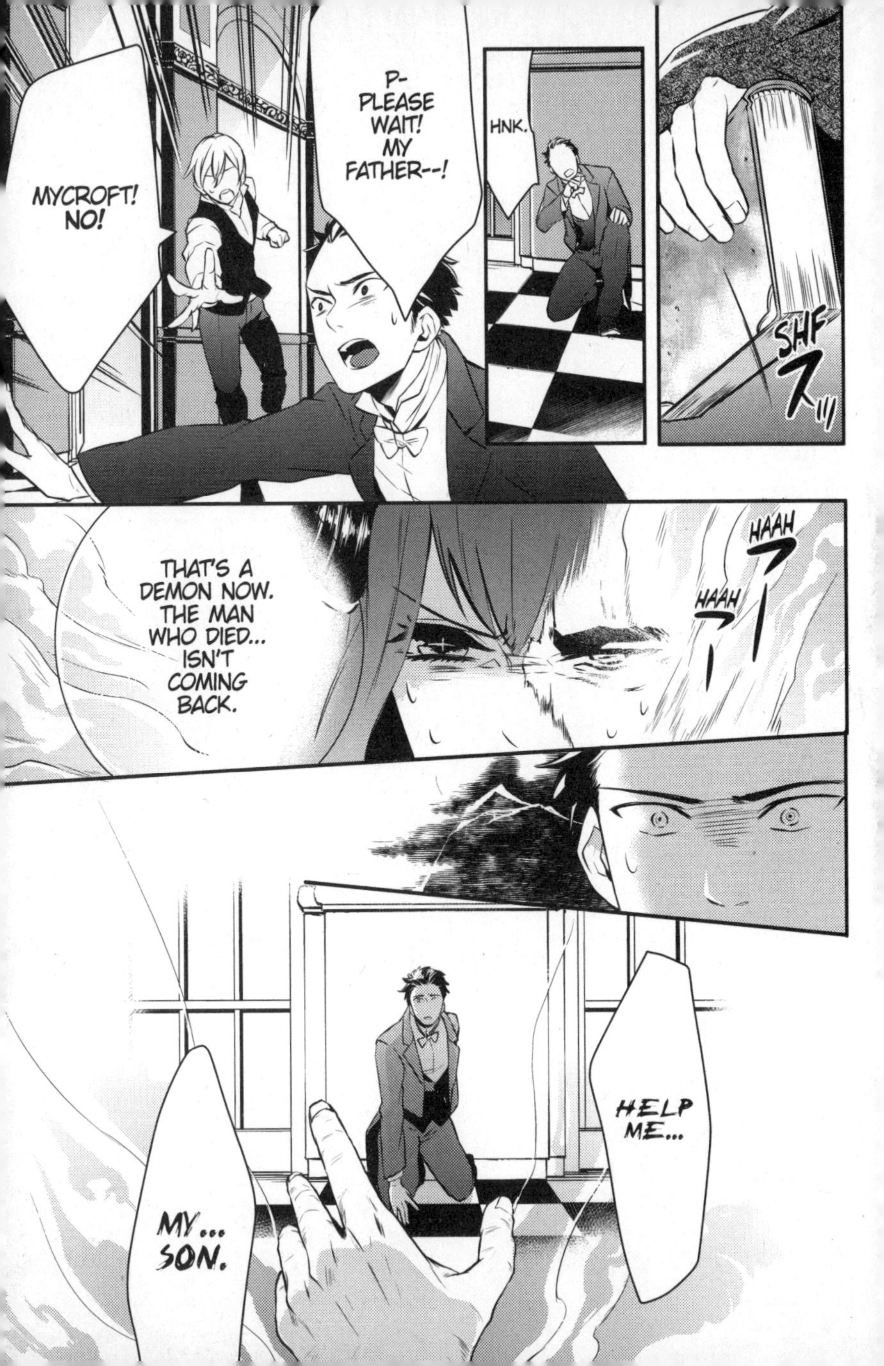
SHF
スッ
HNK.
P-PLEASE WAIT! MY FATHER--!
MYCROFT! NO!
HAAH
HAAH
THAT'S A DEMON NOW. THE MAN WHO DIED... ISN'T COMING BACK.
HELP ME...
MY... SON.

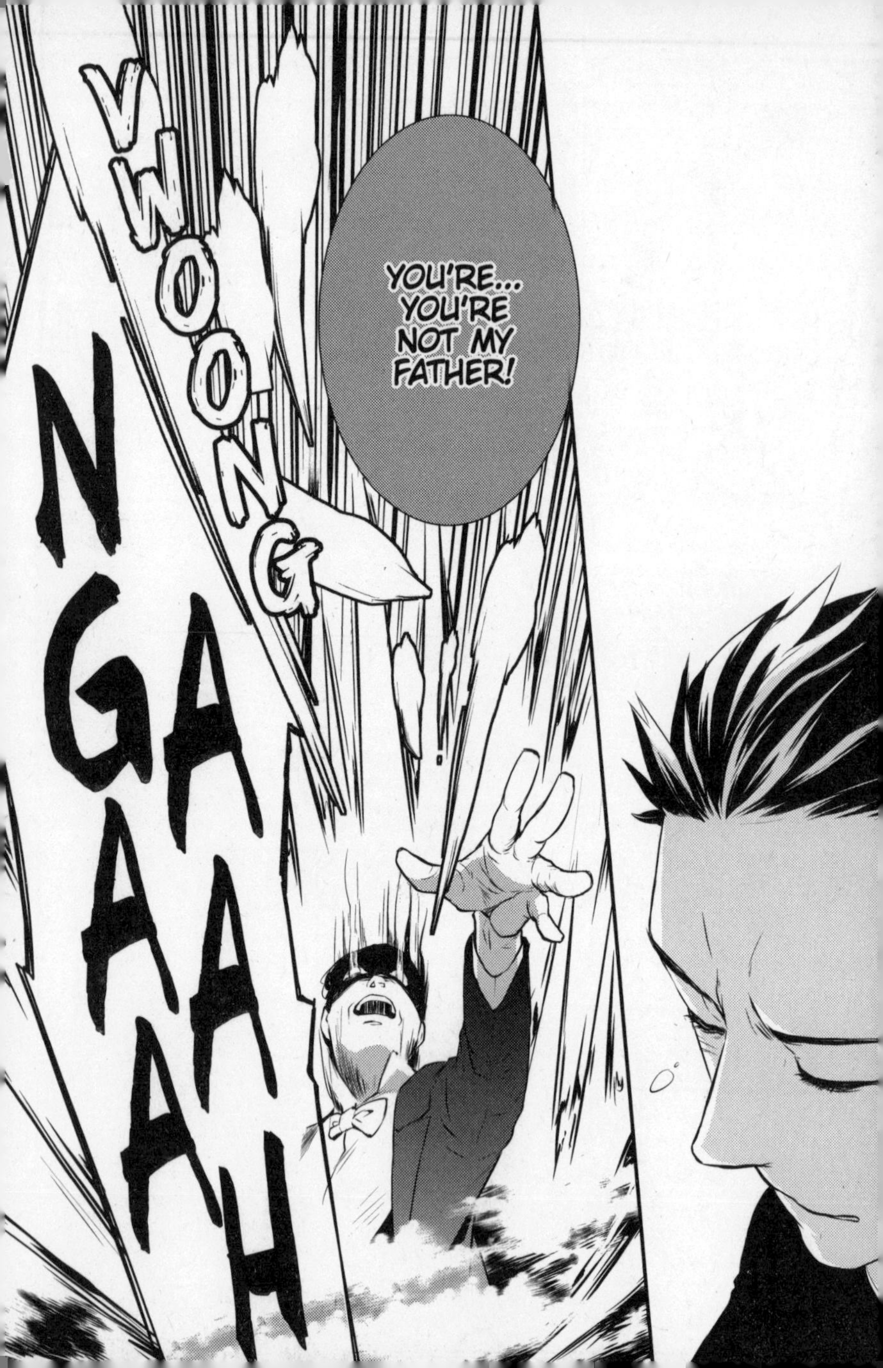
YOU'RE... YOU'RE NOT MY FATHER!
VWOOONG
NGAAAAH

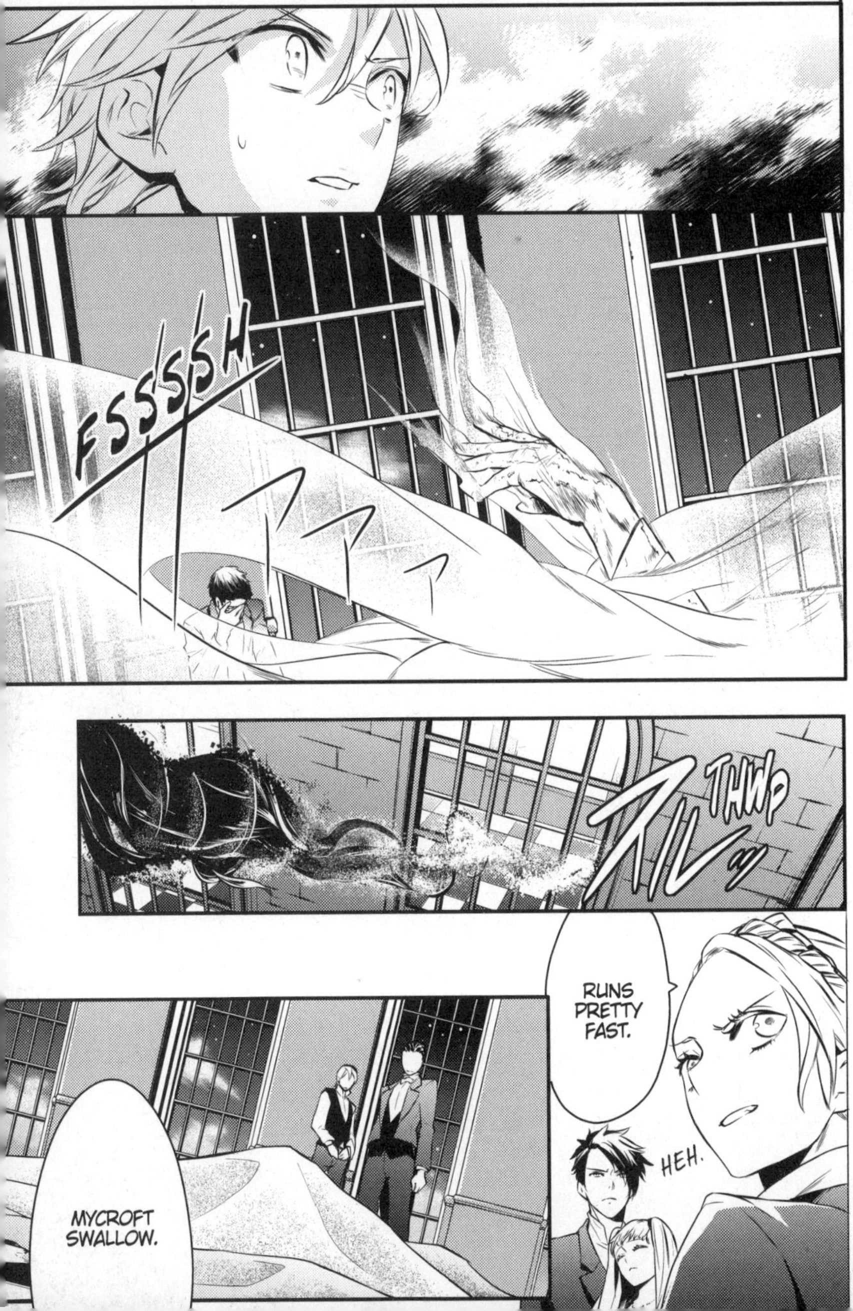
FSSSSH
THWP
RUNS PRETTY FAST.
HEH.
MYCROFT SWALLOW.

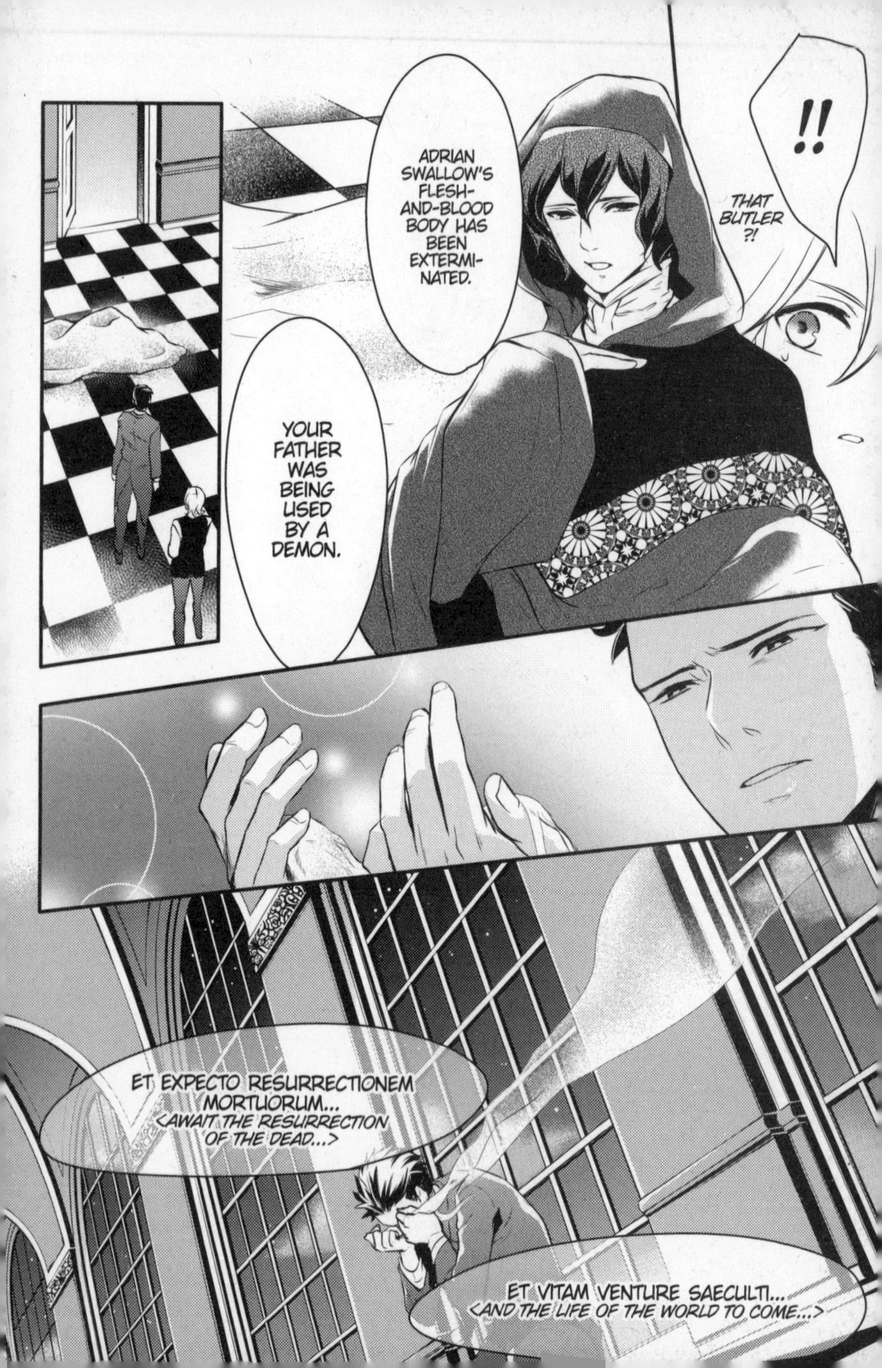
!!
THAT BUTLER?!
ADRIAN SWALLOW'S FLESH-AND-BLOOD BODY HAS BEEN EXTERMINATED.
YOUR FATHER WAS BEING USED BY A DEMON.
ET EXPECTO RESURRECTIONEM MORTUORUM... <AWAIT THE RESURRECTION OF THE DEAD...>
ET VITAM VENTURE SAECULTI... <AND THE LIFE OF THE WORLD TO COME...>

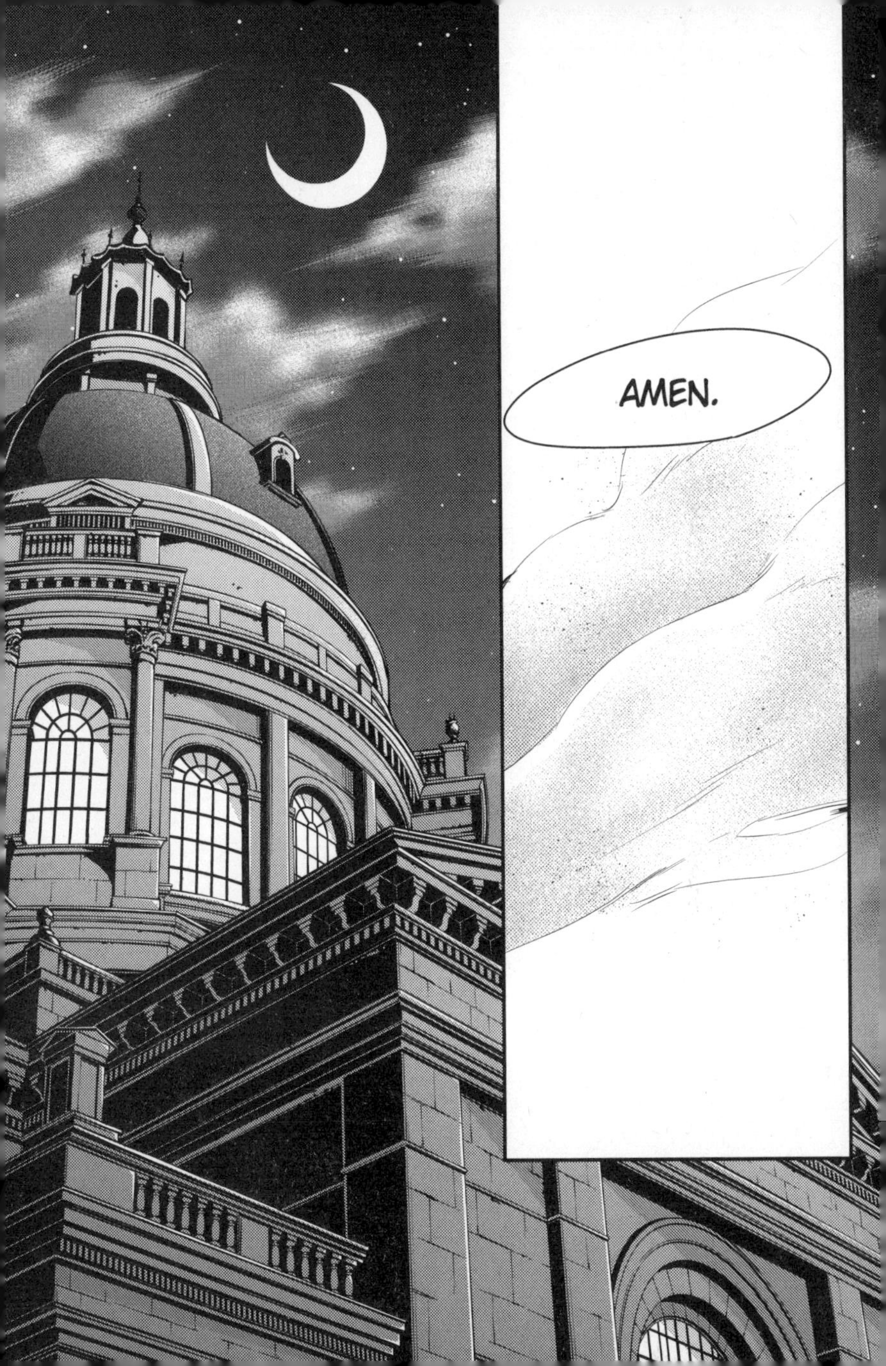
AMEN.

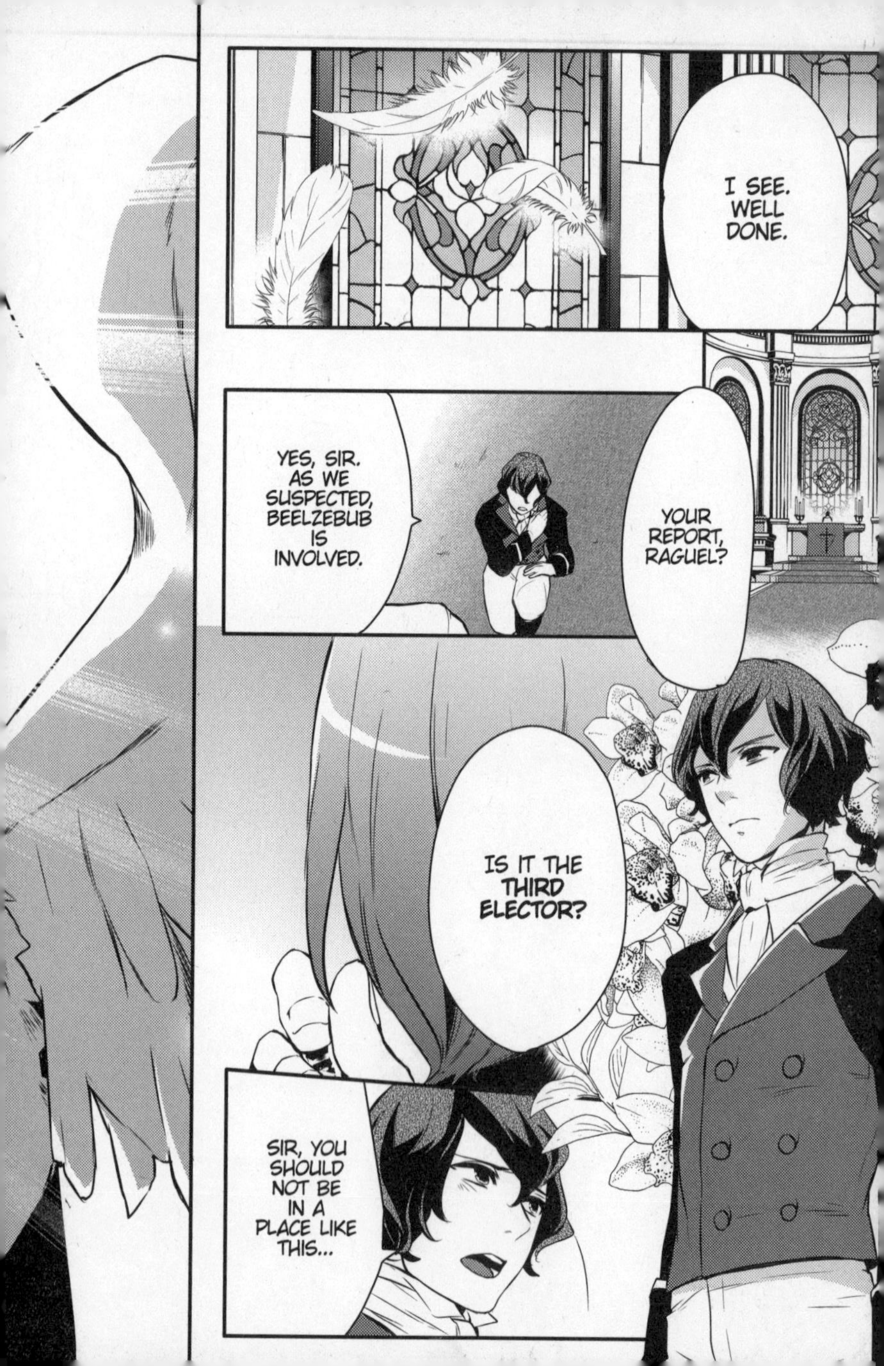
I SEE. WELL DONE.
YOUR REPORT, RAGUEL?
YES, SIR. AS WE SUSPECTED, BEELZEBUB IS INVOLVED.
IS IT THE THIRD ELECTOR?
SIR, YOU SHOULD NOT BE IN A PLACE LIKE THIS...

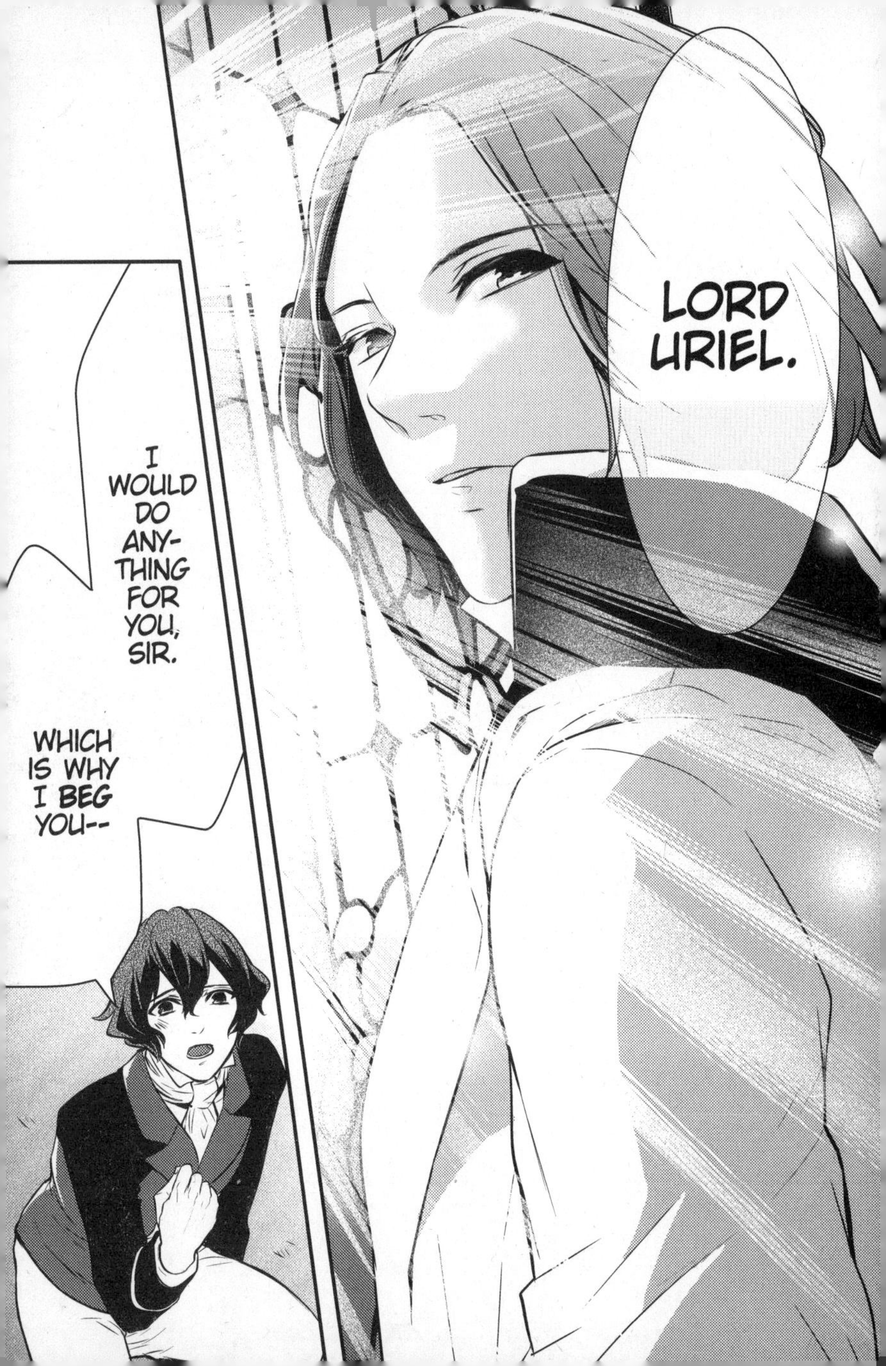
LORD URIEL.
I WOULD DO ANY-THING FOR YOU, SIR.
WHICH IS WHY I BEG YOU--

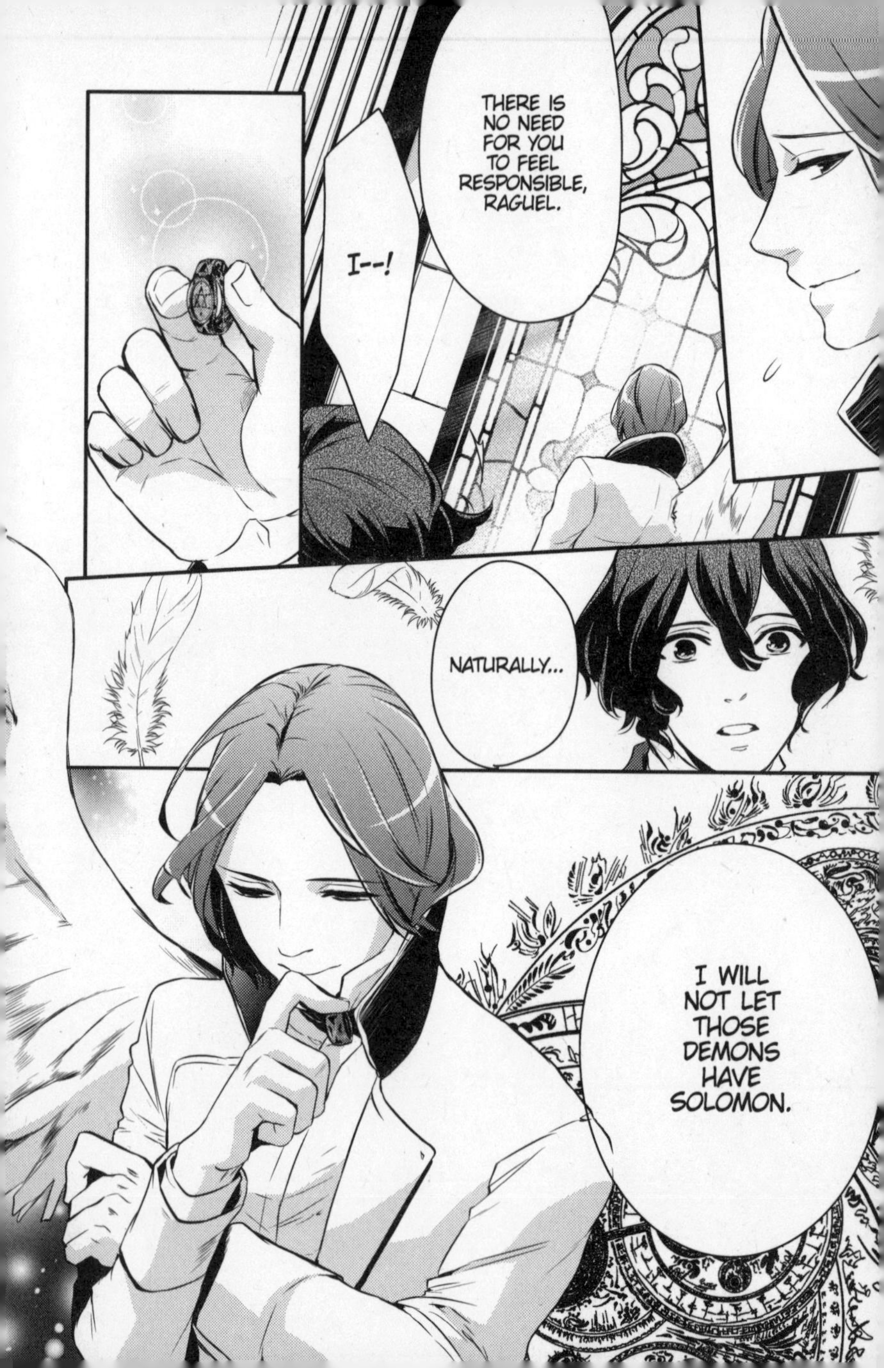
THERE IS NO NEED FOR YOU TO FEEL RESPONSIBLE, RAGUEL.
I--!
NATURALLY...
I WILL NOT LET THOSE DEMONS HAVE SOLOMON.

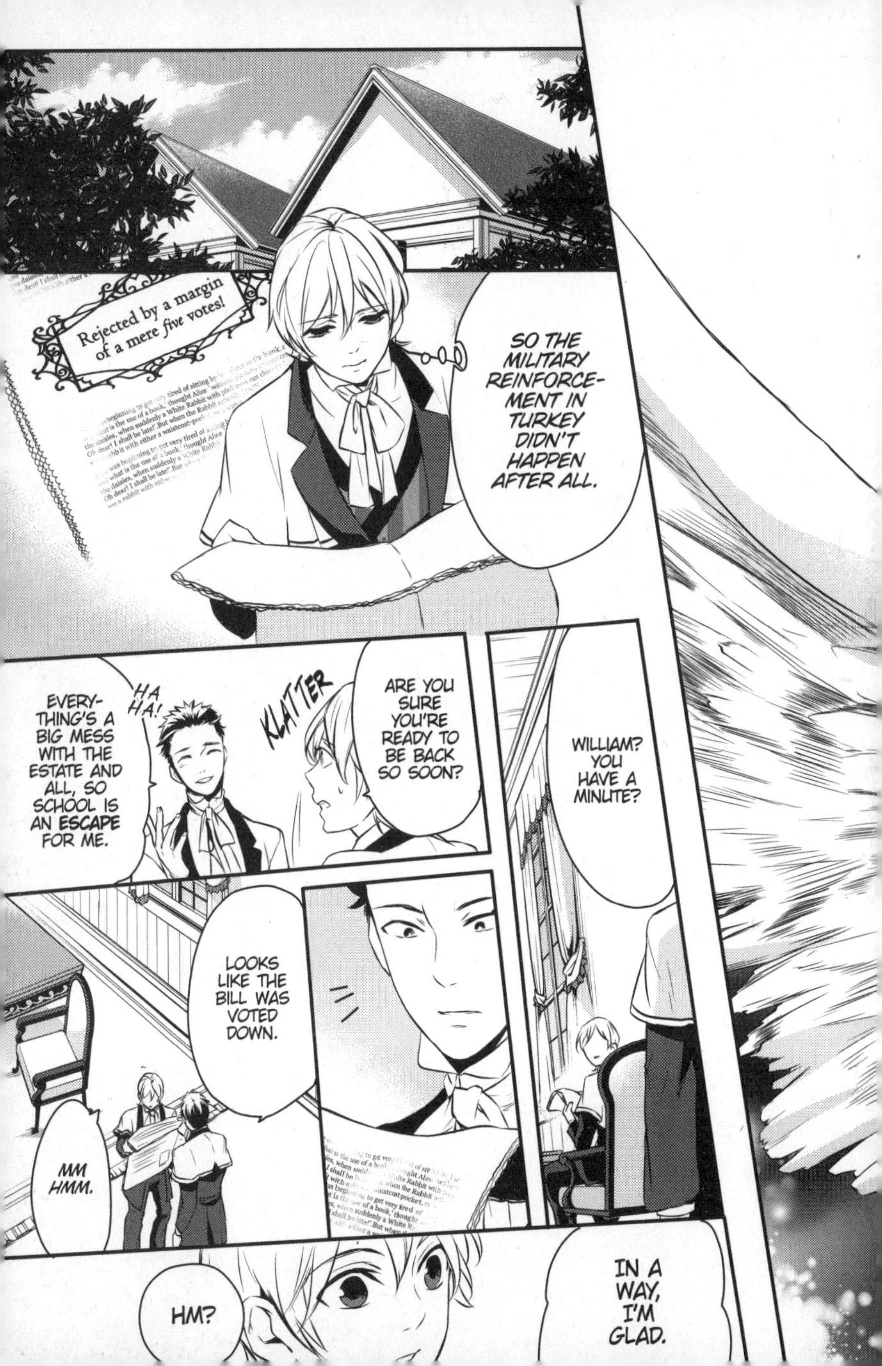
SO THE MILITARY REINFORCEMENT IN TURKEY DIDN'T HAPPEN AFTER ALL.
Rejected by a margin of a mere five votes!
WILLIAM? YOU HAVE A MINUTE?
ARE YOU SURE YOU'RE READY TO BE BACK SO SOON?
KLATTER
HA HA!
EVERYTHING'S A BIG MESS WITH THE ESTATE AND ALL, SO SCHOOL IS AN ESCAPE FOR ME.
LOOKS LIKE THE BILL WAS VOTED DOWN.
MM HMM.
IN A WAY, I'M GLAD.
HM?

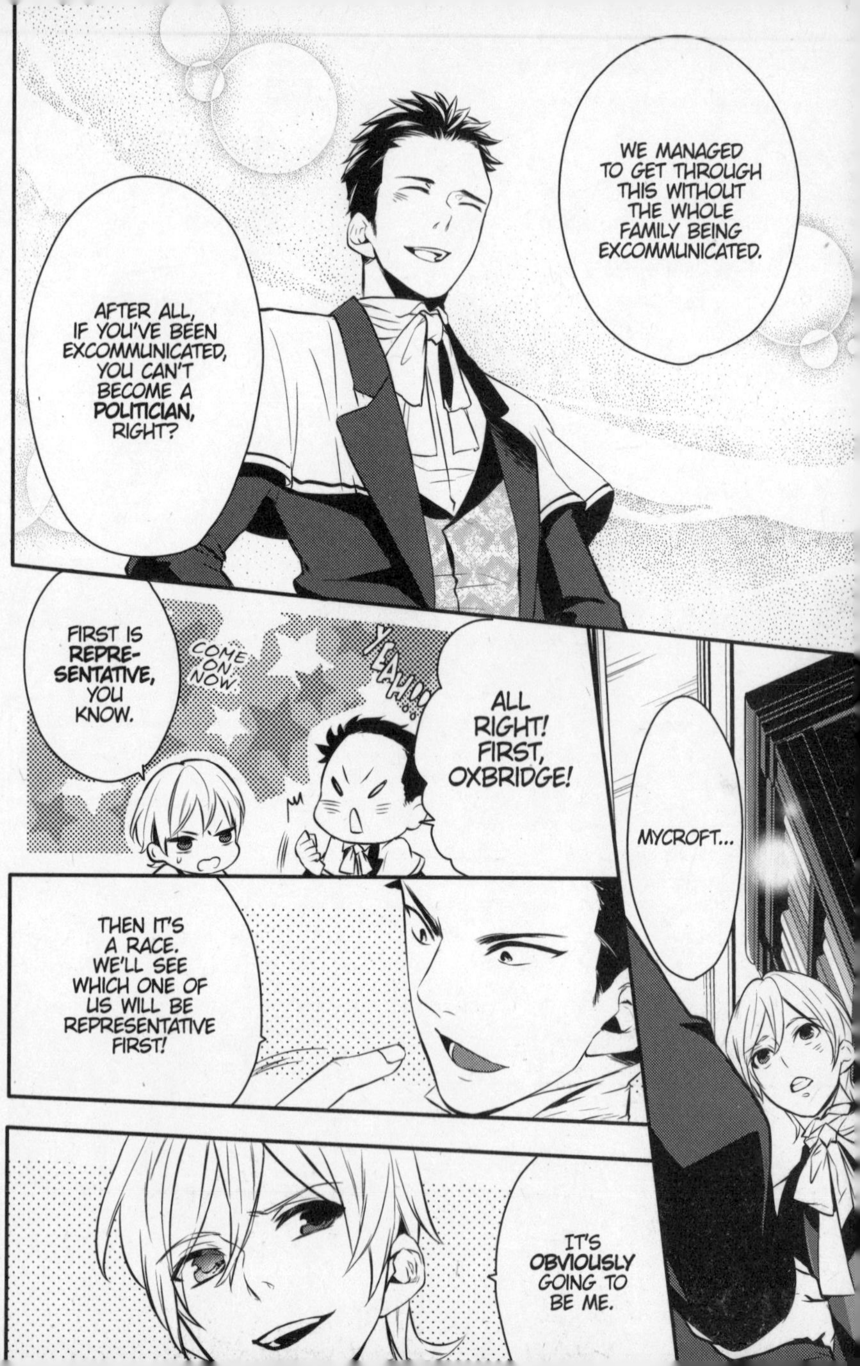
WE MANAGED TO GET THROUGH THIS WITHOUT THE WHOLE FAMILY BEING EXCOMMUNICATED.
AFTER ALL, IF YOU'VE BEEN EXCOMMUNICATED, YOU CAN'T BECOME A **POLITICIAN,** RIGHT?
MYCROFT...
ALL RIGHT! FIRST, OXBRIDGE!
YEAH!
COME ON NOW.
FIRST IS **REPRE-SENTATIVE,** YOU KNOW.
THEN IT'S A RACE. WE'LL SEE WHICH ONE OF US WILL BE REPRESENTATIVE FIRST!
IT'S **OBVIOUSLY** GOING TO BE ME.

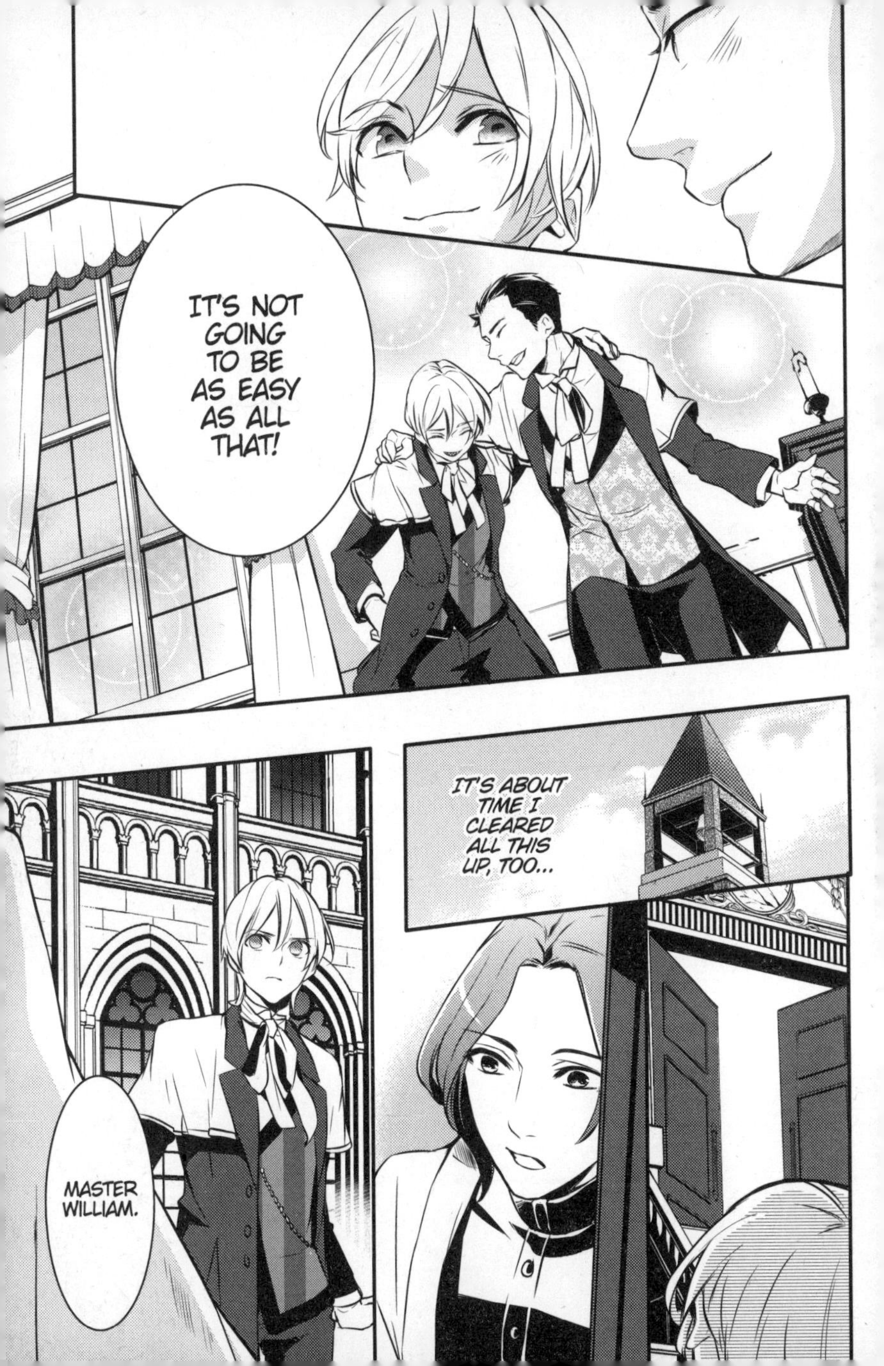
IT'S NOT GOING TO BE AS EASY AS ALL THAT!
IT'S ABOUT TIME I CLEARED ALL THIS UP, TOO...
MASTER WILLIAM.

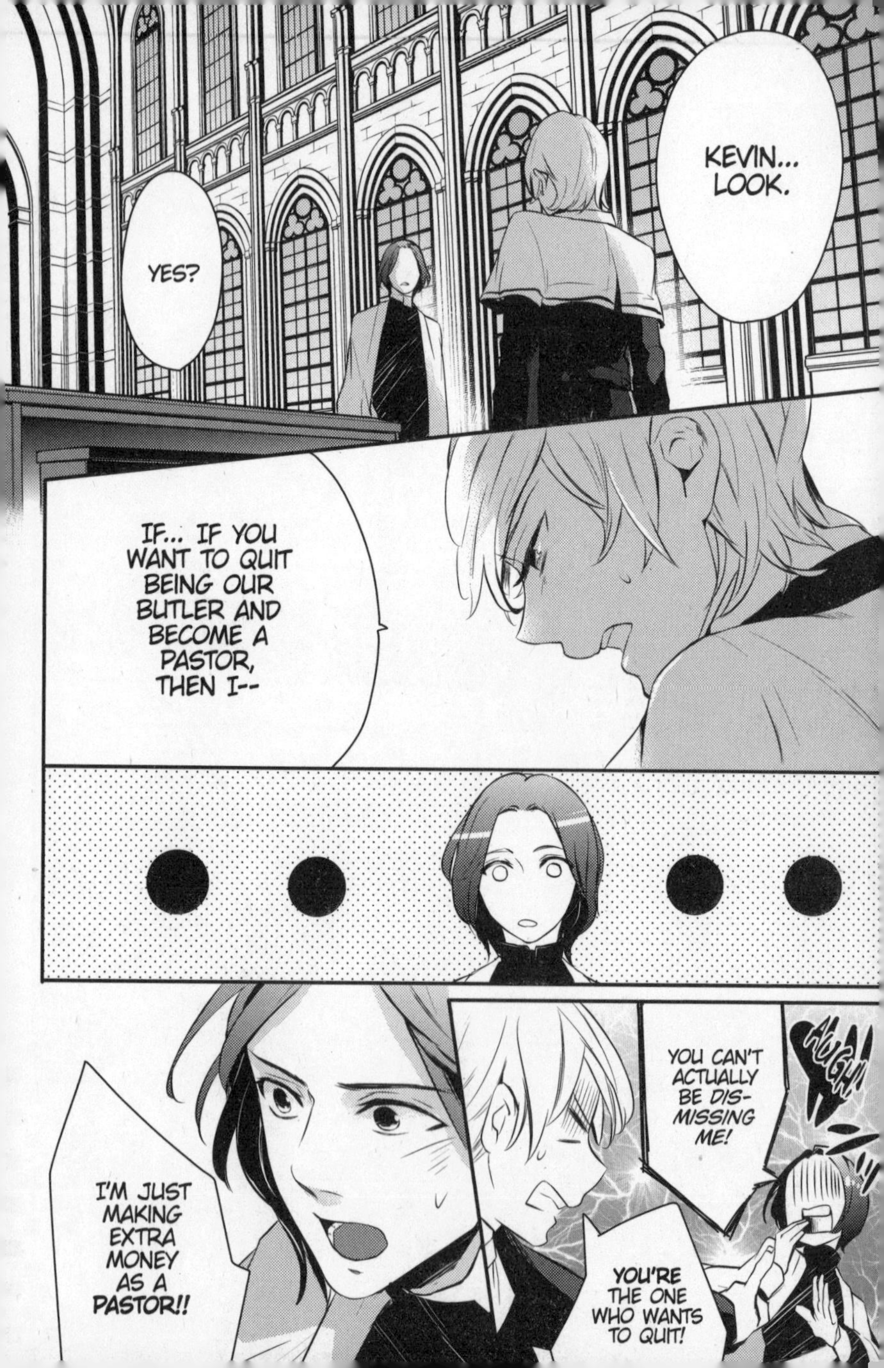
KEVIN... LOOK.
YES?
IF... IF YOU WANT TO QUIT BEING OUR BUTLER AND BECOME A PASTOR, THEN I--
AUGH!!
YOU CAN'T ACTUALLY BE DIS-MISSING ME!
YOU'RE THE ONE WHO WANTS TO QUIT!
I'M JUST MAKING EXTRA MONEY AS A PASTOR!!

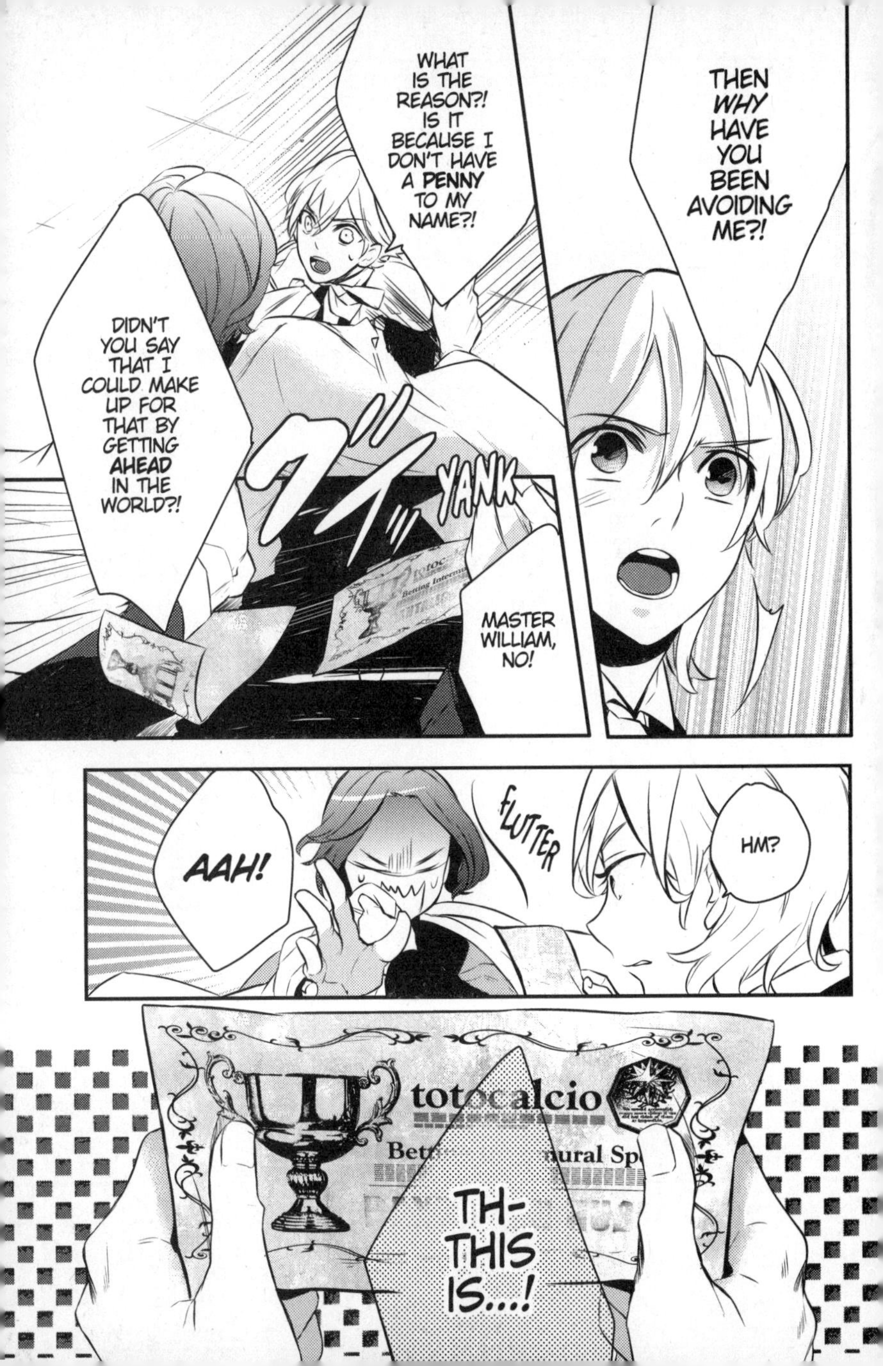
THEN WHY HAVE YOU BEEN AVOIDING ME?!
WHAT IS THE REASON?! IS IT BECAUSE I DON'T HAVE A PENNY TO MY NAME?!
DIDN'T YOU SAY THAT I COULD MAKE UP FOR THAT BY GETTING AHEAD IN THE WORLD?!
YANK
MASTER WILLIAM, NO!
HM?
FLUTTER
AAH!
totocalcio
TH-THIS IS...!

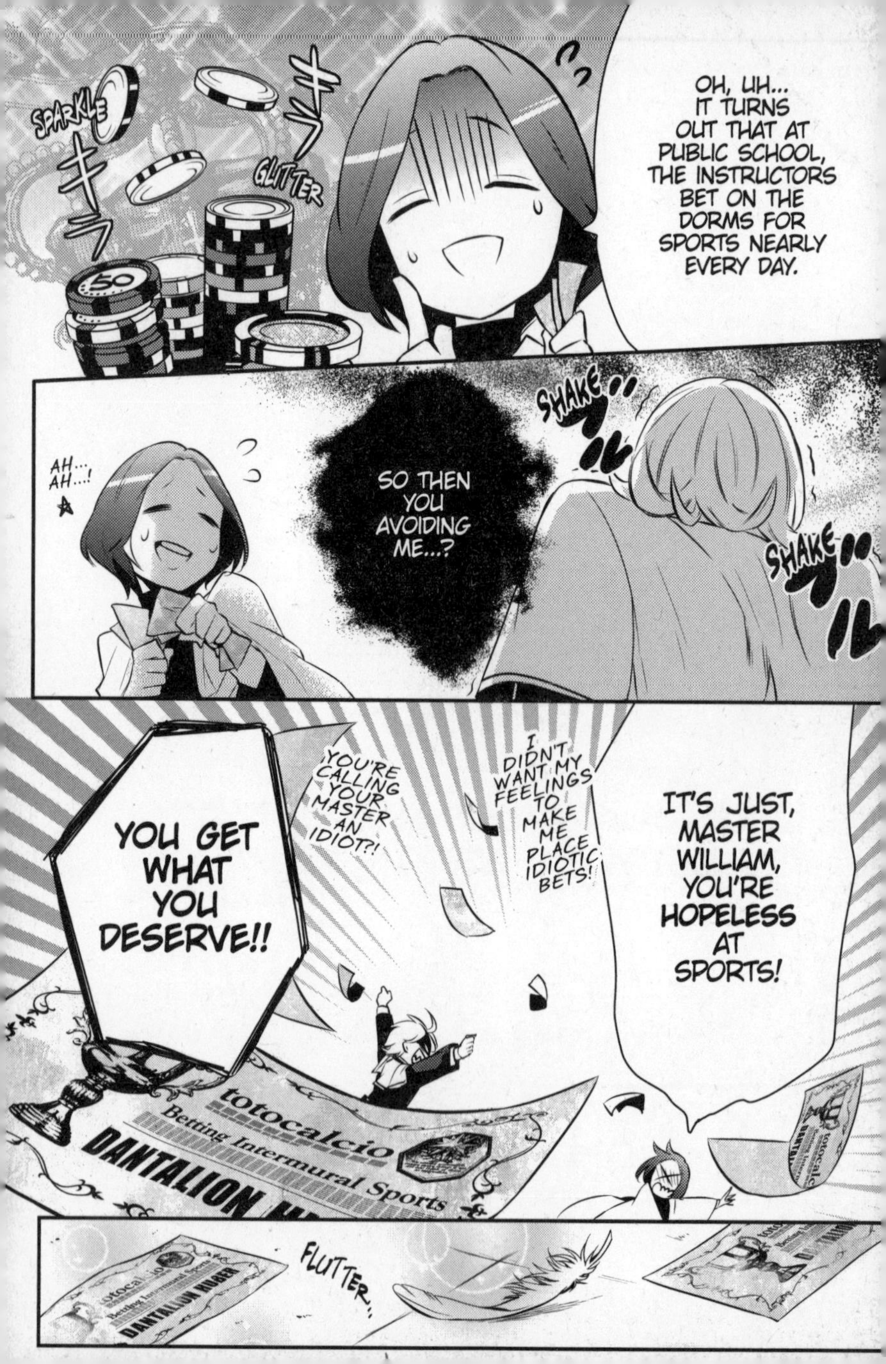
OH, UH... IT TURNS OUT THAT AT PUBLIC SCHOOL, THE INSTRUCTORS BET ON THE DORMS FOR SPORTS NEARLY EVERY DAY.
GLITTER
SPARKLE
50
SHAKE
SHAKE
SO THEN YOU AVOIDING ME...?
AH... AH...!
IT'S JUST, MASTER WILLIAM, YOU'RE HOPELESS AT SPORTS!
I DIDN'T WANT MY FEELINGS TO MAKE ME PLACE IDIOTIC BETS!
YOU'RE CALLING YOUR MASTER AN IDIOT?!
YOU GET WHAT YOU DESERVE!!
totocalcio
Betting Intermural Sports
FLUTTER...
totocalcio
Betting Intermural Sports
DANTALION HUBER

魔界王子

devils and realist

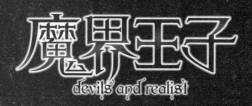

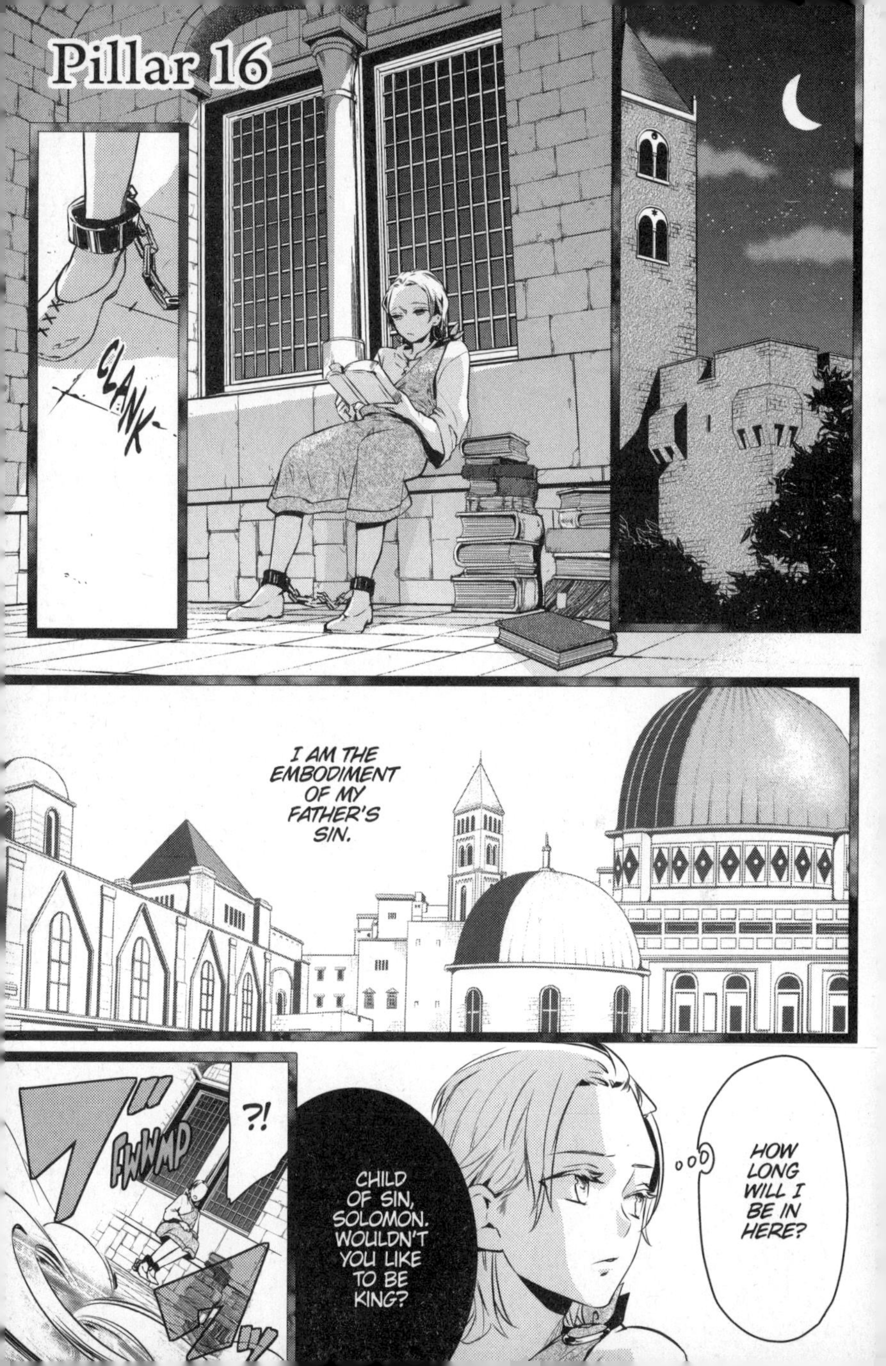
Pillar 16
CLANK
I AM THE EMBODIMENT OF MY FATHER'S SIN.
HOW LONG WILL I BE IN HERE?
CHILD OF SIN, SOLOMON. WOULDN'T YOU LIKE TO BE KING?
?!
FWWMP

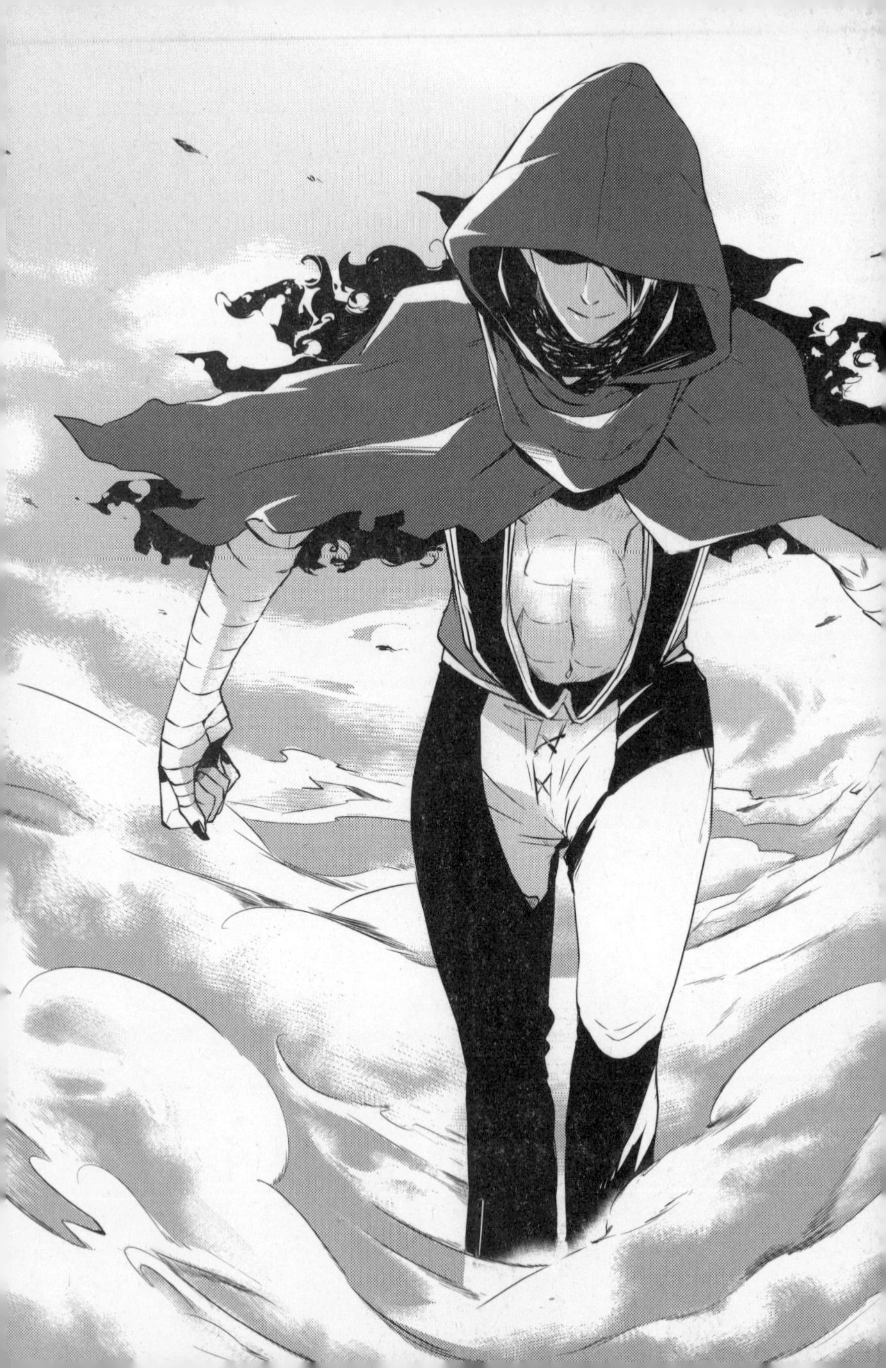

Pillar 16

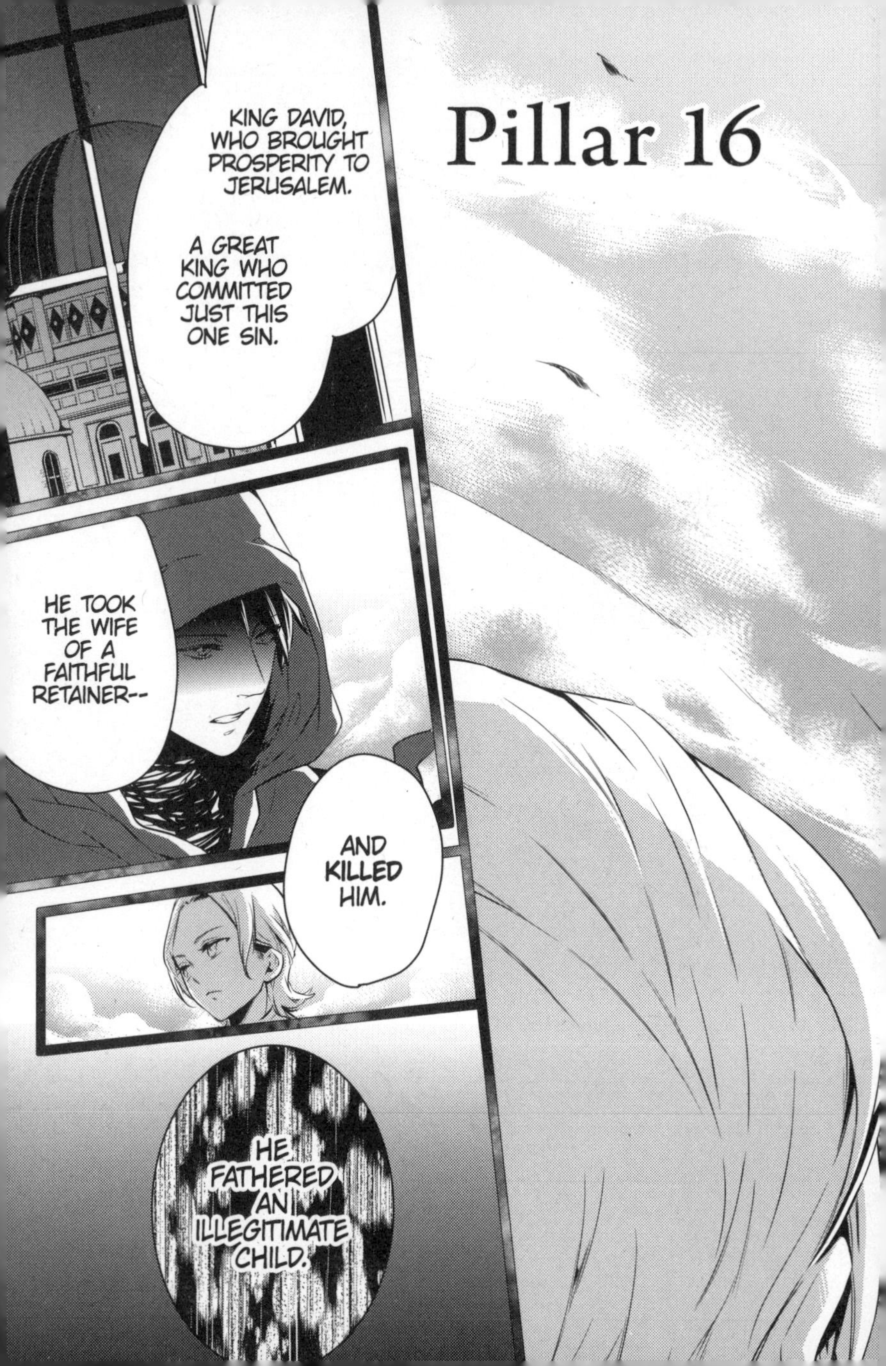
KING DAVID, WHO BROUGHT PROSPERITY TO JERUSALEM.
A GREAT KING WHO COMMITTED JUST THIS ONE SIN.
HE TOOK THE WIFE OF A FAITHFUL RETAINER--
AND KILLED HIM.
HE FATHERED AN ILLEGITIMATE CHILD.

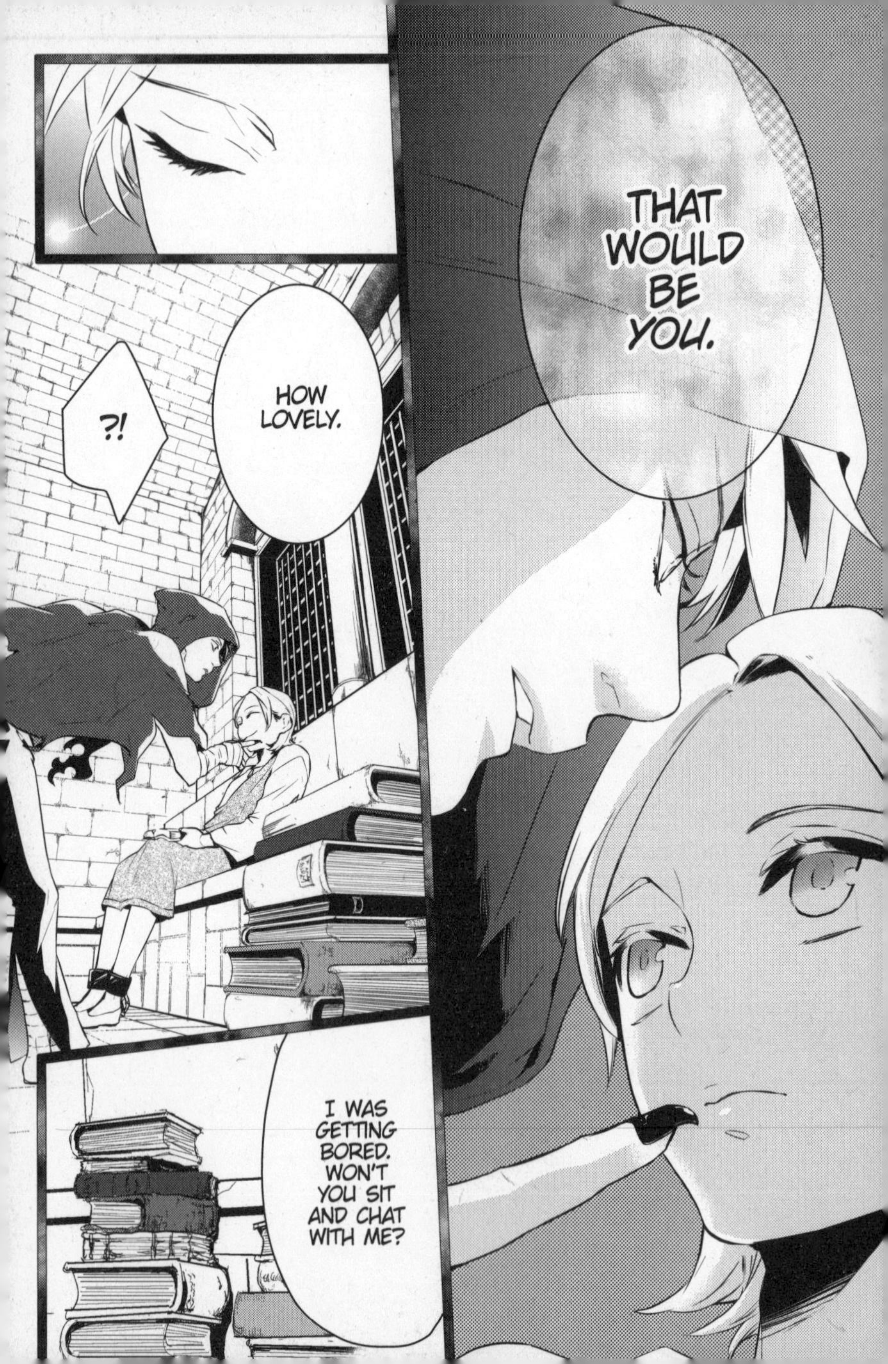
THAT WOULD BE YOU.
HOW LOVELY.
?!
I WAS GETTING BORED. WON'T YOU SIT AND CHAT WITH ME?

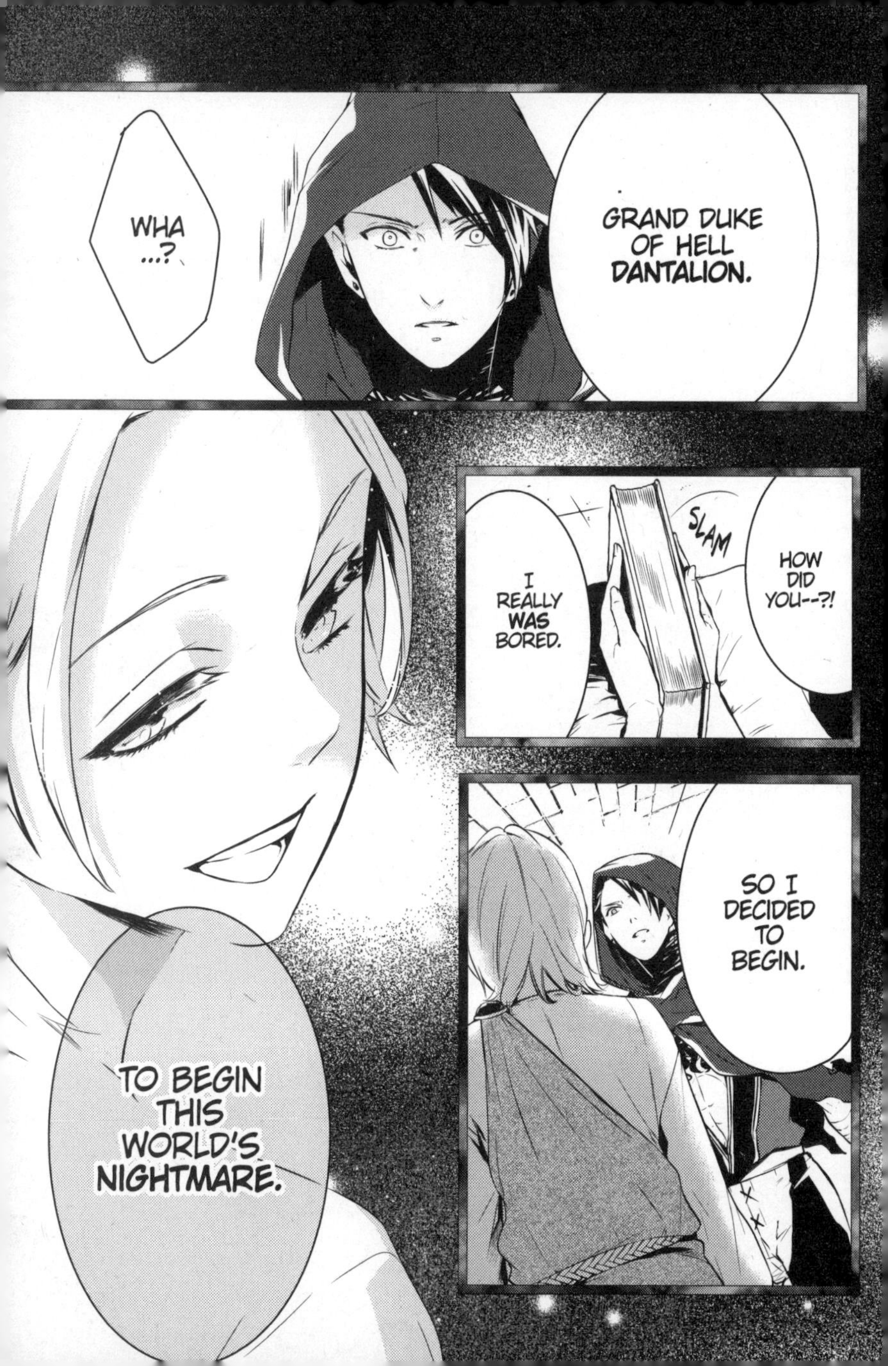
GRAND DUKE OF HELL DANTALION.
WHA ...?
HOW DID YOU--?!
SLAM
I REALLY WAS BORED.
SO I DECIDED TO BEGIN.
TO BEGIN THIS WORLD'S NIGHTMARE.

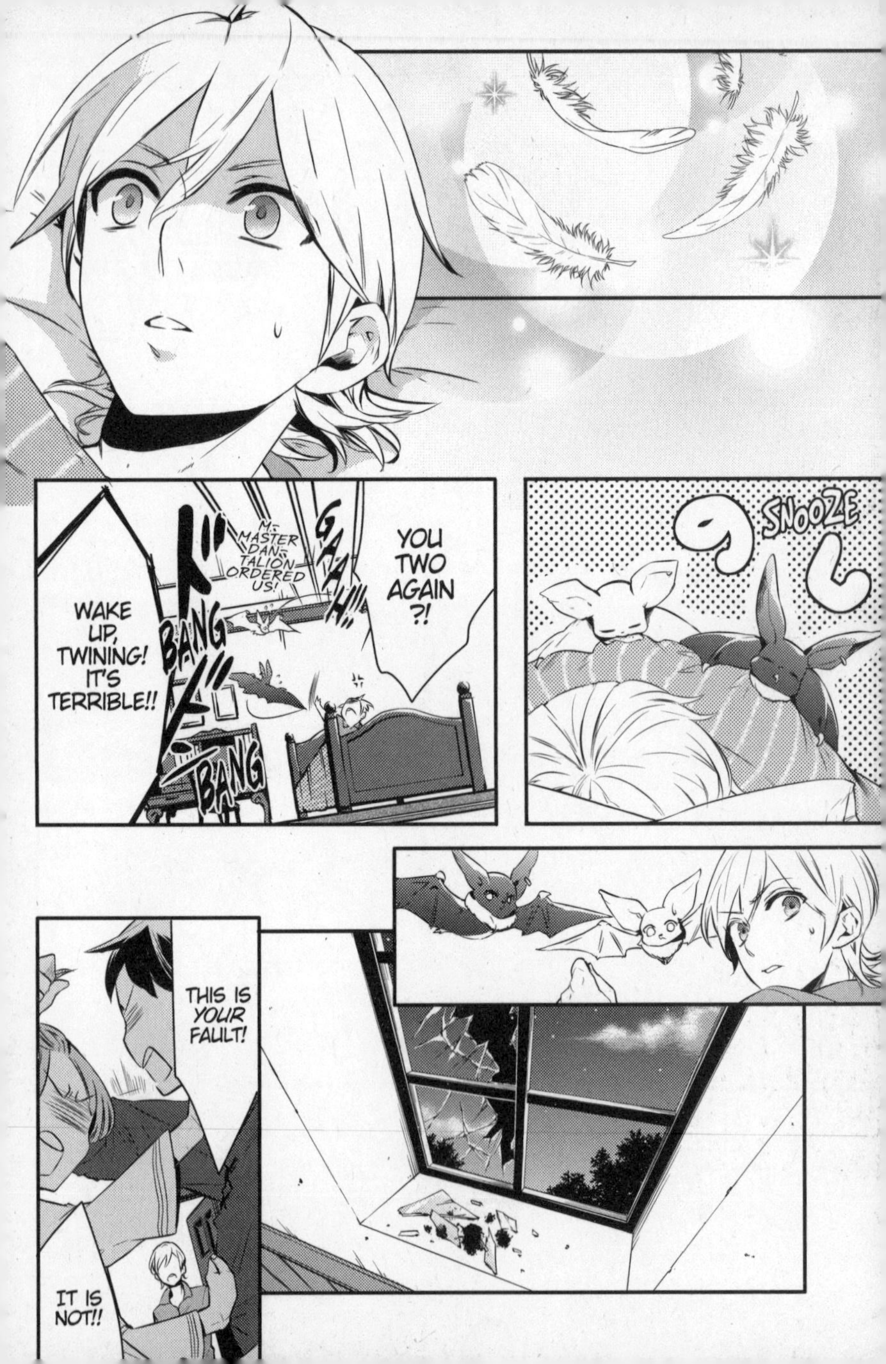
SNOOZE
YOU TWO AGAIN?!
GAAAH!!
M-MASTER DAN-TALION ORDERED US!
WAKE UP, TWINING! IT'S TERRIBLE!!
BANG
BANG
THIS IS YOUR FAULT!
IT IS NOT!!

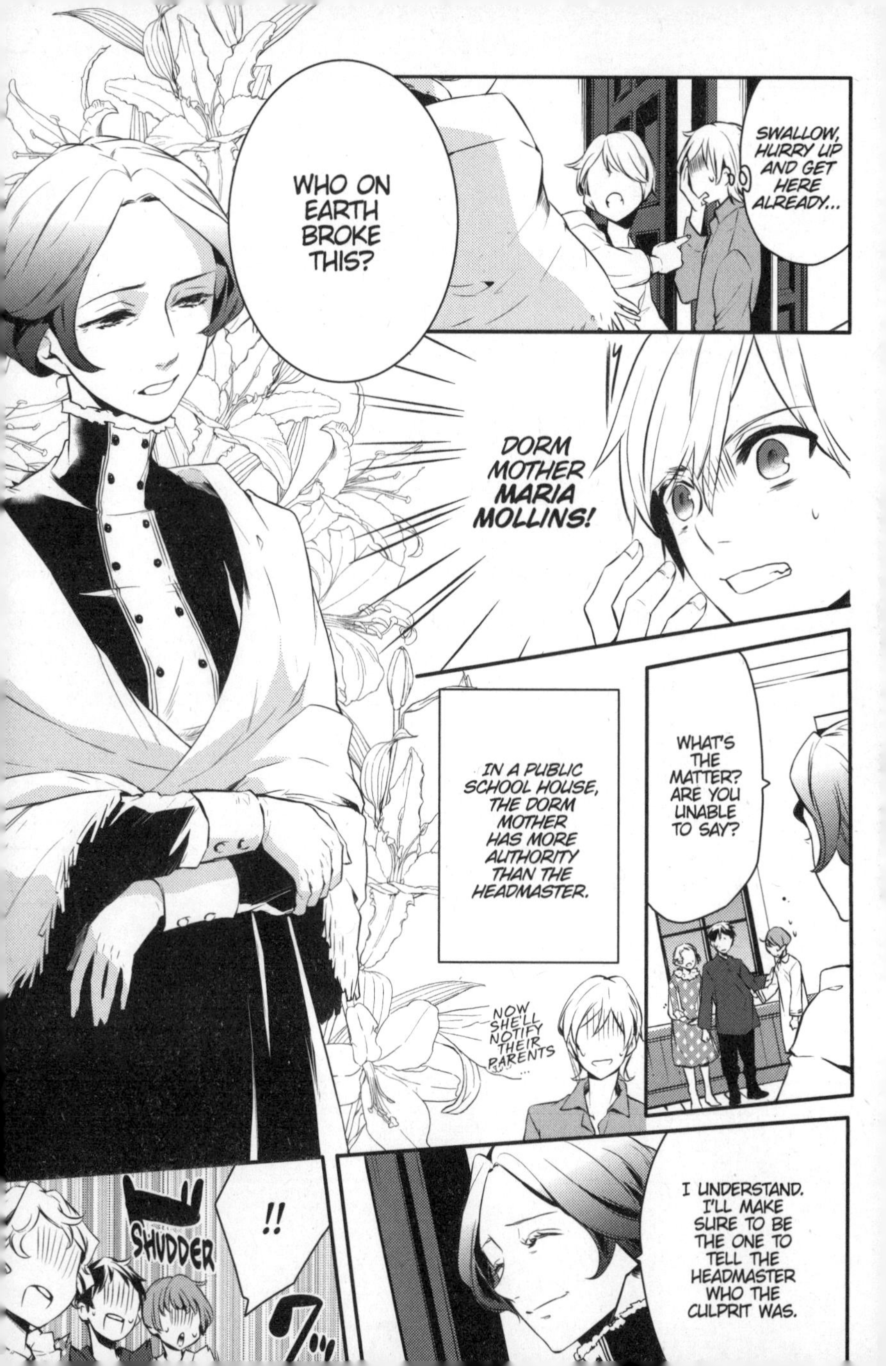
SWALLOW, HURRY UP AND GET HERE ALREADY...
WHO ON EARTH BROKE THIS?
DORM MOTHER MARIA MOLLINS!
WHAT'S THE MATTER? ARE YOU UNABLE TO SAY?
IN A PUBLIC SCHOOL HOUSE, THE DORM MOTHER HAS MORE AUTHORITY THAN THE HEADMASTER.
NOW SHE'LL NOTIFY THEIR PARENTS...
I UNDERSTAND. I'LL MAKE SURE TO BE THE ONE TO TELL THE HEADMASTER WHO THE CULPRIT WAS.
!!
SHUDDER

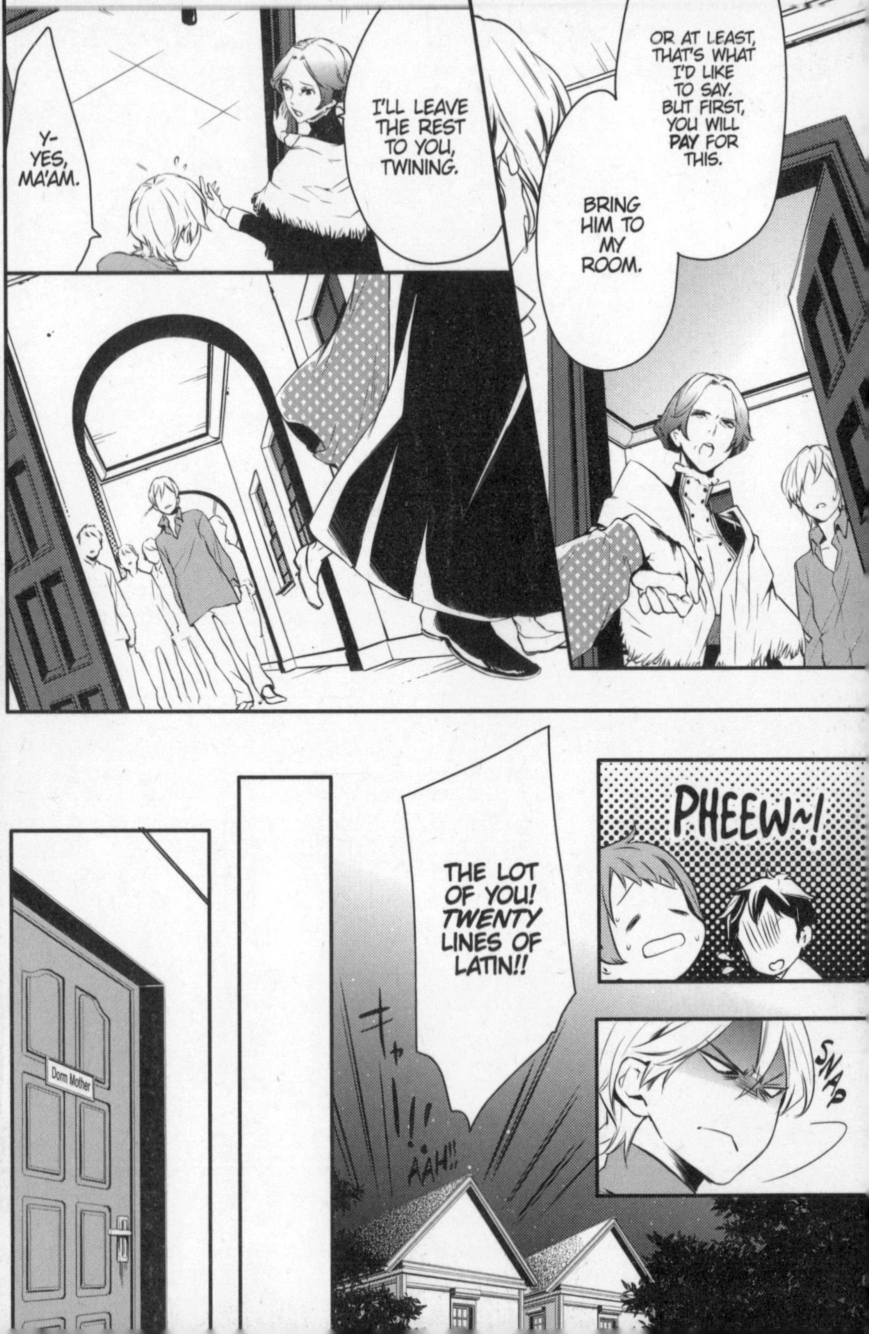
OR AT LEAST, THAT'S WHAT I'D LIKE TO SAY. BUT FIRST, YOU WILL PAY FOR THIS.
BRING HIM TO MY ROOM.
I'LL LEAVE THE REST TO YOU, TWINING.
Y- YES, MA'AM.
PHEEW~!
SNAP
THE LOT OF YOU! TWENTY LINES OF LATIN!!
キャ!!
AAH!!
Dorm Mother

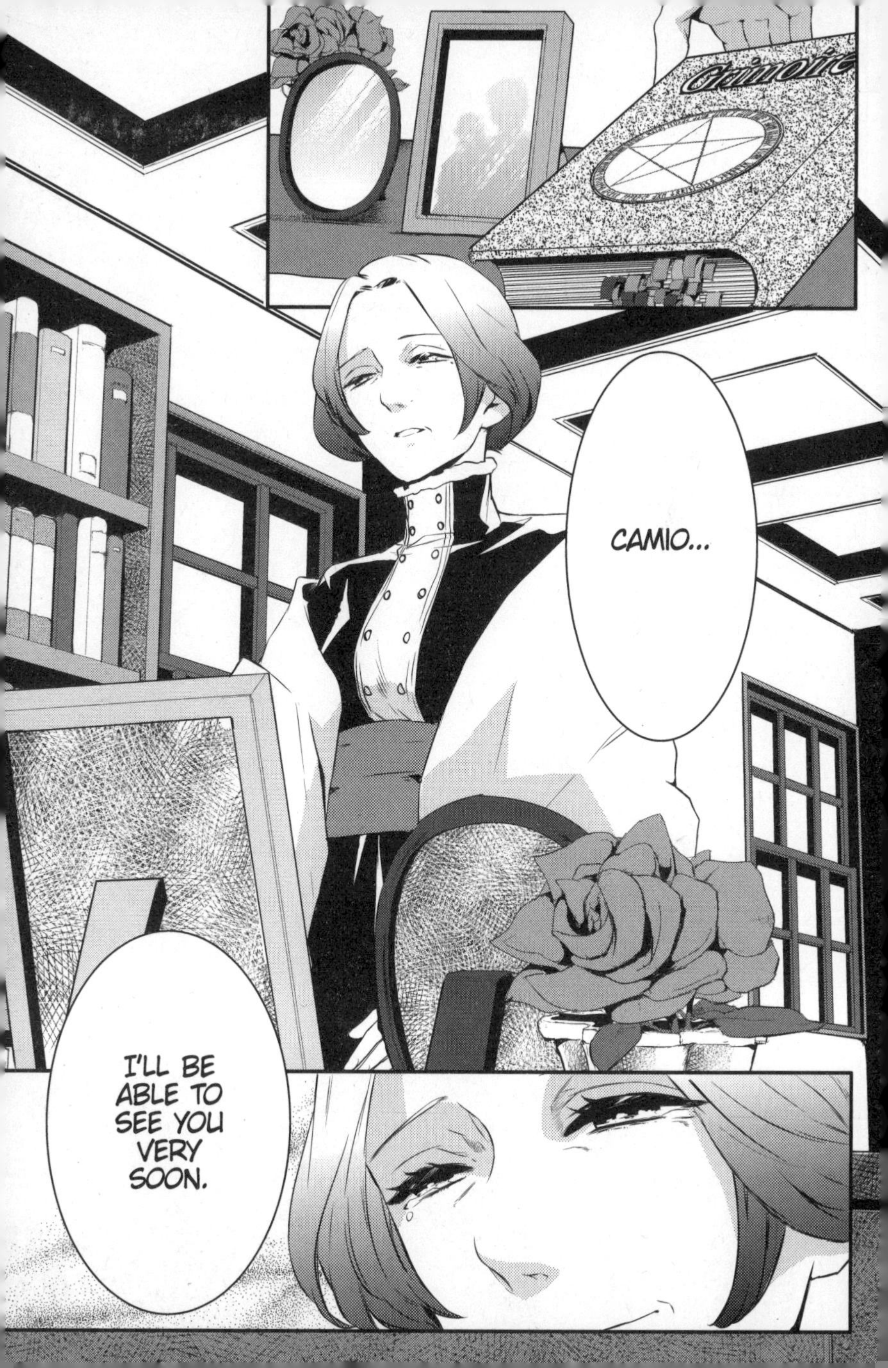
Grimoire
CAMIO...
I'LL BE ABLE TO SEE YOU VERY SOON.

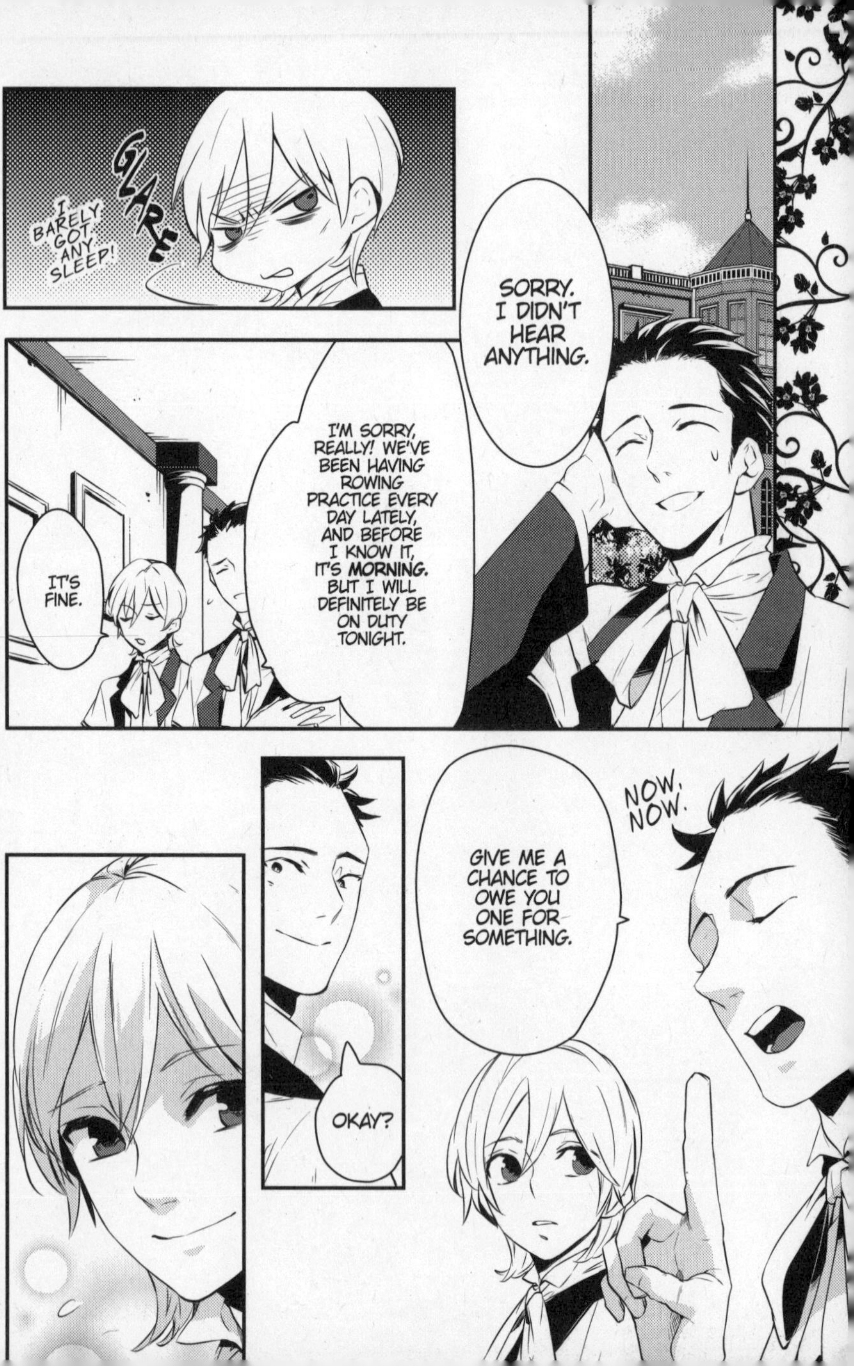
SORRY. I DIDN'T HEAR ANYTHING.
GLARE
I BARELY GOT ANY SLEEP!
I'M SORRY, REALLY! WE'VE BEEN HAVING ROWING PRACTICE EVERY DAY LATELY, AND BEFORE I KNOW IT, IT'S **MORNING**. BUT I WILL DEFINITELY BE ON DUTY TONIGHT.
IT'S FINE.
NOW, NOW.
GIVE ME A CHANCE TO OWE YOU ONE FOR SOMETHING.
OKAY?

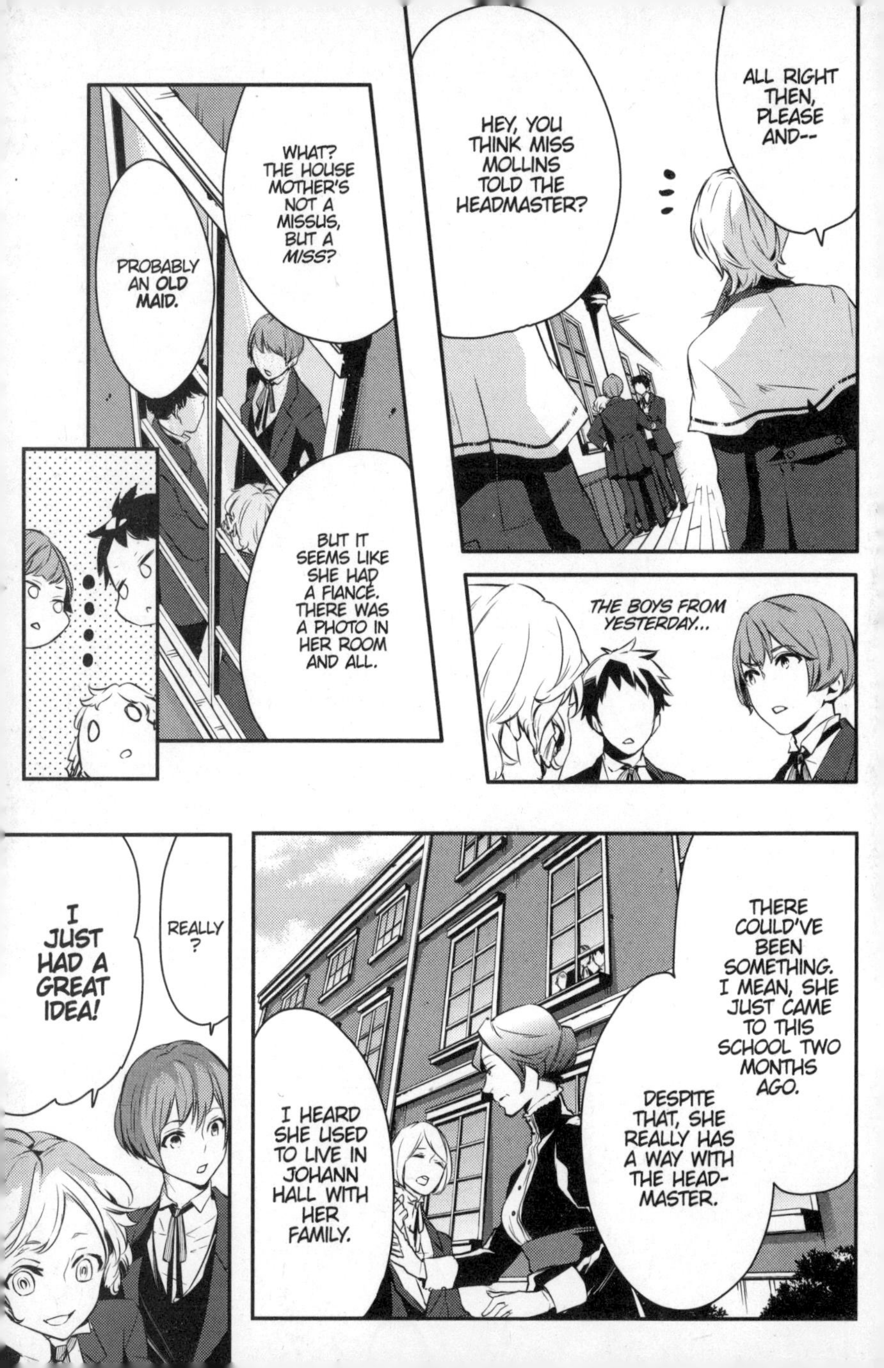
ALL RIGHT THEN, PLEASE AND--
HEY, YOU THINK MISS MOLLINS TOLD THE HEADMASTER?
THE BOYS FROM YESTERDAY...
WHAT? THE HOUSE MOTHER'S NOT A MISSUS, BUT A MISS?
PROBABLY AN OLD MAID.
BUT IT SEEMS LIKE SHE HAD A FIANCÉ. THERE WAS A PHOTO IN HER ROOM AND ALL.
THERE COULD'VE BEEN SOMETHING. I MEAN, SHE JUST CAME TO THIS SCHOOL TWO MONTHS AGO.
DESPITE THAT, SHE REALLY HAS A WAY WITH THE HEAD-MASTER.
I HEARD SHE USED TO LIVE IN JOHANN HALL WITH HER FAMILY.
REALLY?
I JUST HAD A GREAT IDEA!

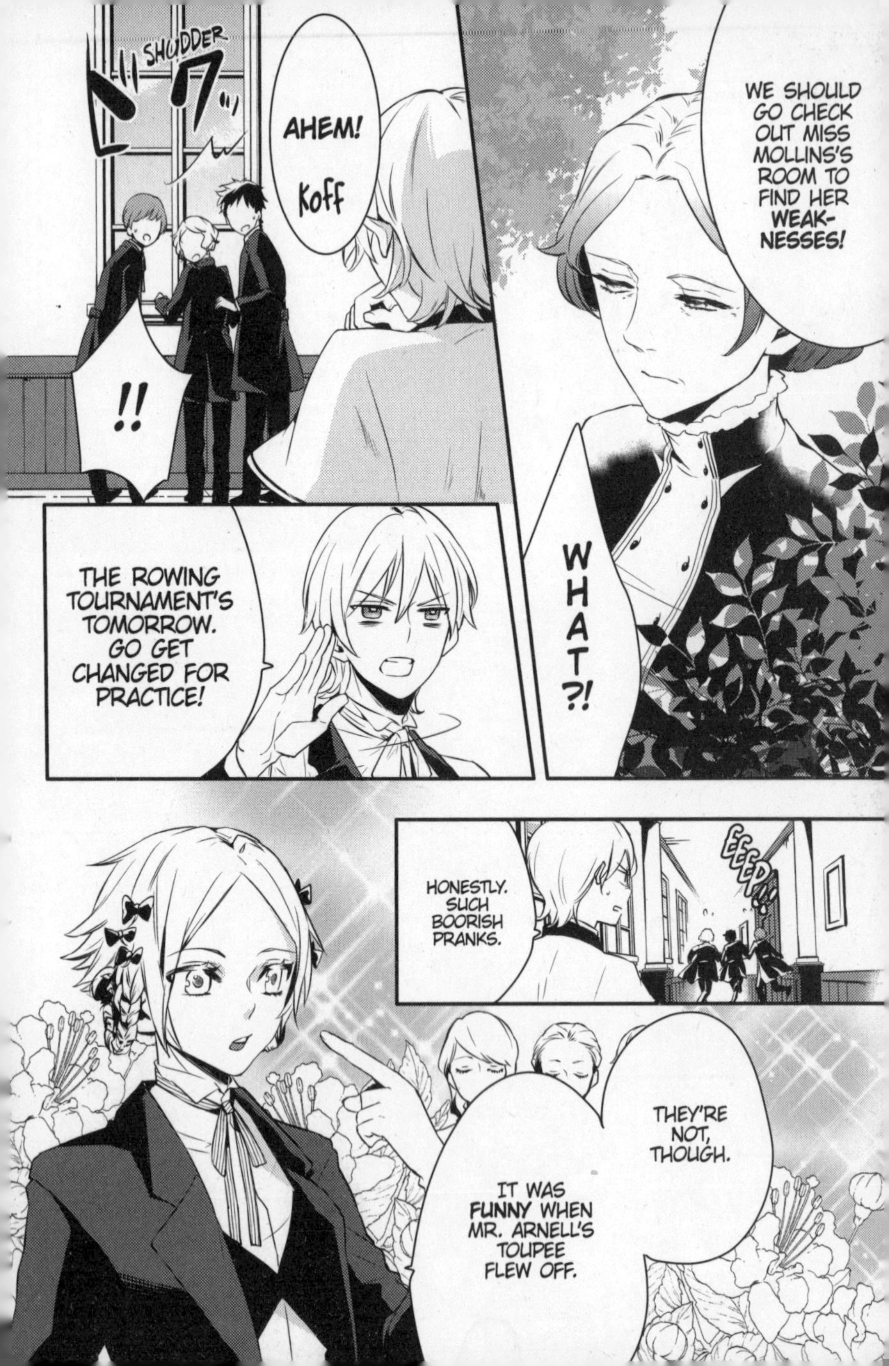
WE SHOULD GO CHECK OUT MISS MOLLINS'S ROOM TO FIND HER WEAKNESSES!
WHAT?!
SHUDDER
AHEM!
Koff
!!
THE ROWING TOURNAMENT'S TOMORROW. GO GET CHANGED FOR PRACTICE!
EEEP!!
HONESTLY. SUCH BOORISH PRANKS.
THEY'RE NOT, THOUGH.
IT WAS FUNNY WHEN MR. ARNELL'S TOUPEE FLEW OFF.

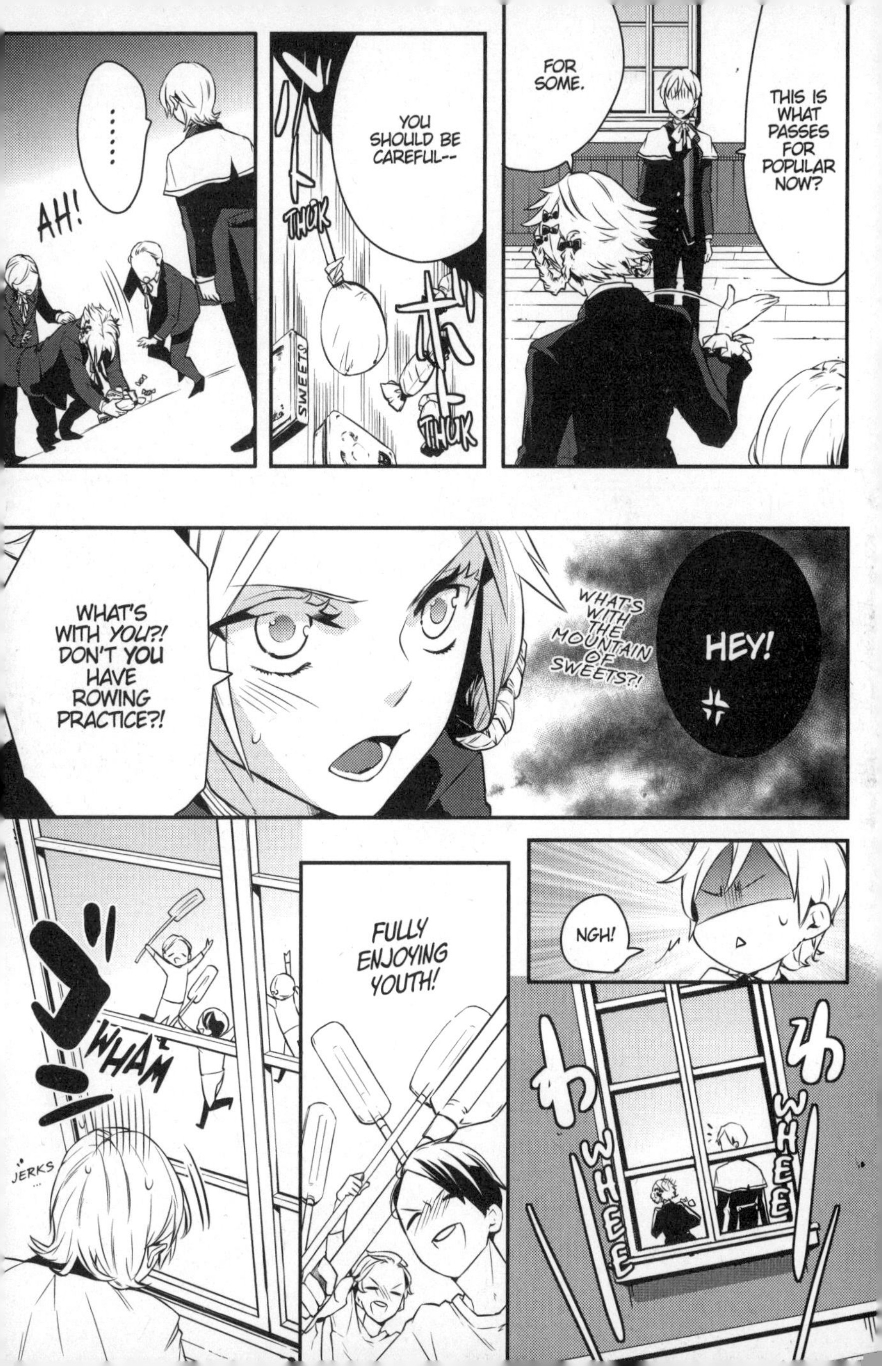
THIS IS WHAT PASSES FOR POPULAR NOW?
FOR SOME.
YOU SHOULD BE CAREFUL--
THUK
THUK
......
AH!
HEY!
WHAT'S WITH THE MOUNTAIN OF SWEETS?!
WHAT'S WITH YOU?! DON'T YOU HAVE ROWING PRACTICE?!
NGH!
WHEE
WHEE
FULLY ENJOYING YOUTH!
WHAM
JERKS ...

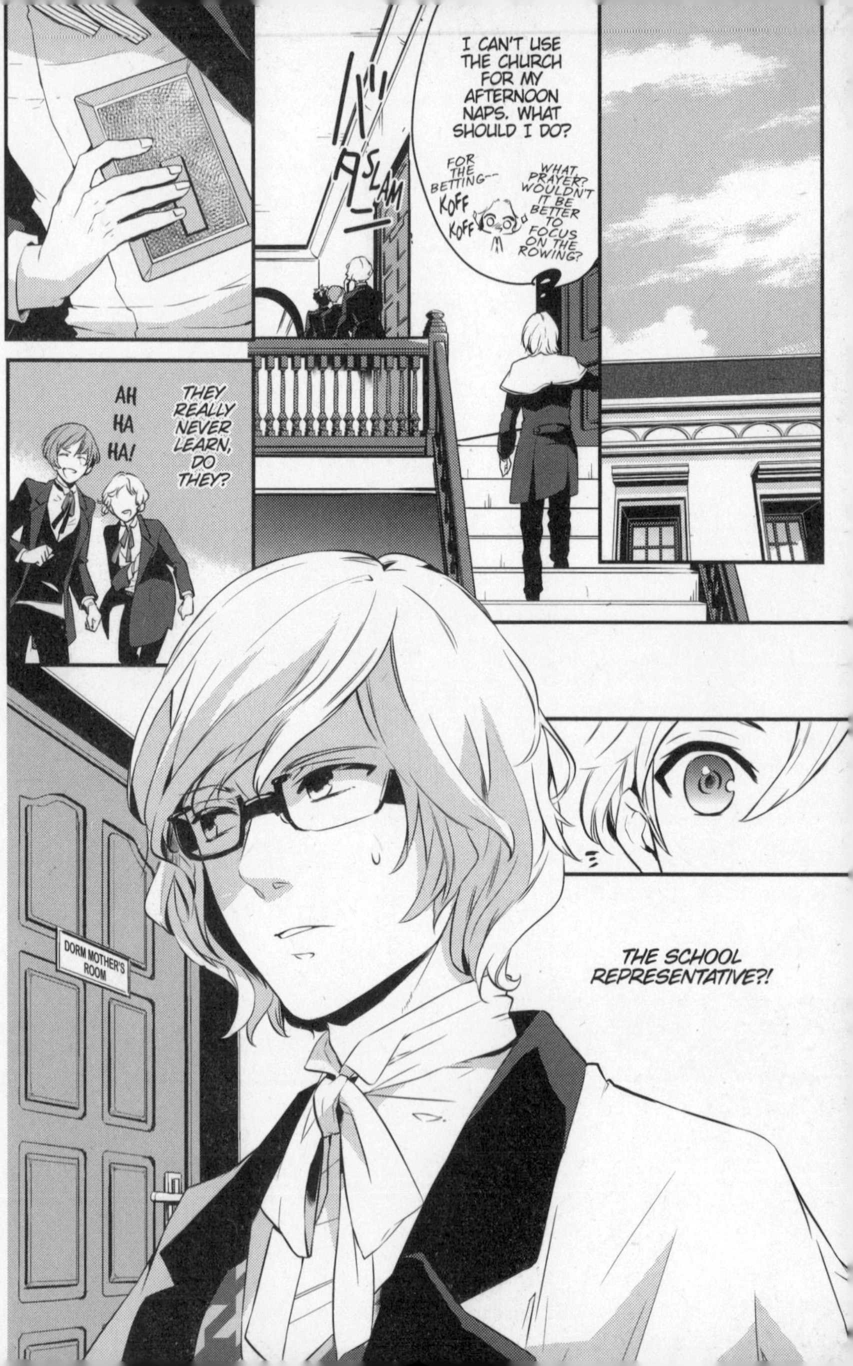
I CAN'T USE THE CHURCH FOR MY AFTERNOON NAPS. WHAT SHOULD I DO?
WHAT, PRAYER? WOULDN'T IT BE BETTER TO FOCUS ON THE ROWING?
FOR THE BETTING-- KOFF KOFF
SLAM
THEY REALLY NEVER LEARN, DO THEY?
AH HA HA!
THE SCHOOL REPRESENTATIVE?!
DORM MOTHER'S ROOM

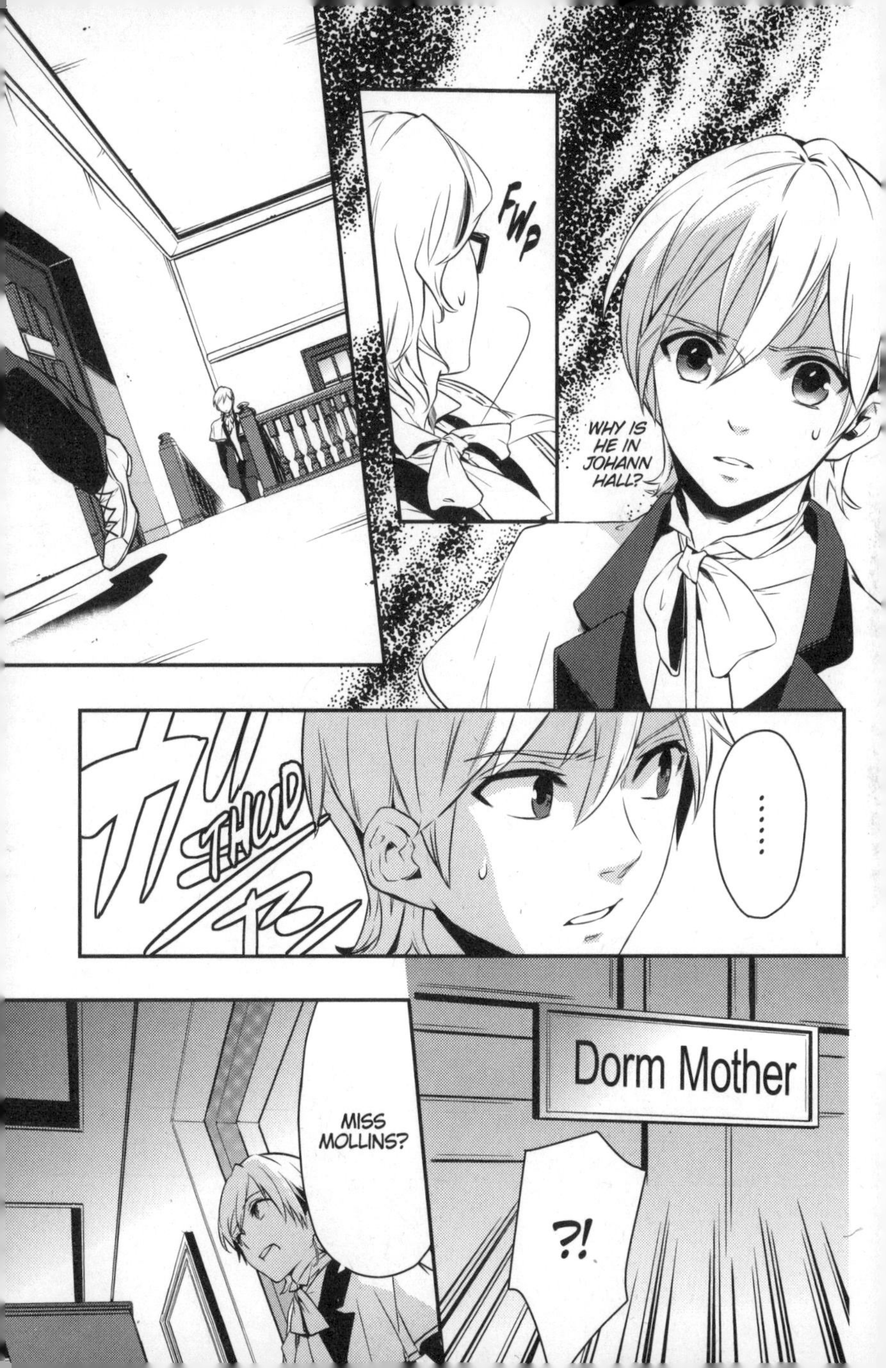
WHY IS HE IN JOHANN HALL?
FWP
......
THUD
Dorm Mother
?!
MISS MOLLINS?

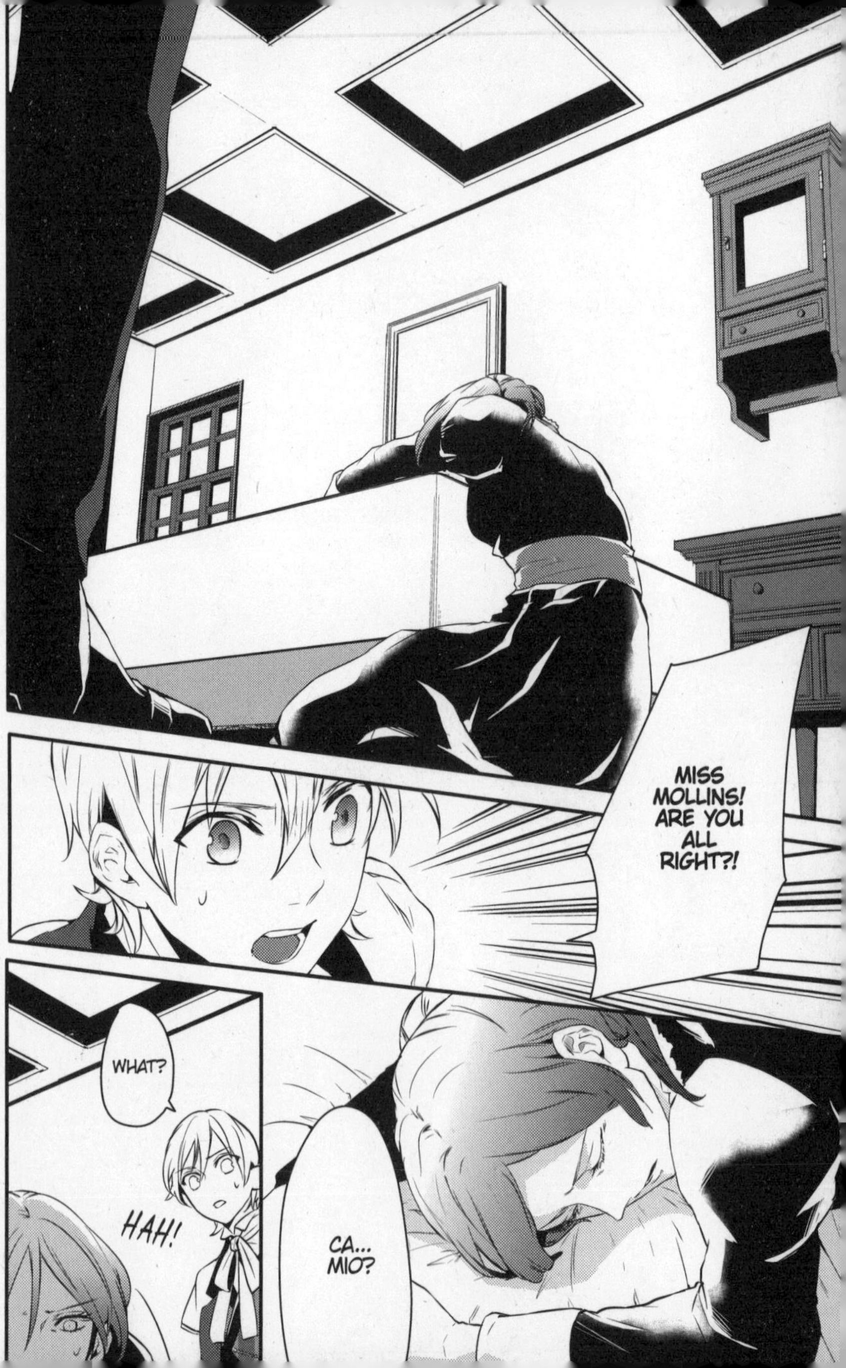
MISS MOLLINS! ARE YOU ALL RIGHT?!
CA... MIO?
WHAT?
HAH!

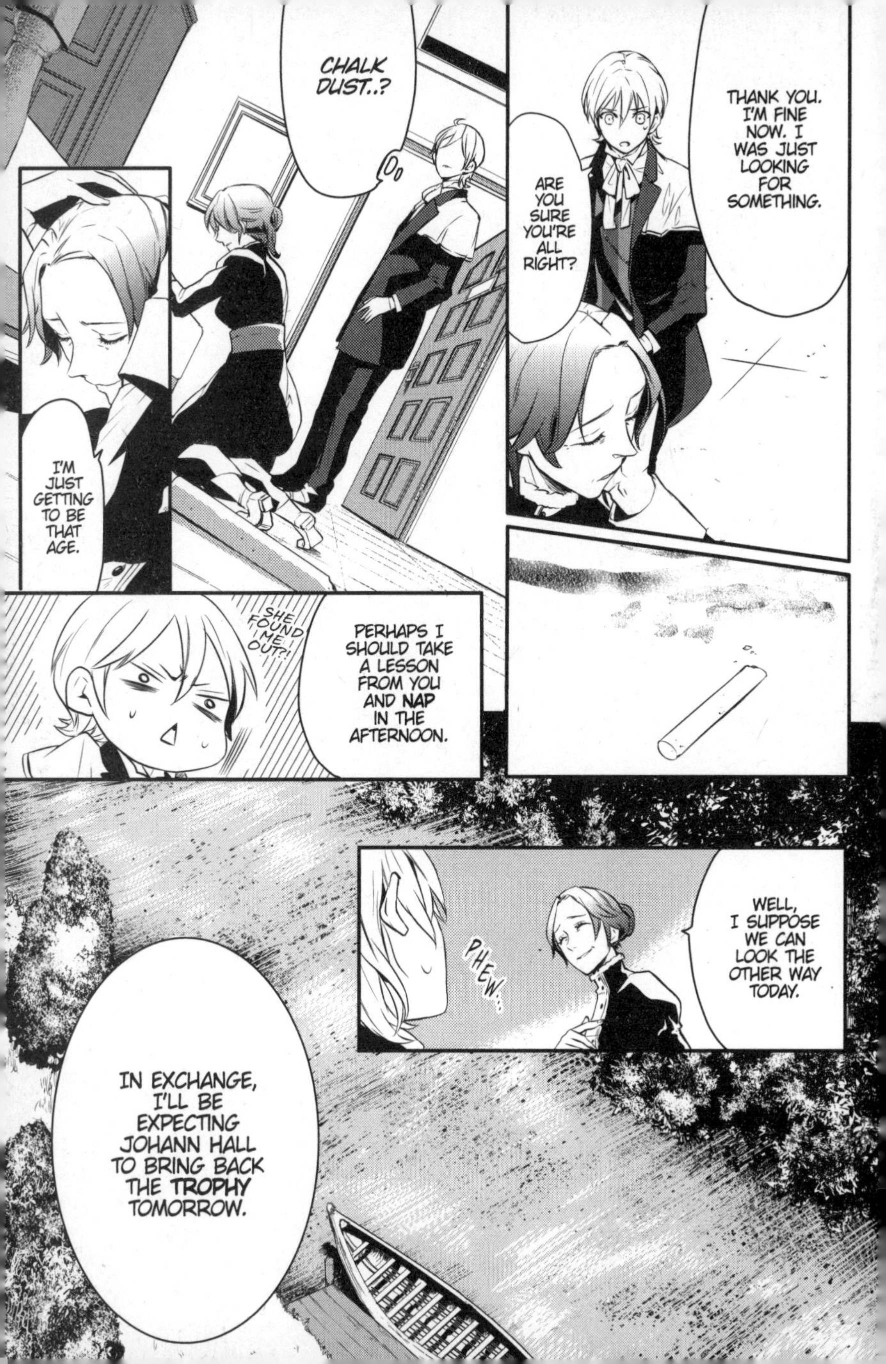
THANK YOU. I'M FINE NOW. I WAS JUST LOOKING FOR SOMETHING.
ARE YOU SURE YOU'RE ALL RIGHT?
CHALK DUST..?
Oo
I'M JUST GETTING TO BE THAT AGE.
PERHAPS I SHOULD TAKE A LESSON FROM YOU AND NAP IN THE AFTERNOON.
SHE FOUND ME OUT?!
WELL, I SUPPOSE WE CAN LOOK THE OTHER WAY TODAY.
PHEW..
IN EXCHANGE, I'LL BE EXPECTING JOHANN HALL TO BRING BACK THE TROPHY TOMORROW.

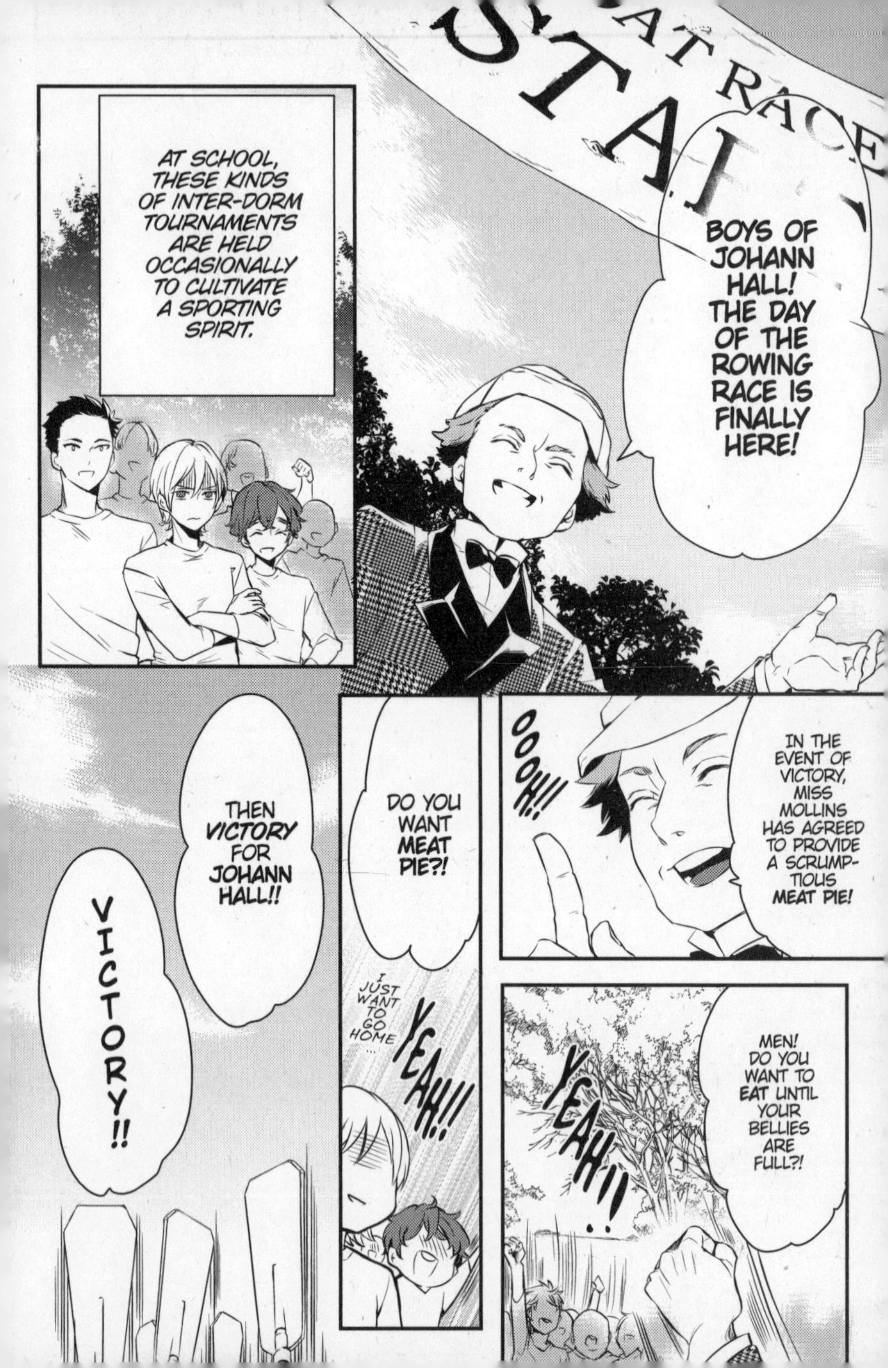

AT RACE
BOYS OF JOHANN HALL! THE DAY OF THE ROWING RACE IS FINALLY HERE!
AT SCHOOL, THESE KINDS OF INTER-DORM TOURNAMENTS ARE HELD OCCASIONALLY TO CULTIVATE A SPORTING SPIRIT.
IN THE EVENT OF VICTORY, MISS MOLLINS HAS AGREED TO PROVIDE A SCRUMP-TIOUS MEAT PIE!
OOOOH!!
MEN! DO YOU WANT TO EAT UNTIL YOUR BELLIES ARE FULL?!
YEAH!!
DO YOU WANT MEAT PIE?!
YEAH!!
I JUST WANT TO GO HOME...
THEN VICTORY FOR JOHANN HALL!!
VICTORY!!

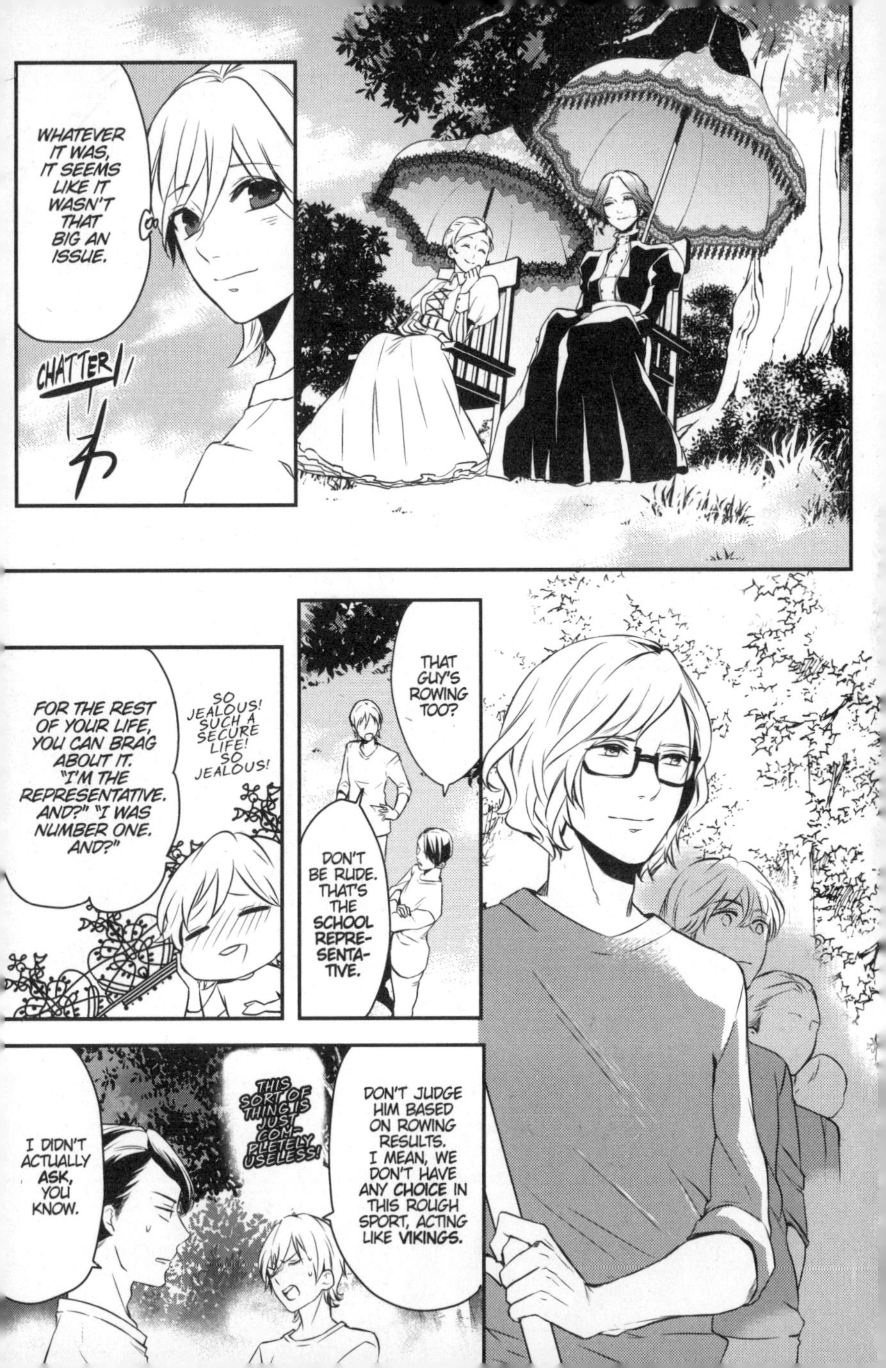
WHATEVER IT WAS, IT SEEMS LIKE IT WASN'T THAT BIG AN ISSUE.
CHATTER
THAT GUY'S ROWING TOO?
DON'T BE RUDE. THAT'S THE SCHOOL REPRESENTATIVE.
FOR THE REST OF YOUR LIFE, YOU CAN BRAG ABOUT IT. "I'M THE REPRESENTATIVE. AND?" "I WAS NUMBER ONE. AND?"
SO JEALOUS! SUCH A SECURE LIFE! SO JEALOUS!
DON'T JUDGE HIM BASED ON ROWING RESULTS. I MEAN, WE DON'T HAVE ANY CHOICE IN THIS ROUGH SPORT, ACTING LIKE VIKINGS.
THIS SORT OF THING IS JUST COMPLETELY USELESS!
I DIDN'T ACTUALLY ASK, YOU KNOW.

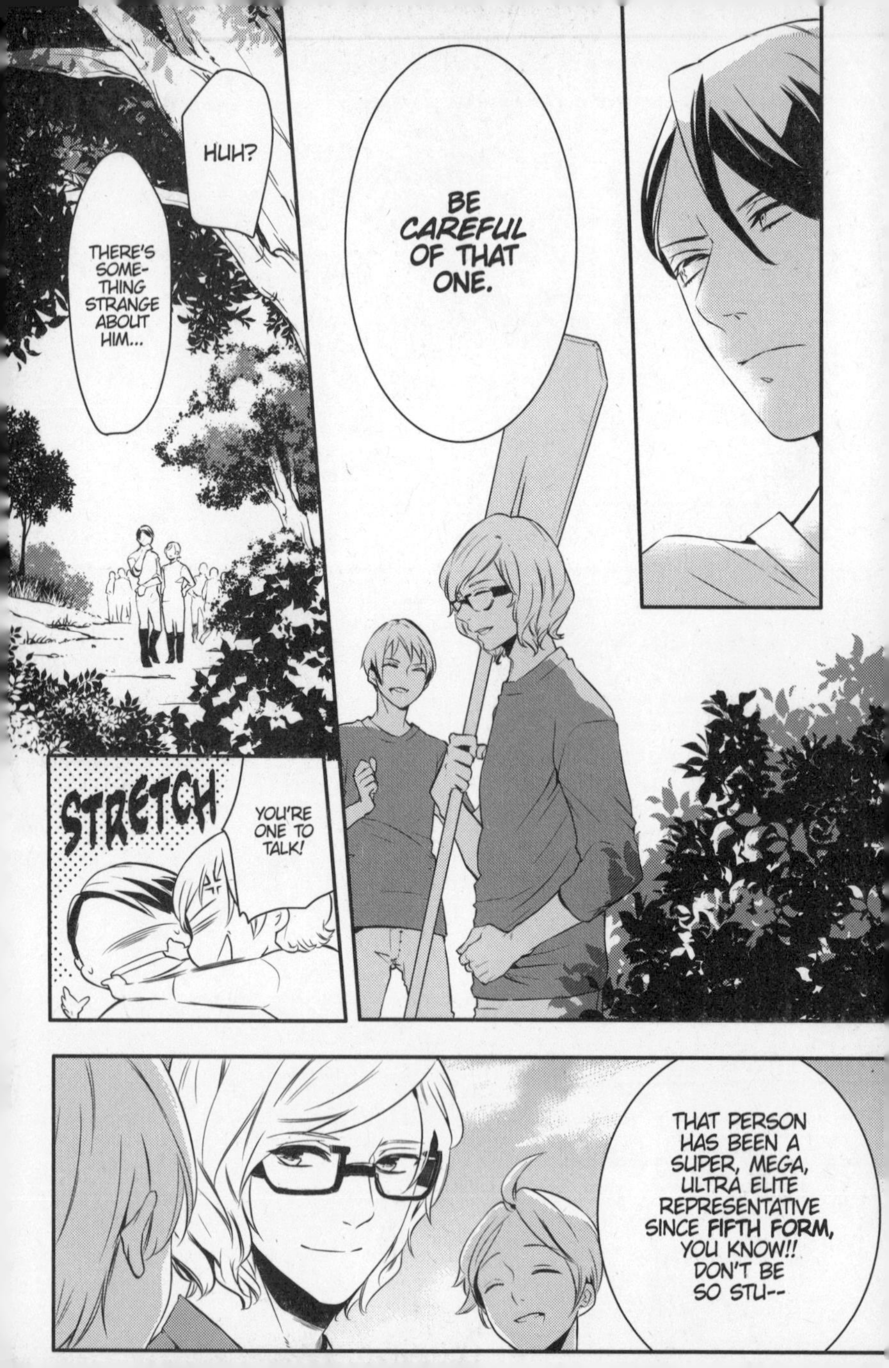
BE CAREFUL OF THAT ONE.
HUH?
THERE'S SOME-THING STRANGE ABOUT HIM...
YOU'RE ONE TO TALK!
STRETCH
THAT PERSON HAS BEEN A SUPER, MEGA, ULTRA ELITE REPRESENTATIVE SINCE FIFTH FORM, YOU KNOW!! DON'T BE SO STU--

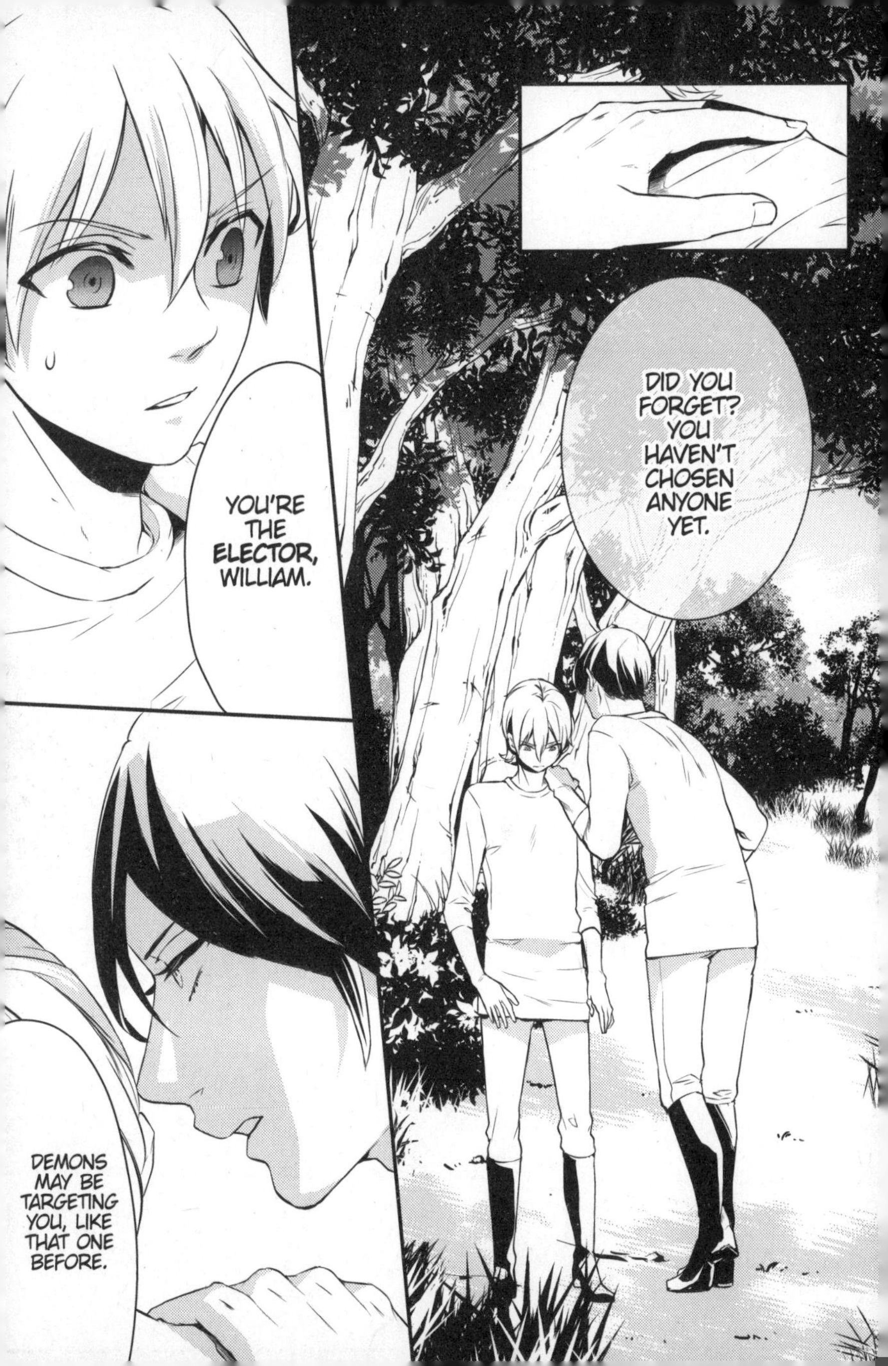
DID YOU FORGET? YOU HAVEN'T CHOSEN ANYONE YET.
YOU'RE THE ELECTOR, WILLIAM.
DEMONS MAY BE TARGETING YOU, LIKE THAT ONE BEFORE.

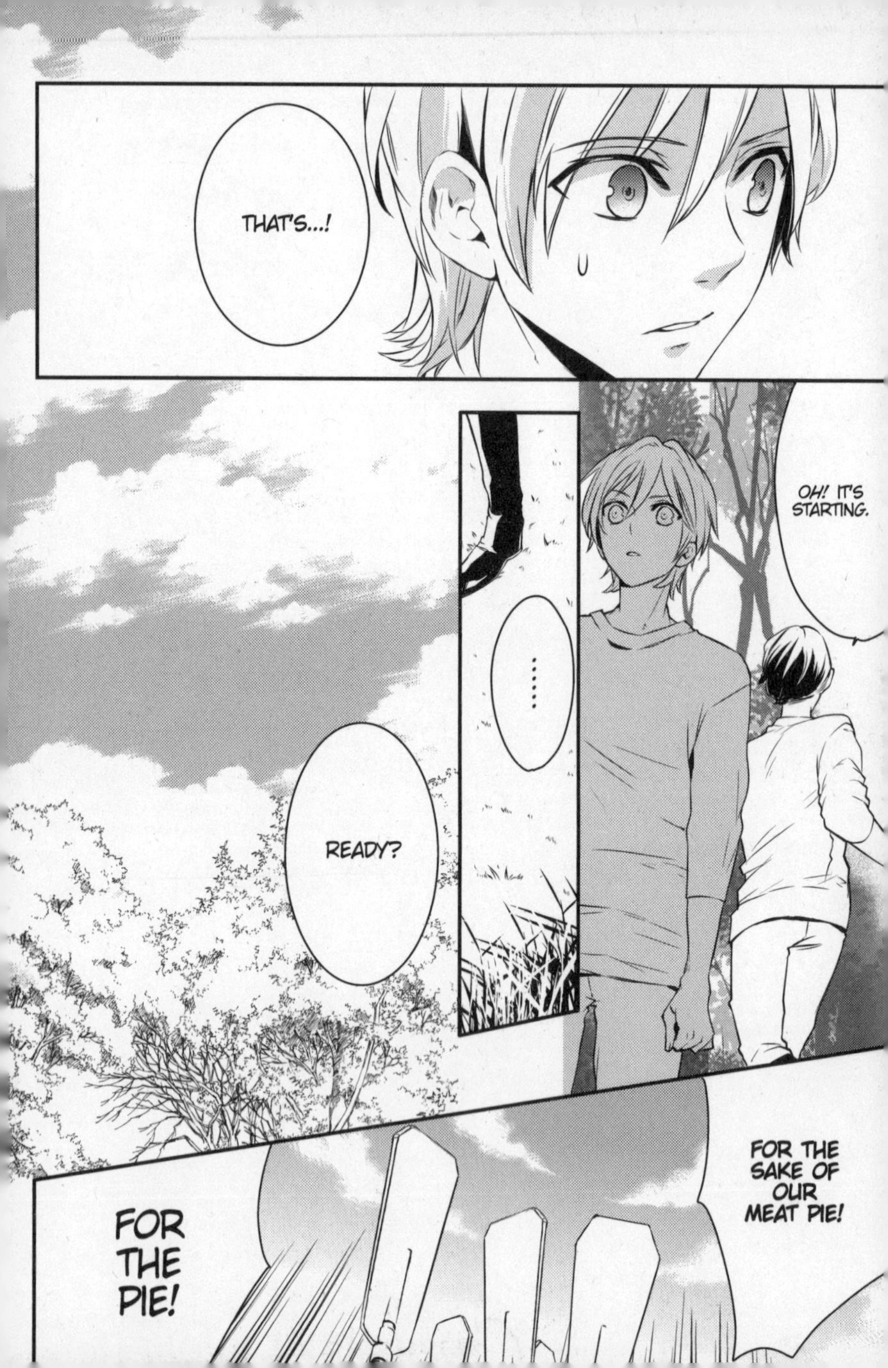
THAT'S...!
OH! IT'S STARTING.
......
READY?
FOR THE SAKE OF OUR MEAT PIE!
FOR THE PIE!

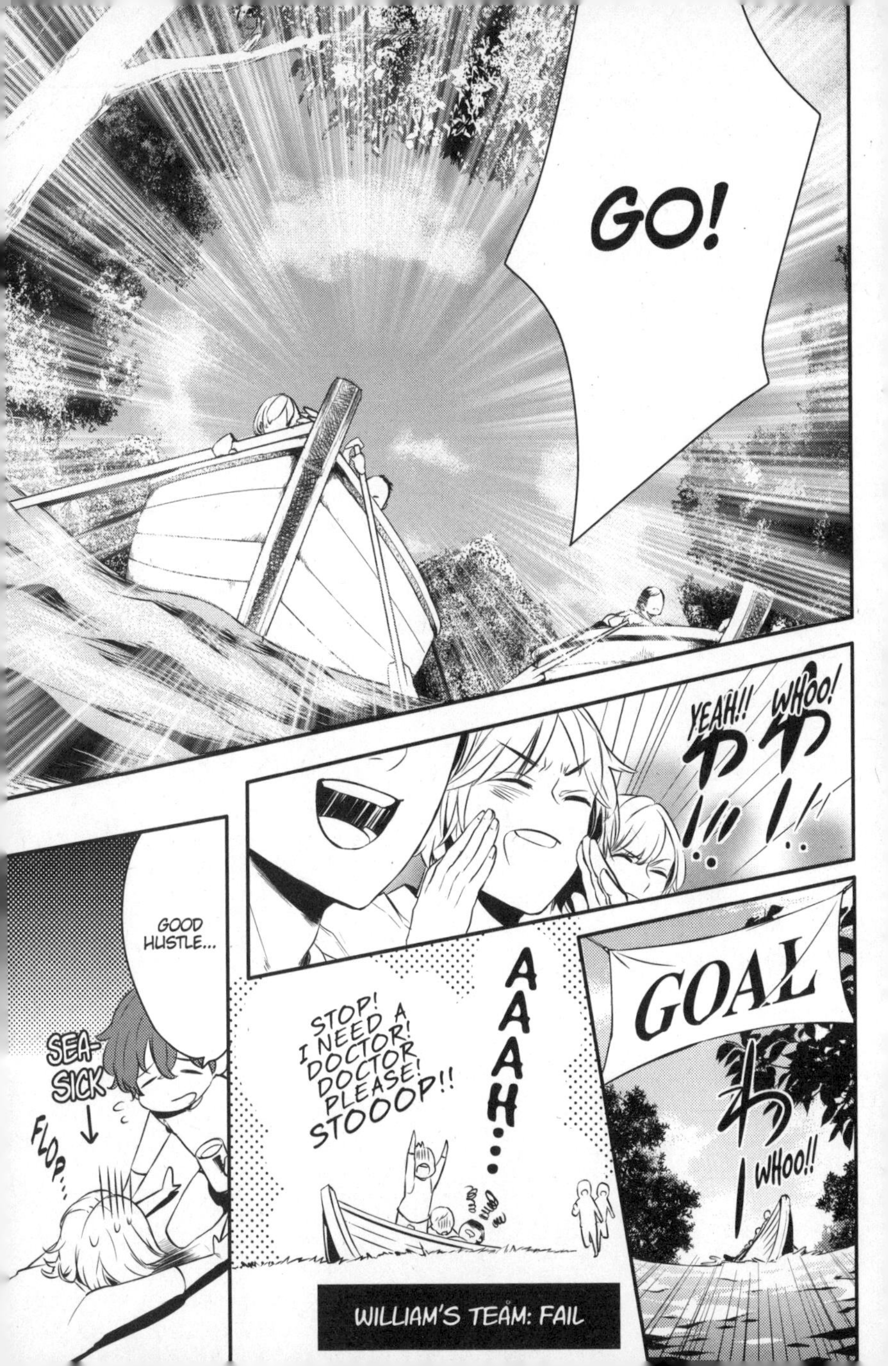
GO!
YEAH!!
WHOO!
GOAL
WHOO!!
AAAAH...
STOP! I NEED A DOCTOR! DOCTOR PLEASE! STOOOP!!
WILLIAM'S TEAM: FAIL
GOOD HUSTLE...
SEA-SICK
FLOP...

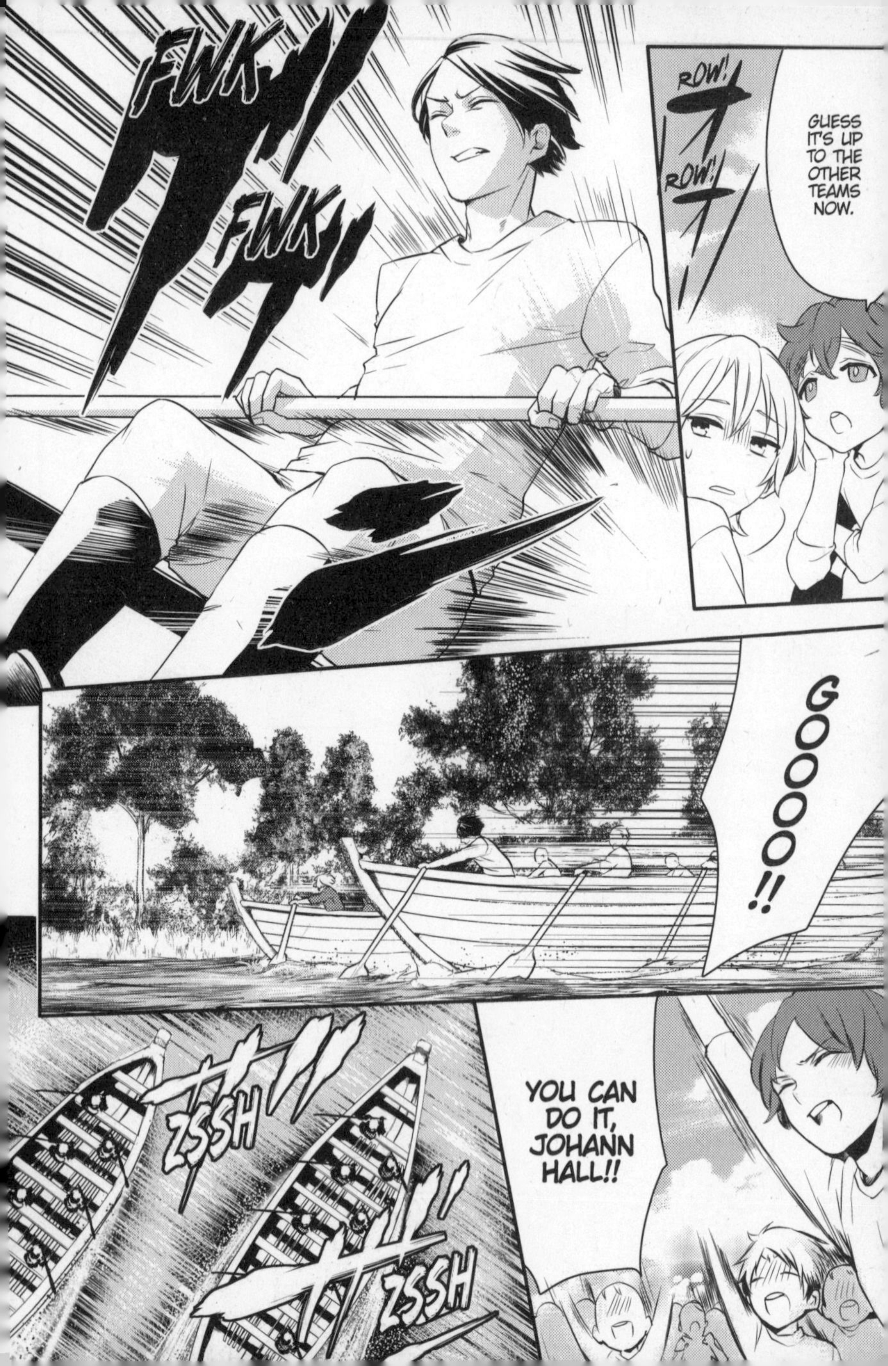
ROW!
ROW!
GUESS IT'S UP TO THE OTHER TEAMS NOW.
FWK
FWK
GOOOOO!!
YOU CAN DO IT, JOHANN HALL!!
ZSSH
ZSSH

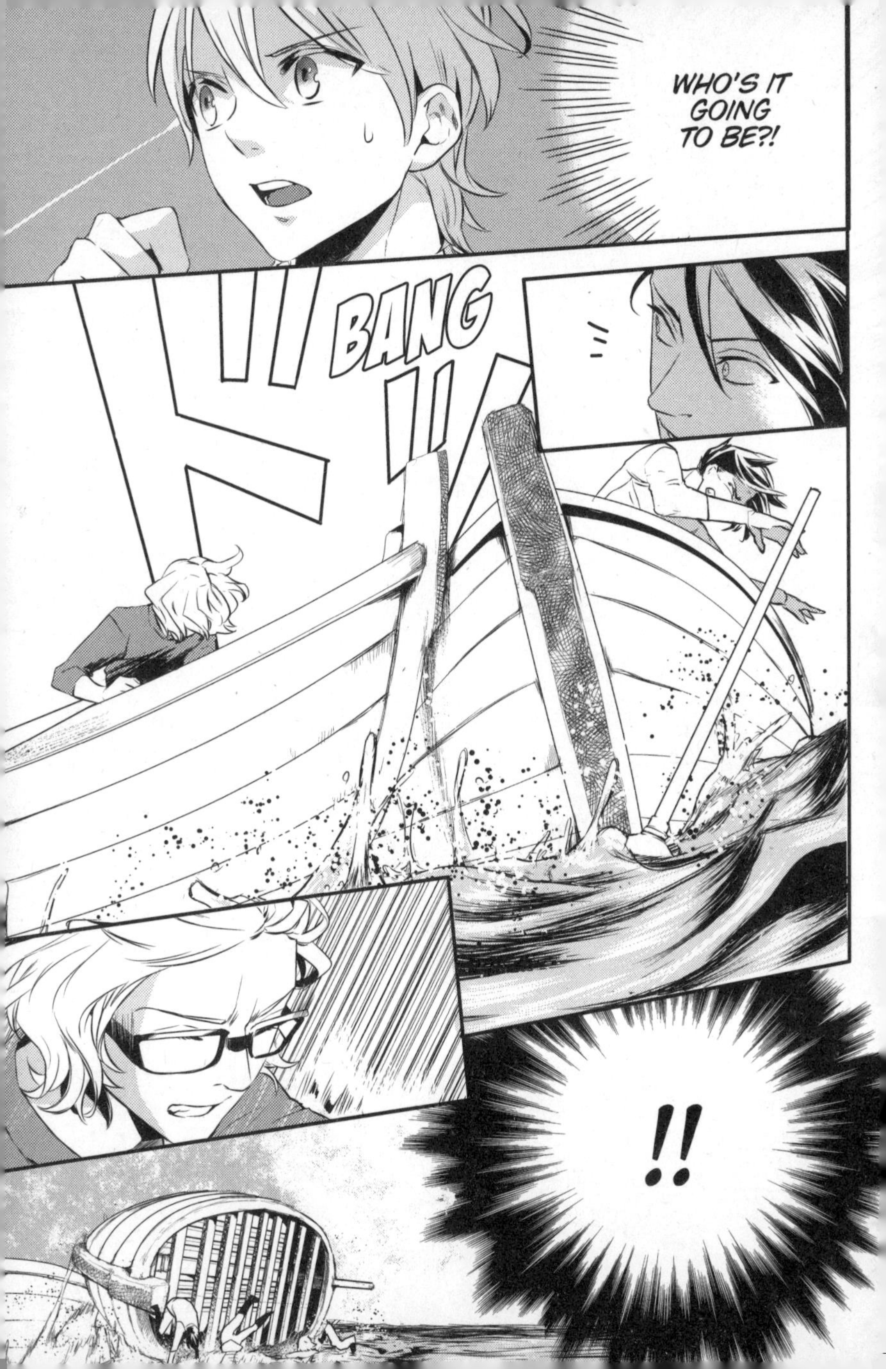
WHO'S IT GOING TO BE?!
BANG
!!

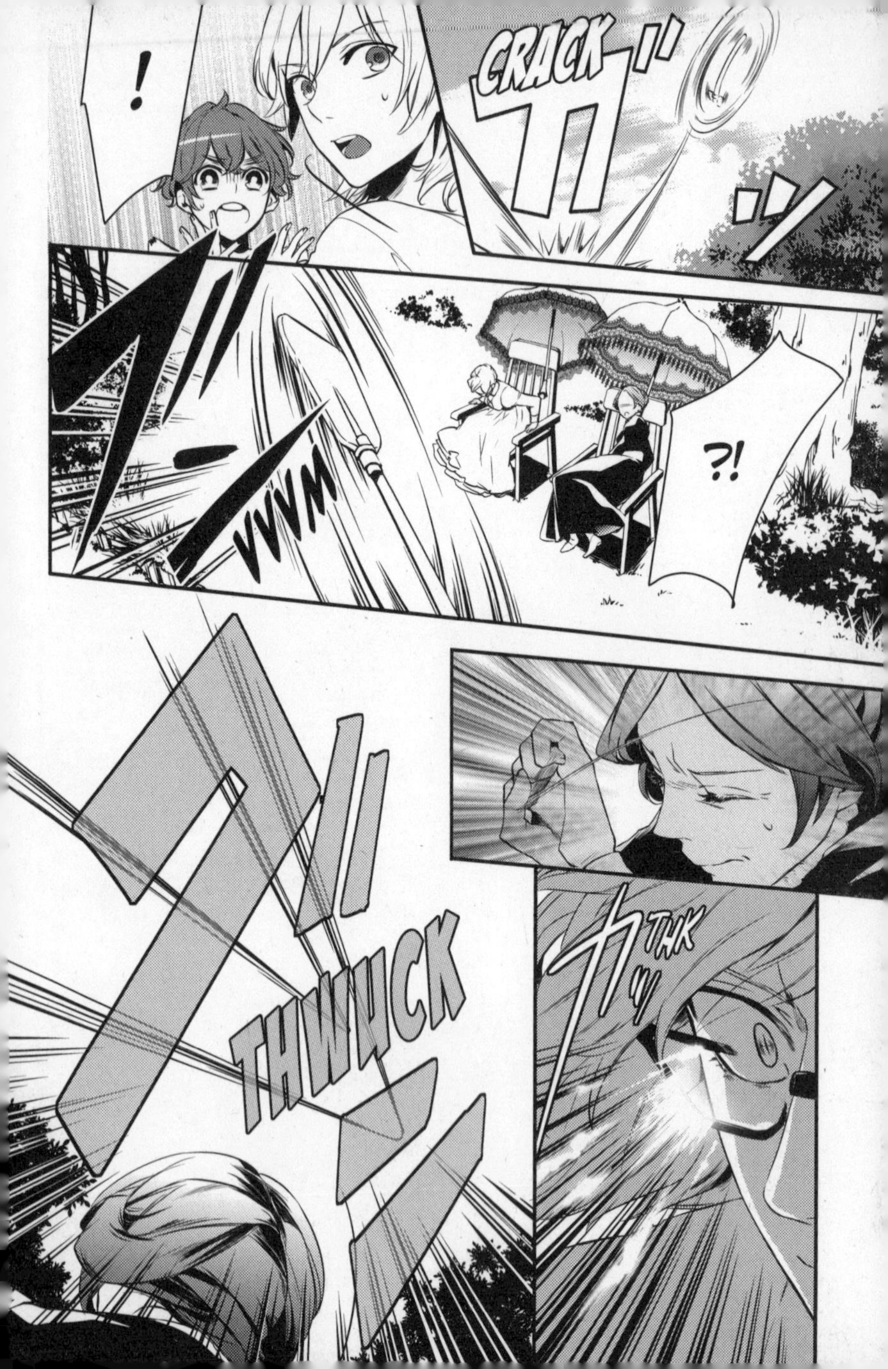
CRACK
!
?!
VVVM
THK
THWUCK

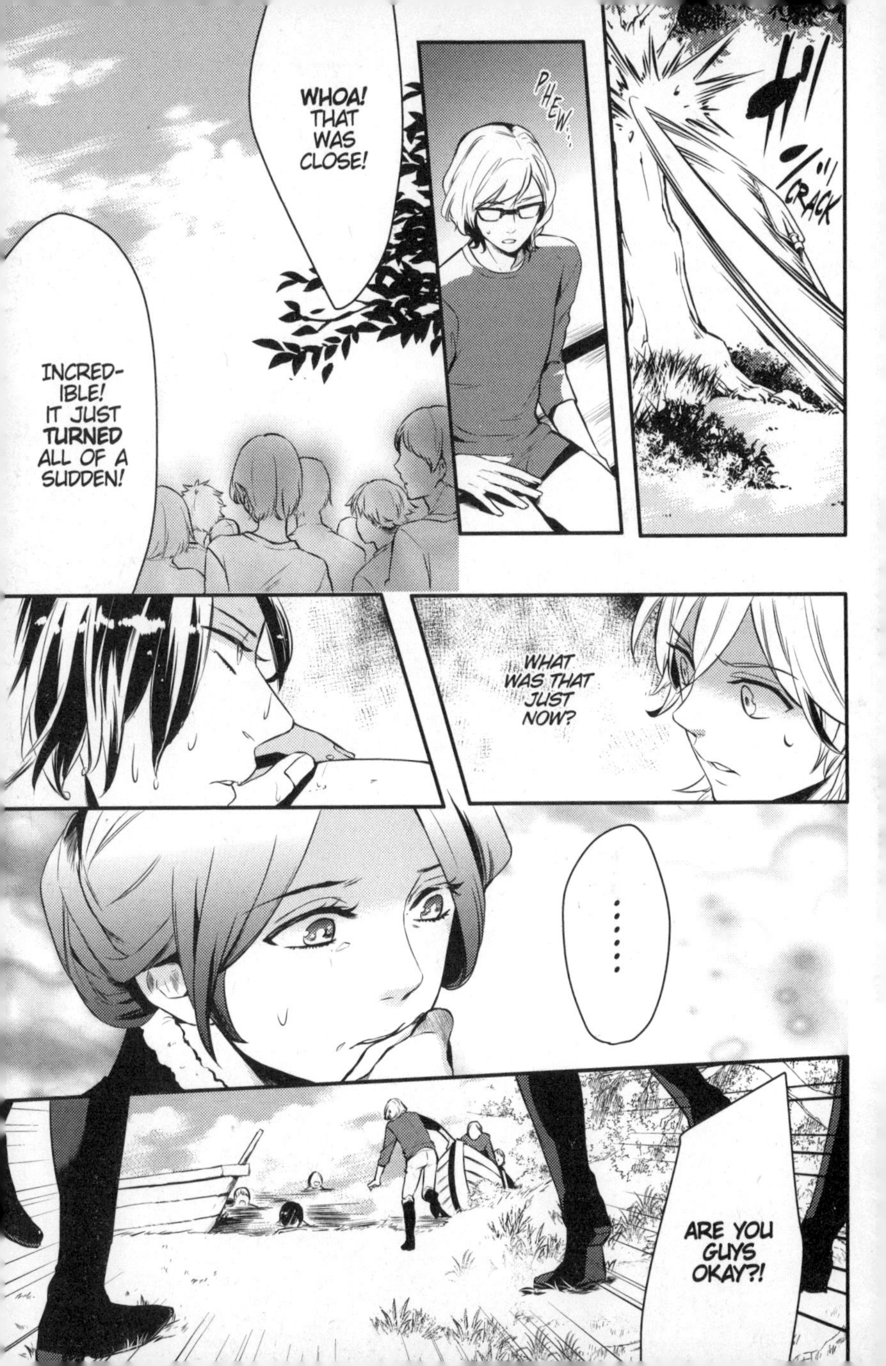
CRACK
PHEW..
WHOA! THAT WAS CLOSE!
INCRED-IBLE! IT JUST TURNED ALL OF A SUDDEN!
WHAT WAS THAT JUST NOW?
......
ARE YOU GUYS OKAY?!

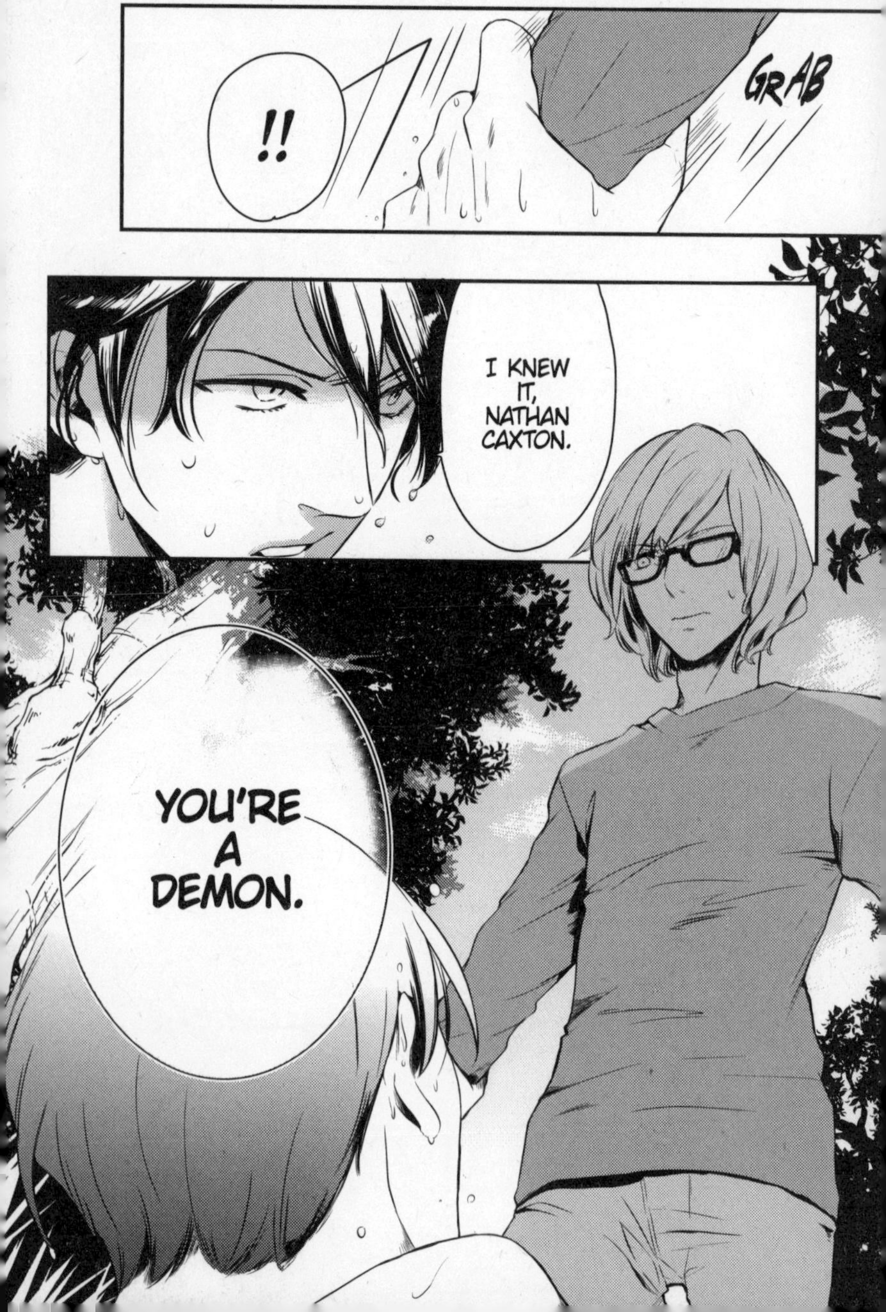
GRAB
!!
I KNEW IT, NATHAN CAXTON.
YOU'RE A DEMON.

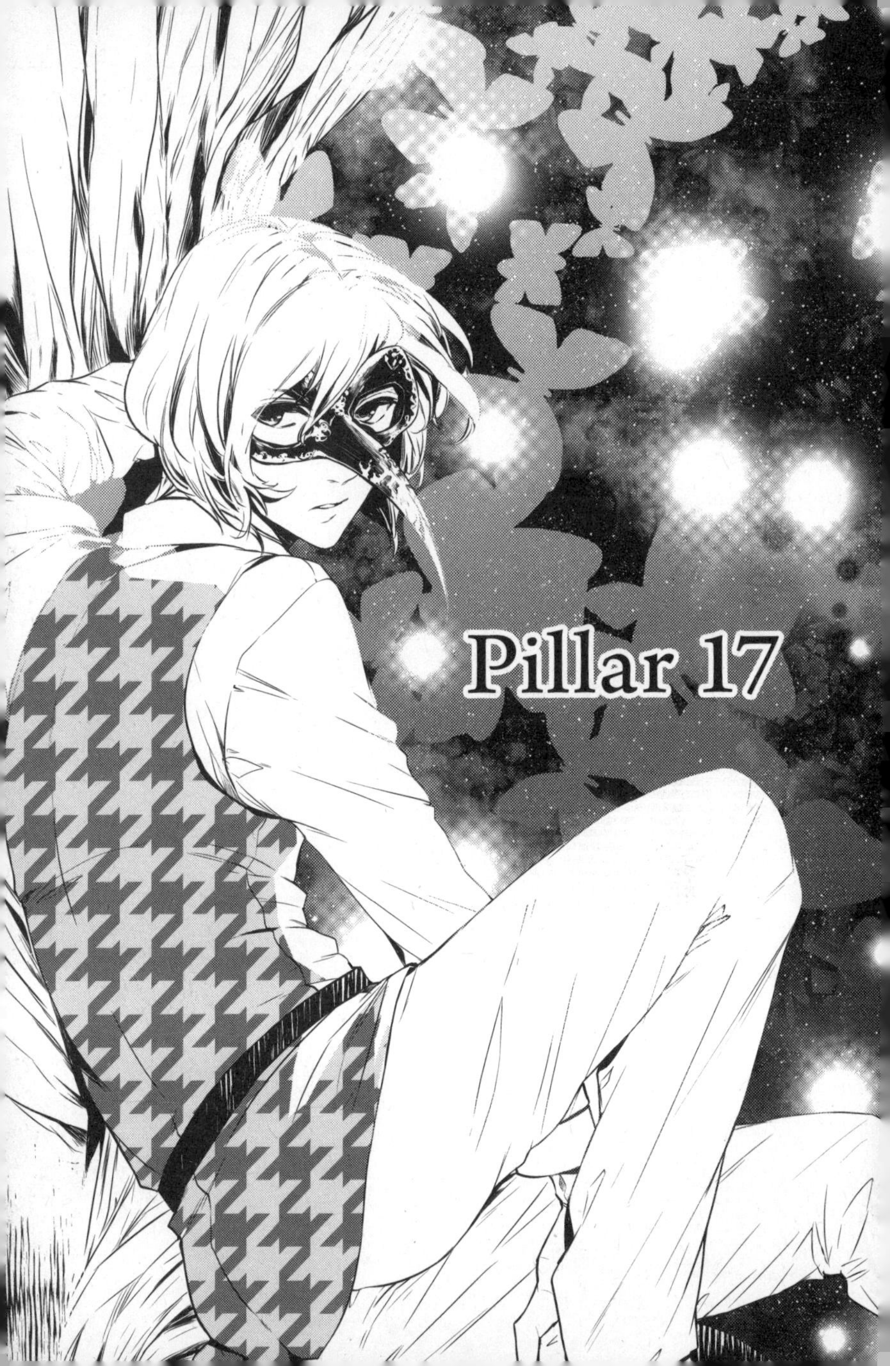
Pillar 17

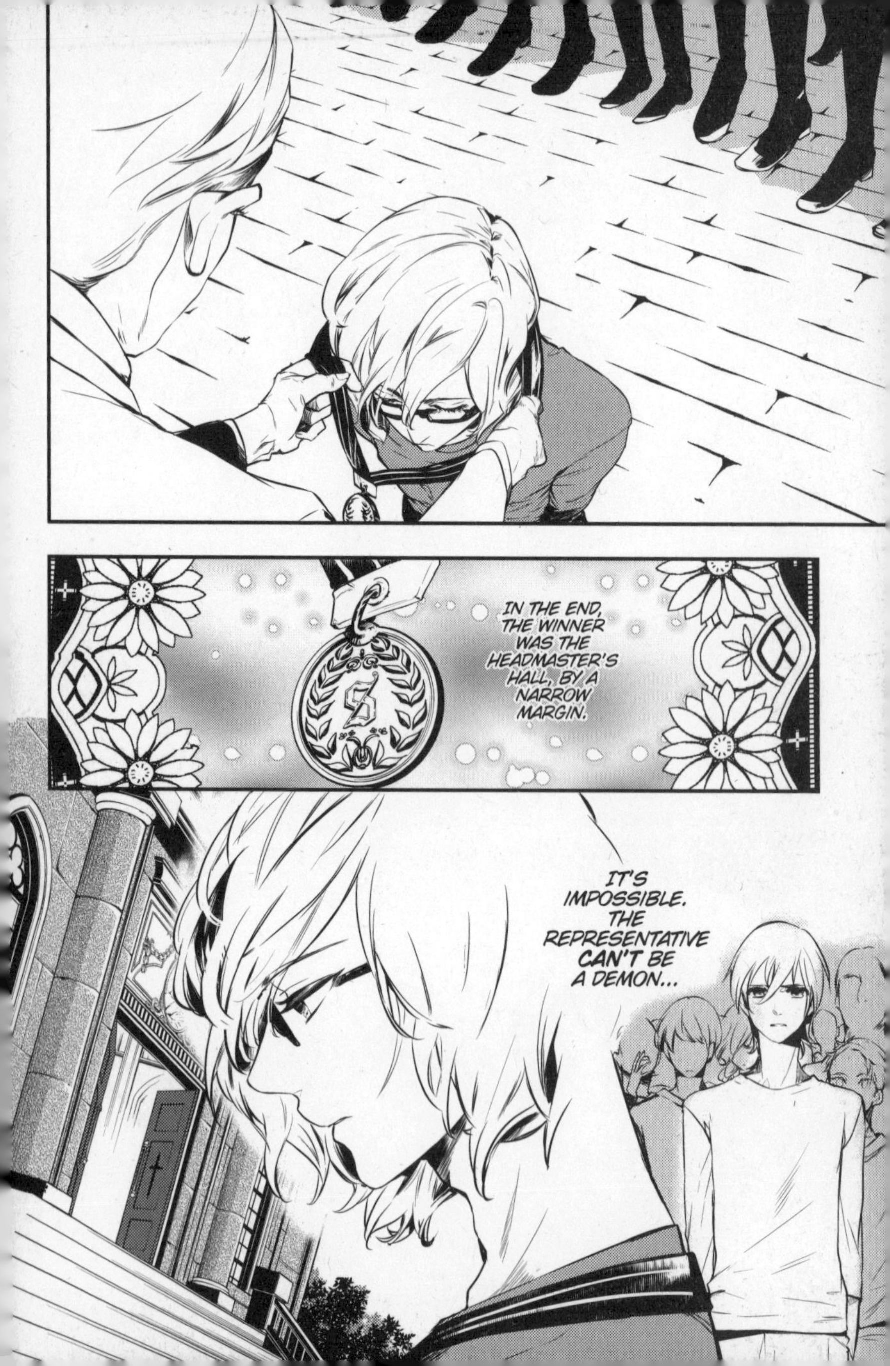
IN THE END, THE WINNER WAS THE HEADMASTER'S HALL, BY A NARROW MARGIN.
IT'S IMPOSSIBLE. THE REPRESENTATIVE CAN'T BE A DEMON...

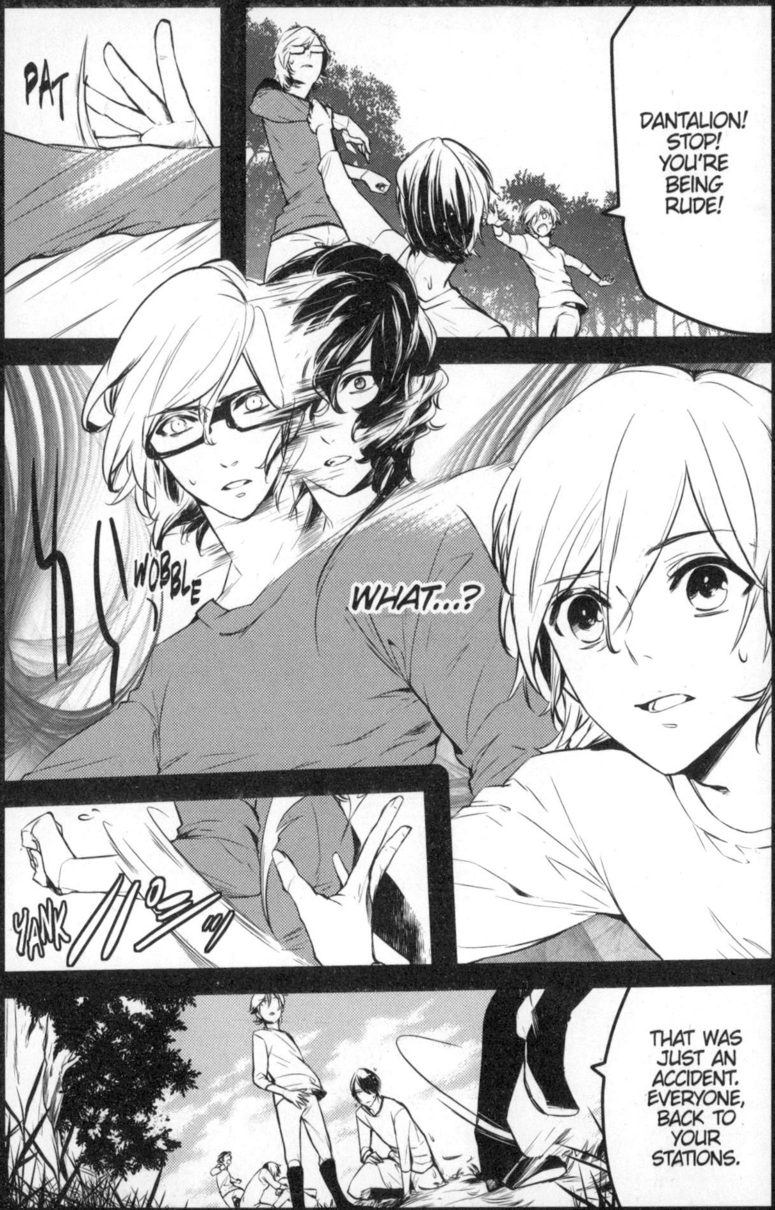
DANTALION! STOP! YOU'RE BEING RUDE!
PAT
WHAT...?
WOBBLE
YANK
THAT WAS JUST AN ACCIDENT. EVERYONE, BACK TO YOUR STATIONS.

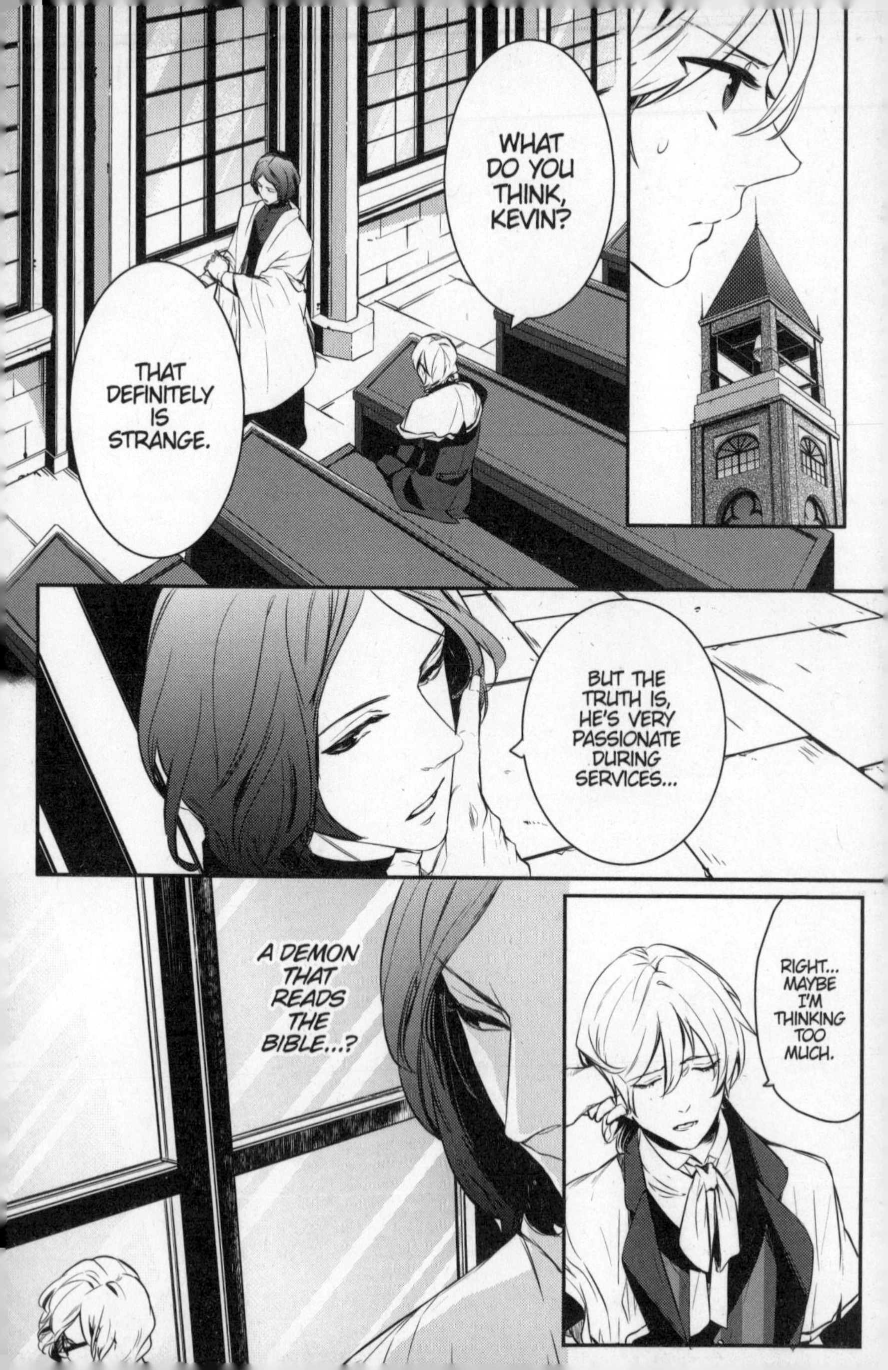
WHAT DO YOU THINK, KEVIN?
THAT DEFINITELY IS STRANGE.
BUT THE TRUTH IS, HE'S VERY PASSIONATE DURING SERVICES...
RIGHT... MAYBE I'M THINKING TOO MUCH.
A DEMON THAT READS THE BIBLE...?

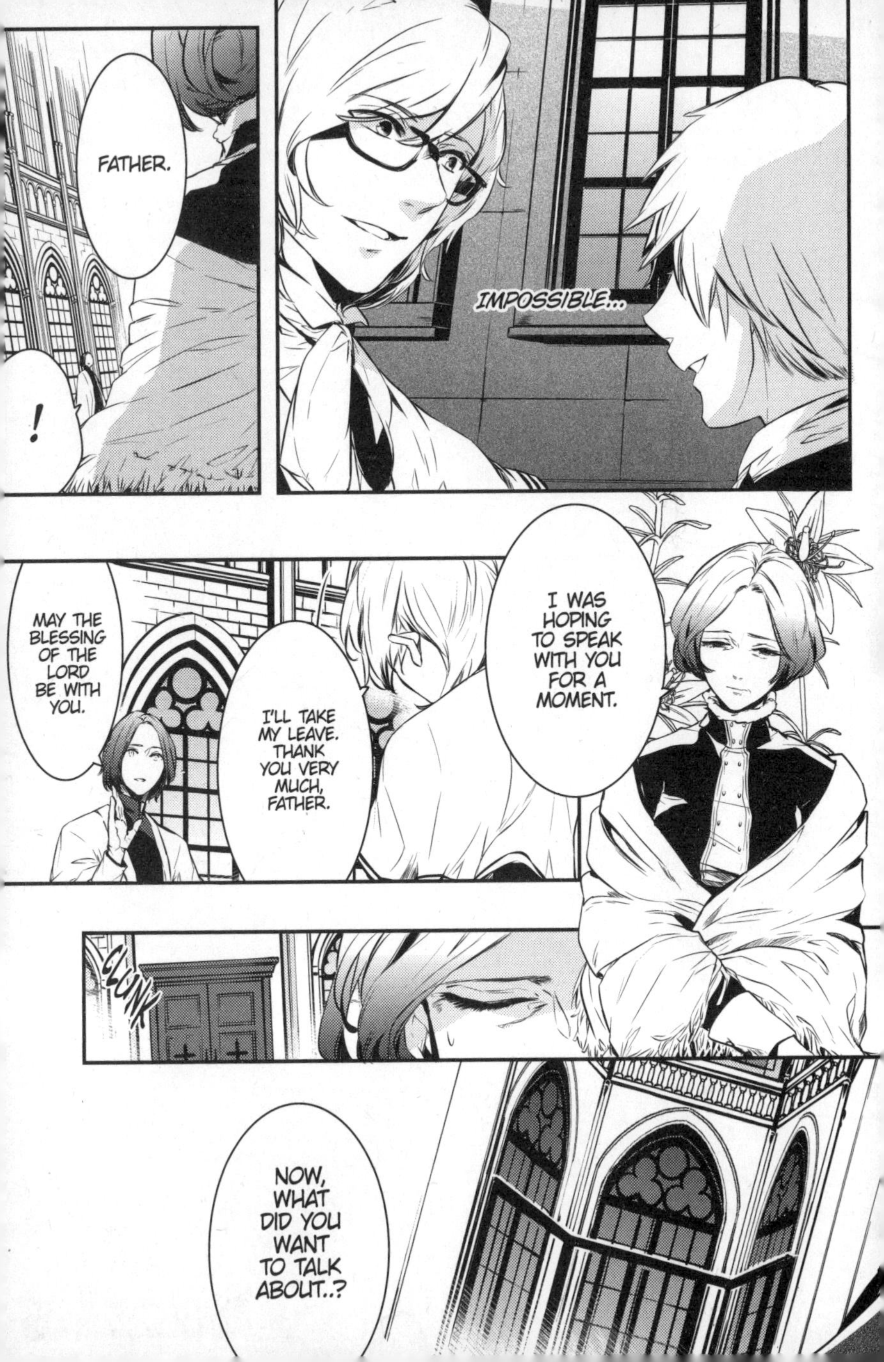
IMPOSSIBLE...
FATHER.
!
I WAS HOPING TO SPEAK WITH YOU FOR A MOMENT.
I'LL TAKE MY LEAVE. THANK YOU VERY MUCH, FATHER.
MAY THE BLESSING OF THE LORD BE WITH YOU.
CLUNK
NOW, WHAT DID YOU WANT TO TALK ABOUT..?

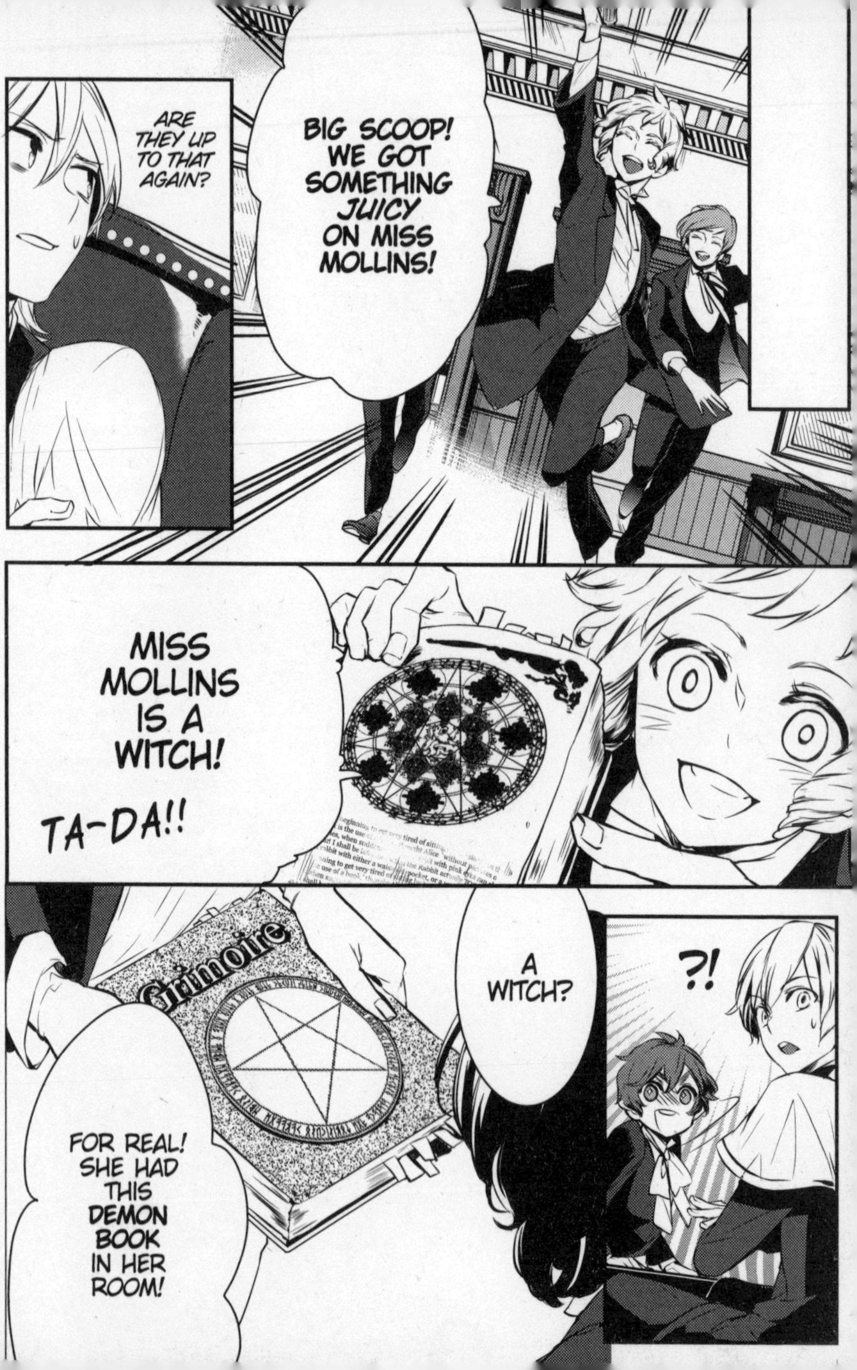
BIG SCOOP! WE GOT SOMETHING JUICY ON MISS MOLLINS!
ARE THEY UP TO THAT AGAIN?
MISS MOLLINS IS A WITCH!
TA-DA!!
?!
A WITCH?
Grimoire
FOR REAL! SHE HAD THIS DEMON BOOK IN HER ROOM!

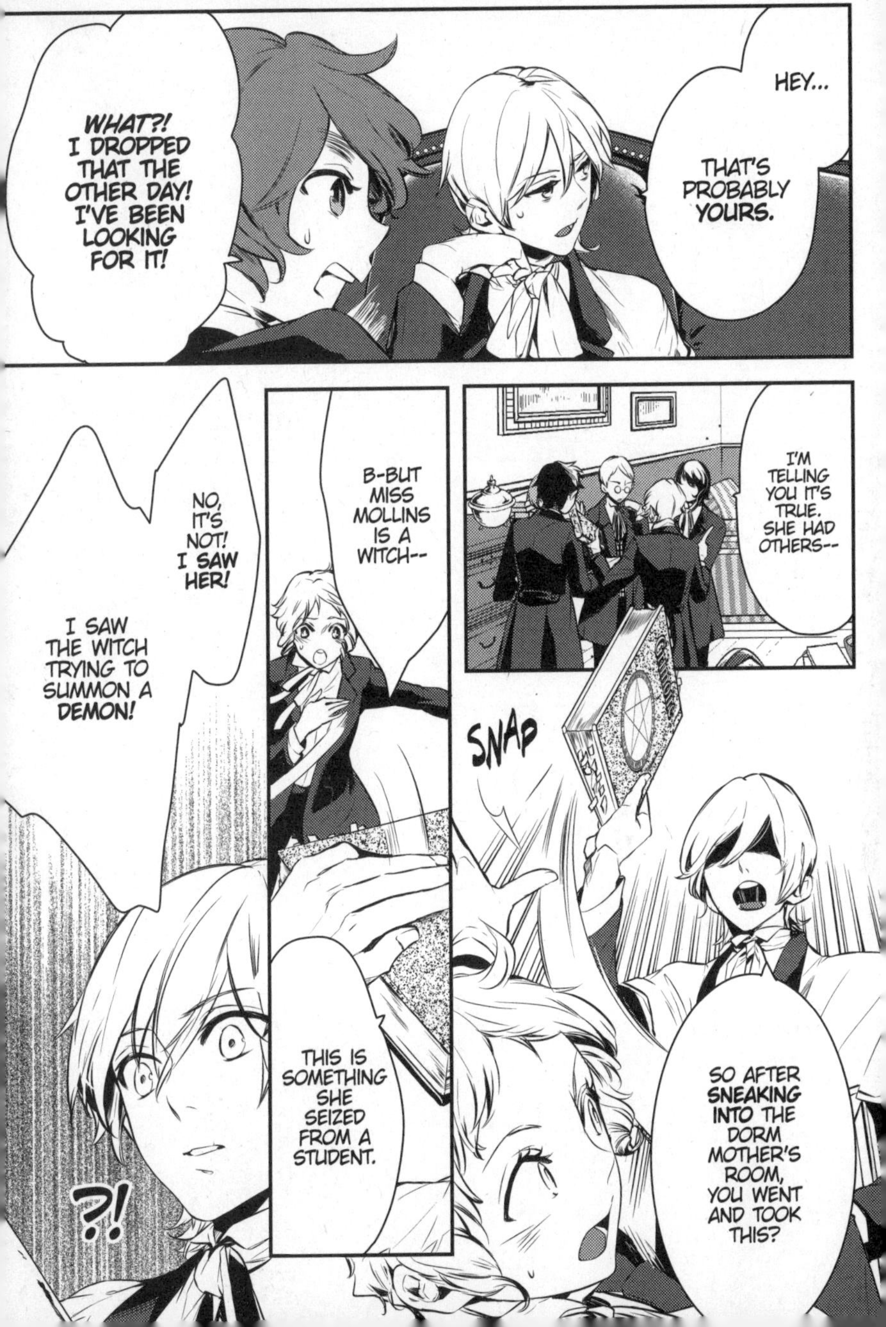
HEY...
THAT'S PROBABLY YOURS.
WHAT?! I DROPPED THAT THE OTHER DAY! I'VE BEEN LOOKING FOR IT!
I'M TELLING YOU IT'S TRUE. SHE HAD OTHERS--
B-BUT MISS MOLLINS IS A WITCH--
NO, IT'S NOT! I SAW HER!
I SAW THE WITCH TRYING TO SUMMON A DEMON!
SNAP
SO AFTER SNEAKING INTO THE DORM MOTHER'S ROOM, YOU WENT AND TOOK THIS?
THIS IS SOMETHING SHE SEIZED FROM A STUDENT.
?!

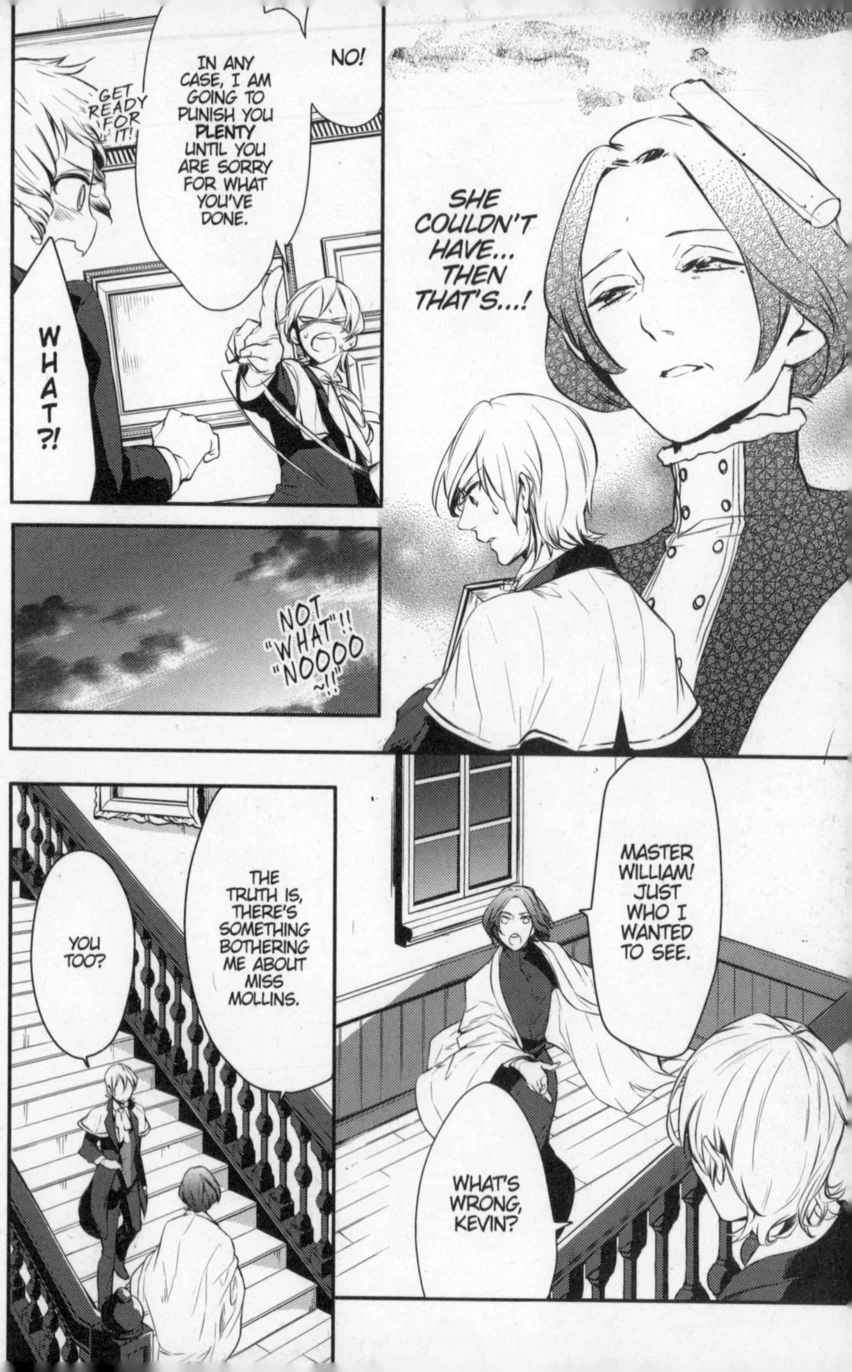
SHE COULDN'T HAVE... THEN THAT'S...!
NO!
IN ANY CASE, I AM GOING TO PUNISH YOU PLENTY UNTIL YOU ARE SORRY FOR WHAT YOU'VE DONE.
GET READY FOR IT!
WHAT?!
NOT "WHAT"!! "NOOOO~!!"
MASTER WILLIAM! JUST WHO I WANTED TO SEE.
WHAT'S WRONG, KEVIN?
THE TRUTH IS, THERE'S SOMETHING BOTHERING ME ABOUT MISS MOLLINS.
YOU TOO?

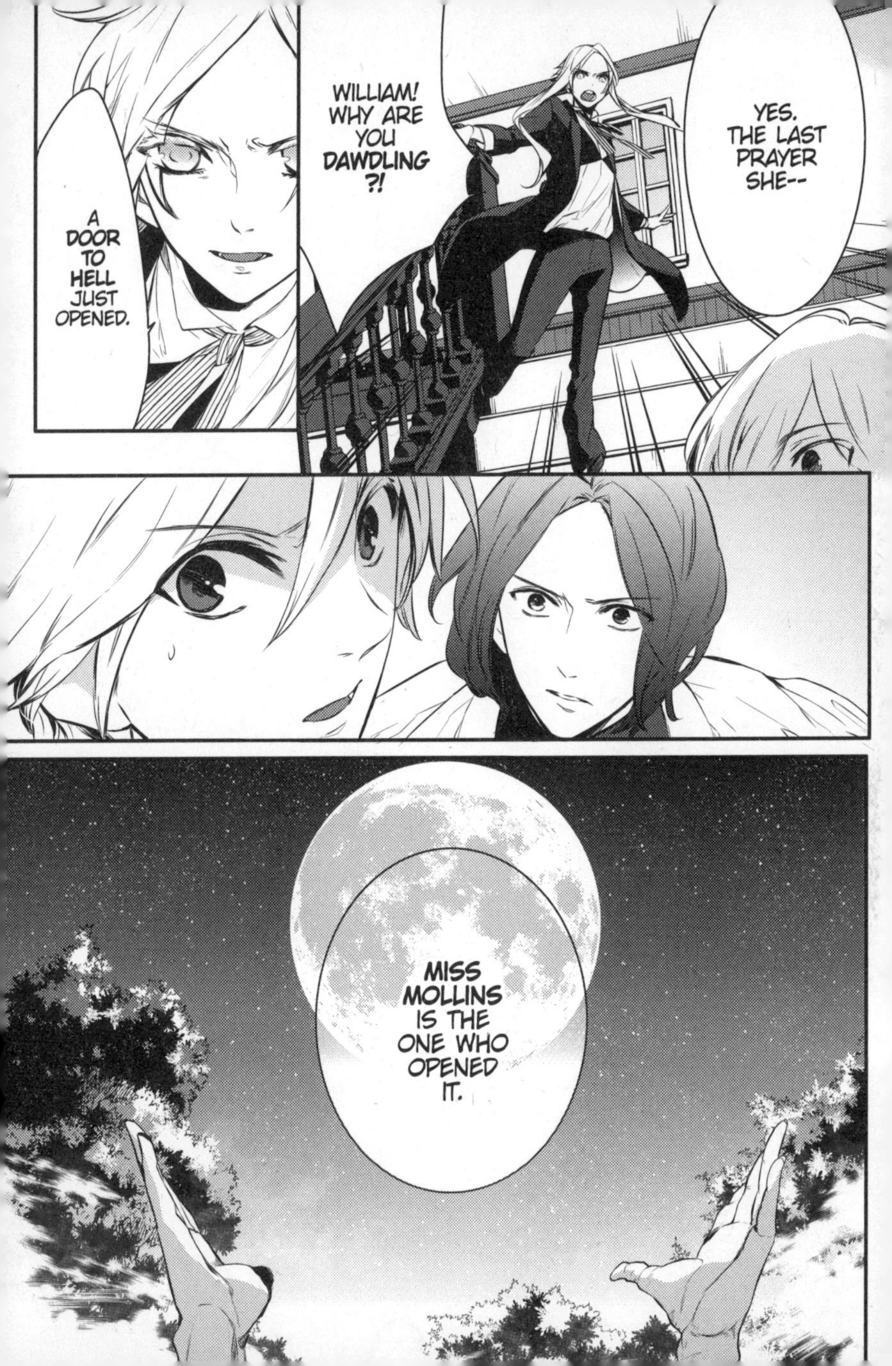
YES. THE LAST PRAYER SHE--
WILLIAM! WHY ARE YOU DAWDLING?!
A DOOR TO HELL JUST OPENED.
MISS MOLLINS IS THE ONE WHO OPENED IT.

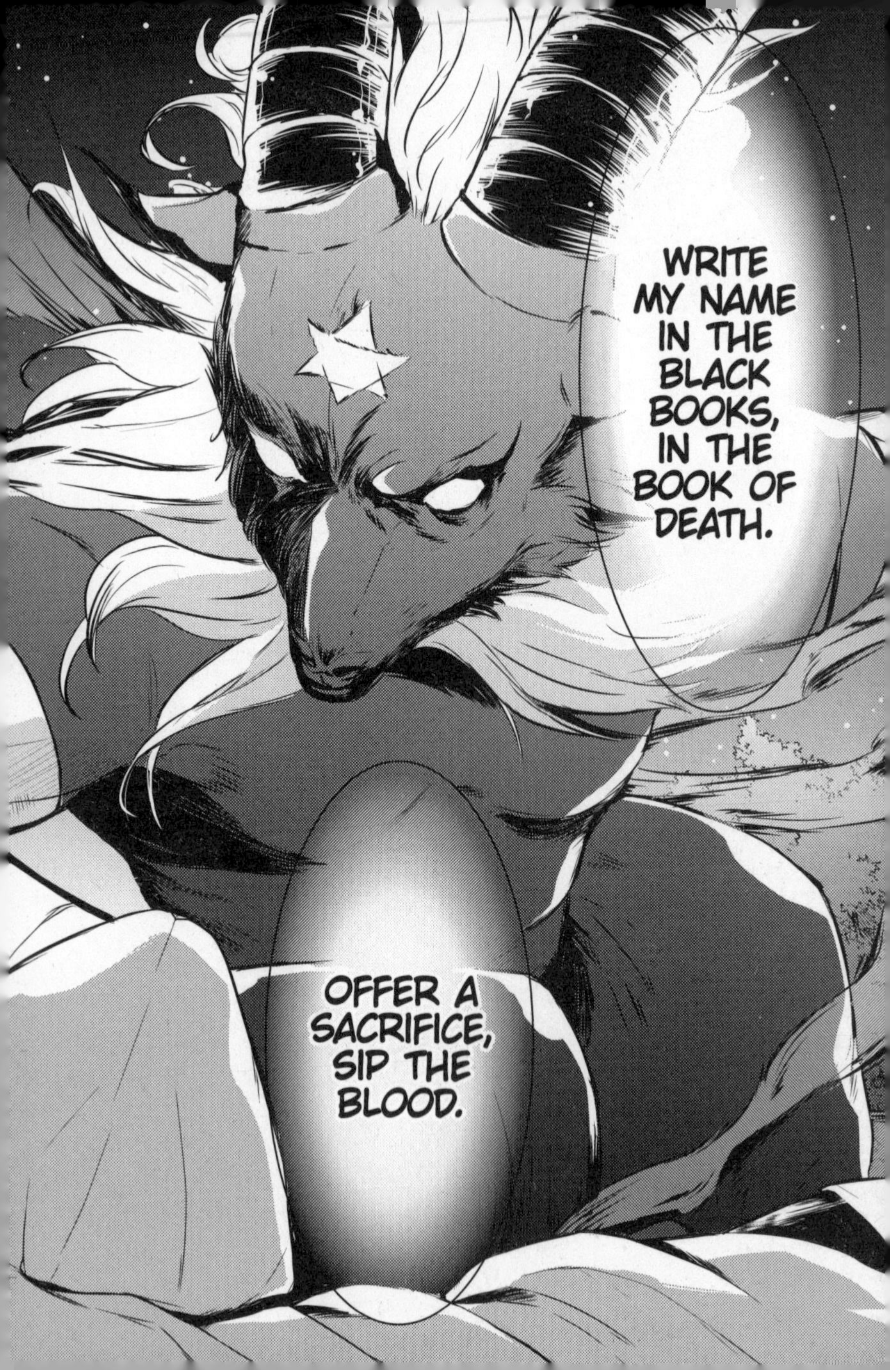
WRITE MY NAME IN THE BLACK BOOKS, IN THE BOOK OF DEATH.
OFFER A SACRIFICE, SIP THE BLOOD.

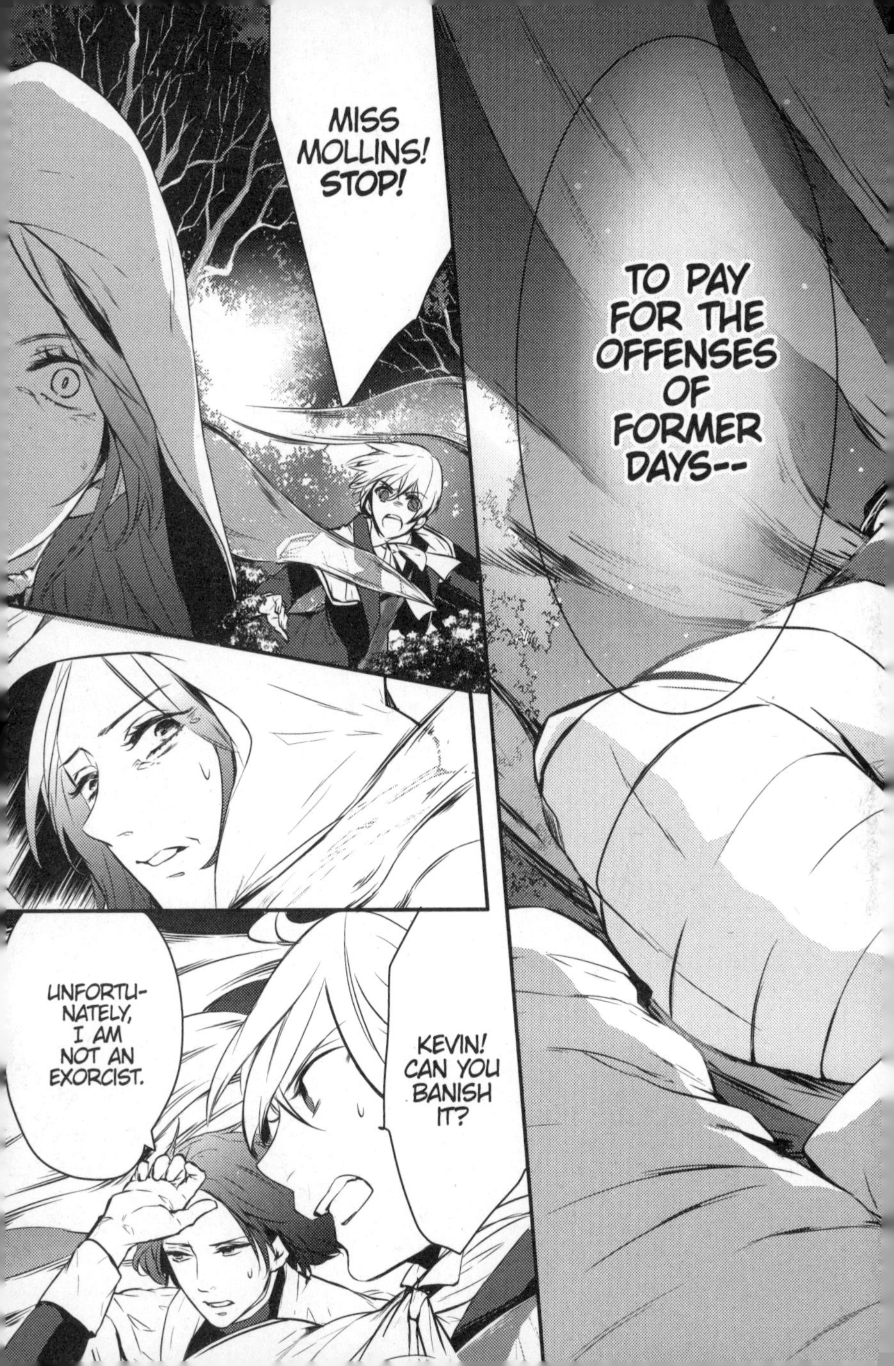
TO PAY FOR THE OFFENSES OF FORMER DAYS--
MISS MOLLINS! STOP!
KEVIN! CAN YOU BANISH IT?
UNFORTU-NATELY, I AM NOT AN EXORCIST.

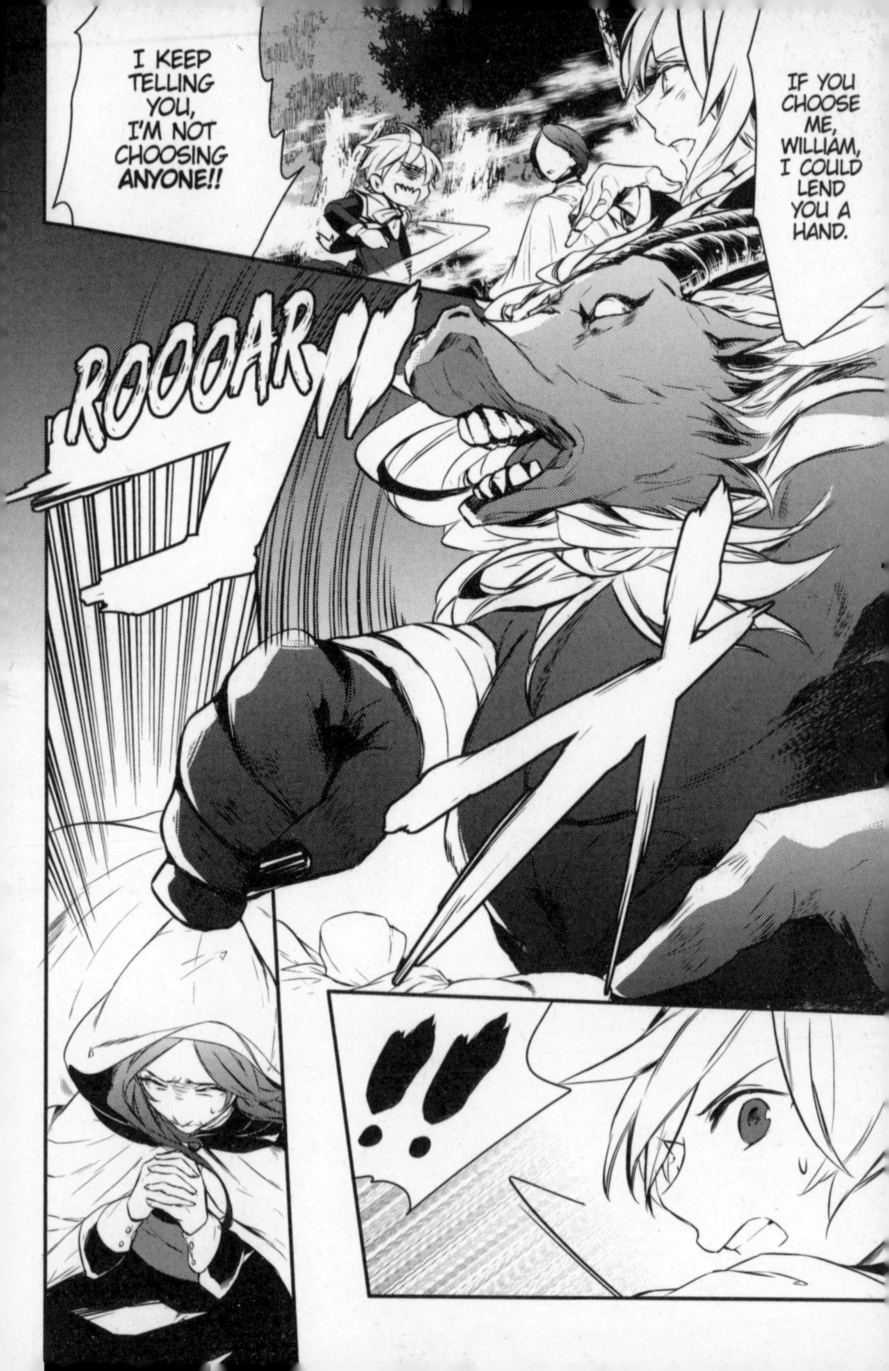
IF YOU CHOOSE ME, WILLIAM, I COULD LEND YOU A HAND.
I KEEP TELLING YOU, I'M NOT CHOOSING ANYONE!!
ROOOAR
!!

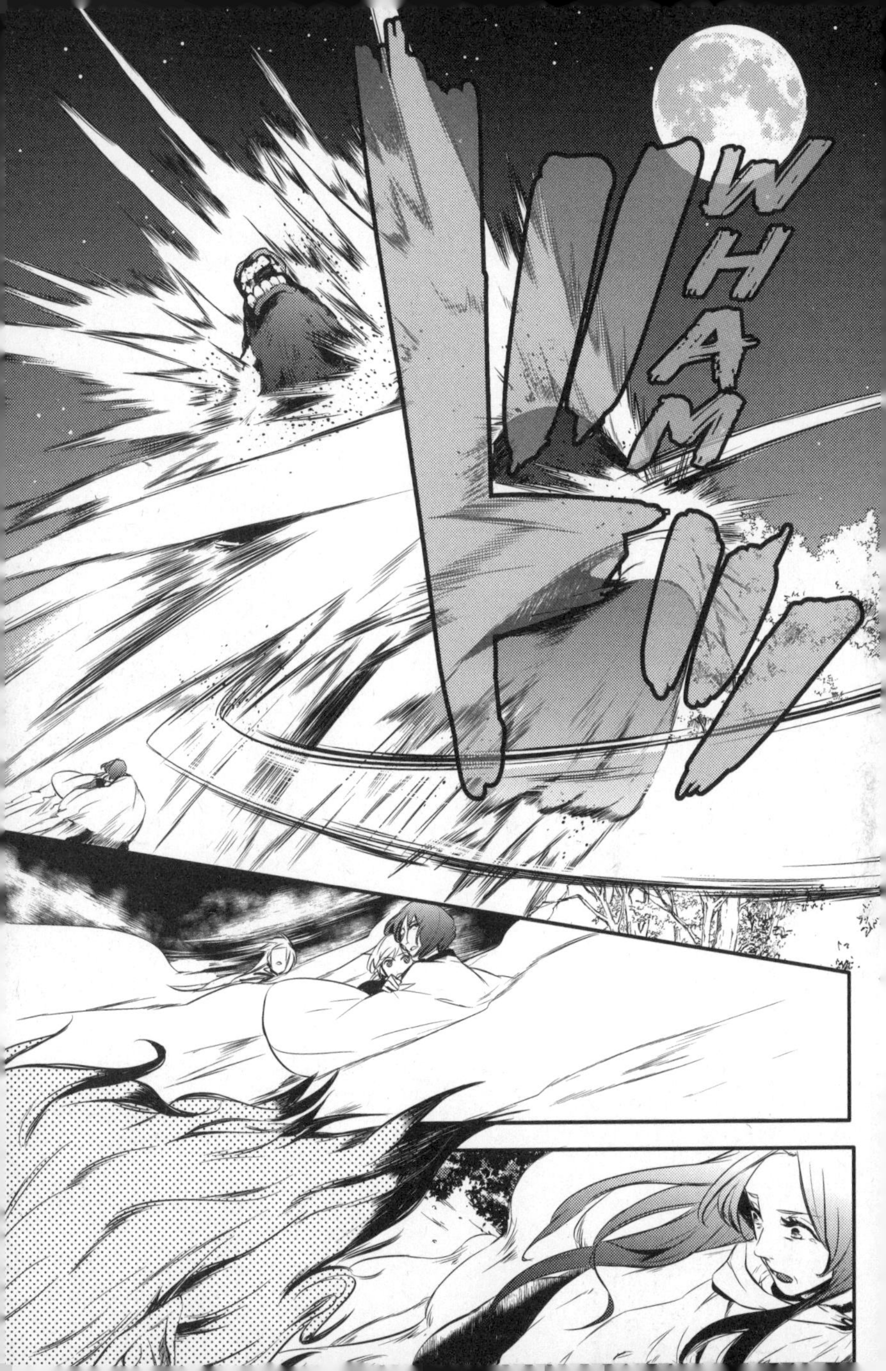
WHAM

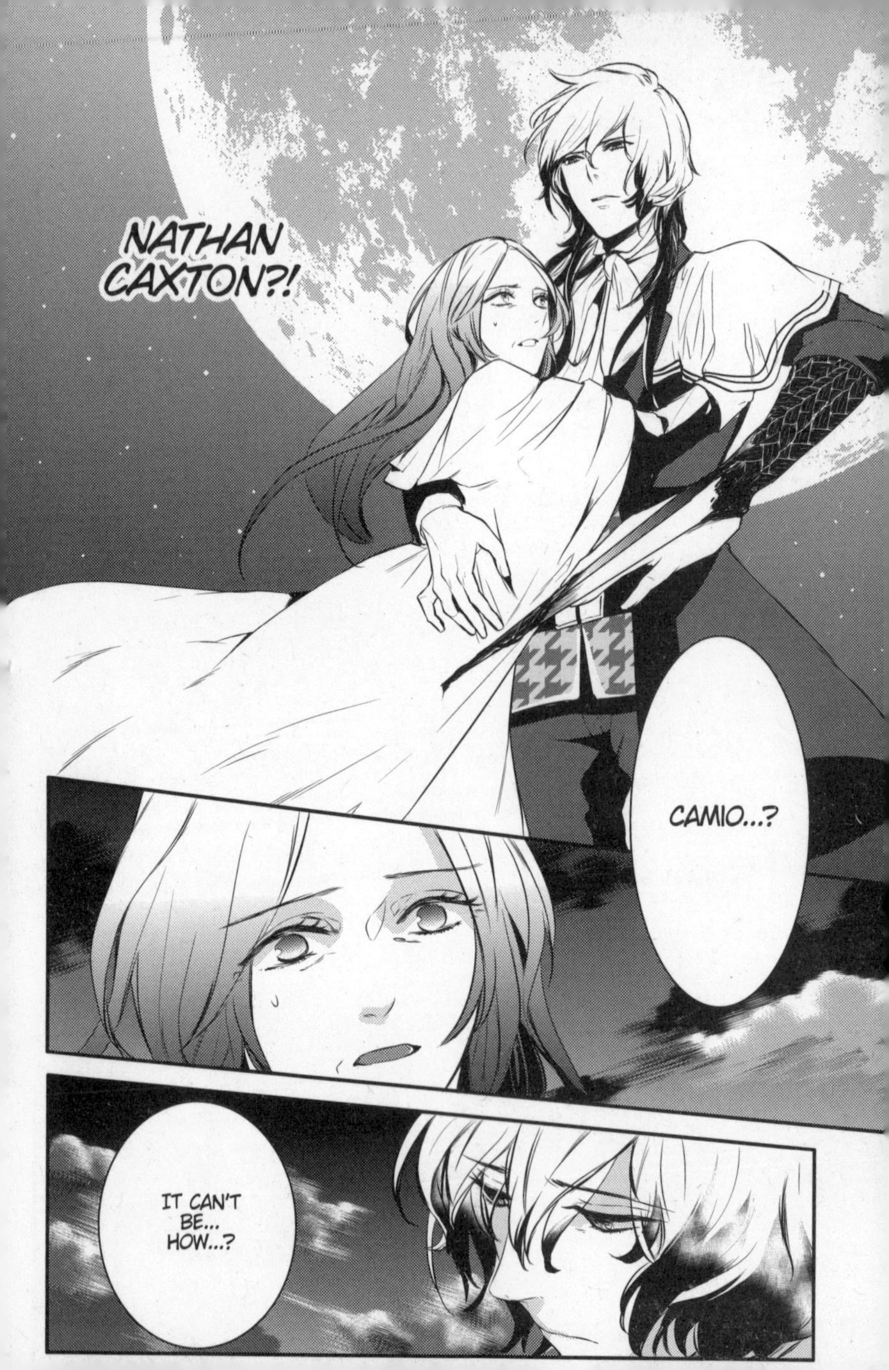
NATHAN CAXTON?!
CAMIO...?
IT CAN'T BE... HOW...?

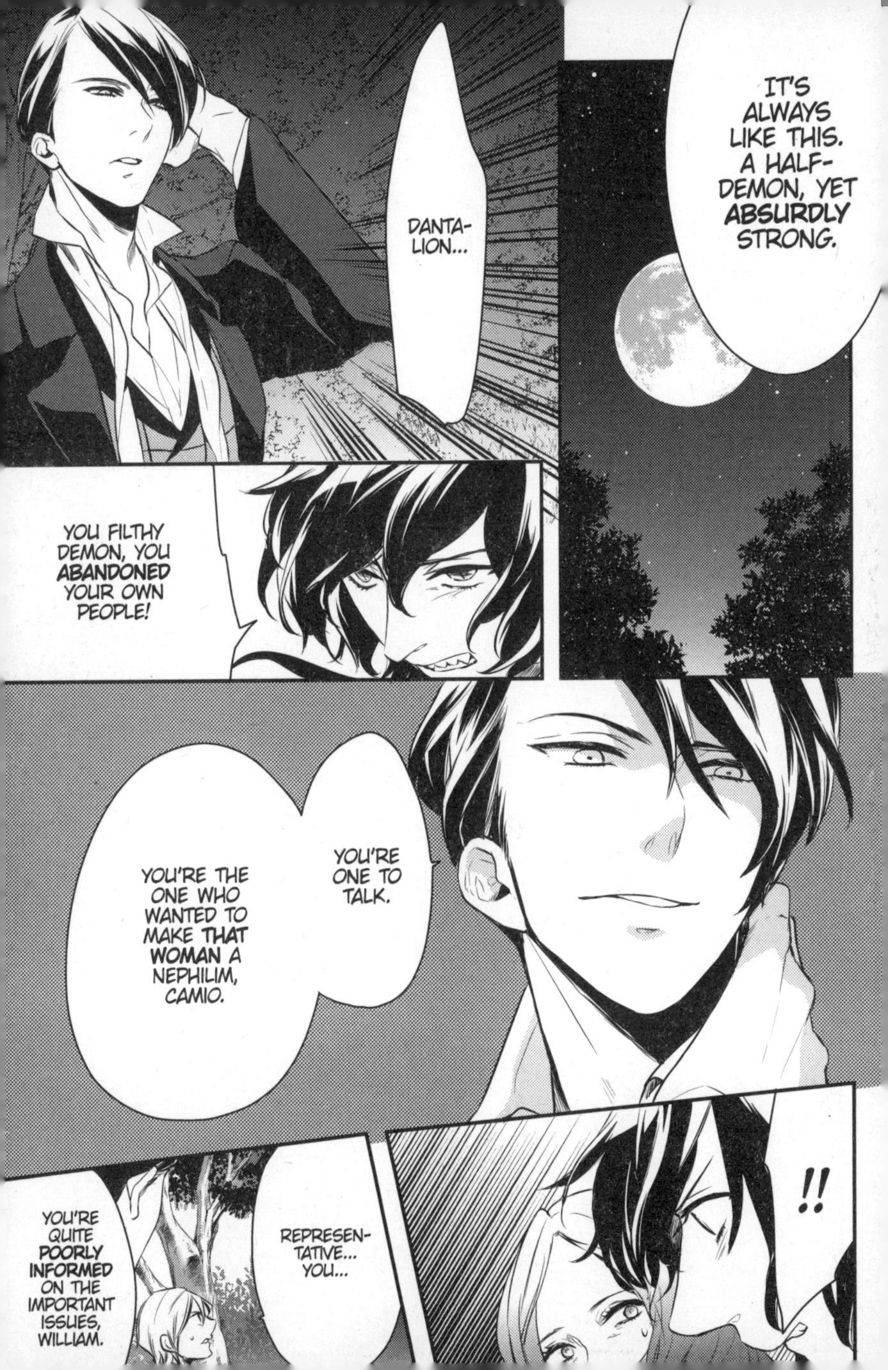
IT'S ALWAYS LIKE THIS. A HALF-DEMON, YET ABSURDLY STRONG.
DANTA-LION...
YOU FILTHY DEMON, YOU ABANDONED YOUR OWN PEOPLE!
YOU'RE ONE TO TALK.
YOU'RE THE ONE WHO WANTED TO MAKE THAT WOMAN A NEPHILIM, CAMIO.
!!
REPRESEN-TATIVE... YOU...
YOU'RE QUITE POORLY INFORMED ON THE IMPORTANT ISSUES, WILLIAM.

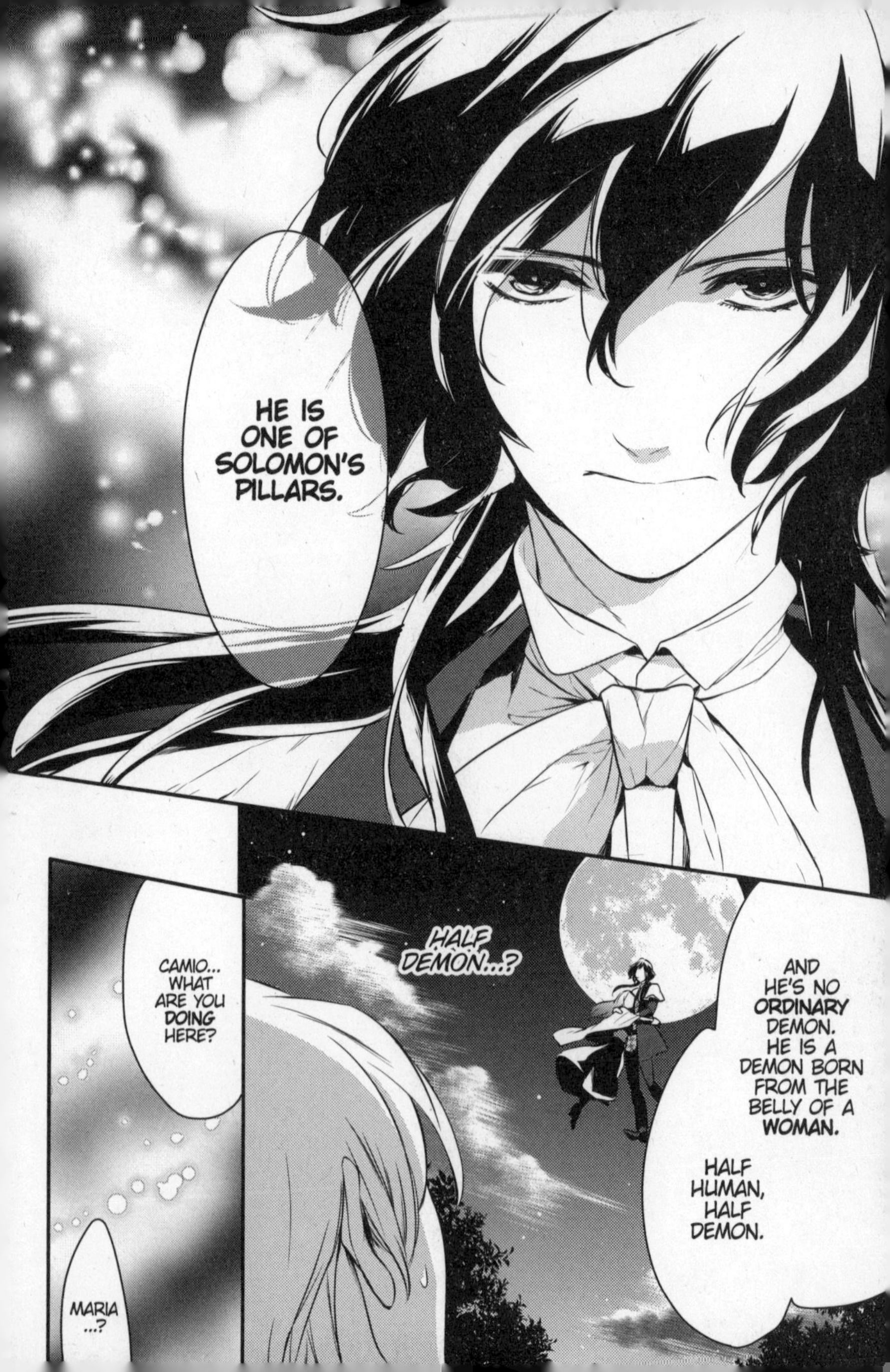
HE IS ONE OF SOLOMON'S PILLARS.
AND HE'S NO ORDINARY DEMON. HE IS A DEMON BORN FROM THE BELLY OF A WOMAN.
HALF HUMAN, HALF DEMON.
HALF DEMON...?
CAMIO... WHAT ARE YOU DOING HERE?
MARIA ...?

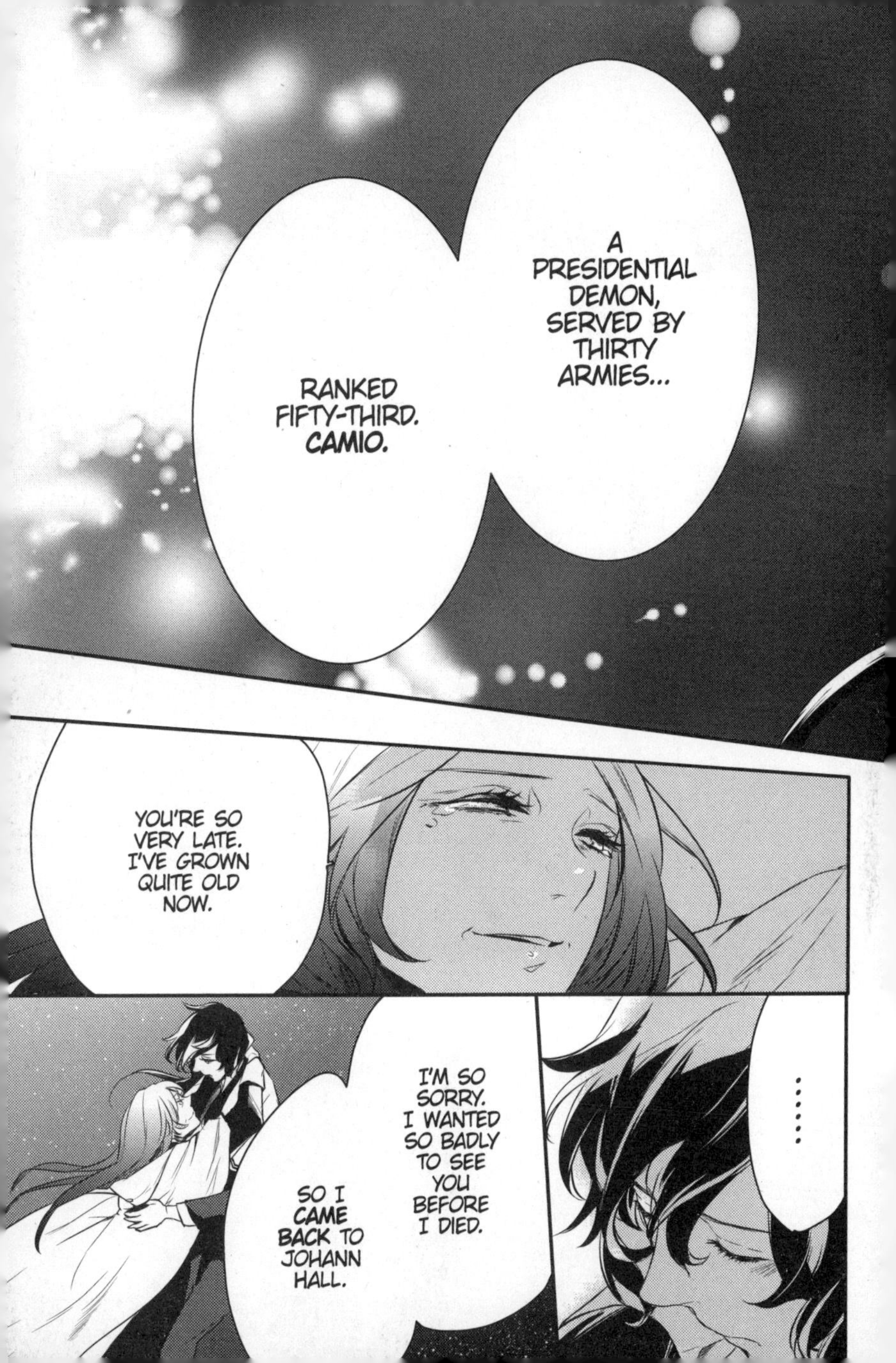
A PRESIDENTIAL DEMON, SERVED BY THIRTY ARMIES...
RANKED FIFTY-THIRD. CAMIO.
YOU'RE SO VERY LATE. I'VE GROWN QUITE OLD NOW.
......
I'M SO SORRY. I WANTED SO BADLY TO SEE YOU BEFORE I DIED.
SO I CAME BACK TO JOHANN HALL.

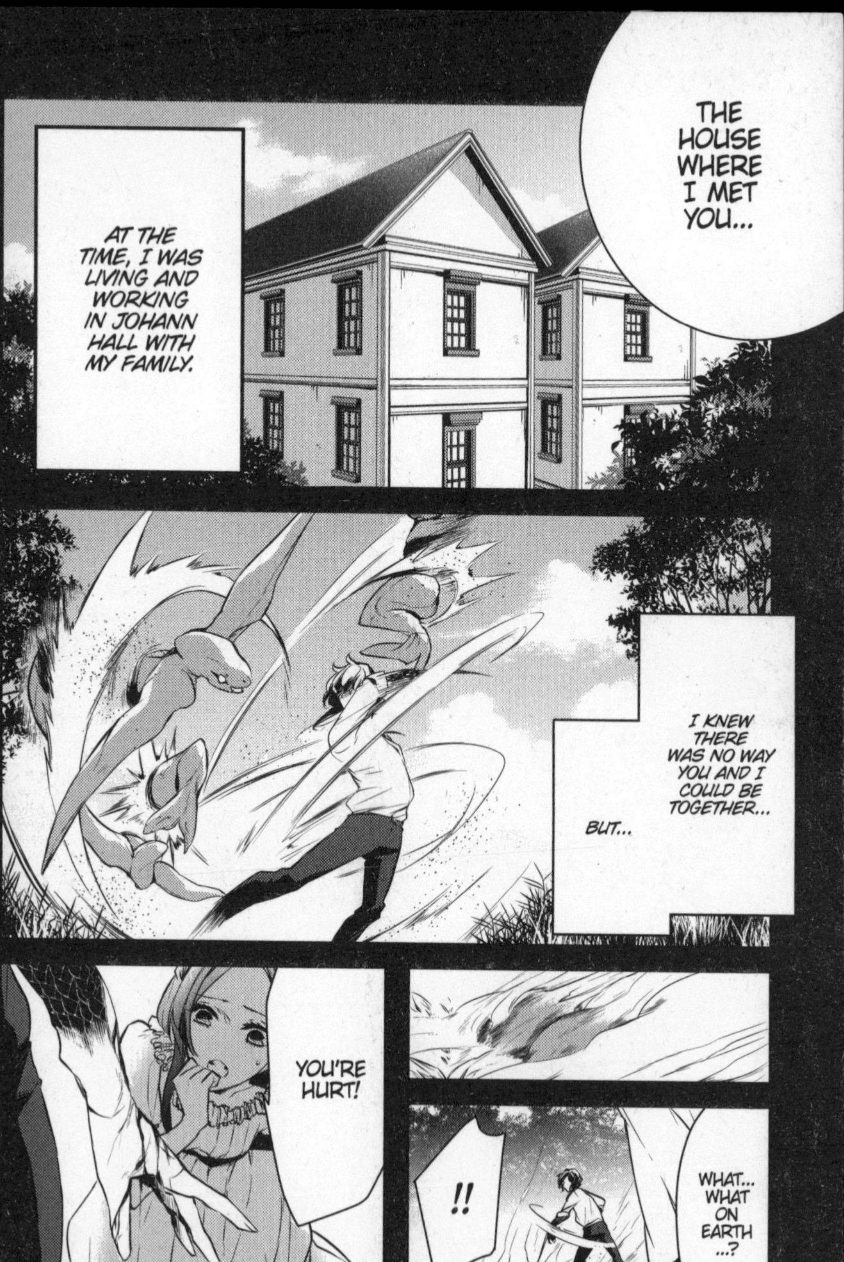
THE HOUSE WHERE I MET YOU...
AT THE TIME, I WAS LIVING AND WORKING IN JOHANN HALL WITH MY FAMILY.
I KNEW THERE WAS NO WAY YOU AND I COULD BE TOGETHER...
BUT...
WHAT... WHAT ON EARTH ...?
!!
YOU'RE HURT!

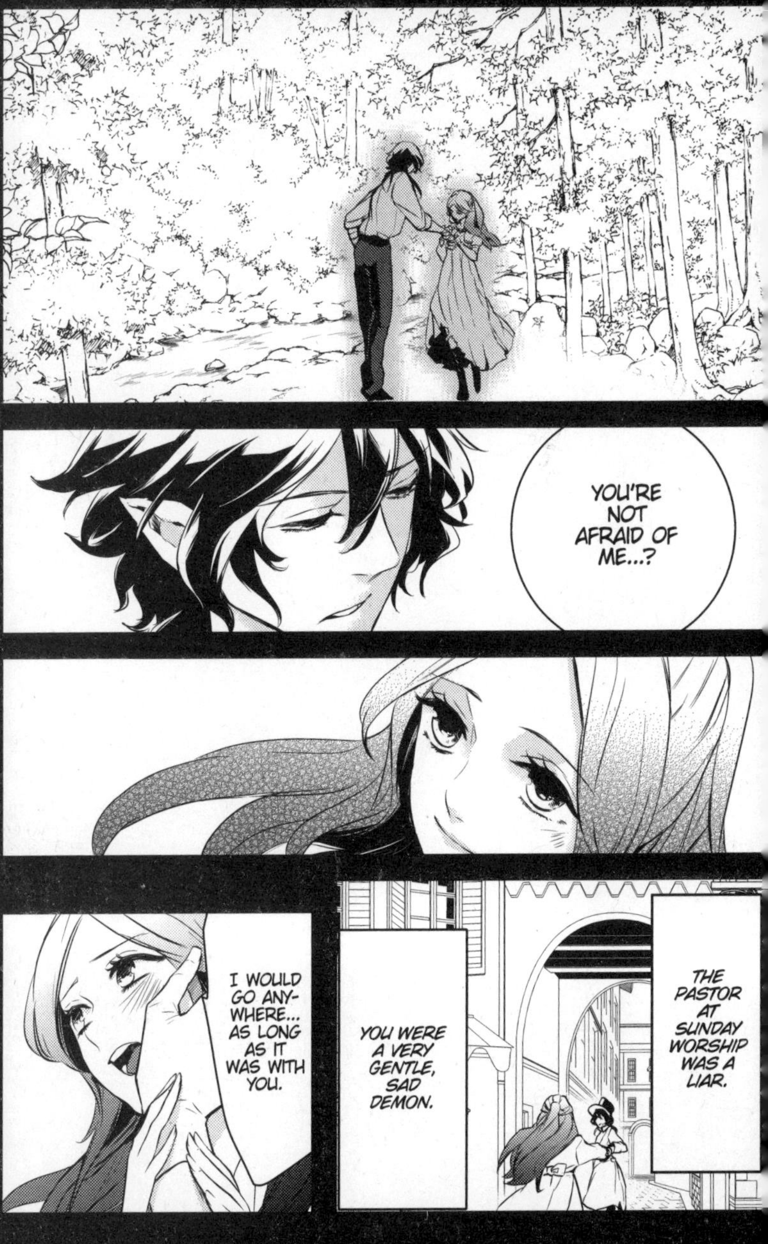
YOU'RE NOT AFRAID OF ME...?
THE PASTOR AT SUNDAY WORSHIP WAS A LIAR.
YOU WERE A VERY GENTLE, SAD DEMON.
I WOULD GO ANYWHERE... AS LONG AS IT WAS WITH YOU.

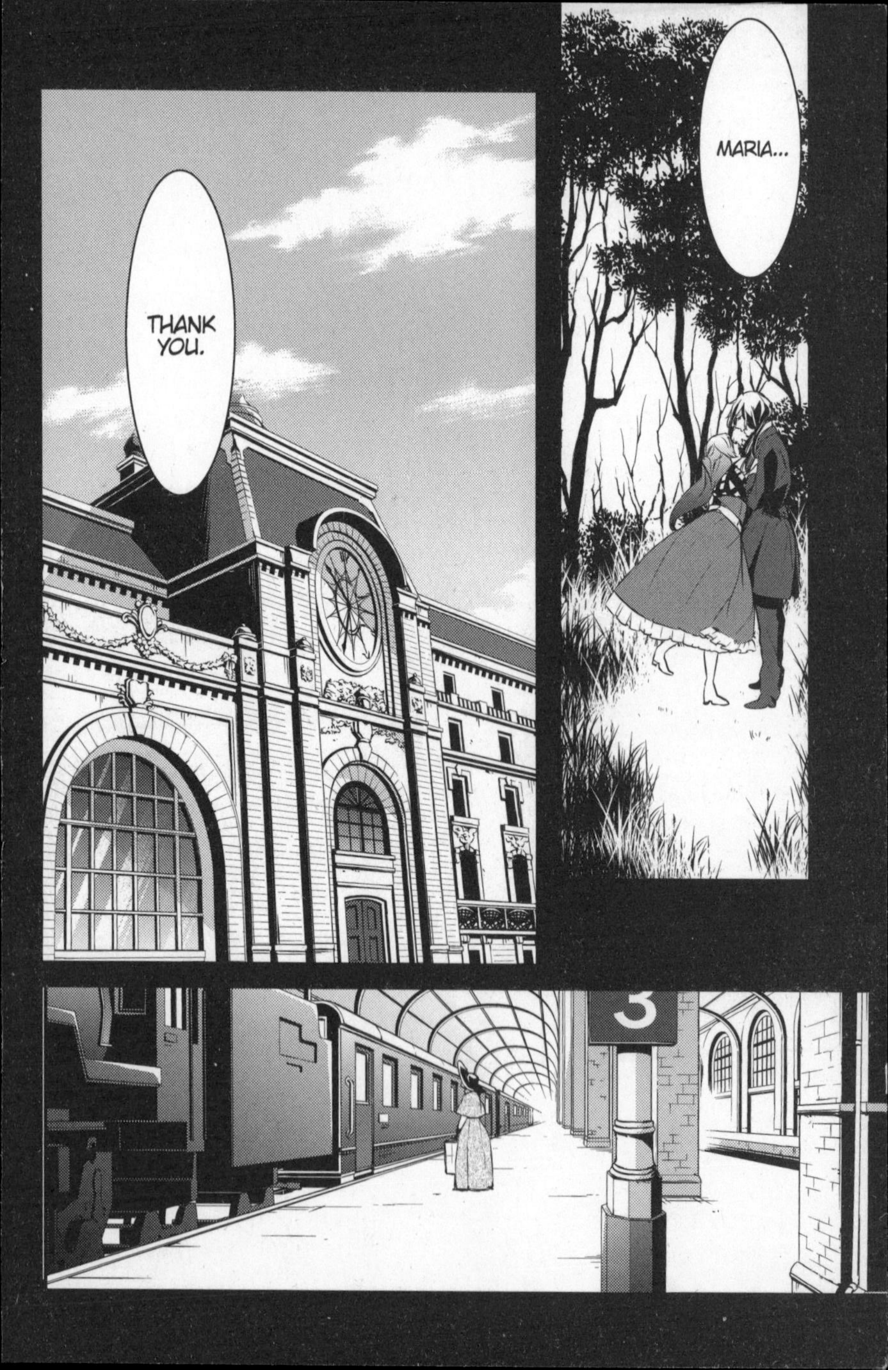
MARIA...
THANK YOU.

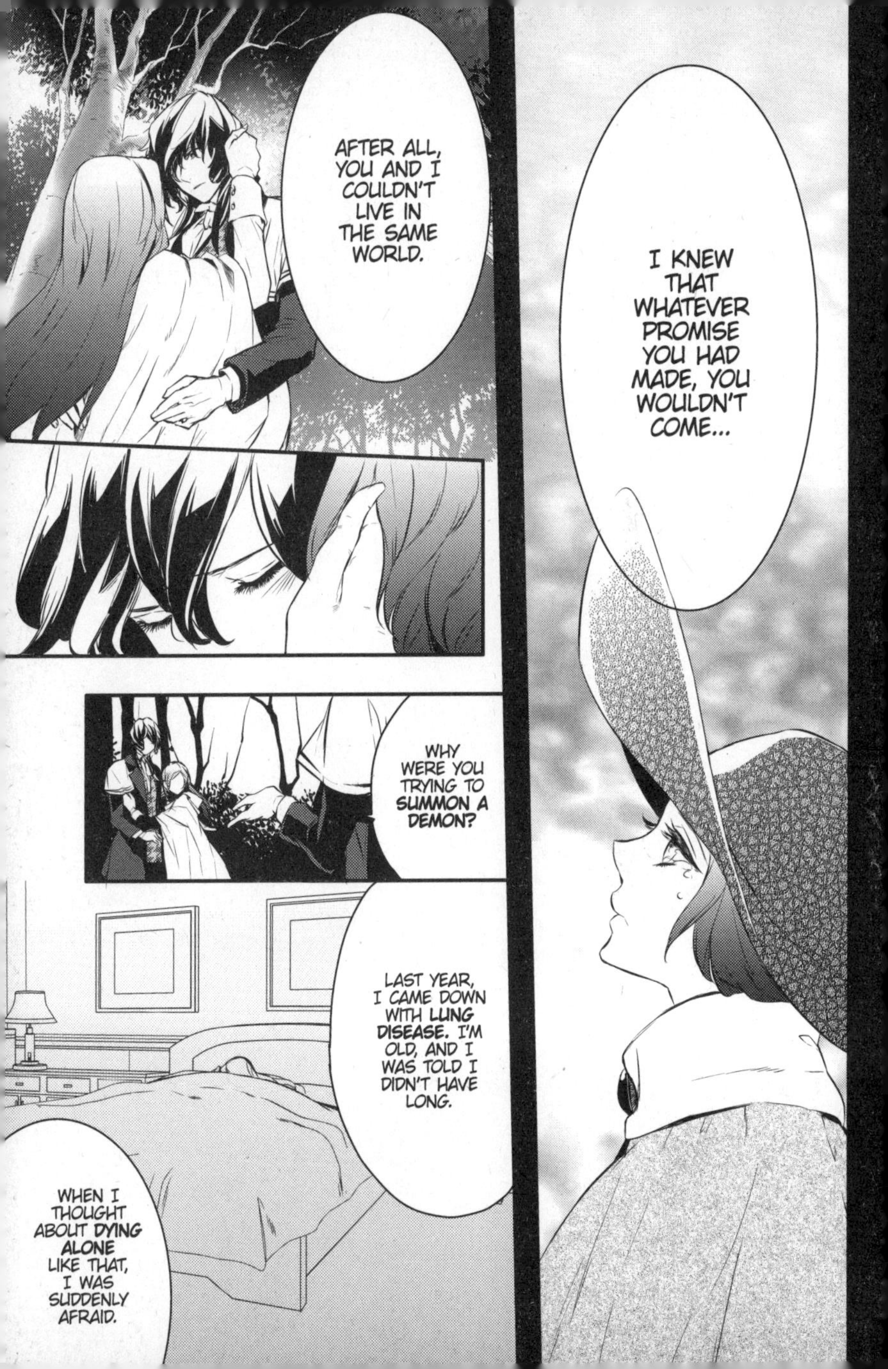
I KNEW THAT WHATEVER PROMISE YOU HAD MADE, YOU WOULDN'T COME...
AFTER ALL, YOU AND I COULDN'T LIVE IN THE SAME WORLD.
WHY WERE YOU TRYING TO SUMMON A DEMON?
LAST YEAR, I CAME DOWN WITH LUNG DISEASE. I'M OLD, AND I WAS TOLD I DIDN'T HAVE LONG.
WHEN I THOUGHT ABOUT DYING ALONE LIKE THAT, I WAS SUDDENLY AFRAID.

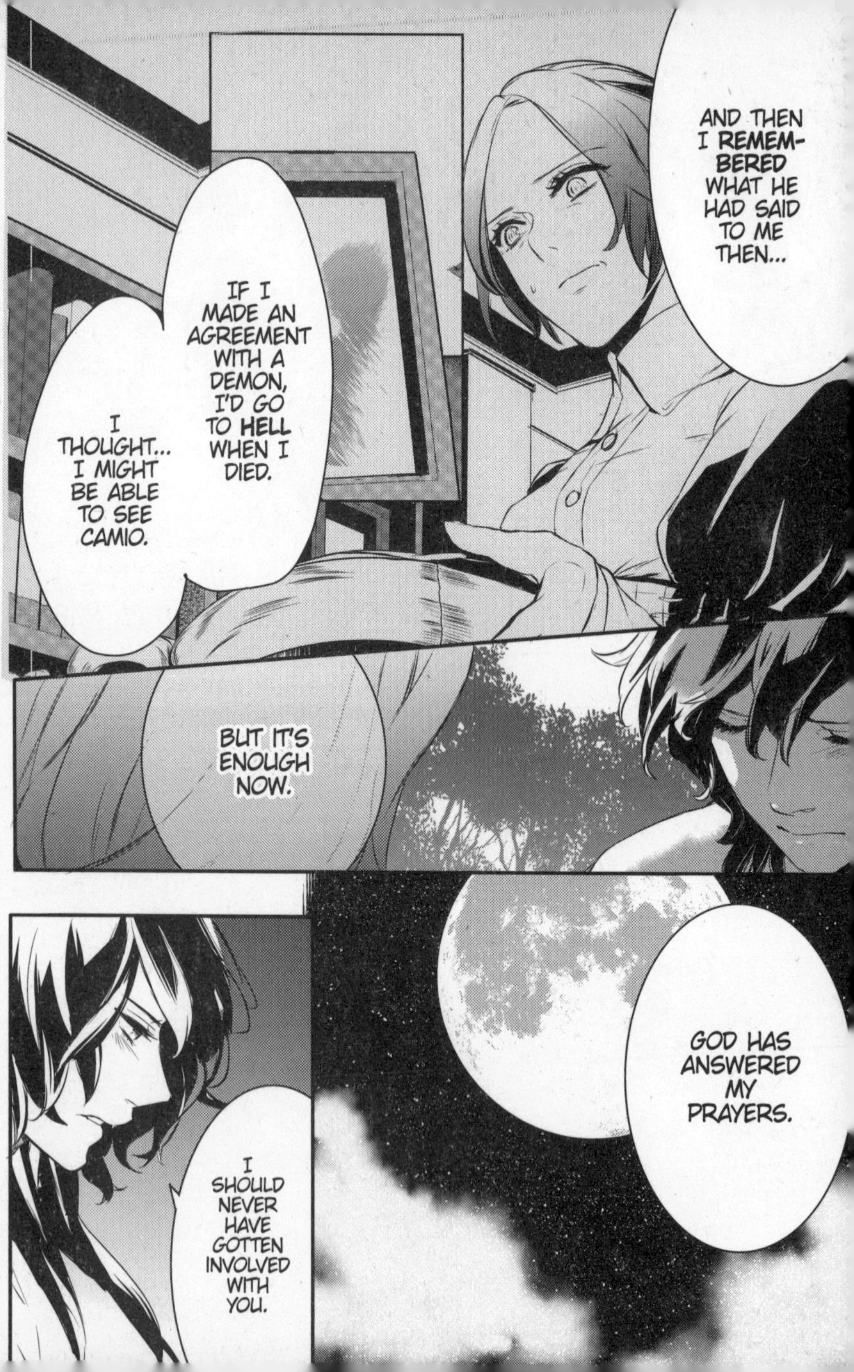
AND THEN I REMEMBERED WHAT HE HAD SAID TO ME THEN...
IF I MADE AN AGREEMENT WITH A DEMON, I'D GO TO HELL WHEN I DIED.
I THOUGHT... I MIGHT BE ABLE TO SEE CAMIO.
BUT IT'S ENOUGH NOW.
GOD HAS ANSWERED MY PRAYERS.
I SHOULD NEVER HAVE GOTTEN INVOLVED WITH YOU.

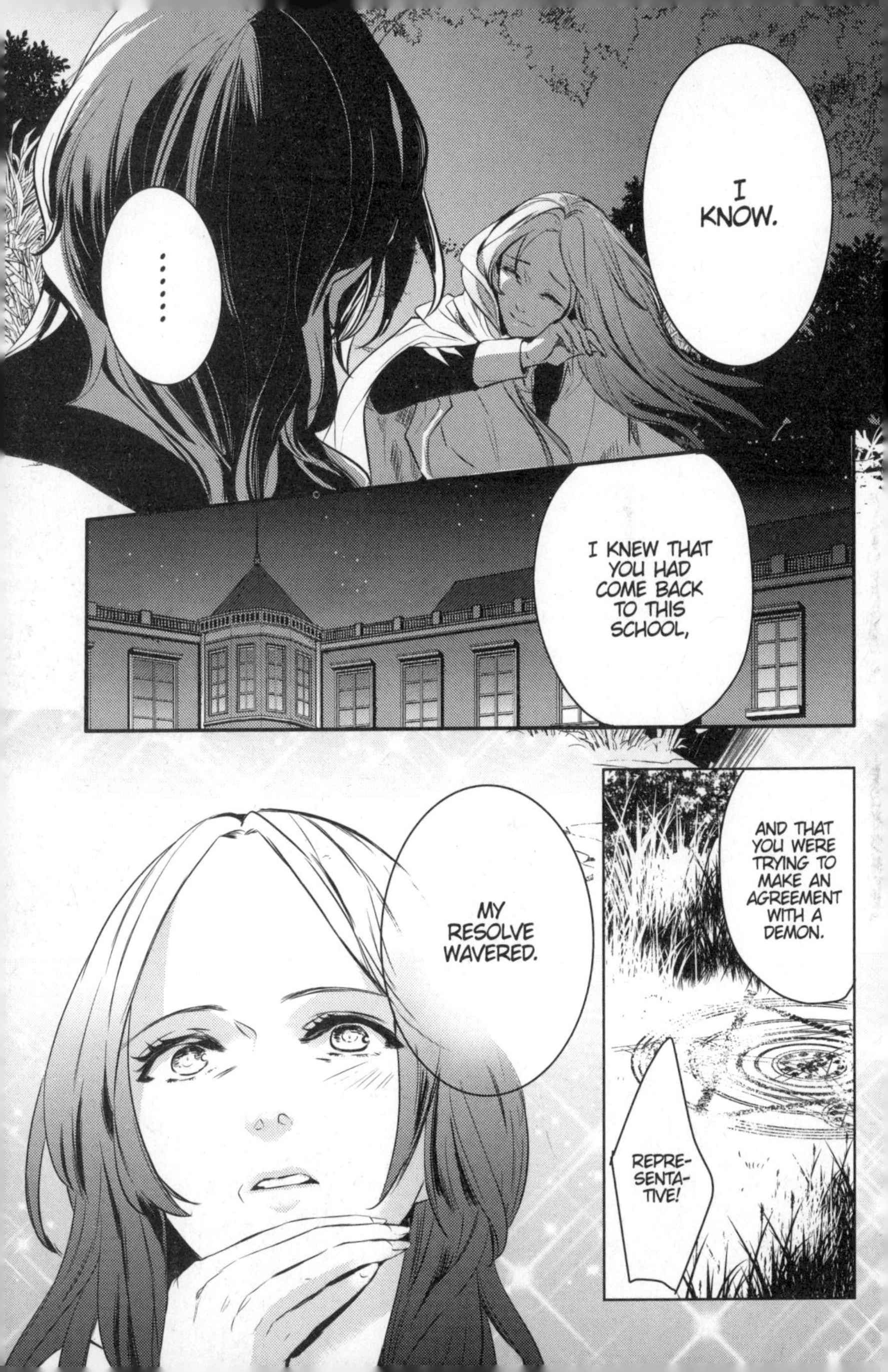
I KNOW.
……
I KNEW THAT YOU HAD COME BACK TO THIS SCHOOL,
AND THAT YOU WERE TRYING TO MAKE AN AGREEMENT WITH A DEMON.
REPRE-SENTA-TIVE!
MY RESOLVE WAVERED.

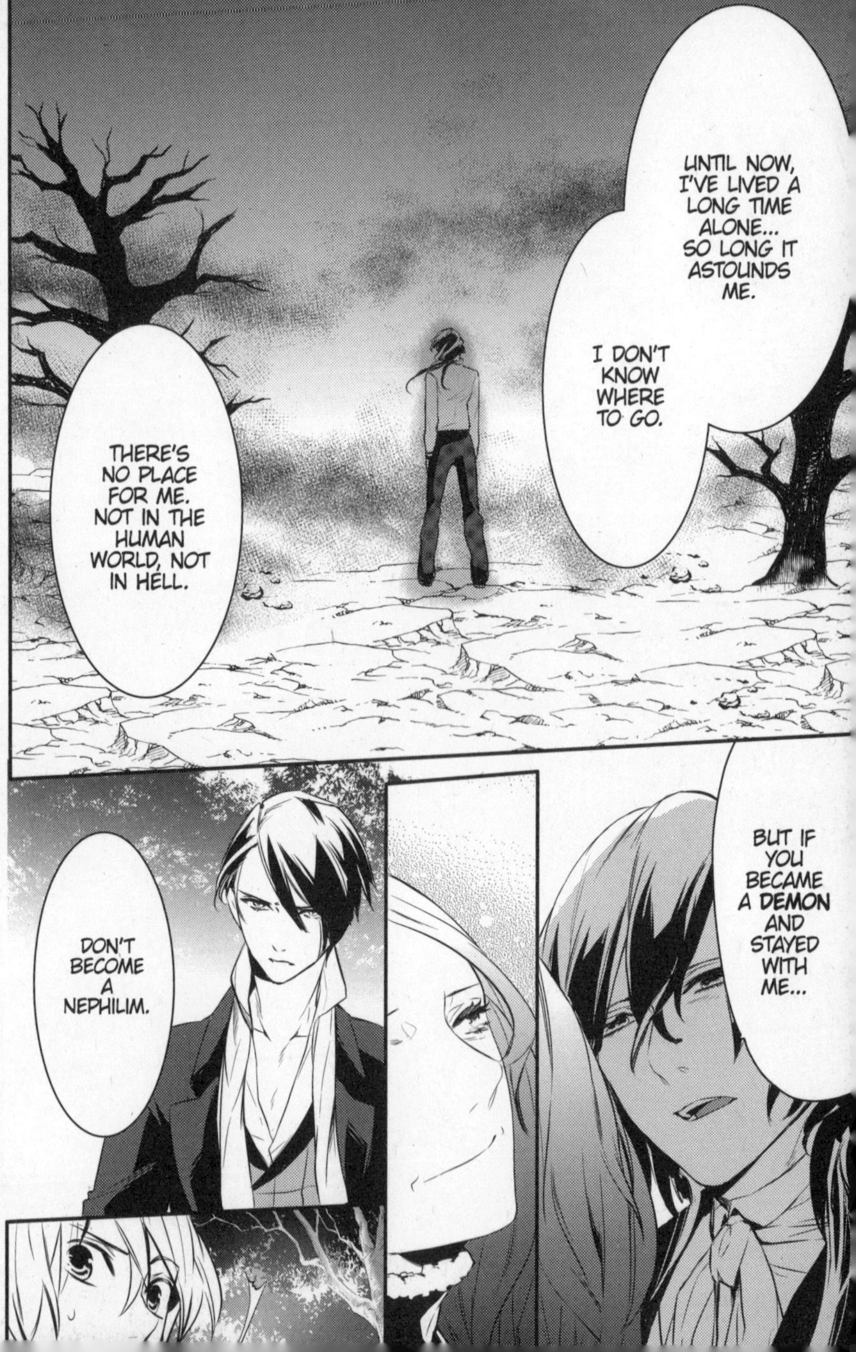
UNTIL NOW, I'VE LIVED A LONG TIME ALONE... SO LONG IT ASTOUNDS ME.
I DON'T KNOW WHERE TO GO.
THERE'S NO PLACE FOR ME. NOT IN THE HUMAN WORLD, NOT IN HELL.
BUT IF YOU BECAME A DEMON AND STAYED WITH ME...
DON'T BECOME A NEPHILIM.

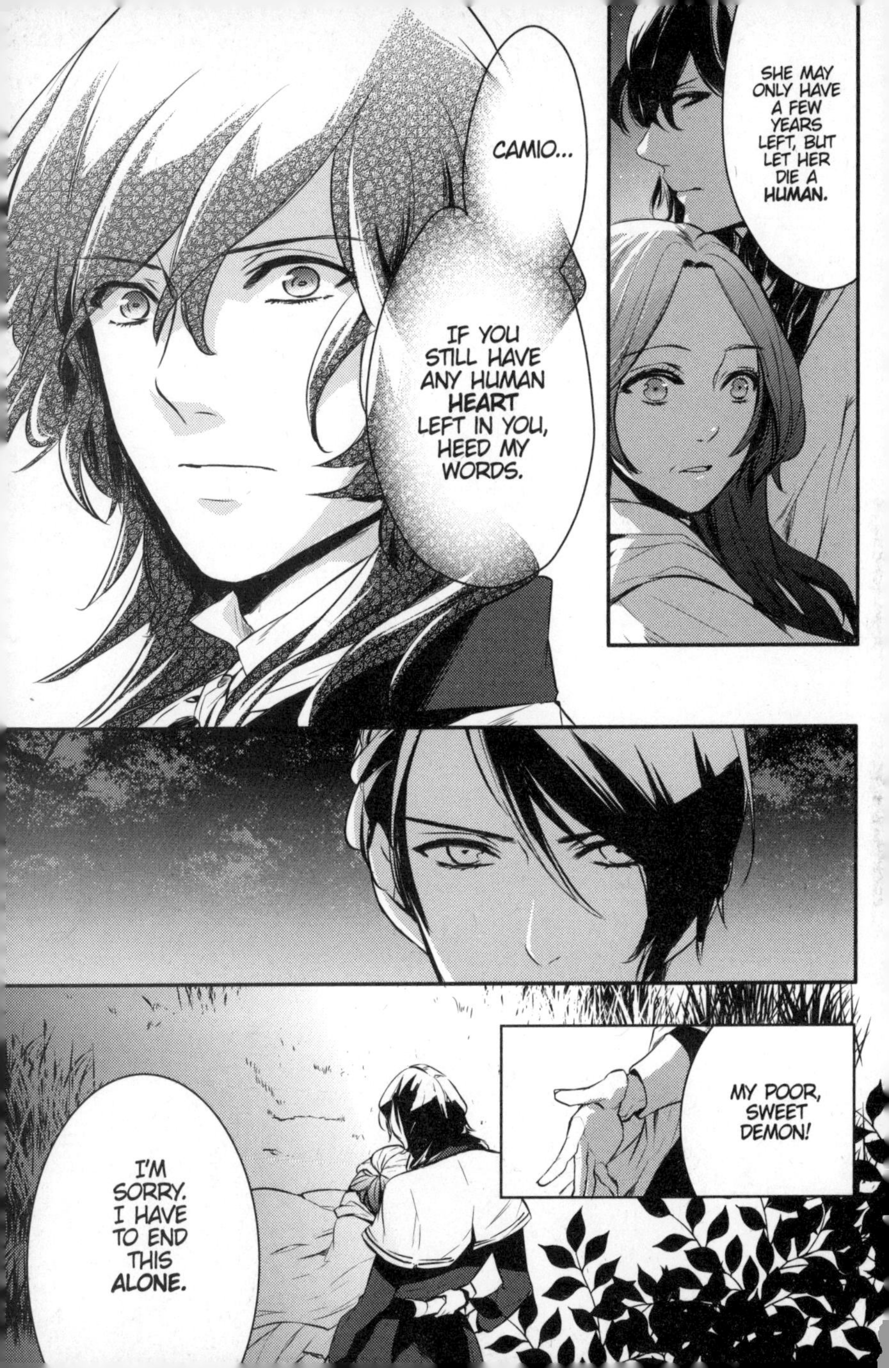
SHE MAY ONLY HAVE A FEW YEARS LEFT, BUT LET HER DIE A HUMAN.
CAMIO...
IF YOU STILL HAVE ANY HUMAN HEART LEFT IN YOU, HEED MY WORDS.
MY POOR, SWEET DEMON!
I'M SORRY. I HAVE TO END THIS ALONE.

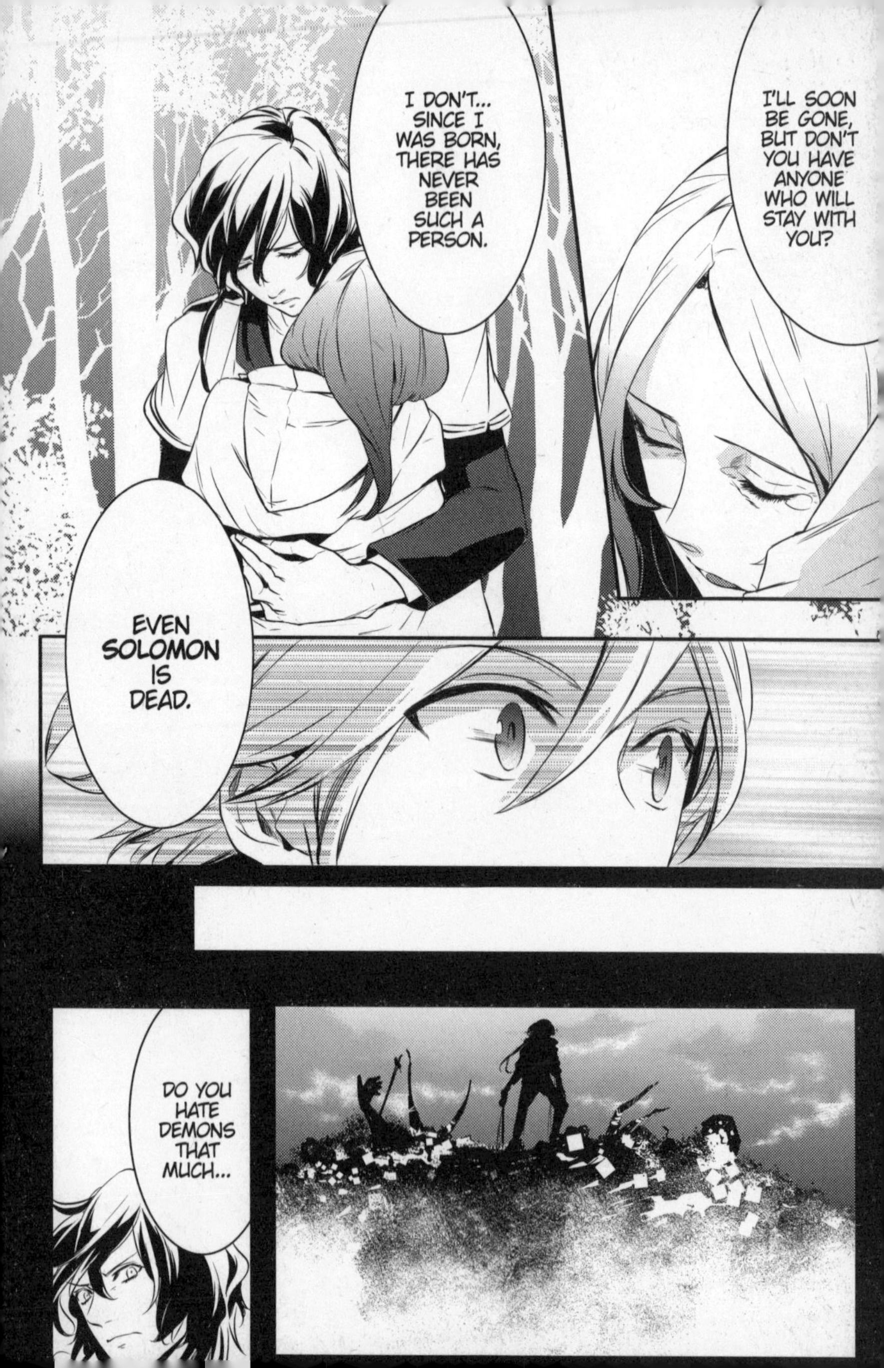
I'LL SOON BE GONE, BUT DON'T YOU HAVE ANYONE WHO WILL STAY WITH YOU?
I DON'T... SINCE I WAS BORN, THERE HAS NEVER BEEN SUCH A PERSON.
EVEN SOLOMON IS DEAD.
DO YOU HATE DEMONS THAT MUCH...

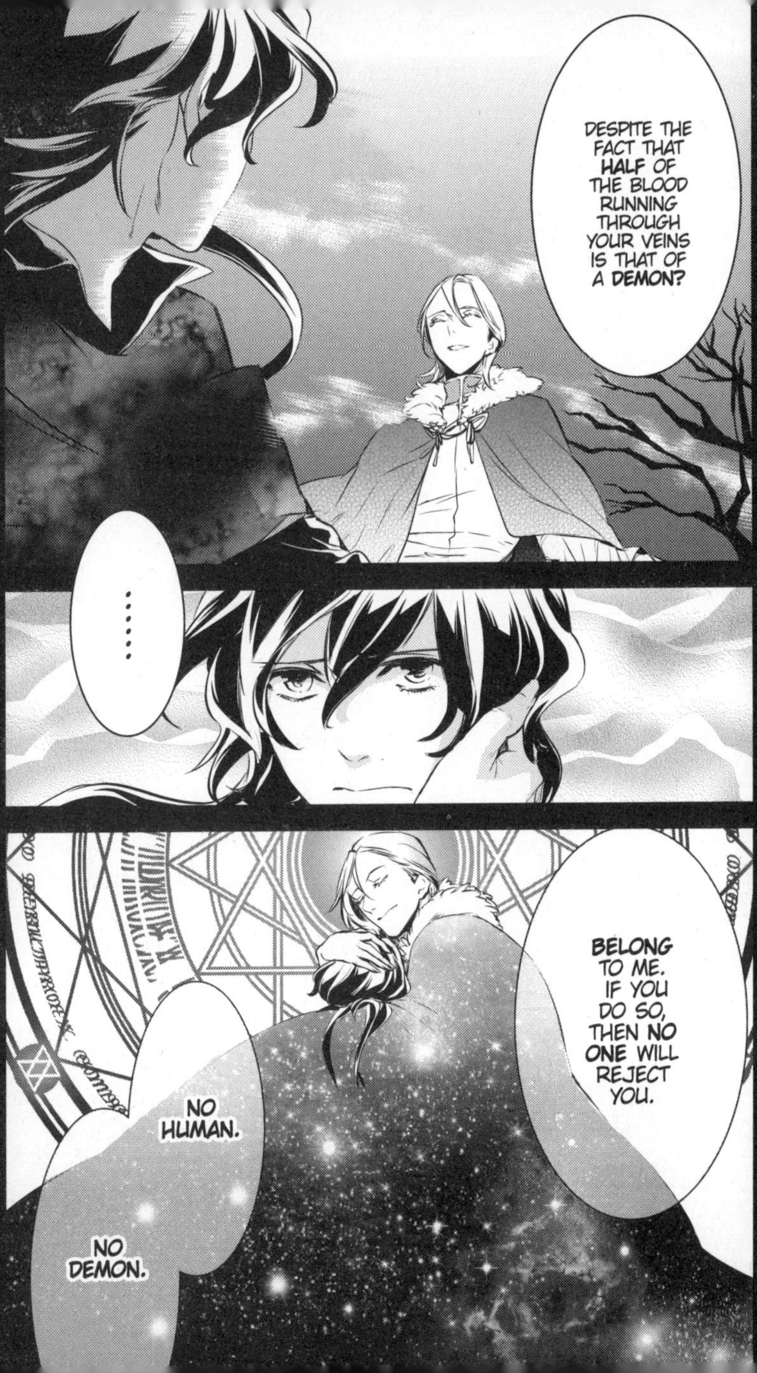
DESPITE THE FACT THAT HALF OF THE BLOOD RUNNING THROUGH YOUR VEINS IS THAT OF A DEMON?
......
BELONG TO ME. IF YOU DO SO, THEN NO ONE WILL REJECT YOU.
NO HUMAN.
NO DEMON.

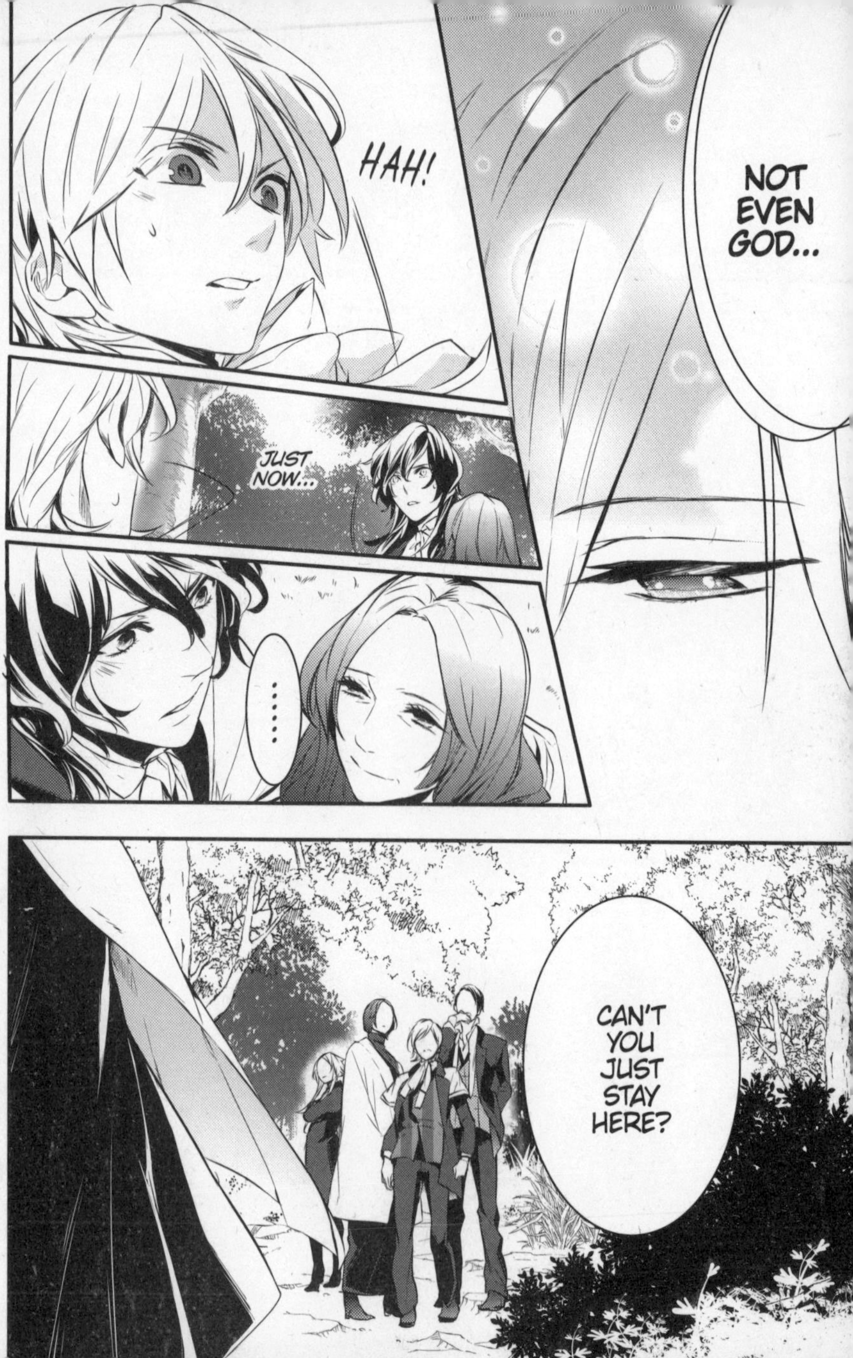
NOT EVEN GOD...
HAH!
JUST NOW...
......
CAN'T YOU JUST STAY HERE?

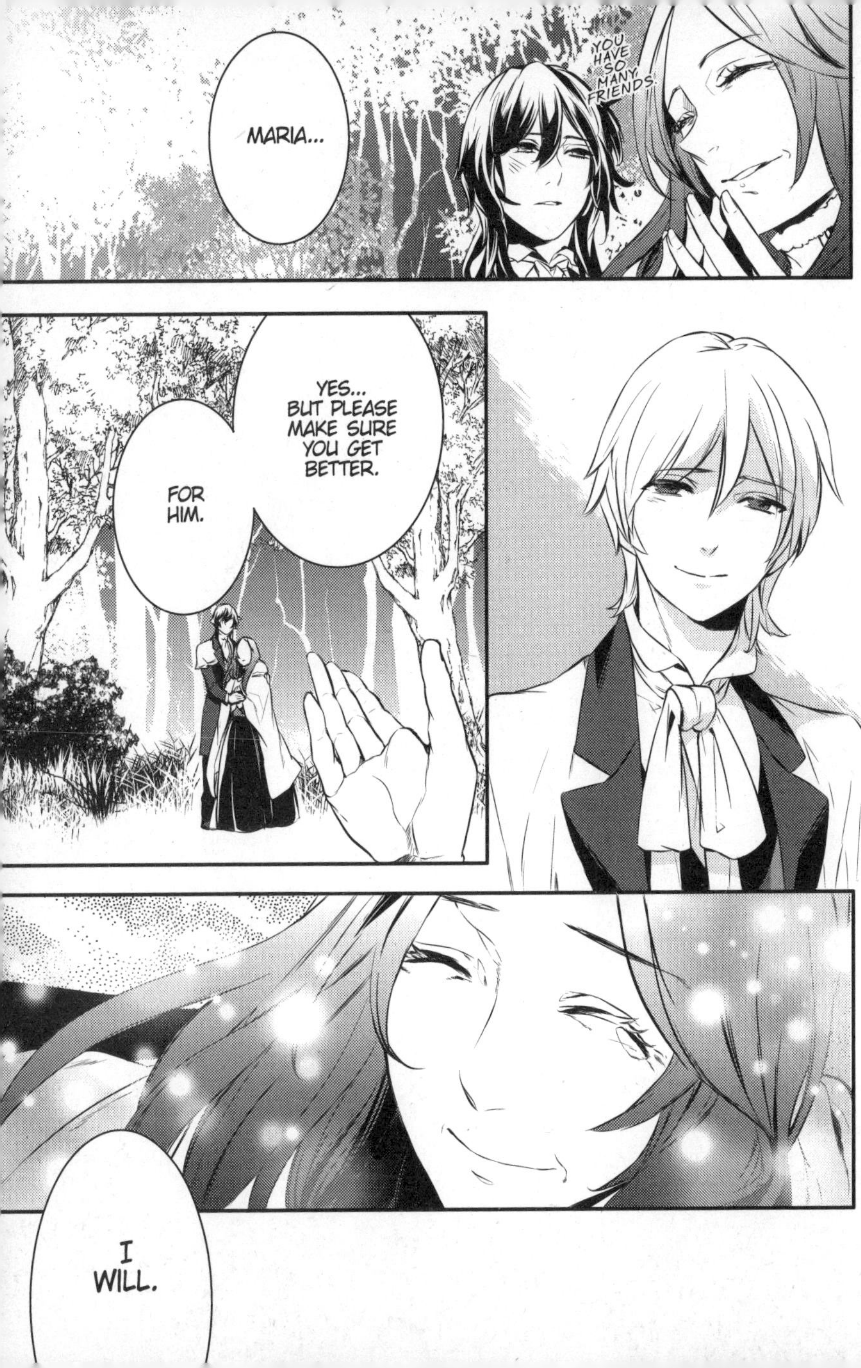
YOU HAVE SO MANY FRIENDS.
MARIA...
YES... BUT PLEASE MAKE SURE YOU GET BETTER.
FOR HIM.
I WILL.

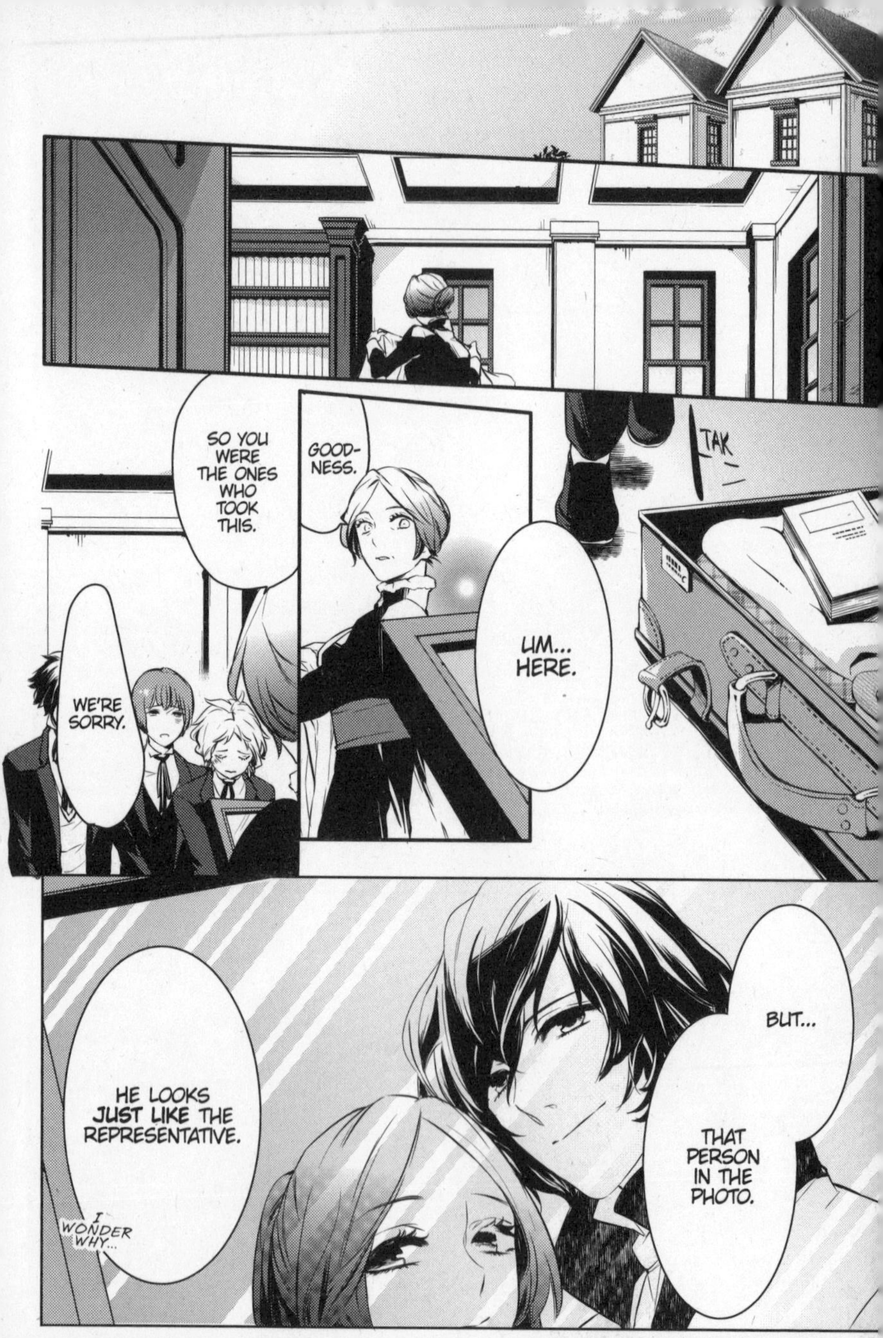
TAK
UM... HERE.
GOODNESS.
SO YOU WERE THE ONES WHO TOOK THIS.
WE'RE SORRY.
BUT...
THAT PERSON IN THE PHOTO.
HE LOOKS JUST LIKE THE REPRESENTATIVE.
I WONDER WHY...

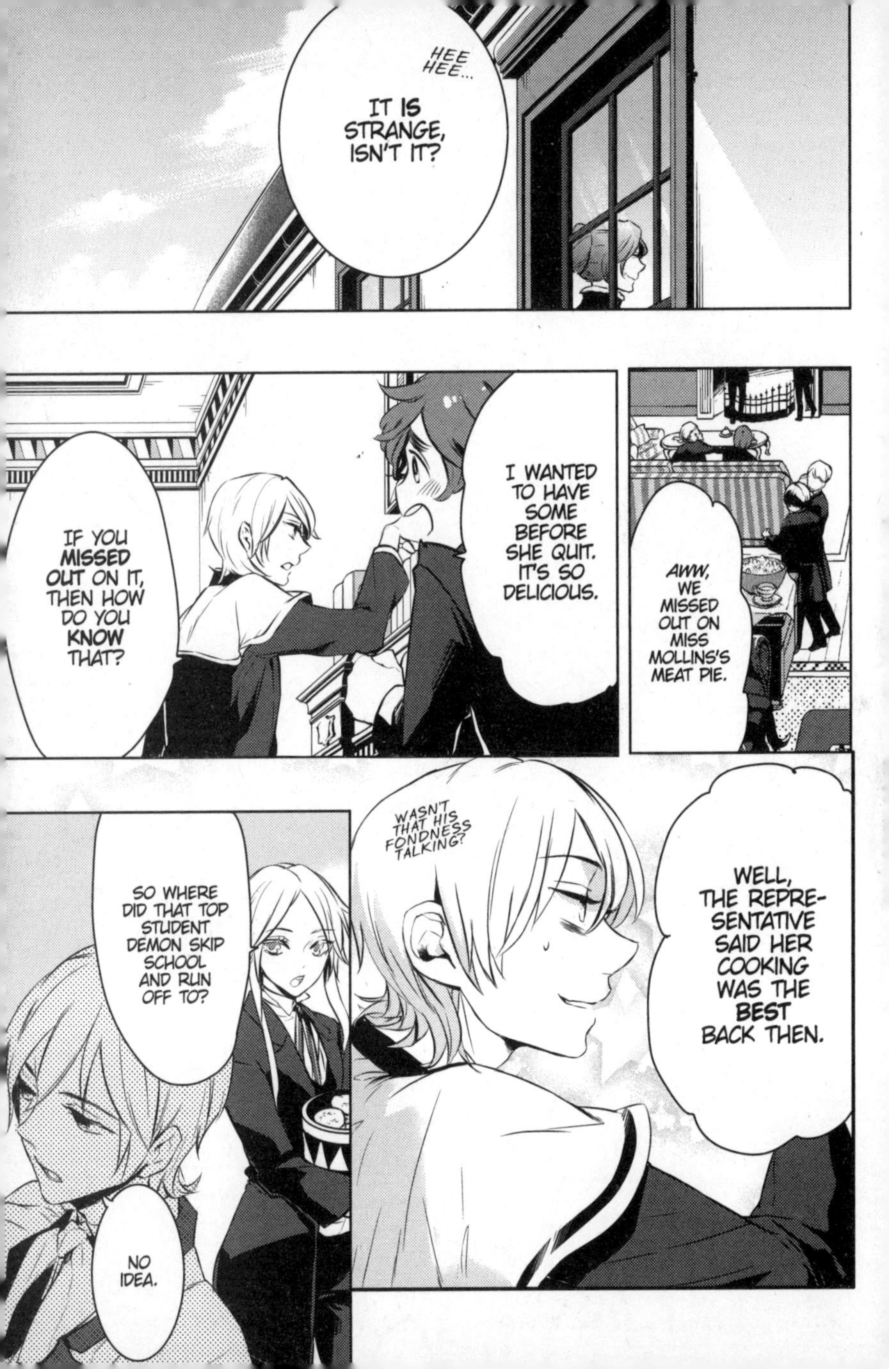
HEE HEE...
IT IS STRANGE, ISN'T IT?
AWW, WE MISSED OUT ON MISS MOLLINS'S MEAT PIE.
I WANTED TO HAVE SOME BEFORE SHE QUIT. IT'S SO DELICIOUS.
IF YOU MISSED OUT ON IT, THEN HOW DO YOU KNOW THAT?
WELL, THE REPRE-SENTATIVE SAID HER COOKING WAS THE BEST BACK THEN.
WASN'T THAT HIS FONDNESS TALKING?
SO WHERE DID THAT TOP STUDENT DEMON SKIP SCHOOL AND RUN OFF TO?
NO IDEA.

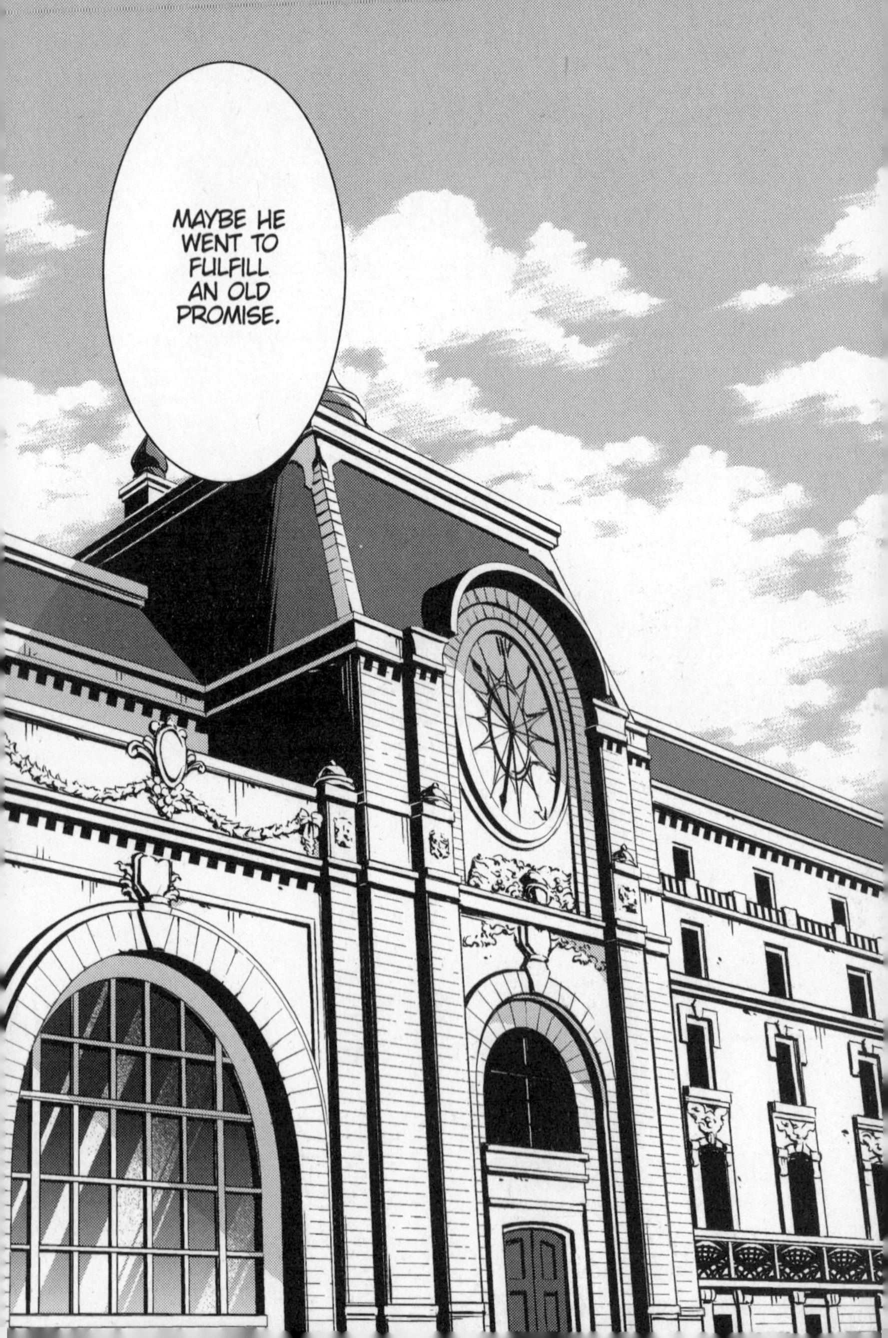
MAYBE HE WENT TO FULFILL AN OLD PROMISE.

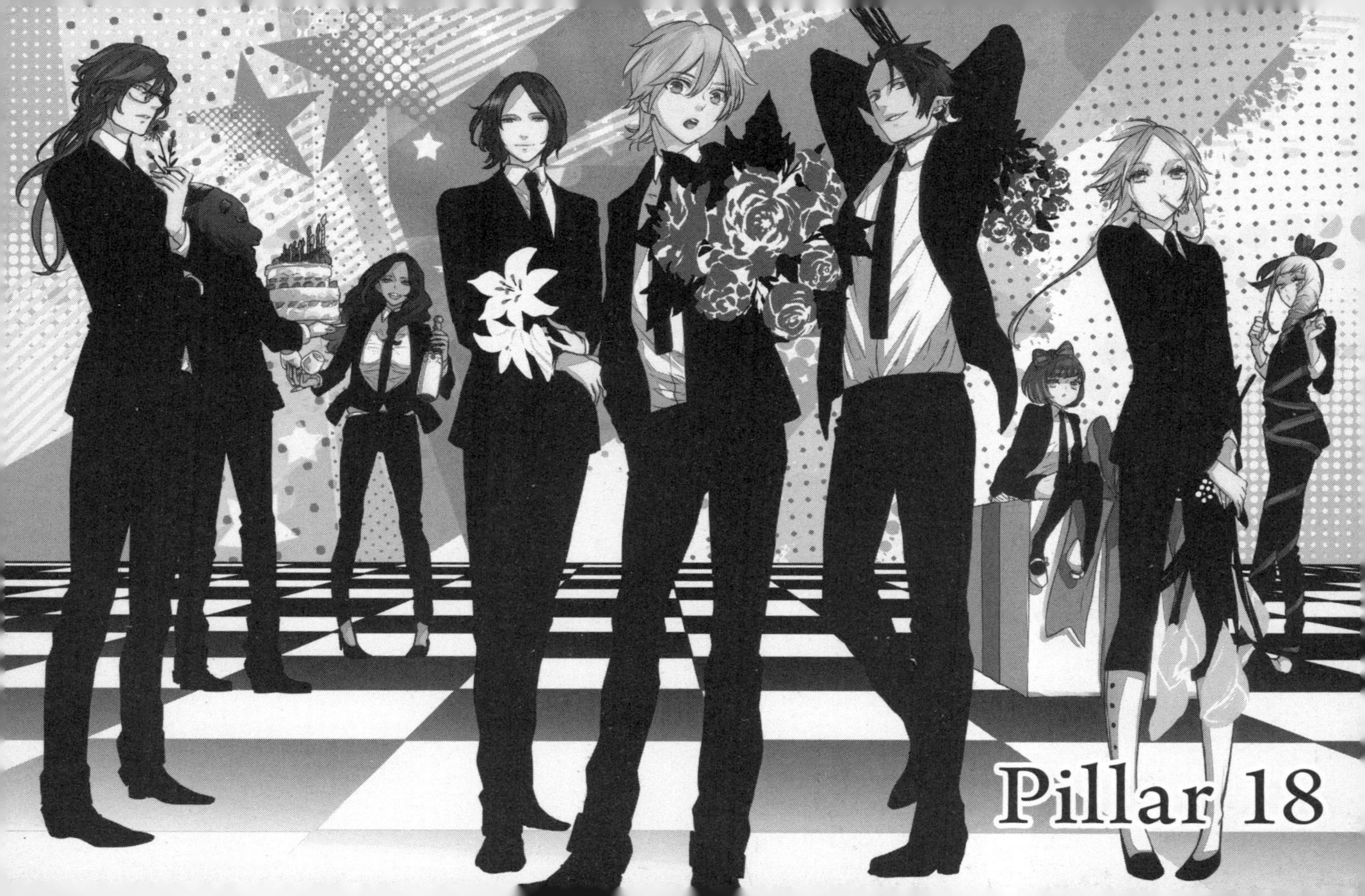
Pillar 18

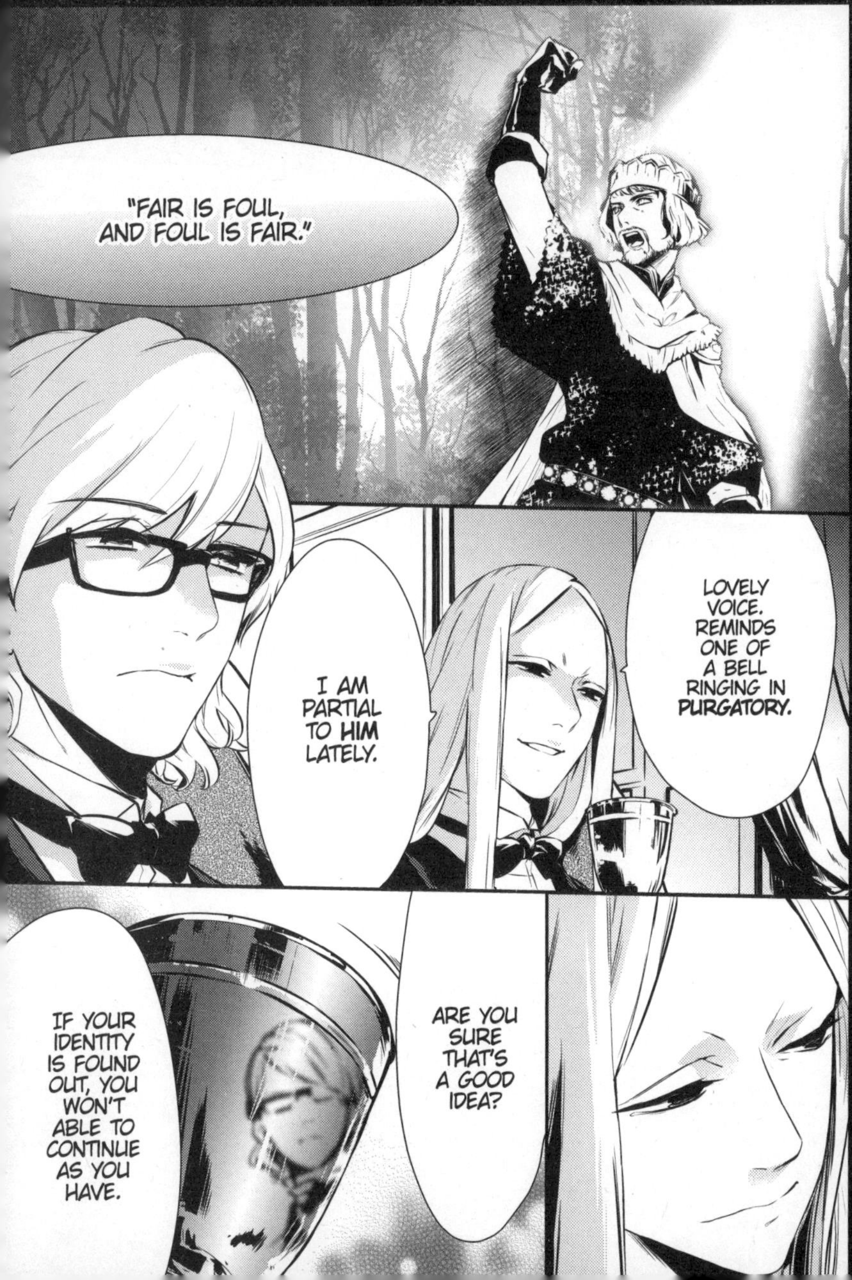
"FAIR IS FOUL, AND FOUL IS FAIR."
LOVELY VOICE. REMINDS ONE OF A BELL RINGING IN PURGATORY.
I AM PARTIAL TO HIM LATELY.
ARE YOU SURE THAT'S A GOOD IDEA?
IF YOUR IDENTITY IS FOUND OUT, YOU WON'T ABLE TO CONTINUE AS YOU HAVE.

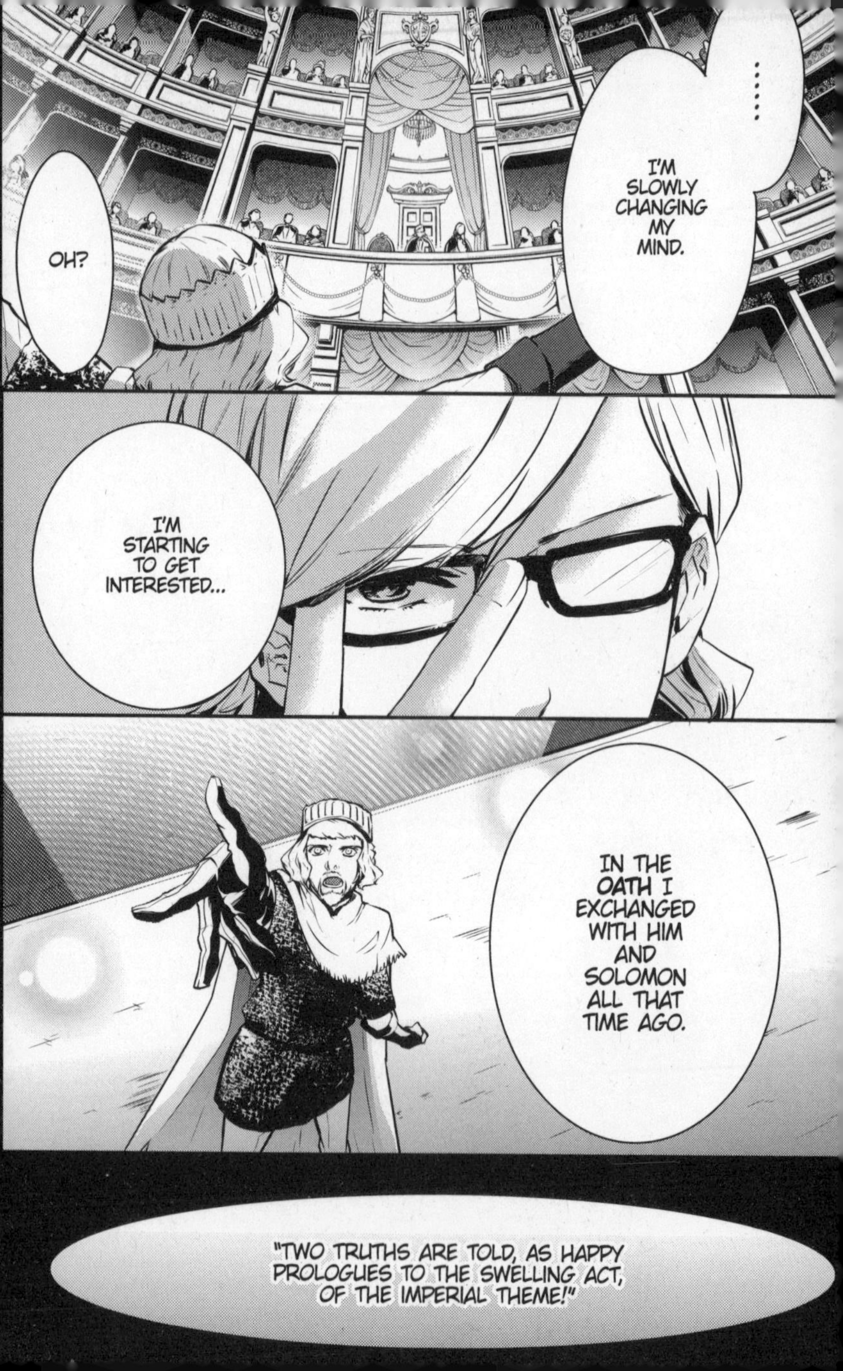
......
I'M SLOWLY CHANGING MY MIND.
OH?
I'M STARTING TO GET INTERESTED...
IN THE OATH I EXCHANGED WITH HIM AND SOLOMON ALL THAT TIME AGO.
"TWO TRUTHS ARE TOLD, AS HAPPY PROLOGUES TO THE SWELLING ACT, OF THE IMPERIAL THEME!"

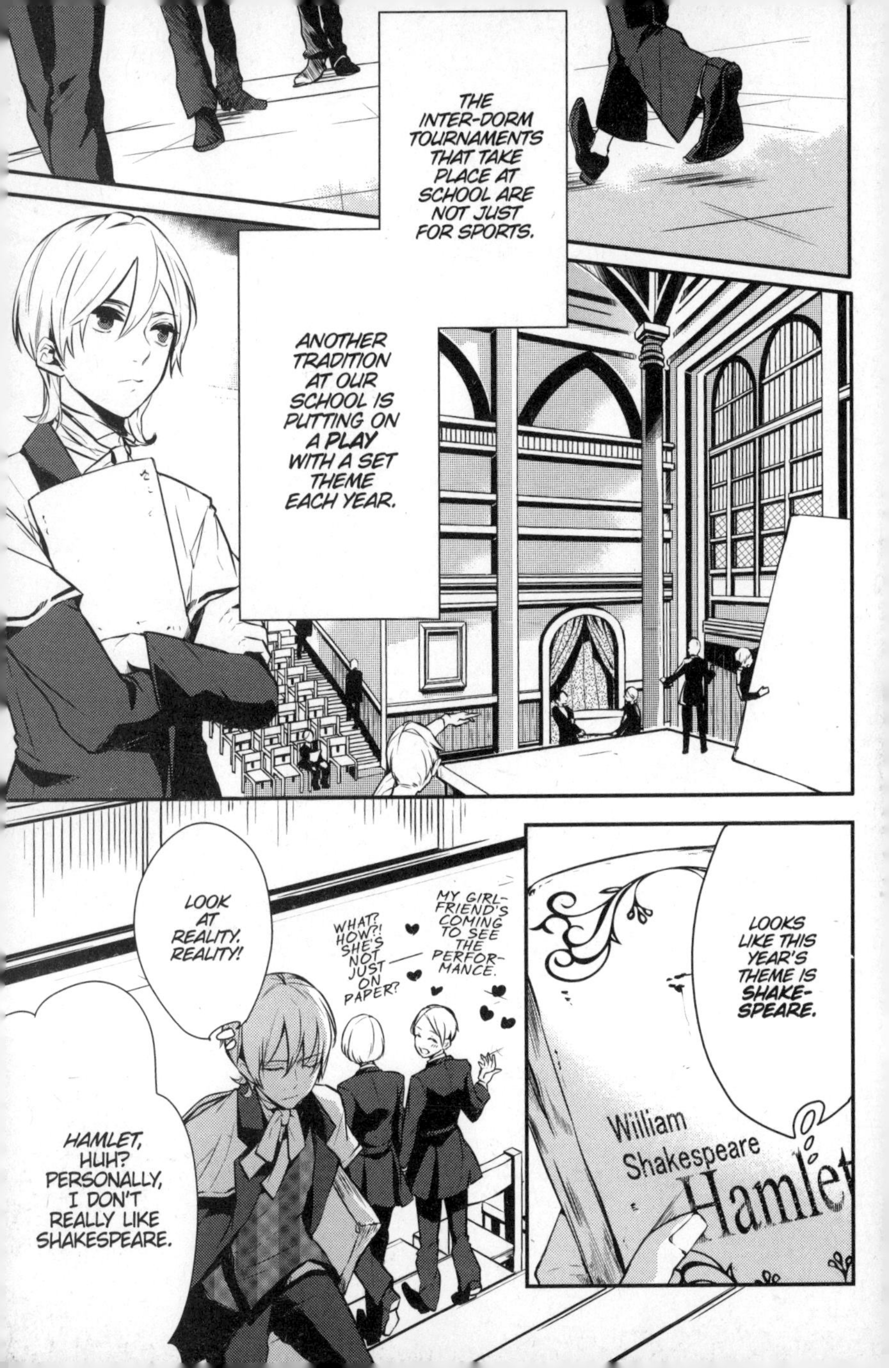
THE INTER-DORM TOURNAMENTS THAT TAKE PLACE AT SCHOOL ARE NOT JUST FOR SPORTS.
ANOTHER TRADITION AT OUR SCHOOL IS PUTTING ON A **PLAY** WITH A SET THEME EACH YEAR.
LOOKS LIKE THIS YEAR'S THEME IS **SHAKESPEARE.**
William Shakespeare
Hamlet
MY GIRLFRIEND'S COMING TO SEE THE PERFORMANCE.
WHAT? HOW?! SHE'S NOT JUST ON PAPER?
LOOK AT REALITY. REALITY!
HAMLET, HUH? PERSONALLY, I DON'T REALLY LIKE SHAKESPEARE.

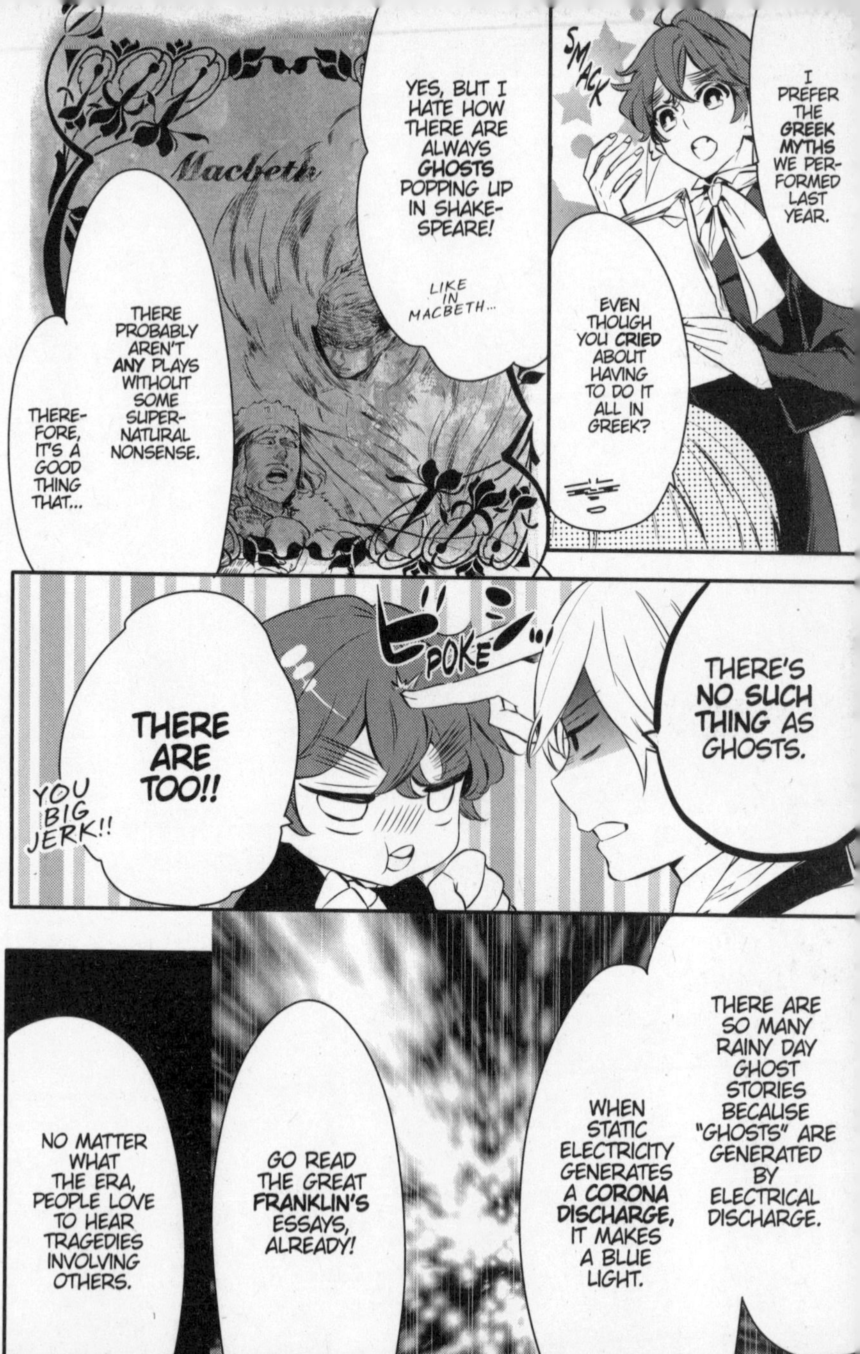

I PREFER THE GREEK MYTHS WE PERFORMED LAST YEAR.
SMACK
EVEN THOUGH YOU CRIED ABOUT HAVING TO DO IT ALL IN GREEK?
YES, BUT I HATE HOW THERE ARE ALWAYS GHOSTS POPPING UP IN SHAKE-SPEARE!
Macbeth
LIKE IN MACBETH...
THERE PROBABLY AREN'T ANY PLAYS WITHOUT SOME SUPER-NATURAL NONSENSE.
THERE-FORE, IT'S A GOOD THING THAT...
THERE'S NO SUCH THING AS GHOSTS.
POKE
THERE ARE TOO!!
YOU BIG JERK!!
THERE ARE SO MANY RAINY DAY GHOST STORIES BECAUSE "GHOSTS" ARE GENERATED BY ELECTRICAL DISCHARGE.
WHEN STATIC ELECTRICITY GENERATES A CORONA DISCHARGE, IT MAKES A BLUE LIGHT.
GO READ THE GREAT FRANKLIN'S ESSAYS, ALREADY!
NO MATTER WHAT THE ERA, PEOPLE LOVE TO HEAR TRAGEDIES INVOLVING OTHERS.

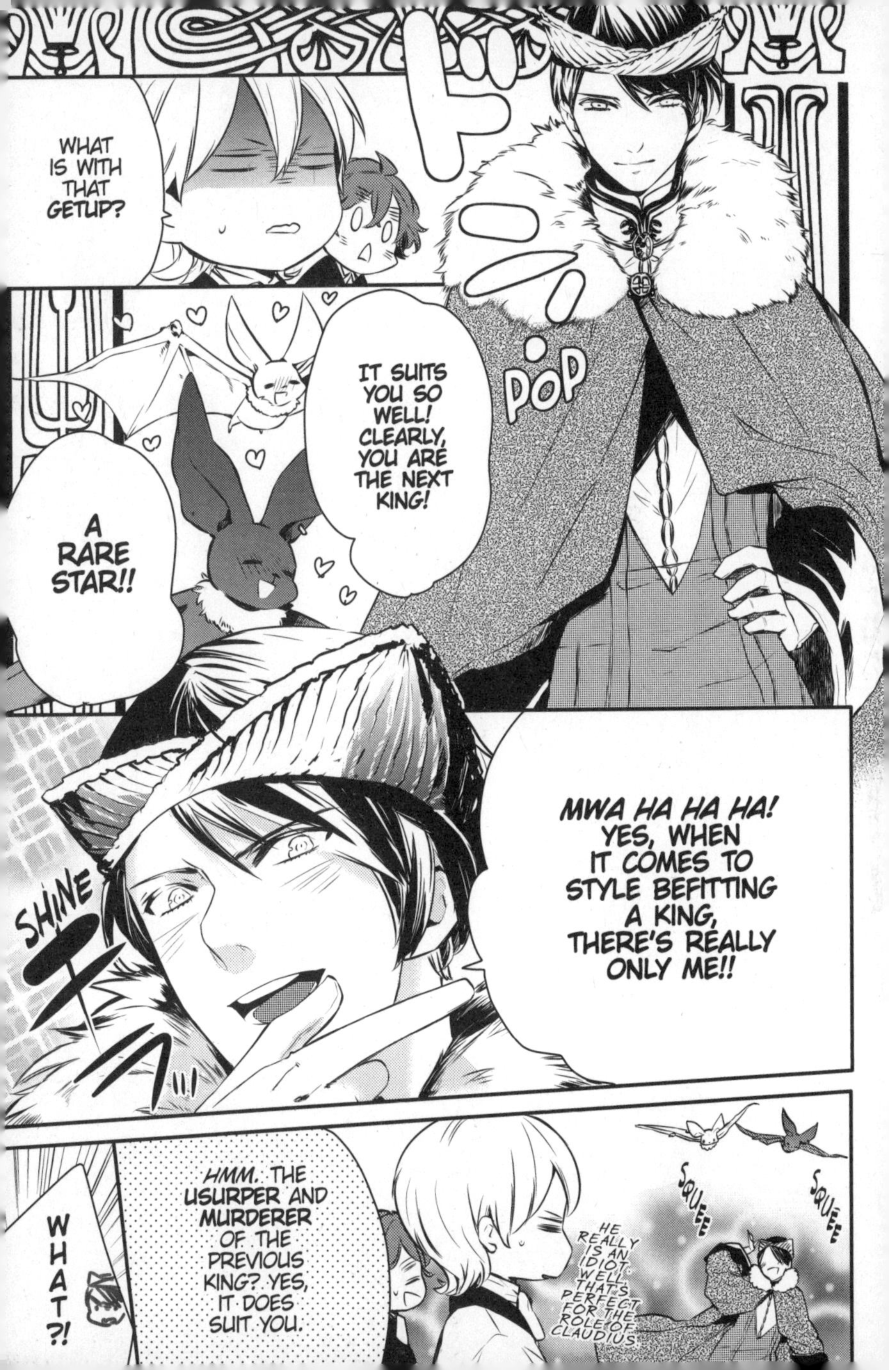
POP
WHAT IS WITH THAT GETUP?
IT SUITS YOU SO WELL! CLEARLY, YOU ARE THE NEXT KING!
A RARE STAR!!
MWA HA HA HA! YES, WHEN IT COMES TO STYLE BEFITTING A KING, THERE'S REALLY ONLY ME!!
SHINE
SQUEE
SQUEE
HE REALLY IS AN IDIOT. WELL, THAT'S PERFECT FOR THE ROLE OF CLAUDIUS.
HMM. THE USURPER AND MURDERER OF THE PREVIOUS KING? YES, IT DOES SUIT YOU.
WHAT?!

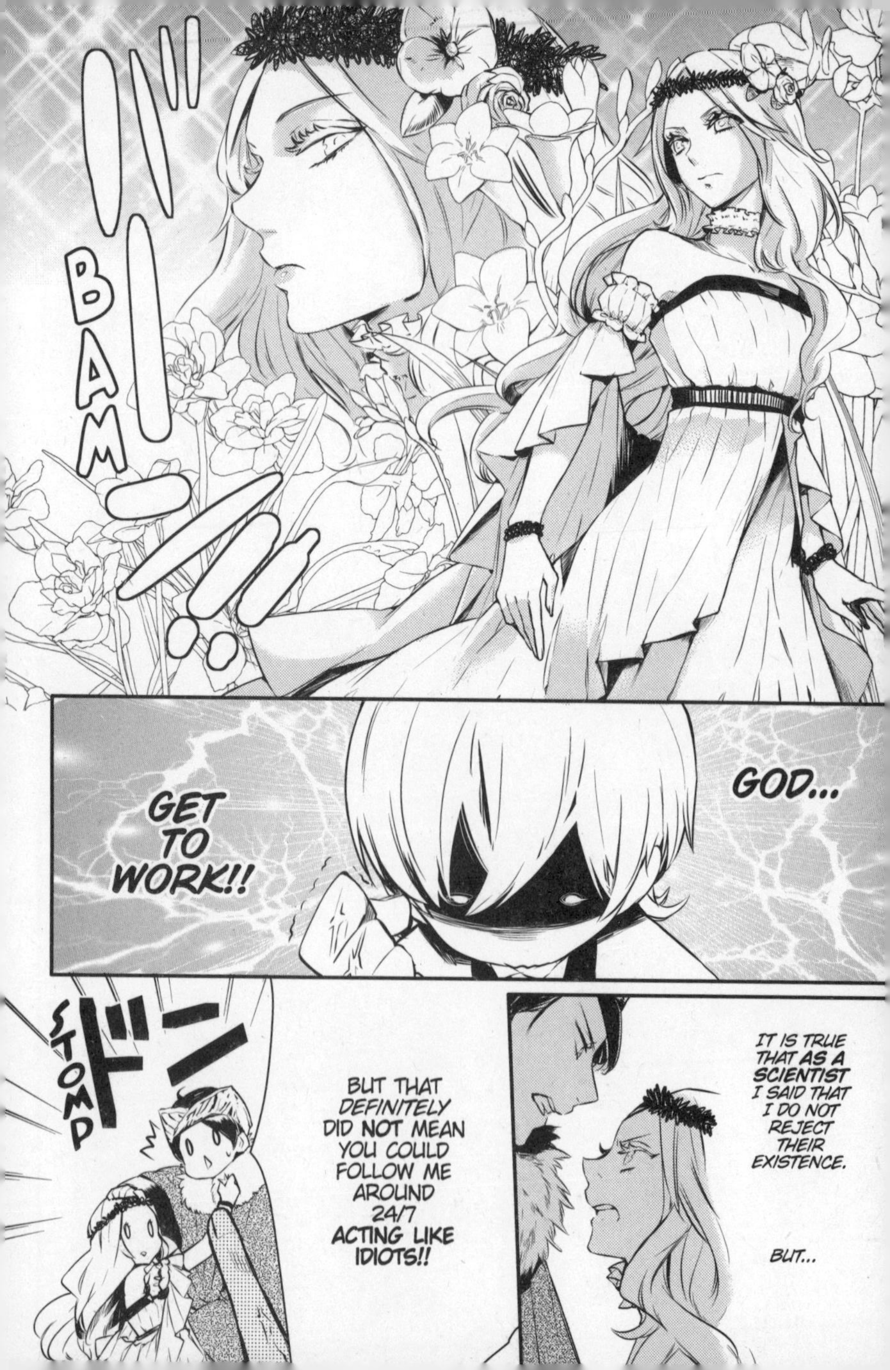
BAM
GOD...
GET TO WORK!!
IT IS TRUE THAT AS A SCIENTIST I SAID THAT I DO NOT REJECT THEIR EXISTENCE.
BUT...
STOMP
BUT THAT DEFINITELY DID NOT MEAN YOU COULD FOLLOW ME AROUND 24/7 ACTING LIKE IDIOTS!!

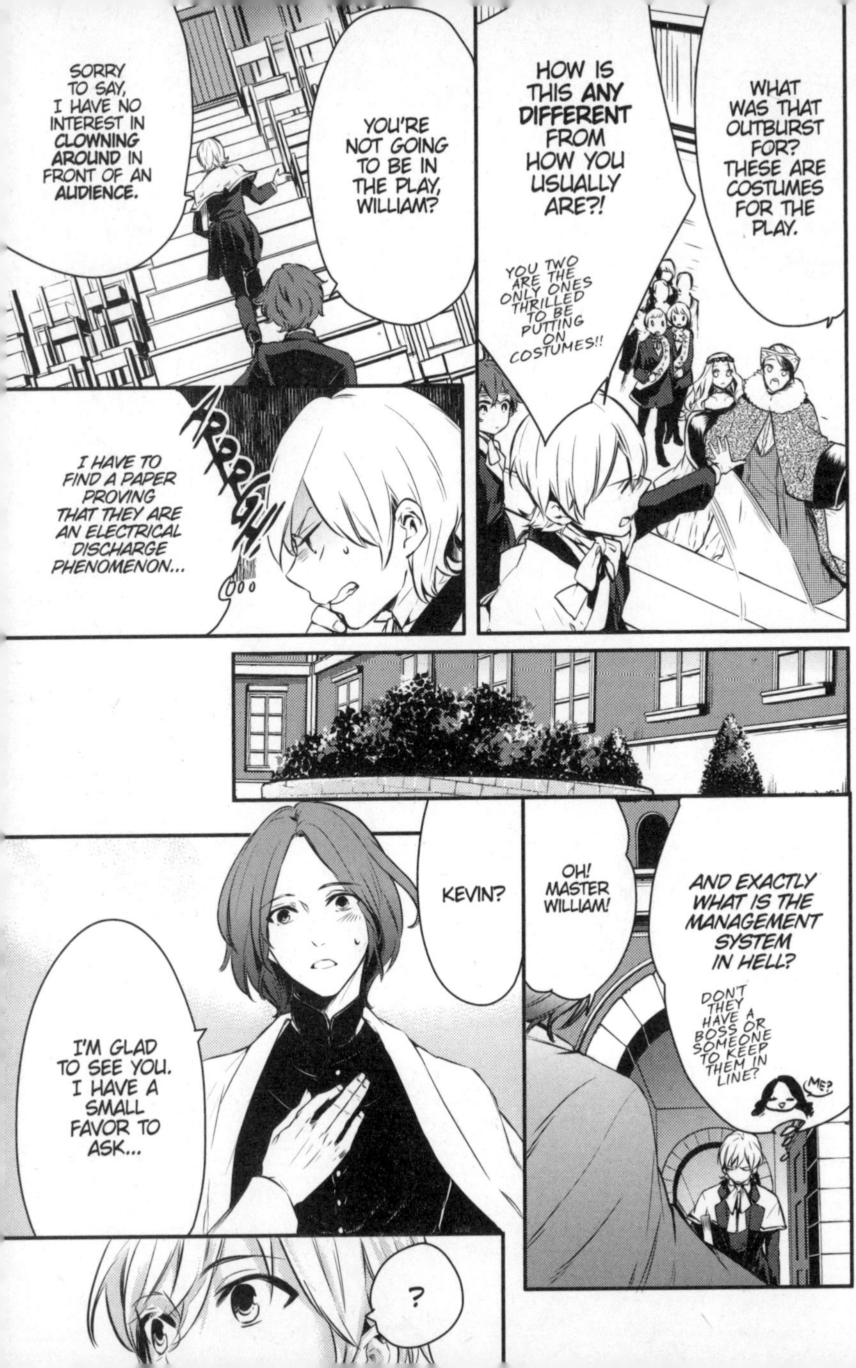
WHAT WAS THAT OUTBURST FOR? THESE ARE COSTUMES FOR THE PLAY.
HOW IS THIS ANY DIFFERENT FROM HOW YOU USUALLY ARE?!
YOU TWO ARE THE ONLY ONES THRILLED TO BE PUTTING ON COSTUMES!!
YOU'RE NOT GOING TO BE IN THE PLAY, WILLIAM?
SORRY TO SAY, I HAVE NO INTEREST IN CLOWNING AROUND IN FRONT OF AN AUDIENCE.
ARRRGH!
I HAVE TO FIND A PAPER PROVING THAT THEY ARE AN ELECTRICAL DISCHARGE PHENOMENON...
AND EXACTLY WHAT IS THE MANAGEMENT SYSTEM IN HELL?
DON'T THEY HAVE A BOSS OR SOMEONE TO KEEP THEM IN LINE?
ME?
OH! MASTER WILLIAM!
KEVIN?
I'M GLAD TO SEE YOU. I HAVE A SMALL FAVOR TO ASK...
?

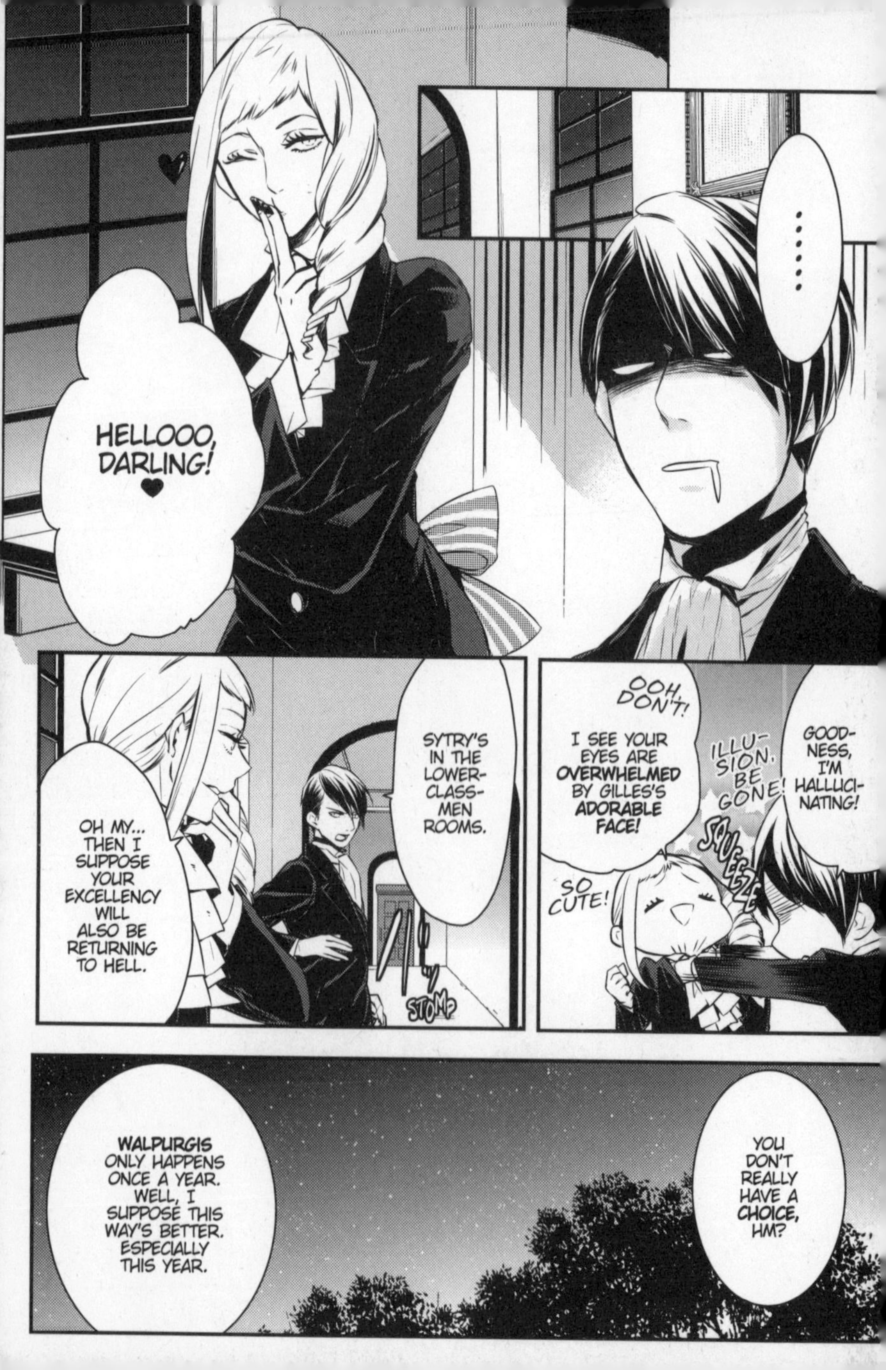
......
HELLOOO, DARLING! ♥
GOODNESS, I'M HALLUCINATING!
ILLUSION, BE GONE!
OOH, DON'T!
I SEE YOUR EYES ARE **OVERWHELMED** BY GILLES'S **ADORABLE FACE!**
SQUEEZE
SO CUTE!
SYTRY'S IN THE LOWER-CLASSMEN ROOMS.
STOMP
OH MY... THEN I SUPPOSE YOUR EXCELLENCY WILL ALSO BE RETURNING TO HELL.
YOU DON'T REALLY HAVE A **CHOICE,** HM?
WALPURGIS ONLY HAPPENS ONCE A YEAR. WELL, I SUPPOSE THIS WAY'S BETTER. ESPECIALLY THIS YEAR.

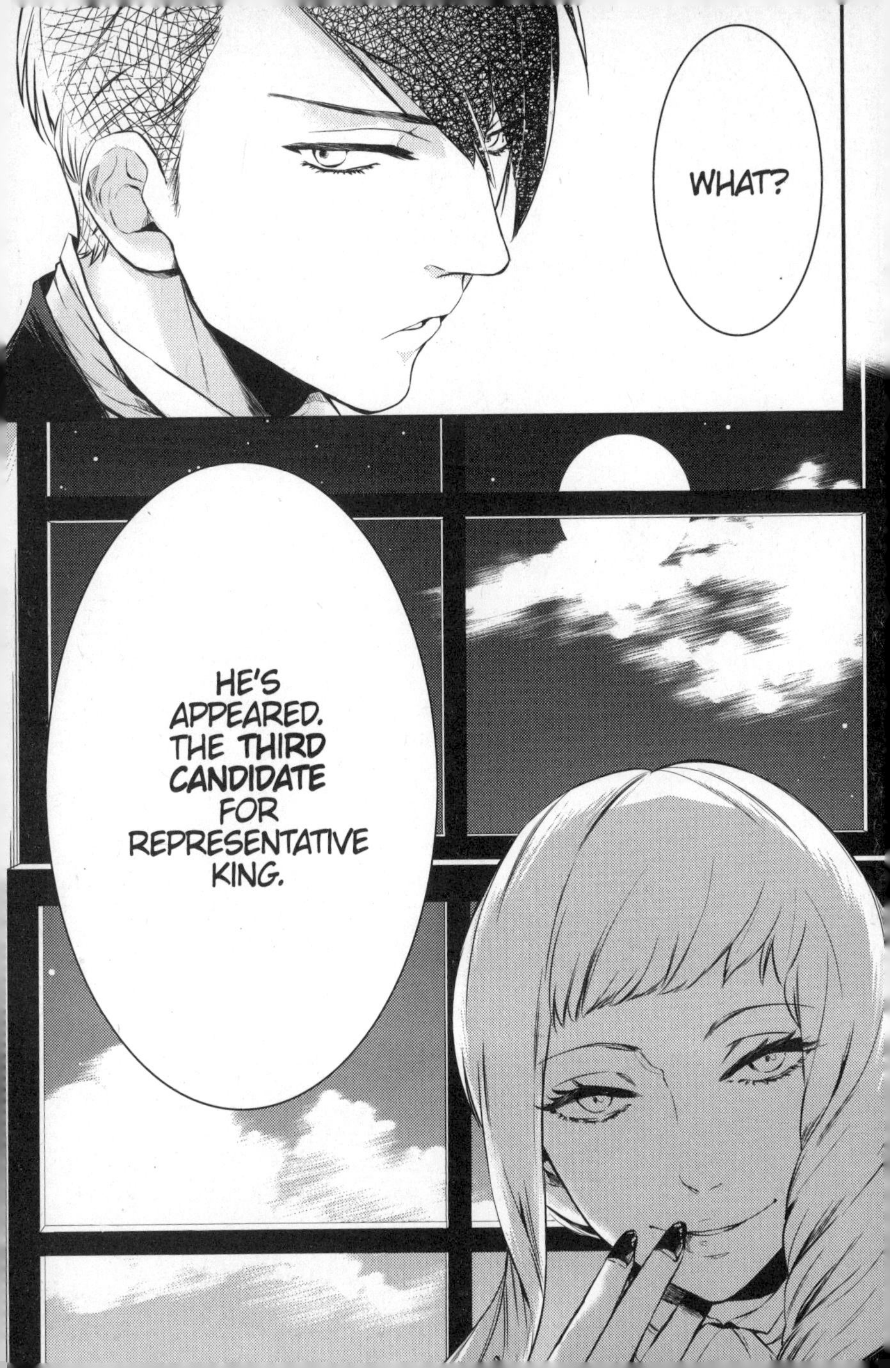
WHAT?
HE'S APPEARED. THE THIRD CANDIDATE FOR REPRESENTATIVE KING.

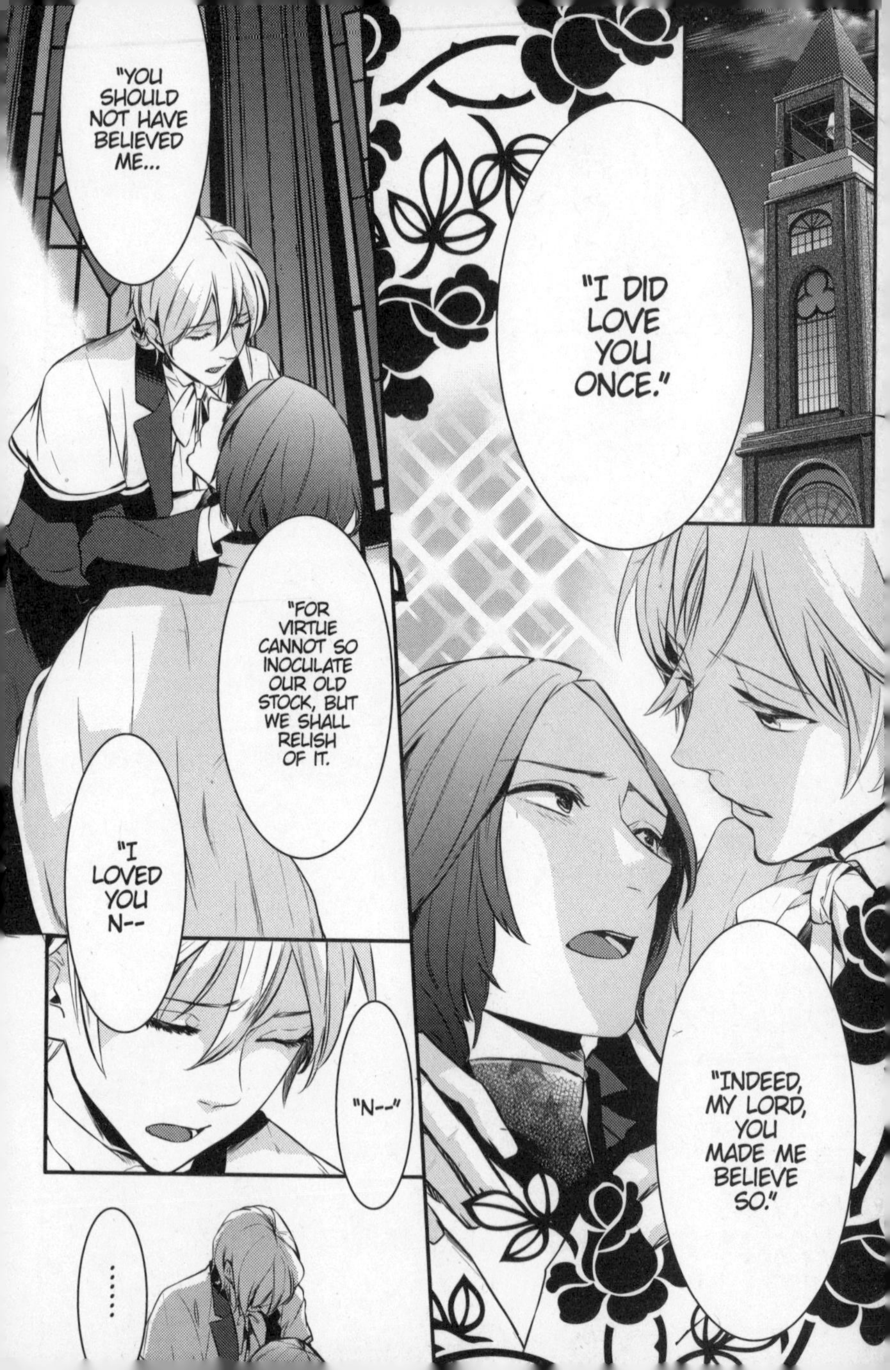
"I DID LOVE YOU ONCE."
"INDEED, MY LORD, YOU MADE ME BELIEVE SO."
"YOU SHOULD NOT HAVE BELIEVED ME...
"FOR VIRTUE CANNOT SO INOCULATE OUR OLD STOCK, BUT WE SHALL RELISH OF IT.
"I LOVED YOU N--
"N--"
......

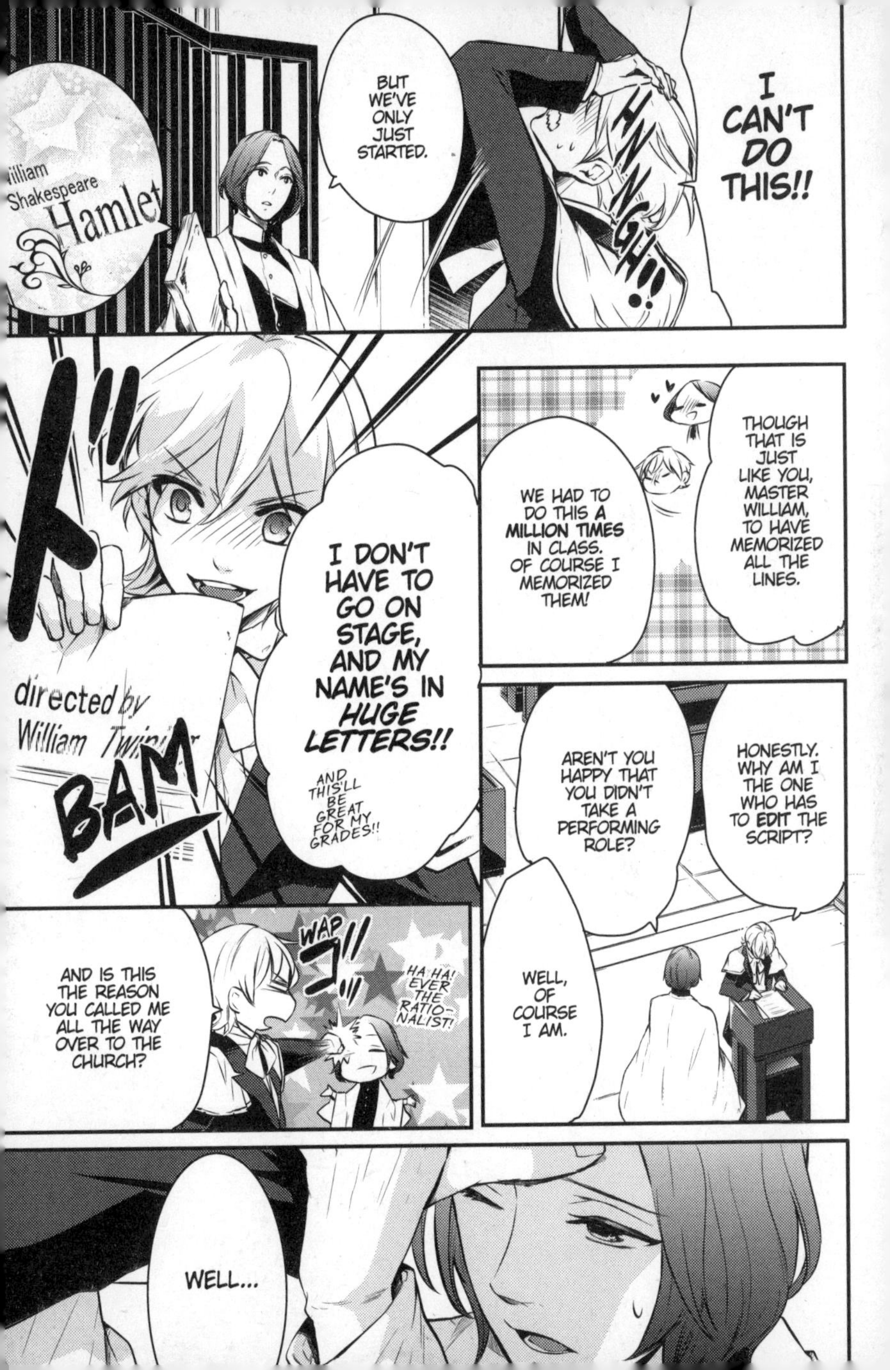

I CAN'T DO THIS!!
HNNNGH!!
BUT WE'VE ONLY JUST STARTED.
William Shakespeare Hamlet
THOUGH THAT IS JUST LIKE YOU, MASTER WILLIAM, TO HAVE MEMORIZED ALL THE LINES.
WE HAD TO DO THIS A MILLION TIMES IN CLASS. OF COURSE I MEMORIZED THEM!
HONESTLY. WHY AM I THE ONE WHO HAS TO EDIT THE SCRIPT?
AREN'T YOU HAPPY THAT YOU DIDN'T TAKE A PERFORMING ROLE?
WELL, OF COURSE I AM.
I DON'T HAVE TO GO ON STAGE, AND MY NAME'S IN HUGE LETTERS!!
AND THIS'LL BE GREAT FOR MY GRADES!!
directed by William Twini
BAM
AND IS THIS THE REASON YOU CALLED ME ALL THE WAY OVER TO THE CHURCH?
WAP
HA HA! EVER THE RATIO-NALIST!
WELL...

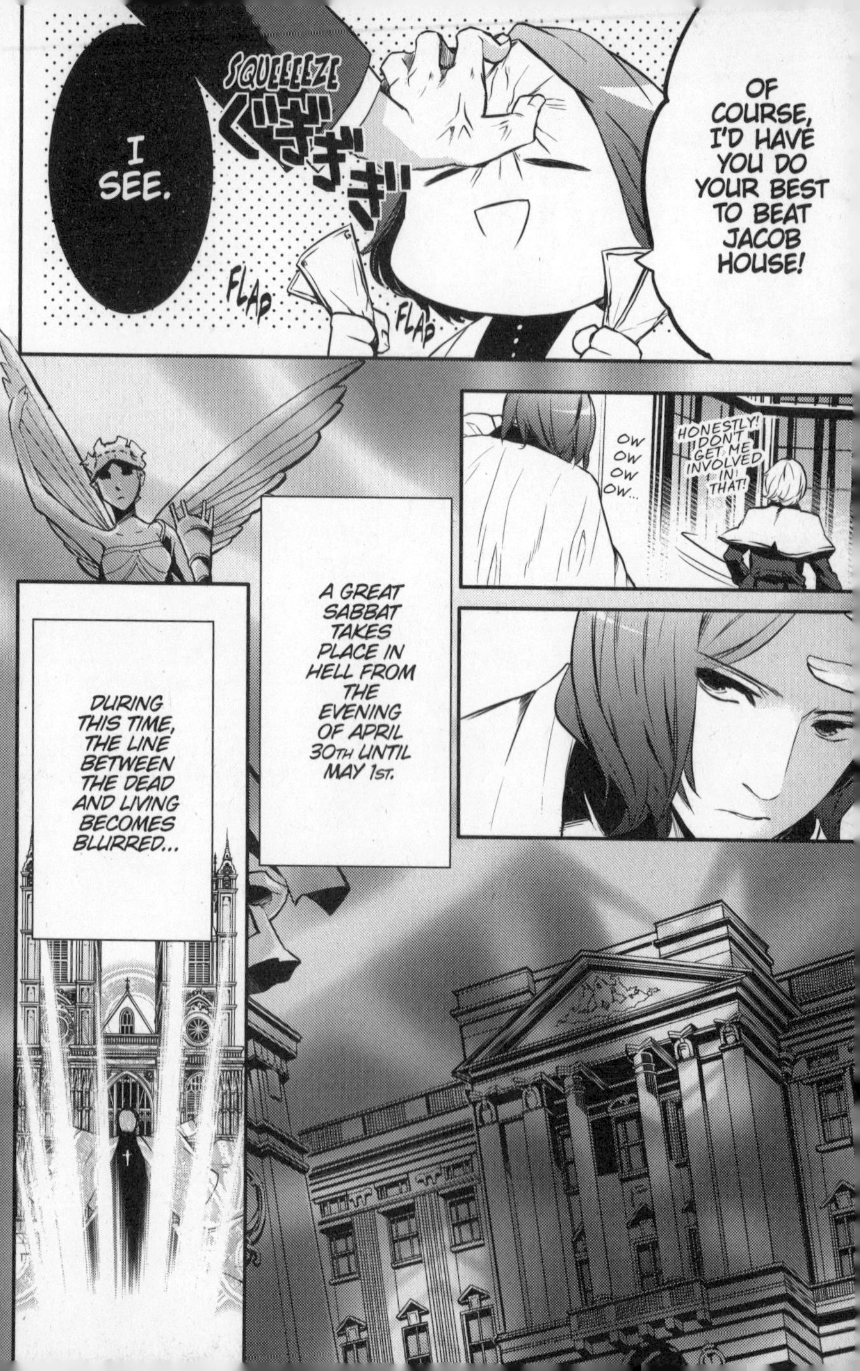
OF COURSE, I'D HAVE YOU DO YOUR BEST TO BEAT JACOB HOUSE!
SQUEEEEZE
ぐぎぎぎ
FLAP
FLAP
I SEE.
HONESTLY! DONT GET ME INVOLVED IN THAT!
OW OW OW OW...
A GREAT SABBAT TAKES PLACE IN HELL FROM THE EVENING OF APRIL 30TH UNTIL MAY 1ST.
DURING THIS TIME, THE LINE BETWEEN THE DEAD AND LIVING BECOMES BLURRED...

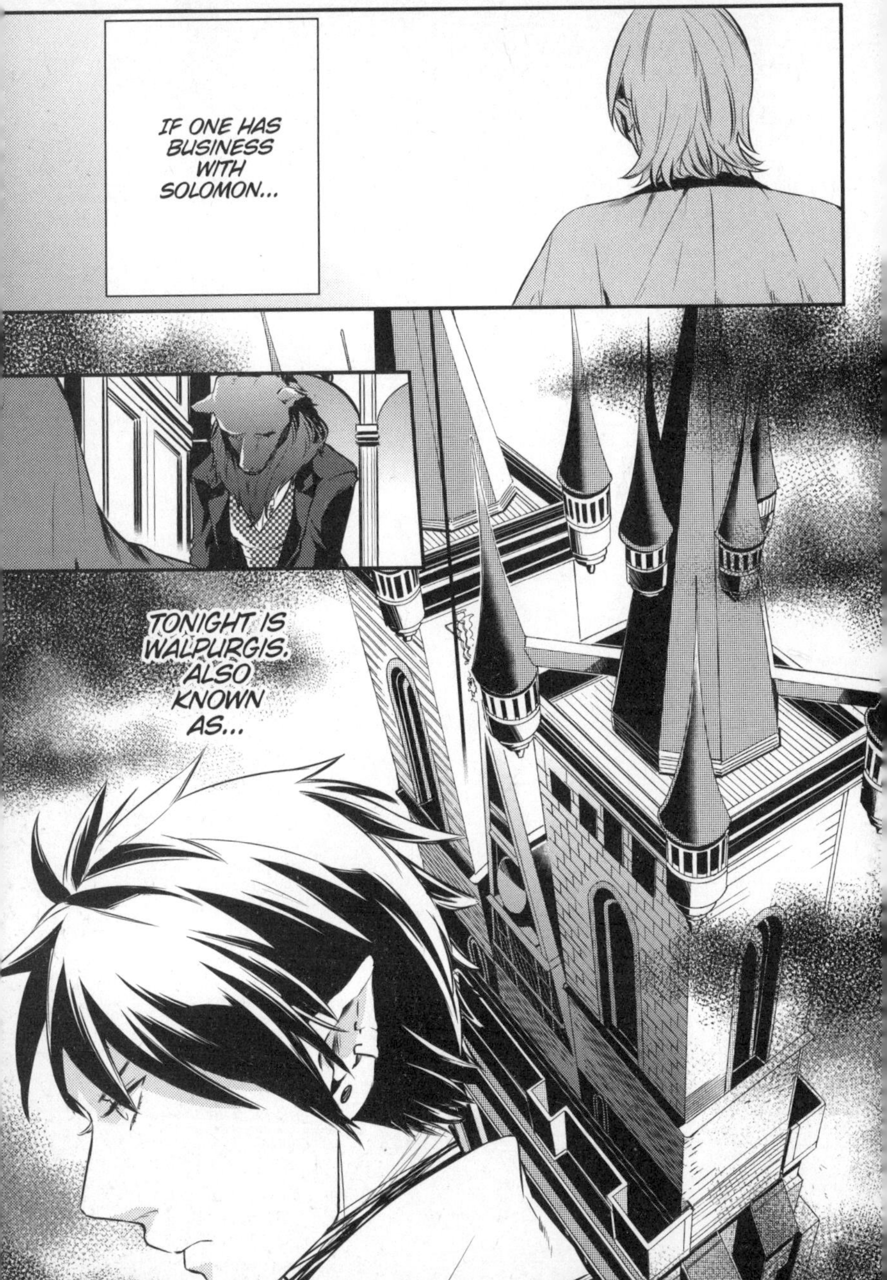
IF ONE HAS BUSINESS WITH SOLOMON...
TONIGHT IS WALPURGIS. ALSO KNOWN AS...

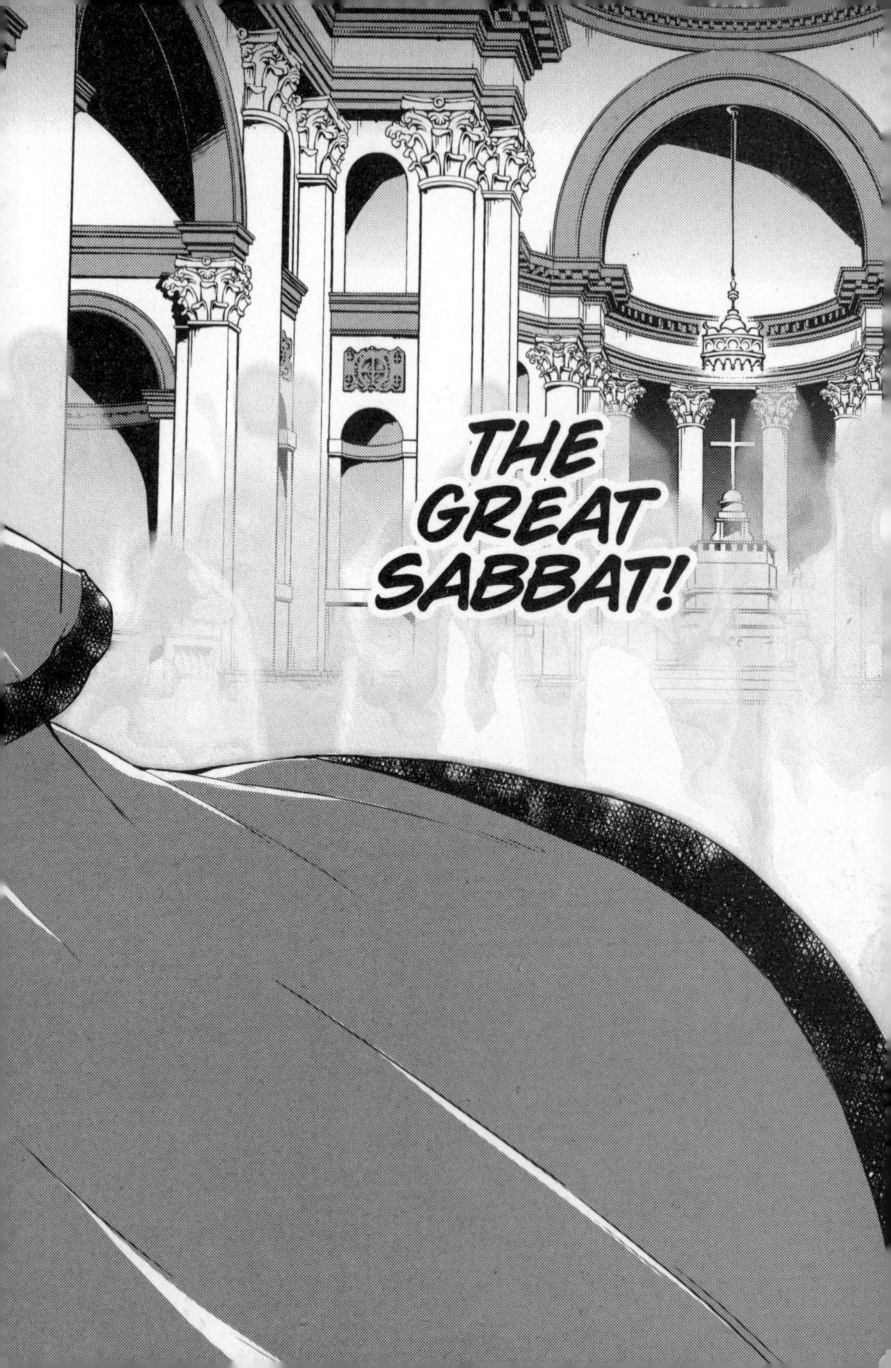
THE GREAT SABBAT!

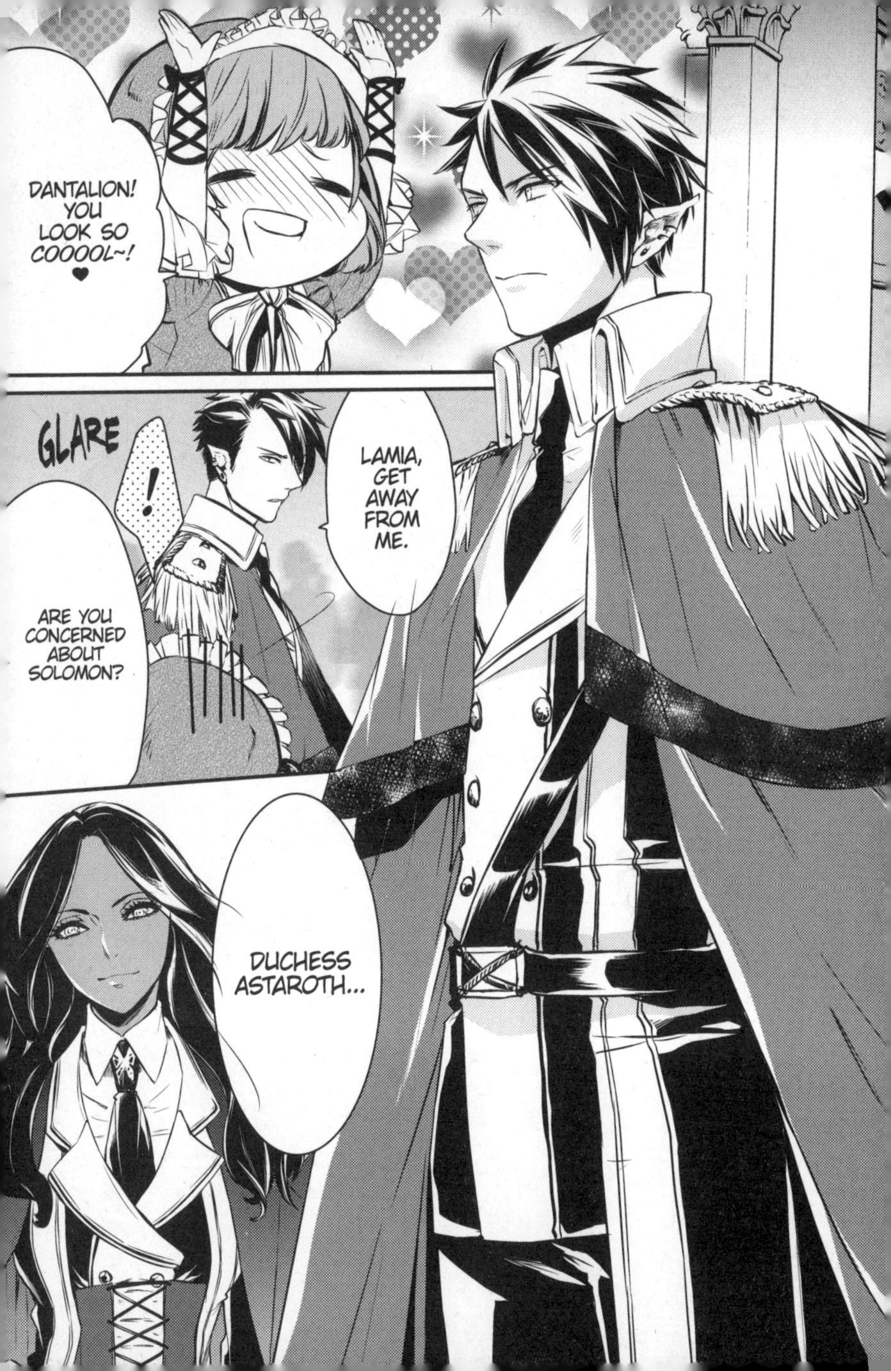
DANTALION! YOU LOOK SO COOOOL~! ❤
LAMIA, GET AWAY FROM ME.
GLARE
!
ARE YOU CONCERNED ABOUT SOLOMON?
DUCHESS ASTAROTH...

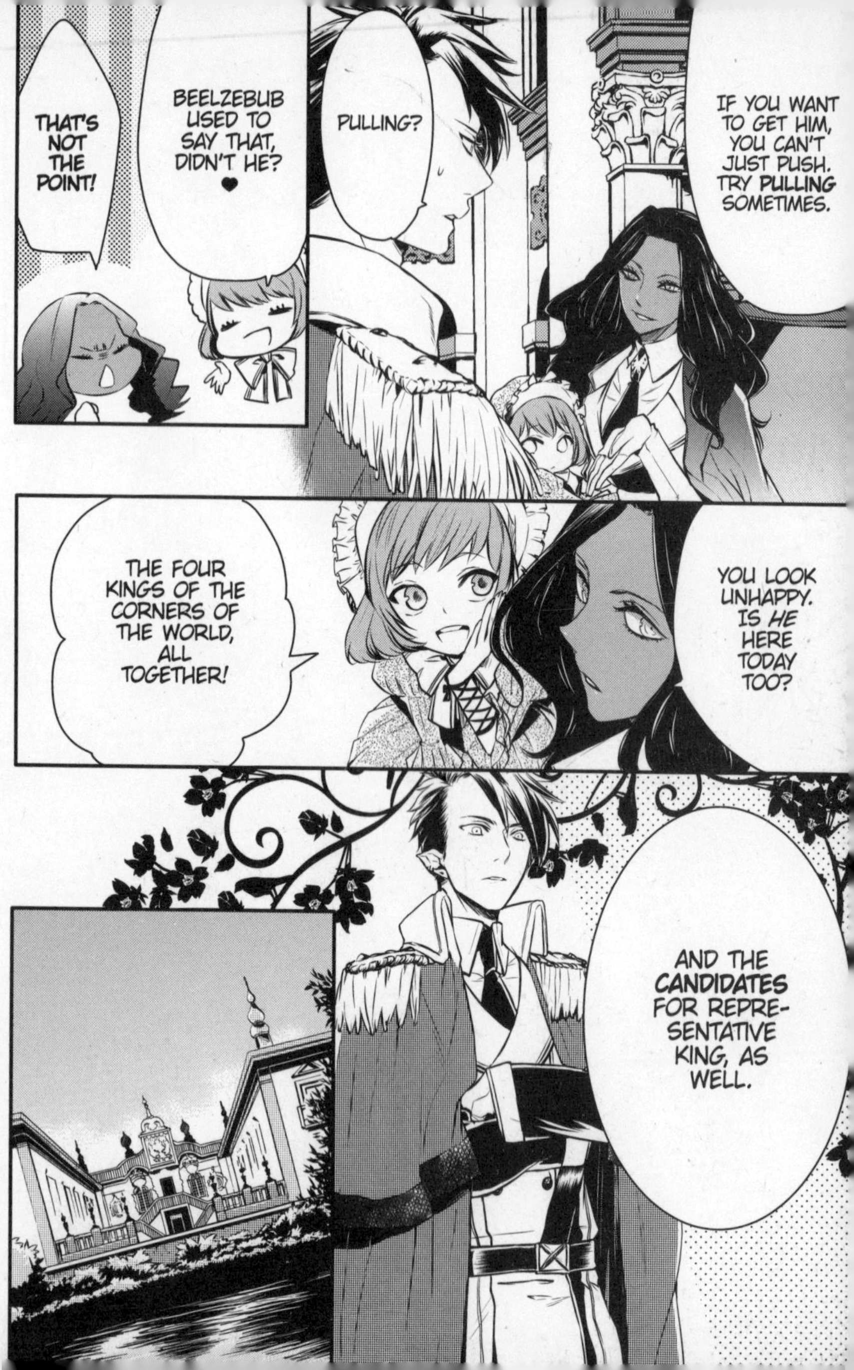
IF YOU WANT TO GET HIM, YOU CAN'T JUST PUSH. TRY **PULLING** SOMETIMES.
PULLING?
BEELZEBUB USED TO SAY THAT, DIDN'T HE? ♥
THAT'S NOT THE POINT!
YOU LOOK UNHAPPY. IS *HE* HERE TODAY TOO?
THE FOUR KINGS OF THE CORNERS OF THE WORLD, ALL TOGETHER!
AND THE CANDIDATES FOR REPRE- SENTATIVE KING, AS WELL.

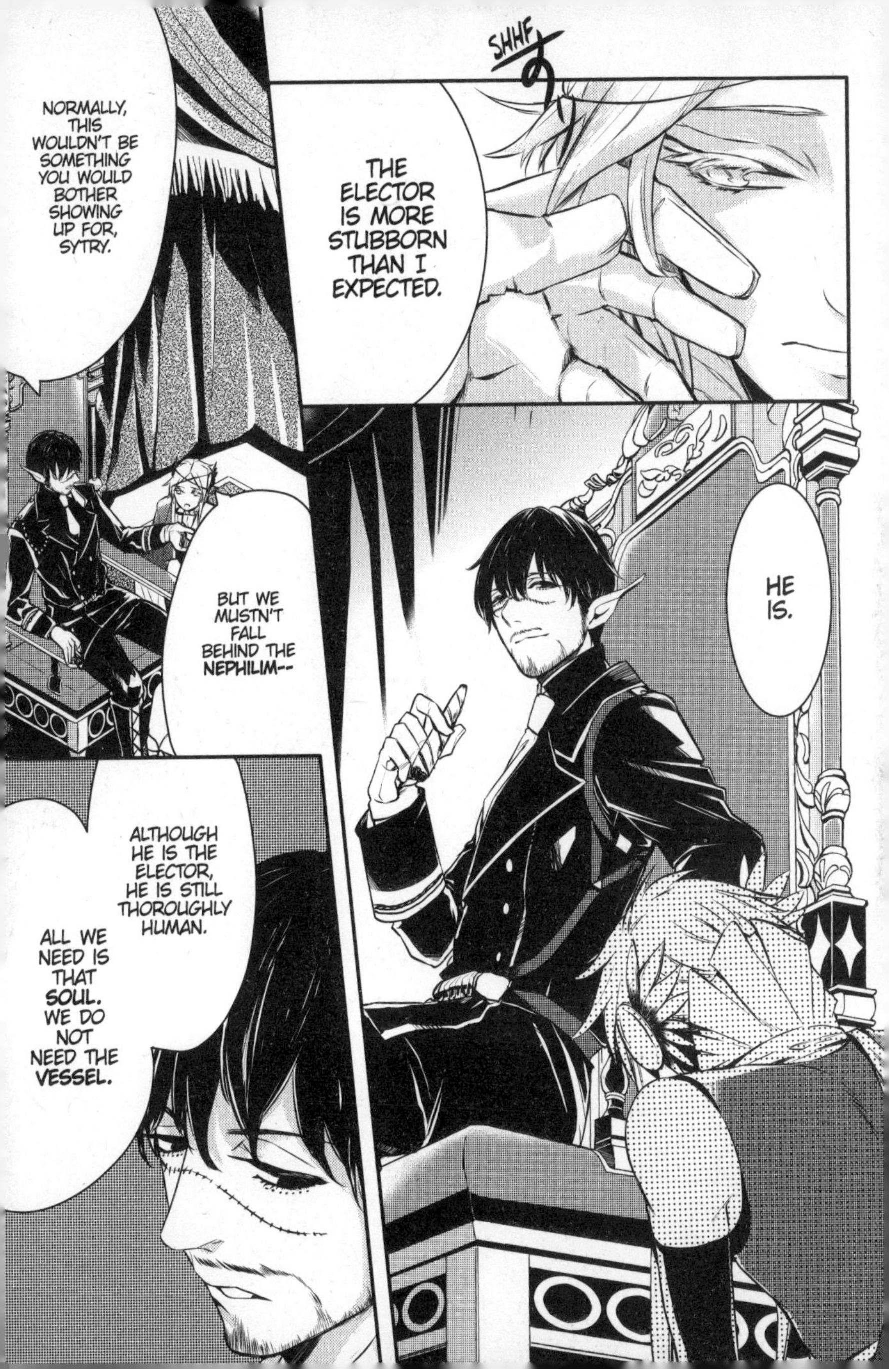
SHHF
THE ELECTOR IS MORE STUBBORN THAN I EXPECTED.
NORMALLY, THIS WOULDN'T BE SOMETHING YOU WOULD BOTHER SHOWING UP FOR, SYTRY.
BUT WE MUSTN'T FALL BEHIND THE NEPHILIM--
HE IS.
ALTHOUGH HE IS THE ELECTOR, HE IS STILL THOROUGHLY HUMAN.
ALL WE NEED IS THAT SOUL. WE DO NOT NEED THE VESSEL.

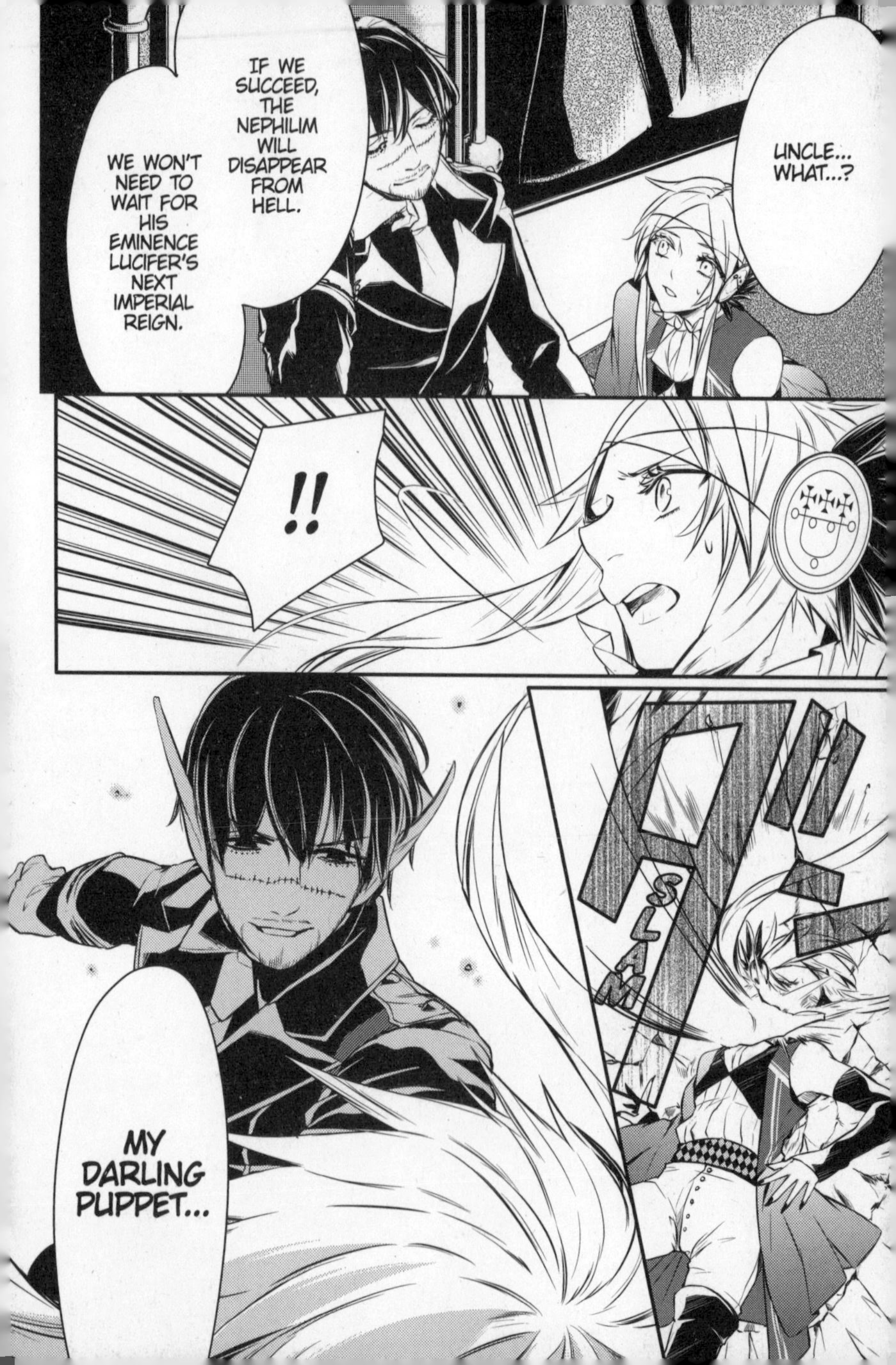
UNCLE... WHAT...?
IF WE SUCCEED, THE NEPHILIM WILL DISAPPEAR FROM HELL.
WE WON'T NEED TO WAIT FOR HIS EMINENCE LUCIFER'S NEXT IMPERIAL REIGN.
!!
SLAM
MY DARLING PUPPET...

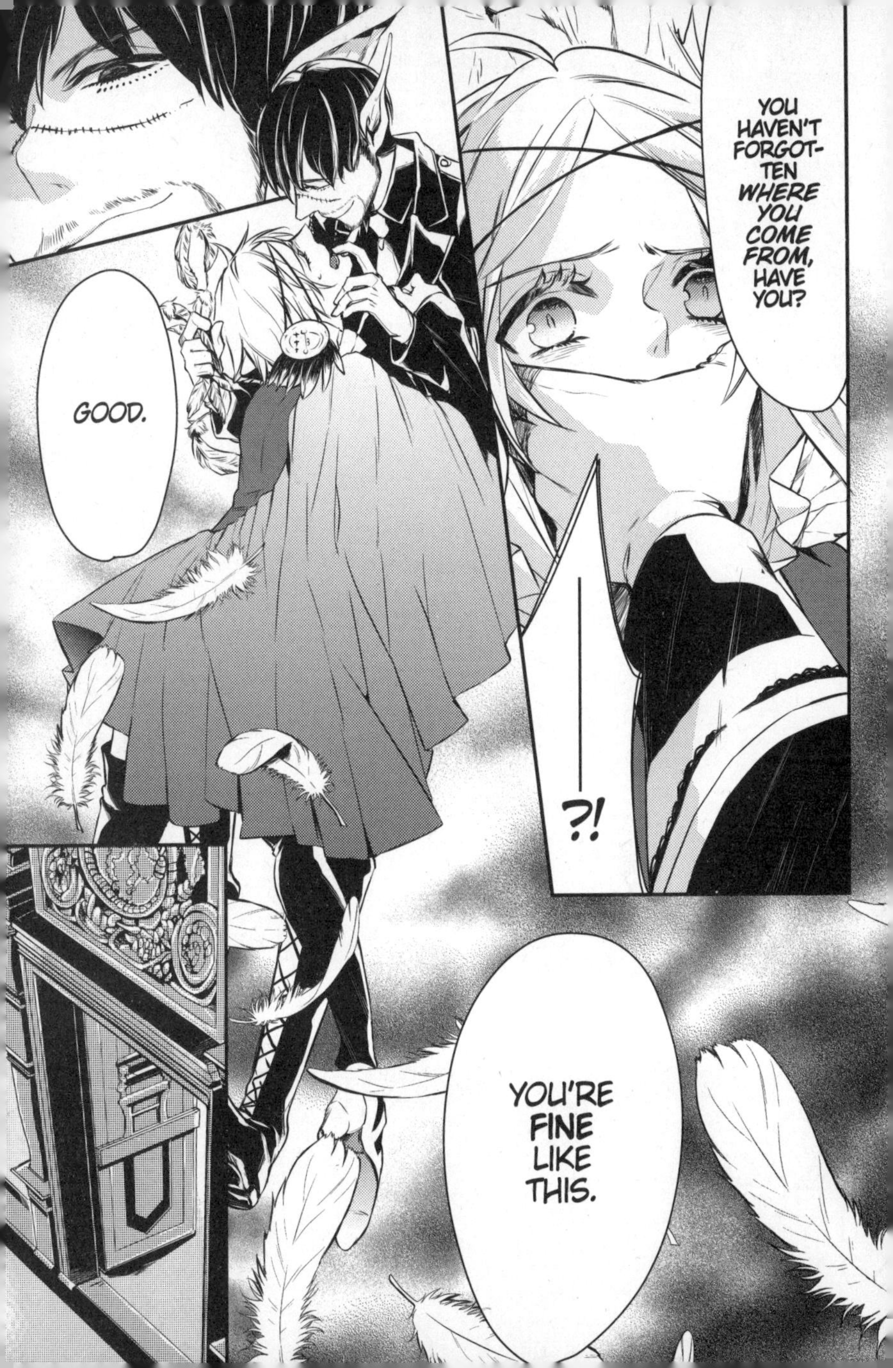
YOU HAVEN'T FORGOT-TEN *WHERE* YOU COME FROM, HAVE YOU?
——?!
GOOD.
YOU'RE FINE LIKE THIS.

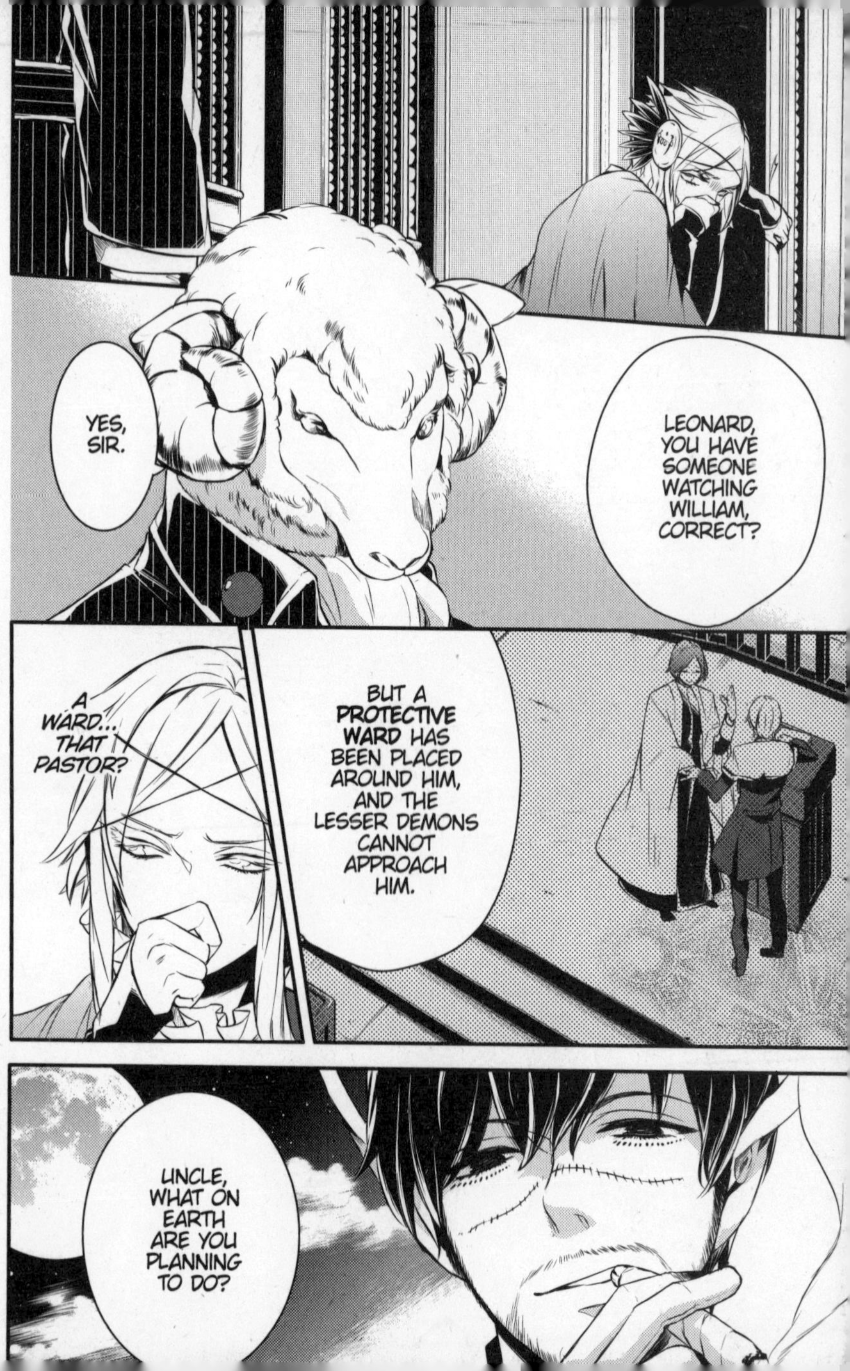
LEONARD, YOU HAVE SOMEONE WATCHING WILLIAM, CORRECT?
YES, SIR.
BUT A PROTECTIVE WARD HAS BEEN PLACED AROUND HIM, AND THE LESSER DEMONS CANNOT APPROACH HIM.
A WARD... THAT PASTOR?
UNCLE, WHAT ON EARTH ARE YOU PLANNING TO DO?

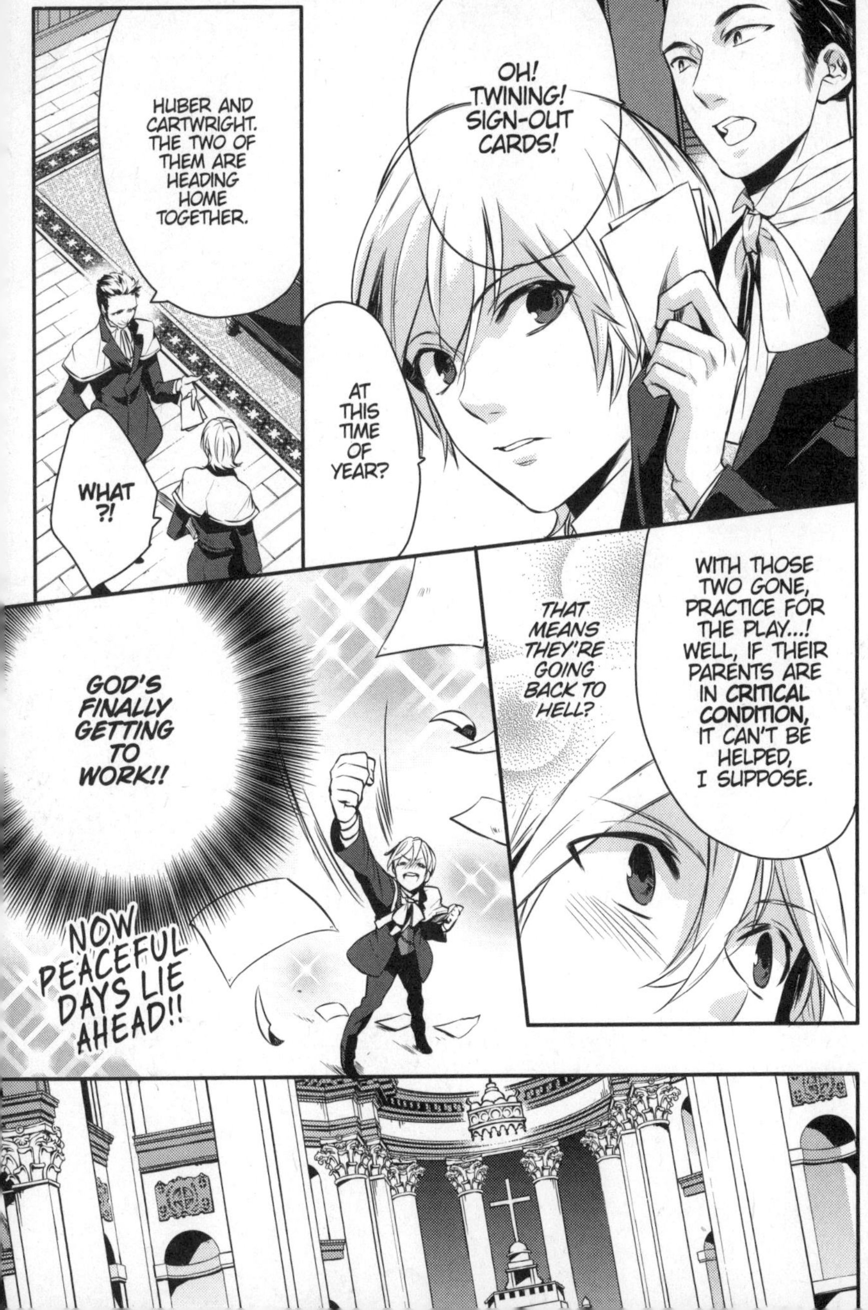
OH! TWINING! SIGN-OUT CARDS!
AT THIS TIME OF YEAR?
HUBER AND CARTWRIGHT. THE TWO OF THEM ARE HEADING HOME TOGETHER.
WHAT ?!
WITH THOSE TWO GONE, PRACTICE FOR THE PLAY...! WELL, IF THEIR PARENTS ARE IN CRITICAL CONDITION, IT CAN'T BE HELPED, I SUPPOSE.
THAT MEANS THEY'RE GOING BACK TO HELL?
GOD'S FINALLY GETTING TO WORK!!
NOW PEACEFUL DAYS LIE AHEAD!!

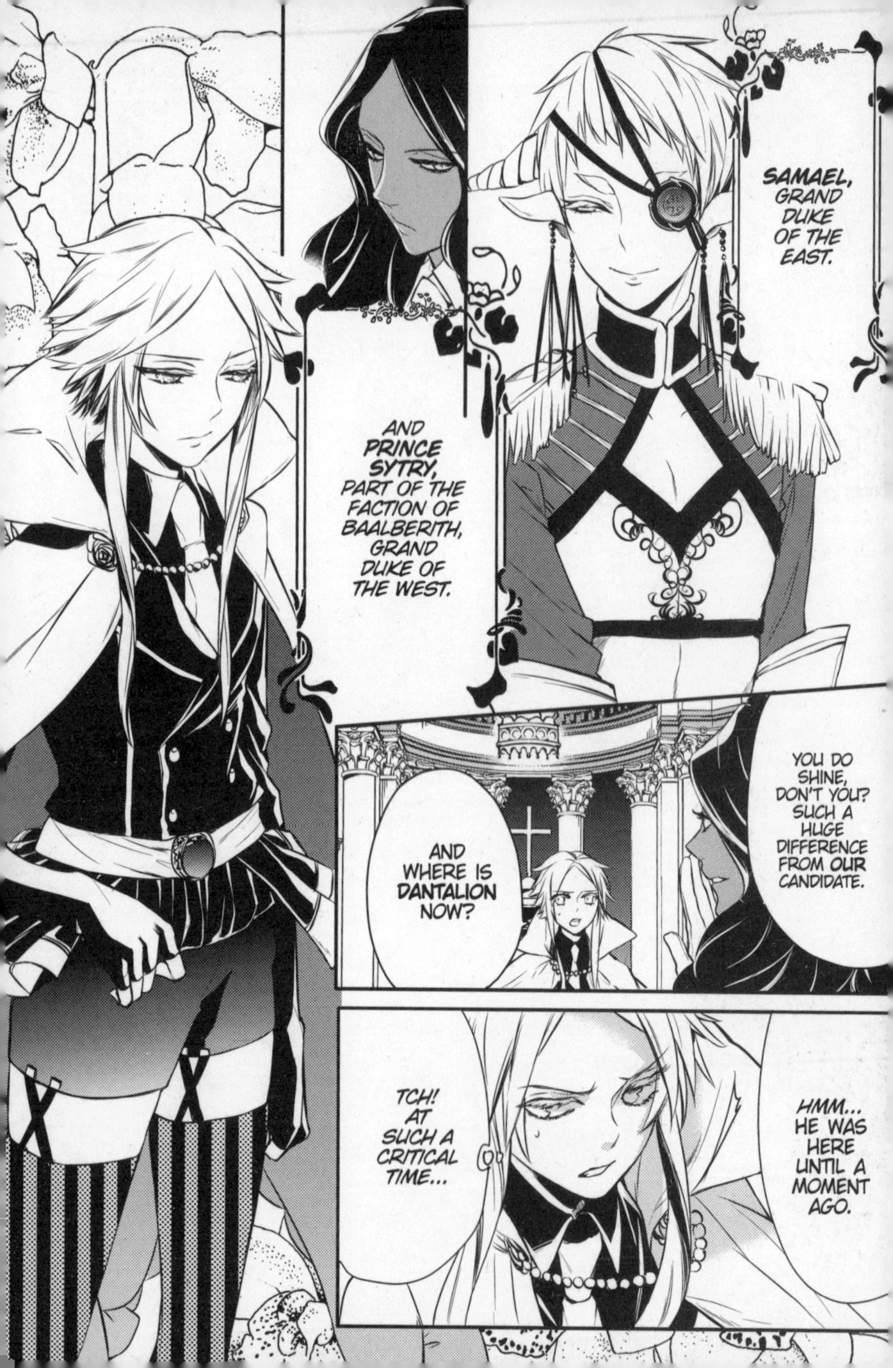
SAMAEL, GRAND DUKE OF THE EAST.
AND PRINCE SYTRY, PART OF THE FACTION OF BAALBERITH, GRAND DUKE OF THE WEST.
YOU DO SHINE, DON'T YOU? SUCH A HUGE DIFFERENCE FROM OUR CANDIDATE.
AND WHERE IS DANTALION NOW?
HMM... HE WAS HERE UNTIL A MOMENT AGO.
TCH! AT SUCH A CRITICAL TIME...

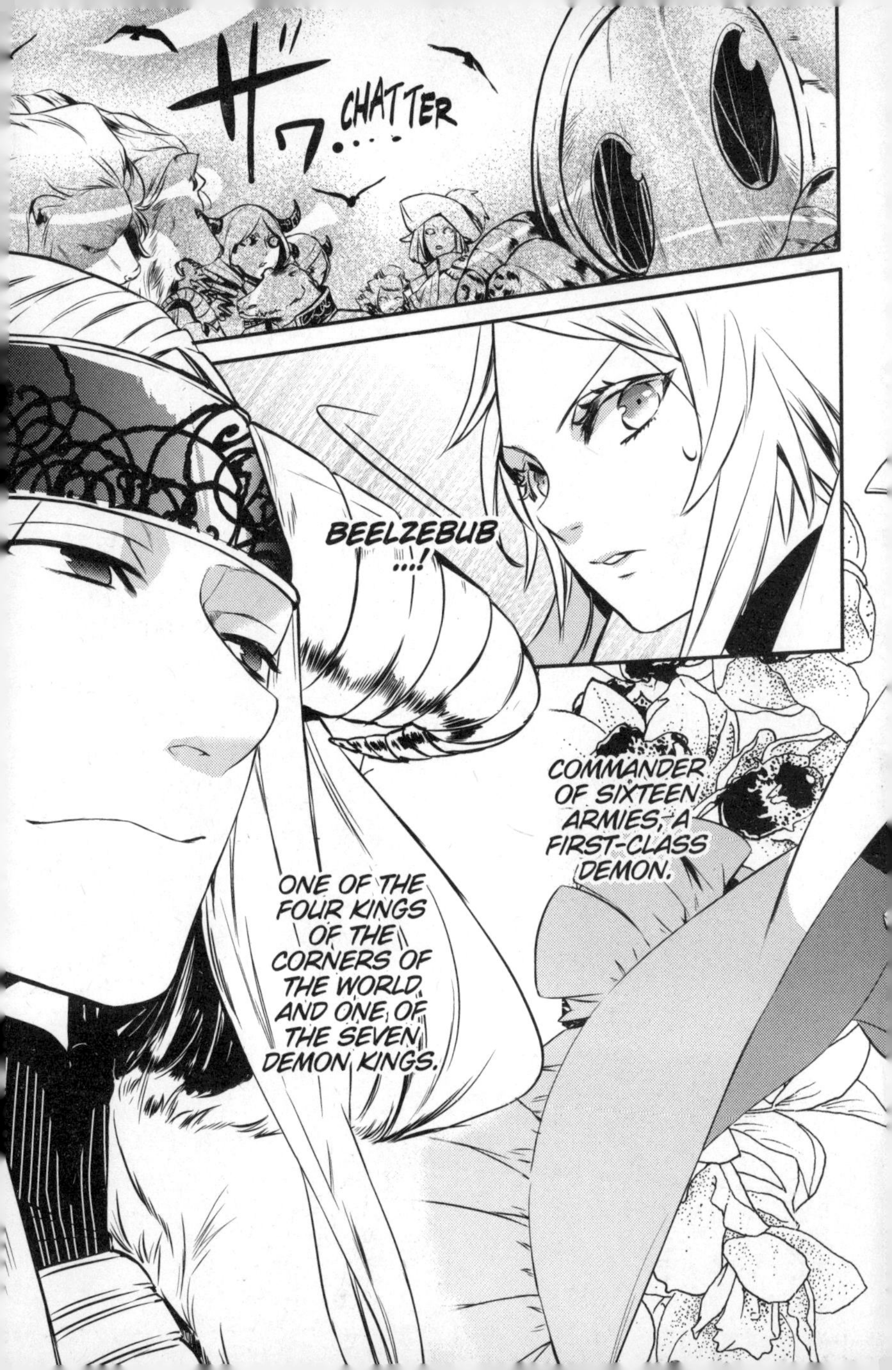
ザワ
CHATTER
BEELZEBUB ...!
COMMANDER OF SIXTEEN ARMIES, A FIRST-CLASS DEMON.
ONE OF THE FOUR KINGS OF THE CORNERS OF THE WORLD AND ONE OF THE SEVEN DEMON KINGS.

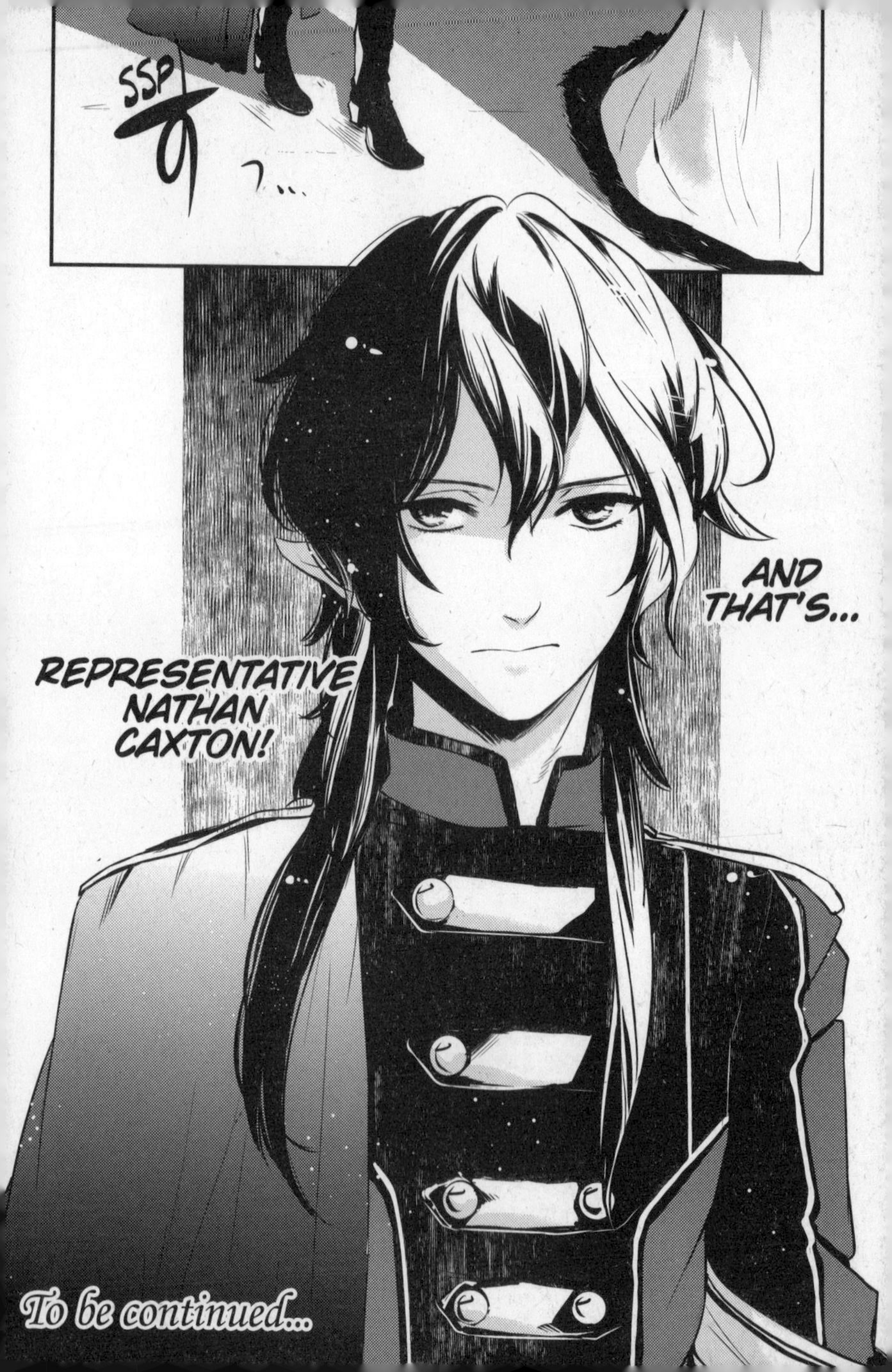
SSP
AND THAT'S...
REPRESENTATIVE NATHAN CAXTON!
To be continued...

魔界王子

devils and realist

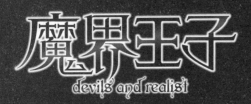

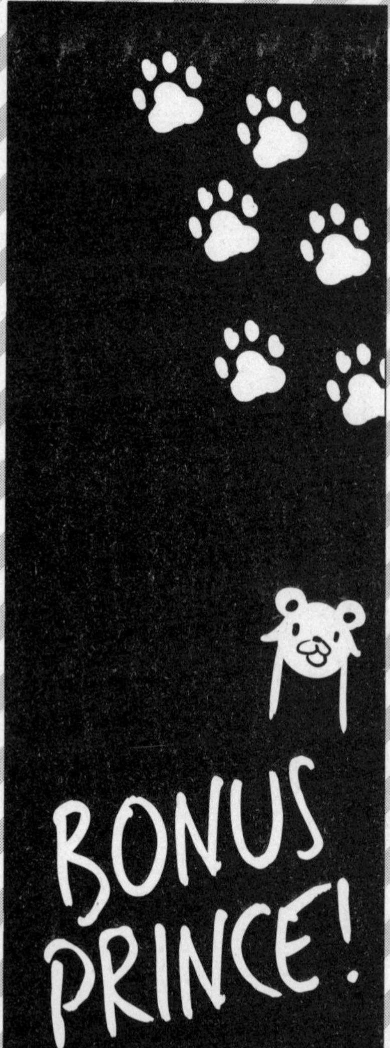
BONUS PRINCE!
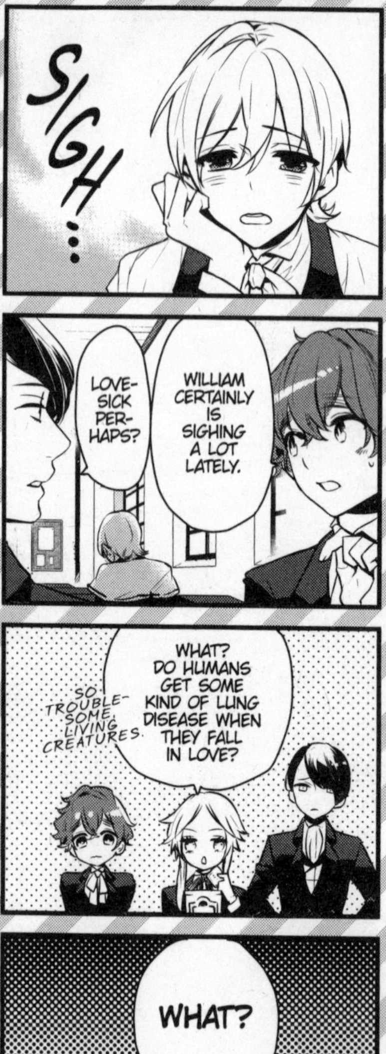
SIGH...
WILLIAM CERTAINLY IS SIGHING A LOT LATELY.
LOVE-SICK PER-HAPS?
WHAT? DO HUMANS GET SOME KIND OF LUNG DISEASE WHEN THEY FALL IN LOVE?
SO TROUBLE-SOME, LIVING CREATURES.
WHAT?

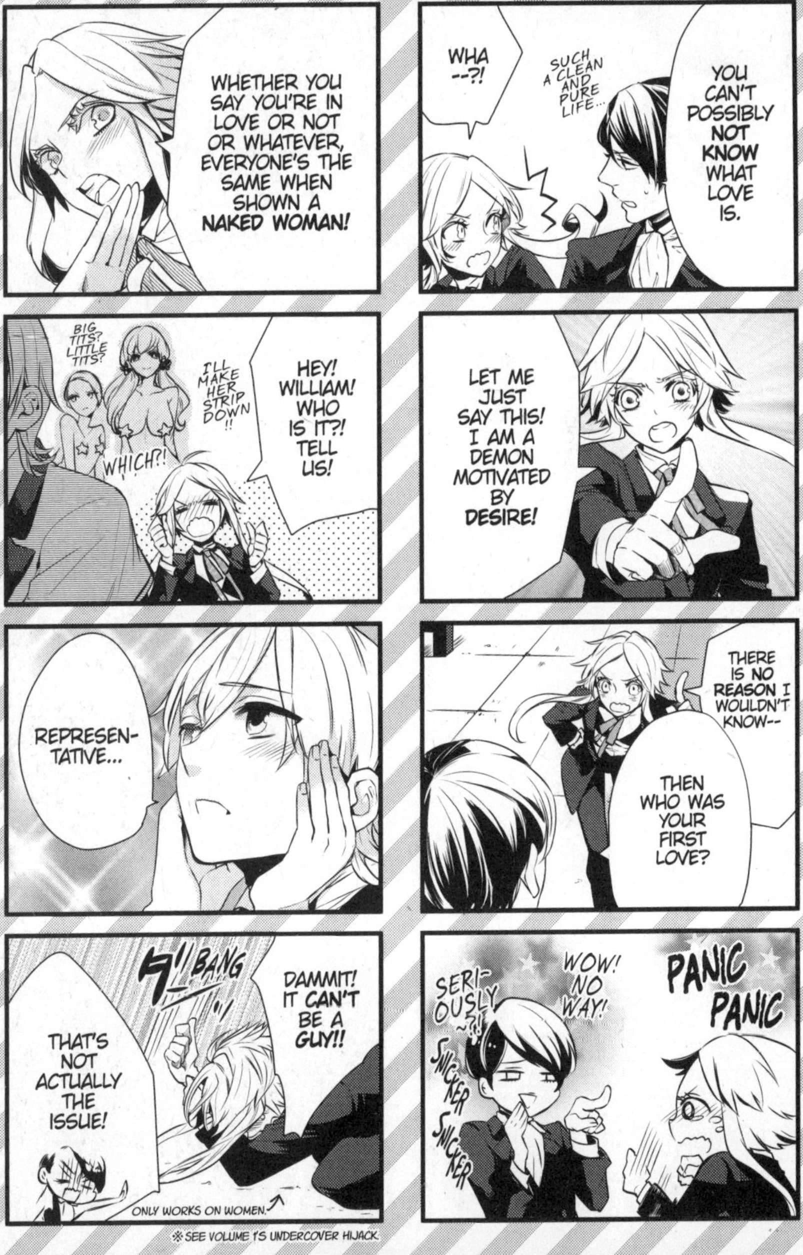
YOU CAN'T POSSIBLY NOT KNOW WHAT LOVE IS.
SUCH A CLEAN AND PURE LIFE...
WHA--?!
WHETHER YOU SAY YOU'RE IN LOVE OR NOT OR WHATEVER, EVERYONE'S THE SAME WHEN SHOWN A NAKED WOMAN!
LET ME JUST SAY THIS! I AM A DEMON MOTIVATED BY DESIRE!
HEY! WILLIAM! WHO IS IT?! TELL US!
I'LL MAKE HER STRIP DOWN!!
BIG TITS? LITTLE TITS?
WHICH?!
THERE IS NO REASON I WOULDN'T KNOW--
THEN WHO WAS YOUR FIRST LOVE?
REPRESEN-TATIVE...
PANIC PANIC
WOW! NO WAY!
SERI-OUSLY~?!
SNICKER SNICKER
DAMMIT! IT CAN'T BE A GUY!!
BANG
THAT'S NOT ACTUALLY THE ISSUE!
ONLY WORKS ON WOMEN.
※SEE VOLUME 1'S UNDERCOVER HIJACK.

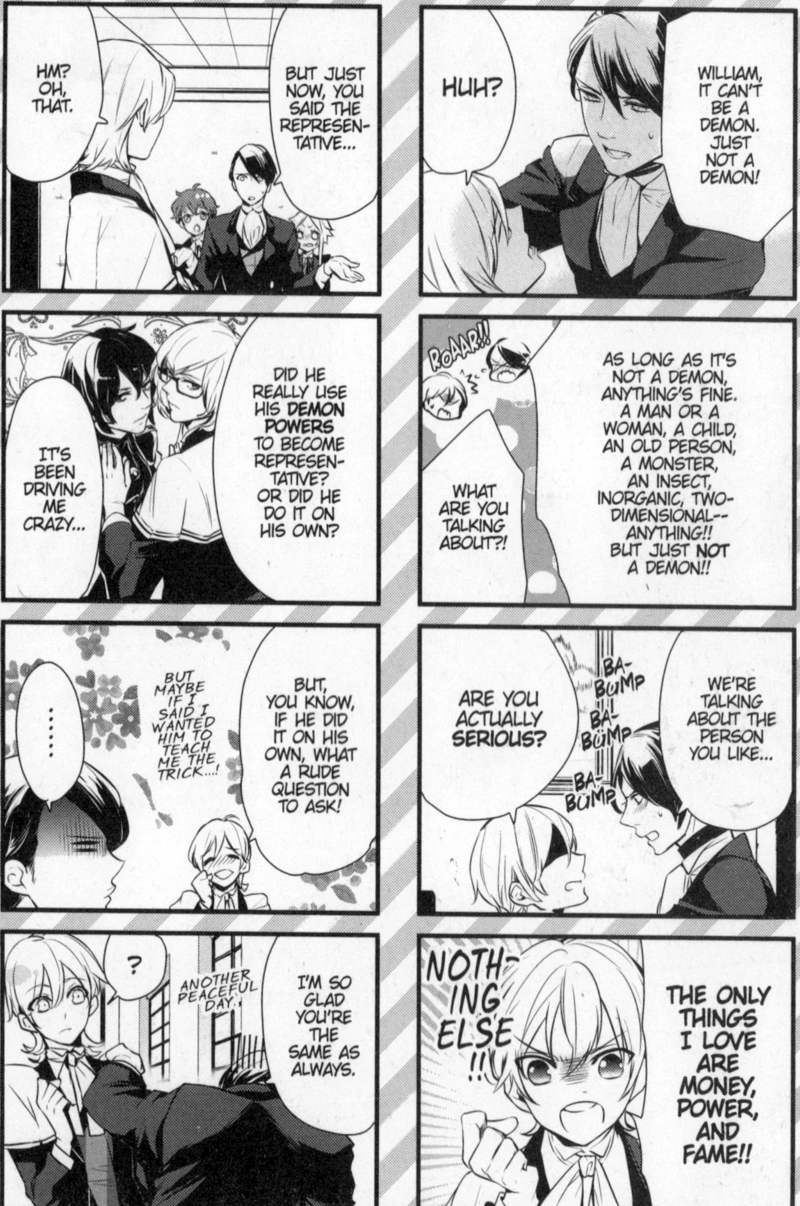
WILLIAM, IT CAN'T BE A DEMON. JUST NOT A DEMON!
HUH?
AS LONG AS IT'S NOT A DEMON, ANYTHING'S FINE. A MAN OR A WOMAN, A CHILD, AN OLD PERSON, A MONSTER, AN INSECT, INORGANIC, TWO-DIMENSIONAL--ANYTHING!! BUT JUST NOT A DEMON!!
WHAT ARE YOU TALKING ABOUT?!
ROAAR!!
WE'RE TALKING ABOUT THE PERSON YOU LIKE...
BA-BUMP BA-BUMP BA-BUMP
ARE YOU ACTUALLY SERIOUS?
THE ONLY THINGS I LOVE ARE MONEY, POWER, AND FAME!!
NOTHING ELSE!!
BUT JUST NOW, YOU SAID THE REPRESENTATIVE...
HM? OH, THAT.
DID HE REALLY USE HIS DEMON POWERS TO BECOME REPRESENTATIVE? OR DID HE DO IT ON HIS OWN?
IT'S BEEN DRIVING ME CRAZY...
BUT, YOU KNOW, IF HE DID IT ON HIS OWN, WHAT A RUDE QUESTION TO ASK!
BUT MAYBE IF I SAID I WANTED HIM TO TEACH ME THE TRICK...!
......
I'M SO GLAD YOU'RE THE SAME AS ALWAYS.
ANOTHER PEACEFUL DAY.
?

END

Afterword

It's the third volume already! Thank you so much for buying it! As of this writing, I haven't actually seen it, but since the covers so far have shown a person and then a demon, maybe next will be a person. Wait, do angels count as people?

I really love ancient history, and I have a little fun putting something related to Egypt or Israel into the work. I set the story in Victorian times. I just hope nothing's anachronistic!

Although I noted in the story (for convenience) that the formerly-human demons are Nephilim, there are also formerly-human angels, of course. People who are referred to as the greats in history, as well as saints, would be famous on this side. Really shining people even take part in the war, and maybe some of them will show up in *Makai Ouji: Devils and Realist* (what?!), but you'll have to check out the next volume for that.

This has been Takadano!

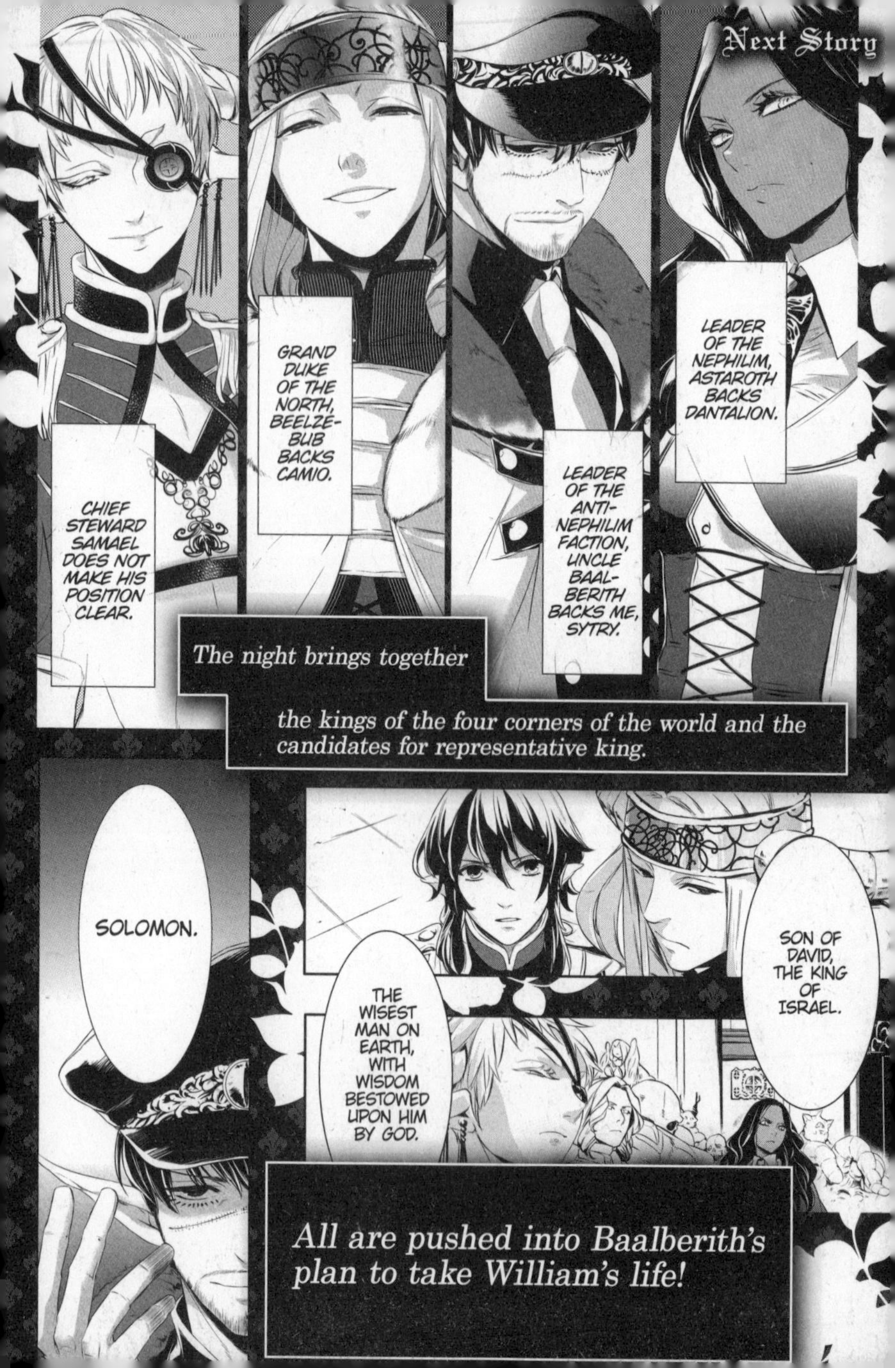
Next Story
LEADER OF THE NEPHILIM, ASTAROTH BACKS DANTALION.
LEADER OF THE ANTI-NEPHILIM FACTION, UNCLE BAAL-BERITH BACKS ME, SYTRY.
GRAND DUKE OF THE NORTH, BEELZE-BUB BACKS CAMIO.
CHIEF STEWARD SAMAEL DOES NOT MAKE HIS POSITION CLEAR.
The night brings together
the kings of the four corners of the world and the candidates for representative king.
SON OF DAVID, THE KING OF ISRAEL.
THE WISEST MAN ON EARTH, WITH WISDOM BESTOWED UPON HIM BY GOD.
SOLOMON.
All are pushed into Baalberith's plan to take William's life!

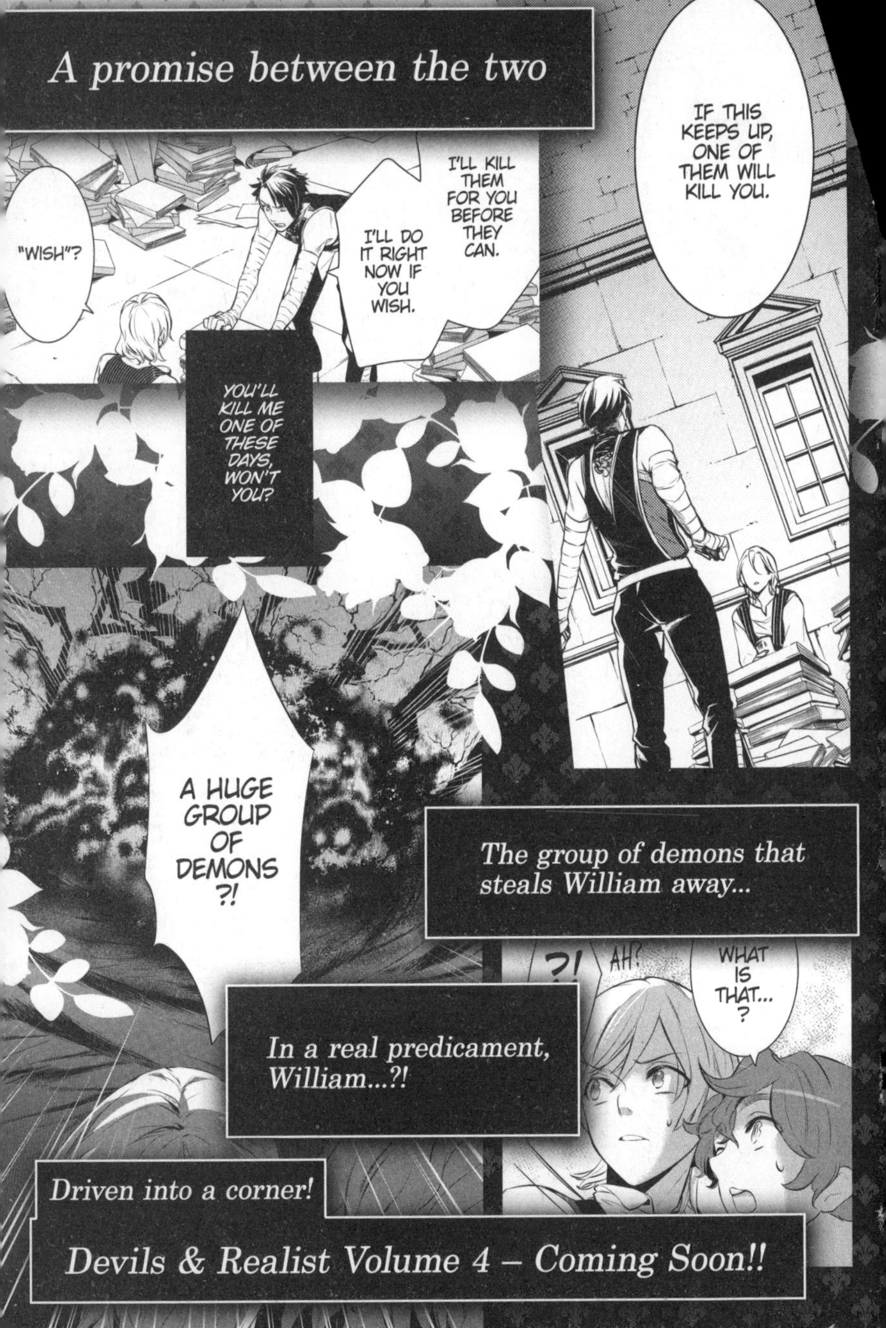
A promise between the two
IF THIS KEEPS UP, ONE OF THEM WILL KILL YOU.
I'LL KILL THEM FOR YOU BEFORE THEY CAN.
I'LL DO IT RIGHT NOW IF YOU WISH.
"WISH"?
YOU'LL KILL ME ONE OF THESE DAYS, WON'T YOU?
The group of demons that steals William away...
WHAT IS THAT...?
AH?
?!
A HUGE GROUP OF DEMONS ?!
In a real predicament, William...?!
Driven into a corner!
Devils & Realist Volume 4 – Coming Soon!!

EVEN SEAS ENTERTAINMENT PRESENTS

Devils and Realist

art by **UTAKO YUKIHIRO** / story by **MADOKA TAKADONO**   VOLUME **3**

TRANSLATION
Jocelyne Allen

ADAPTATION
Danielle King

LETTERING
Roland Amago

LAYOUT
Bambi Eloriaga-Amago

COVER DESIGN
Nicky Lim

PROOFREADER
Lee Otter

MANAGING EDITOR
Adam Arnold

PUBLISHER
Jason DeAngelis

MAKAI OUJI: DEVILS AND REALIST VOL. 3
© Utako Yukihiro/Madoka Takadono 2011
First published in Japan in 2011 by ICHIJINSHA Inc., Tokyo.
English translation rights arranged with ICHIJINSHA Inc., Tokyo, Japan.

Seven Seas books may be purchased in bulk for educational, business, or
promotional use. For information on bulk purchases, please contact Macmillan
Corporate & Premium Sales Department at 1-800-221-7945 (ext 5442)
or write specialmarkets@macmillan.com.

Seven Seas and the Seven Seas logo are trademarks of
Seven Seas Entertainment, LLC. All rights reserved.

ISBN: 978-1-626920-82-8

Printed in Canada

First Printing: November 2014

10 9 8 7 6 5 4 3 2 1

FOLLOW US ONLINE: *www.gomanga.com*

READING DIRECTIONS

This book reads from *right to left*, Japanese style.
If this is your first time reading manga, you start
reading from the top right panel on each page and
take it from there. If you get lost, just follow the
numbered diagram here. It may seem backwards at
first, but you'll get the hang of it! Have fun!!

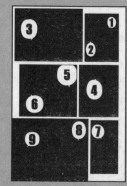